NOV   2006

Driving WITH THE DEVIL

ALSO BY NEAL THOMPSON

Light This Candle: The Life & Times of Alan Shepard —
America's First Spaceman

Driving

WITH THE DEVIL

Southern Moonshine, Detroit Wheels,
and the Birth of NASCAR

Neal Thompson

Crown Publishers

New York

Published in the United States by Crown Publishers, an imprint of the
Crown Publishing Group, a division of Random House, Inc., New York.
www.crownpublishing.com

Crown is a trademark and the Crown colophon is a registered trademark
of Random House, Inc.

Grateful acknowledgment is made to the following for permission to reprint
previously published material: Alfred Publishing Co., Inc.: Excerpt from "Rapid
Roy (The Stock Car Boy)" by Jim Croce. Copyright © 1972 (Renewed) Denjac
Music Company. Copyright assigned to Croce Publishing in the U.S.A. All
rights outside the U.S.A. administered by Denjac Music Company. All rights re-
served. Reprinted by permission of Alfred Publishing Co., Inc.
Mike Cooley: Excerpt from "Daddy's Cup" by Mike Cooley et al.
Reprinted by permission of Mike Cooley.

Part title photo credits:
Part I. Top, courtesy of Lyons Memorial Library, College of the Ozarks.
Bottom, courtesy of Library of Congress (LC-USZ62-42075).
Part II. Courtesy of Raymond Parks. Part III. Courtesy of Eddie Samples.

Library of Congress Cataloging-in-Publication Data
Thompson, Neal.
Driving with the devil : southern moonshine, Detroit wheels, and the birth of
NASCAR / Neal Thompson—1st ed.
Includes bibliographical references and index.
1. Stock car racing—Southern states—History.   2. Automobile racing—
United States—Biography.   3. Southern states—Social conditions.   I. Title.
GV10209.9.S74T46   2006
796.720975—dc22   2006013292

ISBN-10: 1-4000-8225-0
ISBN-13: 978-1-4000-8225-4
Printed in the United States of America
Design by Lenny Henderson
10 9 8 7 6 5 4 3 2 1
First Edition

For Mary

Contents

PREFACE ix

PART I

1 "NASCAR is no longer a southern sport" 3

2 White lightning 11

3 Henry Ford "created a monster" 25

4 The bootlegger turn 50

5 An "orgy of dust, liquor and noise" 72

6 "All the women screamin' Roy Hall" 101

7 "Yesterday his luck ran out" 123

8 "MIRACULOUS DEATH ESCAPE" 132

PART II

9 Body bags and B-24 bombers 147

10 "It's too late now to bring this crowd under control" 168

11 Henry Ford is dead 194

12 "Next thing we know, NASCAR belongs to Bill France" 226

13 "Racing Car Plunges into Throng" 236

14 An "ambience" of death 264

15 The first race, a bootlegger, and a disqualification 279

16 "It's not cheating if you don't get caught" 295

PART III

17   "No way a Plymouth can beat a Cadillac. No way" 313

18   NASCAR is here to stay: "Like sex, the atom bomb and ice cream" 331

19   "I had to start making a living" 338

     Epilogue: This is what NASCAR has become 355

NOTES 367

SOURCES 389

ACKNOWLEDGMENTS 396

INDEX 399

Where you come from is gone, where you thought you were going to never was there, and where you are is no good unless you can get away from it.
— FLANNERY O'CONNOR

Preface

T he notion to uproot my family, move to the South, and investigate moonshine, NASCAR, and the cultural and historical tethers that bind the two simmered inside me for nearly twenty years. It all began with a college course on the irreverent southern writer Flannery O'Connor, taught by a wonderfully foulmouthed, half-drunk Jesuit priest, which introduced my New Jersey eyes and ears to the mysteries of the South.

After college, I hitchhiked around Ireland for a month. The nation's typically rainy spring weather gave me a brutal cold. So when I arrived, coughing and sneezing, at the remote dairy farm of a classmate's relatives, Farmer Quinlan pulled from the cabinet a jar of clear liquid he called "the mountain dew." He poured some into a cracked mug, added a lemon slice, a cinnamon stick, and topped it with boiling water. The concoction, at once warm and icy, bludgeoned my cold—and I asked for more, please.

A year later, while I was working at a newspaper in southwest Virginia, a laid-back photographer named Gene Dalton gave me my next taste of moonshine. Gene's moonshine looked like red wine and tasted of plum. He explained how some Virginia moonshiners soaked fruit in their liquor to mellow the taste. He also explained how his moonshine had descended from the "poteen" I'd tasted in Ireland. A law-enforcement source of mine, an Alcohol, Tobacco and Firearms agent (and occasional drinking partner) named Jim Silvey, provided the next puzzle piece. Silvey explained how moonshiners—whom he and his ATF colleagues still chased through southern Appalachia—had actually created NASCAR, which in rural Virginia was as popular as the Mets I'd rooted for in exurban New York City.

The South's visceral love of NASCAR was unlike anything I'd seen. The sport transcended class the way baseball did; it attracted working class, middle class, and upper class alike. My friends and neighbors attended a few races a year, alongside businessmen and bikers, truck drivers and farmers, preachers and Boy Scouts and felons; they wore NASCAR T-shirts and slapped bumper stickers on their cars declaring their favorite cars (Ford or Chevy) or favorite racers (usually Dale Earnhardt).

As a New Jersey kid, except for a brief affair with *Speed Racer* cartoon episodes, I'd been more interested in skiing, music, and the Mets than cars and racing. But my father—an engineer and amateur mechanic—loved cars and sometimes took my brother and me to Watkins Glen or Pocono Raceway. His hobby permeated my youth. (Thirty years later, I still have the black Penske cap he brought home from a race.) Sunday afternoons blared with TV races, and his fingernails seemed always stained with engine grease. *Car and Driver* or *Road & Track* magazines littered the coffee table. My mother would shriek when he drove home in another sports car—a Lotus, a Porsche, or an Alfa Romeo— and she'd fret when he went off to weekend driving classes.

Over the years, I found myself occasionally wondering how such devotion to the automobile came about and how, exactly, moonshine begat the sport called *NASCAR*. Memories of my trip to Ireland and my days in rural Virginia, sipping moonshine with Gene Dalton or listening to Jim Silvey talk about a bootlegging arrest fermented inside me for years; something about the links between Ireland (of which I am a naturalized citizen), my car-obsessed father, and the Virginia hill country that I'd learned to love. My curiosity finally reached full boil in the summer of 2001.

My wife and sons and I were vacationing at a South Carolina beach town. One Saturday afternoon, my father-in-law and I went driving in search of a drink and a baseball game on TV and found ourselves inside a nearly windowless roadside pub, where eighteen televisions hung above the lengthy wood bar, with two big screens at each end. All twenty TVs were tuned to various auto races. With only a half dozen other patrons at the bar, we asked the barmaid if we could switch one TV to a baseball game. When I changed the channel—on just one of *twenty* televisions, mind you—a long-haired guy in a tank top slumping against the bar a few stools away, who had seemed dead asleep, suddenly roared to life. "Hey, I was watching that! Where's my race?"

Two weeks after that, on September 11, 2001, I was about to drive to a luncheon near the Pentagon to speak to a group of navy veterans when the phone rang. My wife and I then watched CNN in horror as the towers fell in the city that was once our home. Until that terrible day, I'd been a creature of the blue-state Northeast, a lover of New York, New Jersey, and eastern Pennsylvania. Six weeks later, my wife and I decided not to cancel a long-planned trip to Ireland, where Dubliners bought us drinks and empathized with surprising emotion over our nation's loss on 9/11. When we returned home to Baltimore, it felt somehow in between—not north, not south, but middling.

I felt disconnected and decided to make a change. In mid-2002, I left my job at the *Baltimore Sun,* and our family moved south to the mountainous heart of NASCAR country, to surround ourselves with the history, the culture, the people of NASCAR. We now live a mile from the twisted lane used in *Thunder Road,* the film in which Robert Mitchum plays a too-cool southern whiskey tripper. One of my sons' teachers supplies me moonshine that he buys from a dude named One-Eyed Ronnie. My search for corn whiskey's history, its Irish roots, and its role in creating NASCAR has taken me to the homes of aging racers and bootleggers as I traversed the jagged hollows of northeast Alabama, western North Carolina, and North Georgia, particularly the town of Dawsonville, the former moonshining capital of Appalachia, which produced the nation's first and best stock car racers and still hosts an annual Moonshine Festival.

A few months after we moved to North Carolina, a friend bought for my birthday (which happens to fall on the anniversary of Prohibition's birth and death) a book called *Our Southern Highlanders,* by Horace Kephart, a St. Louis librarian with a serious taste for moonshine. In 1904, Kephart abandoned his family and moved to Appalachia because he "yearned for a strange land and a people that had the charm of originality."

Likewise, I have settled in a strange yet charming land, where my neighbors' attitudes, their taste for adventure, their pickup trucks and lawbreaking and speed, and their unslaked thirst for homemade whiskey seventy-three years past Prohibition are all part of a story that's never been told in full. A story about fearless southern bootleggers and the sport they created, but also a story about the South and its cultural impact on America.

Neal Thompson
January 2006
Asheville, North Carolina

The American really loves nothing but his automobile.
— WILLIAM FAULKNER

We have found God in cars, or if not the true God, one so satisfying,
so powerful and awe-inspiring that the distinction is too fine to matter.
— HARRY CREWS

Me and daddy and my uncle,
we took her home and tore her down,
Checked her out real good and cleaned her up
and bored her out.
Took out all the seats, pulled the carpet off the floor,
knocked out all the glass and we welded up the door. . . .

See, it ain't about the money, or even being number one.
You gotta know when it's all over,
you did the best you coulda done.
And knowin' that it's in you, and you never let it out,
Is worse than blowin' any engine
or any wreck you'll ever have.

It's anybody's race out there
and I learned to run my own.
— THE DRIVE-BY TRUCKERS, "DADDY'S CUP"

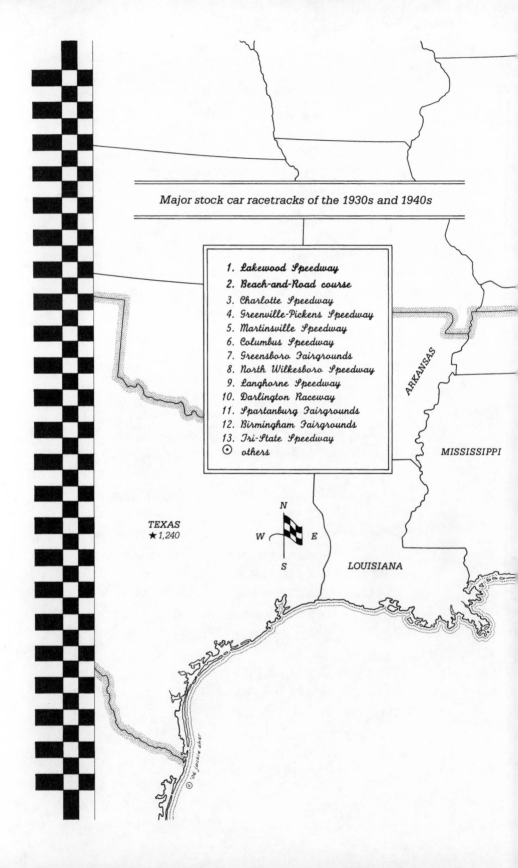

Major stock car racetracks of the 1930s and 1940s

1. Lakewood Speedway
2. Beach-and-Road course
3. Charlotte Speedway
4. Greenville-Pickens Speedway
5. Martinsville Speedway
6. Columbus Speedway
7. Greensboro Fairgrounds
8. North Wilkesboro Speedway
9. Langhorne Speedway
10. Darlington Raceway
11. Spartanburg Fairgrounds
12. Birmingham Fairgrounds
13. Tri-State Speedway
⊙ others

ARKANSAS

MISSISSIPPI

TEXAS
★ 1,240

N
W   E
S

LOUISIANA

© 06 jackie aher

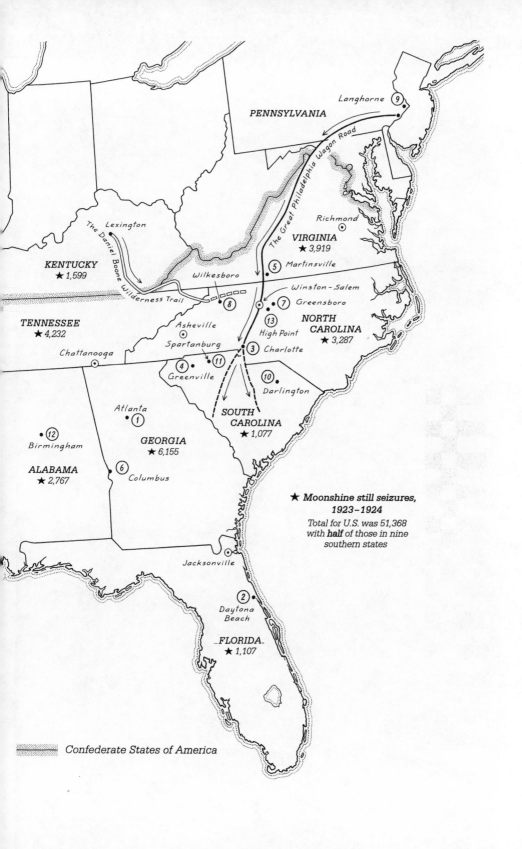

PENNSYLVANIA

Langhorne ⑨

The Great Philadelphia Wagon Road

Richmond ⊙

VIRGINIA
★ 3,919

The Daniel Boone Wilderness Trail

Lexington

⑤ Martinsville

KENTUCKY
★ 1,599

Wilkesboro

Winston-Salem

⑧ ⊙ ⑦ Greensboro

TENNESSEE
★ 4,232

Asheville
⊙
Spartanburg

⑬
High Point

NORTH
CAROLINA
★ 3,287

Chattanooga
⊙

④ ⑪

③ Charlotte

Greenville

⑩
Darlington

Atlanta
①

SOUTH
CAROLINA
★ 1,077

• ⑫
Birmingham

GEORGIA
★ 6,155

ALABAMA
★ 2,767

⑥
Columbus

★ Moonshine still seizures,
1923–1924

Total for U.S. was 51,368
with **half** of those in nine
southern states

Jacksonville
⊙

②
Daytona
Beach

FLORIDA
★ 1,107

Confederate States of America

PART I

Tell about the South. What's it like there?
Why do they live there? Why do they live at all?
— WILLIAM FAULKNER

1

"NASCAR is no longer a southern sport"

The old man has seen a lot. Sometimes too much. Police in his rearview mirror. The inside of jail cells. Friends and family lowered into the ground. Race cars carving deadly paths into crowds. He's seen stacks of money, too—some coming, some going.

Those visions, those memories, all link into a story. The *real* story.

The old man sits behind his orderly desk sipping a Coke, almost as if he's waiting for someone to come through the door and ask, "Tell me what it was like." It is the start of the twenty-first century, but he is dressed in the style of an earlier era: white shirt and narrow black tie, a gray jacket and felt fedora on a nearby hook—the same uniform he's worn since FDR's first term, except for summers, when the fedora is swapped for a straw boater. Raymond Parks is a creature of habit. He doesn't need to be here each day. With moonshining profits earned as a teen, he bought liquor stores, then vending machines, which funded real estate deals and other sources of income (some legal, some not quite). Far from his squalid youth, Parks is worth plenty, more than he could have imagined. He's sold off most of his empire—the houses, the land, the nightclubs, the vending machines, and all of his liquor stores except one. Still, he arrives each morning to putter around the office, make phone calls, check his accounts.

Next door, customers trickle into the one package store Parks has kept, the one he's owned for two-thirds of a century. They buy flasks of Jack Daniels and fifths of Wild Turkey from a brother-in-law who has worked for Parks since World War II. Even now, it's an ironic business for a teetotaler who—as a so-called moonshine "baron" and "king-pin"—used to make, deliver, and profit nicely from illegal corn whiskey. Outside, crews of Georgia road workers jackhammer into his parking lot, part of a road-widening project that brings Atlanta's Northside Drive closer to the bespectacled old man's front door each day.

Parks is ninety-one, though he looks two decades younger. In his twi-light years, this office has become a sanctuary and the place he goes to rummage through the past. The room contains the secrets of NASCAR's origins. On cluttered walls and shelves are the dinged-up and tarnished trophies and loving cups, the yellowed newspaper articles, the vivid black-and-white photographs of men and machines, of crowds and crack-ups, which tell part of the story of how NASCAR came to be.

Take a look: one of Parks's drivers is balanced impossibly on two right wheels in the north turn of the old Beach-and-Road course at Daytona; the wizard mechanic who honed his skills juicing up whiskey cars poses on the fender of a 1939 Ford V-8 coupe outside his "24-Hour" garage, wearing his trademark white T-shirt, white pants, and white socks; a driver stands next to his race car in front of Parks's office / liquor store in 1948, a dozen trophies lined up before him and Miss Atlanta smiling at his side.

Parks is proud of the recent photos, too. It took many years for him to return to the sport he abandoned in 1952. When he did, NASCAR stars such as Dale Earnhardt—his arm affectionately around Parks's shoulder—embraced him as their sport's unsung pioneer.

There were good reasons he'd left the sport a half century earlier. That world contained dark secrets like prison and murder, greed and be-trayal, the frequent maiming of friends and colleagues, their innocent fans, and the violent death of a young child. Parks keeps a few mementos from that chapter of the NASCAR story tucked neatly inside thick black photo albums, home also to faded pictures of whiskey stills, war-ravaged German cities, and a sheet-draped corpse being loaded into a hearse.

The corpse had been Parks's cousin and stock car racing's first true star. He had been like a son to Parks. The day after his greatest racing victory, just as his sport was about to take off, he died. As usual, moonshine was to blame.

Except for Violet—the most beautiful of his five wives, whom he married a decade ago at the age of eighty—Parks is often alone now. He survived his previous wives and his lone son. He outlived all the racers whose careers he launched, including his friend and fellow war veteran Red Byron, who, despite a leg full of Japanese shrapnel, became NASCAR's first champion. He outlived Bill France, too, his wily friend who presided dictator-like over NASCAR's first quarter century. A handful of racers from the 1940s and '50s are still kicking around, but none of the major players from those seminal, post-Depression days before there *was* a NASCAR. Even Dale Earnhardt, the man who brought NASCAR to the masses, is gone, killed at Daytona in 2001.

After abruptly leaving the sport in 1952, Parks watched in awe as NASCAR evolved into something that was unthinkable back in those uneasy years before and after World War II. In the late 1930s, at dusty red-dirt tracks, a victor would be lucky to take home $300 for a win—if the promoter didn't run off with the purse. Now, a single NASCAR racing tire costs more than $300, and a win on any given Sunday is worth half a million.

Over the years, a few hard-core fans, amateur historians, or magazine writers have tracked Parks down. They stop by to scan his photographs, to tap into his memories of the rowdy races on red-clay tracks, the guns and women and fistfights and white liquor, the days before NASCAR existed. Most days, he works in his office alone, or with Violet by his side. He is the sole living keeper of NASCAR's true history, but his memory is fading, and Violet frets about that. In his tenth decade, Parks—the ex-felon, the war veteran, the self-made millionaire and philanthropist—has finally begun to slow down.

The "sport" that Parks helped create became a multi*billion*-dollar industry. It evolved from rural, workingman's domain into an attraction—often an obsession—for eighty million loyal fans. Today's NASCAR, still owned by a single family, is a phenomenon, a churning moneymaker—equal parts Disney, Vegas, and Ringling Brothers—and the second most popular sport in America, with races that regularly attract two hundred thousand spectators. No longer a second-tier event on ESPN2, races are now televised nationally on NBC, TNT, and FOX and in 2007 will begin airing on ABC, ESPN, and other networks, part of a TV contract worth nearly $5 billion.

With the help of sophisticated merchandising, marketing, and soaring corporate sponsorship, NASCAR continues growing beyond the South, faster than ever, becoming more mainstream by the day. NASCAR's red-white-and-blue logo is splashed on cereal boxes in supermarket aisles, on magazine covers, beer cans, clothing, even leather recliners. Try driving any major highway, even in the Northeast, without seeing NASCAR devotions glued to bumpers. Recent additions to the list of $20-million-a-year race car sponsors include Viagra and, reflective of NASCAR's growing female fan base, Brawny paper towels, Tide, and Betty Crocker. In a sign of NASCAR's relentless hunger for profit, it even rescinded a long-standing ban against liquor sponsors to allow Jack Daniels and Jim Beam to endorse cars in 2005.

In 2004, NASCAR's longtime top sponsor—cigarette maker R. J. Reynolds, which had been introduced to NASCAR in 1972 by a convicted moonshiner—was replaced by communications giant Nextel. That $750-million deal symbolized not only the sport's modern era but the continued decline of the South's ideological dominance of the sport. As Richard Petty has said, "NASCAR is no longer a southern sport."

Today, NASCAR's fan base has found a happy home in Los Angeles, Las Vegas, Dallas, Kansas City, and Chicago. Plans are even afoot for a racetrack near New York City. Most fans are college-educated, middle-aged, middle-class homeowners; nearly half are women. At a time when some pro baseball teams play before paltry crowds of a few thousand, attendance at NASCAR events grows by 10 percent a year. Average attendance at a NASCAR Nextel Cup race is nearly 200,000, three times bigger than the average NFL football game. The sport's stars are millionaire celebrities who appear in rock videos, date supermodels, and live in mansions. When Dale Earnhardt died, millions of Americans wept, as did Parks, who was there that day in 2001 when Earnhardt slammed into the wall at Daytona. The prolonged mourning for Earnhardt—the sport's Elvis—opened the eyes of more than a few non–NASCAR fans.

As NASCAR's popularity continues to spread, the sport is becoming a symbol of America itself. But how did NASCAR happen at all? And why? The answers lie in the complicated, whiskey-soaked history of the South.

It's safe to say few of today's NASCAR fans know the name Raymond Parks, nor the monkey named Jocko, the busty pit-road groupies and brash female racers, the moonshining drivers named Fonty, Soapy, Speedy, Smokey, Cannonball, Jap, Cotton, Gober, and Crash. Nor the two intense, freckled friends named Red, one of whom came up with the name NASCAR—the "National Association for Stock Car Auto Racing"—and the other of whom became the sport's first champion. And its second.

Unlike baseball and football, which celebrate their pioneers and early heroes, most of the dirt-poor southerners who founded stock car racing have died or retired into obscurity. There is no Babe Ruth or Ty Cobb, not even an Abner Doubleday. A few NASCAR names from the 1950s and '60s might still resonate among hard-cores: Junior Johnson, Curtis Turner, Fireball Roberts. It's occasionally noted that Richard Petty's father, Lee, and Dale Earnhardt's pop, Ralph, were aggressive, dirt-smeared racing pioneers. But, despite the many books that have proliferated during NASCAR's recent rise to nationwide popularity, the names of Raymond Parks, Red Byron, Red Vogt, Lloyd Seay, and Roy Hall rarely appear in print.

Maybe that's because of NASCAR's dirty little secret: moonshine.

The sport's distant, whiskey-fueled origins are usually wrapped into a neat, vague little clause—". . . *whose early racers were bootleggers* . . ."—about as noncommittal to the deeper truth as crediting pigs for their contribution to football. Today, if the fans know anything about NASCAR's origins, they might know the name Bill France. The tall, megaphone-voiced racer/promoter from D.C. deftly managed to get himself named NASCAR's first president in 1947, then eventually bought out the organization's other top officers and stockholders to make himself sole proprietor of a sport that became his personal dynasty. France is often referred to as NASCAR's "founder," which is oversimplification bordering on fiction. Largely forgotten from the NASCAR story is this: Bill France used to race for, borrow money, and seek advice from a moonshine baron and convicted felon from Atlanta named Raymond Parks.

According to the minutes of the historic 1947 organizational meeting in Daytona Beach at which NASCAR was born, France envisioned an everyman's sport with "distinct possibilities for Sunday shows. . . . We don't know how big it can be if it's handled properly." Many people over the years—including, right from the start, Raymond Parks and the two Reds—have argued that France did *not* handle things properly. NASCAR certainly succeeded far beyond anyone's wildest postwar expectations, thanks in large part to the moonshiners who were its first and best racers. But France held a deep disdain for the whiskey drivers who nurtured NASCAR's gestation and its early years. He worked hard to distance his sport from those roots and was not above blackballing any dissenters, as Parks and both of the Reds discovered.

In striving to create squeaky-clean family entertainment, to the point of downplaying NASCAR's crime-tainted origins, France buried the more dramatic parts of NASCAR's story beneath the all-American mythology he preferred. Efforts to portray stock car racing as a family sport continue to this day. In 2004, Dale Earnhardt Jr. was fined $10,000 for saying "shit" on national television; he declined to apologize, saying that anyone tuned in to a stock car race shouldn't be surprised by a four-letter word. And in 2006, just before the Daytona 500, NASCAR President Mike Helton told reporters in Washington (Bill France's hometown) that "the old Southeastern redneck heritage that we had is no longer in existence." After a backlash from fans, Helton backpedaled, saying NASCAR was "proud of where we came from." Despite the lip service, in its reach to a wider audience, NASCAR seems to be losing its vernacular and, in the words of *The Washington Post*, "shedding its past as if it were an embarrassing family secret."

Bill France, for better or worse, commandeered stock car racing, declared himself its king, appropriated its coffers and history, leaving the real but untidy story behind. He transformed an unruly hobby into a monopoly, then rewrote the past.

This book, therefore, is the previously untold story of how Raymond Parks, his moonshining cousins, and their four-letter-word-using friends from the red-dirt hills of North Georgia helped create the sport that Bill France ultimately made his own.

In the South, where the Great Depression infected deeper and festered longer than elsewhere, there were few escape routes. Folks couldn't venture into the city for a baseball game or a movie because there weren't enough cities, transportation was limited, and the smaller towns rarely had a theater. There were no big-time sports, either (the Braves wouldn't settle in Atlanta until 1965, and the Falcons a year later). It was all cotton fields, unemployed farmers, and Depression-silenced mills, mines, and factories. But if you were lucky enough to have a nearby fairgrounds or an enterprising farmer who'd turned his barren field into a racetrack, maybe you'd have had a chance to stand beside a chicken-wire fence and watch Lloyd Seay in his jacked-up Ford V-8 tearing around the oval, a symbol of power for the powerless. But Seay's racing career would get violently cut short by his moonshining career, and World War II would interrupt the entire sport's progression for nearly five years. It wasn't until after the war that southern racing, helped by an unlikely hero with a war-crippled leg, regained its footing and momentum. The rough, violent years of 1945 through 1950 would then unfold as the most outrageous years of NASCAR's colorful history.

For those who were a part of it, who saw it and felt it, it was incredible.

This is not a book *about* NASCAR. It's the story of what happened in Atlanta, in Daytona Beach, and a handful of smaller southern towns before and after World War II. It's the story of what happened when moonshine and the automobile collided, and how puritanical Henry Ford and the forces of Prohibition and war all inadvertently helped the southern moonshiners and their gnarly sport. NASCAR historians can tell you who led every lap of every race since the organization's first official contest was won in 1948 by a man named Red Byron. But they can't—or won't—say much about what happened in the decade before that. If Abner Doubleday allegedly invented baseball and James Naismith created basketball with peach baskets and soccer balls at a YMCA, then who created NASCAR?

The answer: a bunch of motherless, dirt-poor southern teens driving with the devil in jacked-up Fords full of corn whiskey. Because long before there were stock cars, there were Ford V-8 whiskey cars—the best means of escape a southern boy could wish for.

Well, between Scotch and nothin', I suppose I'd take Scotch.
It's the nearest thing to good moonshine I can find.
— WILLIAM FAULKNER

2

White lightning

More than any of life's pleasures, Benjamin Parks Jr. loved hunting deer. Known to most as Uncle Benny, he stalked northern Georgia's mountains with the century-old muzzle loader he called "Long Susie" and a mule named Becky, in search of his prey. When he died in 1895, at an age estimated to be ninety-five, he'd bagged more than five hundred deer—including, once, two felled by the same bullet.

"A striking figure . . . trim and well-knit" is how an Atlanta newspaper reporter once described Parks. "Evidently a good man yet." Well into his eighties, Parks was able to entertain his many grandkids by walking on his hands. In his nineties, he still hunted deer, walking many miles alongside Becky.

Uncle Benny Parks was born in Virginia, son of a Revolutionary War soldier. The family had come from Scotland and northern Ireland, and like many antiauthority Scots, Irish, and hybrid Scots-Irish of the 1700s and 1800s, Parks required some distance from the federal government in Washington and the puritans of the Northeast. When he was old enough, he left home, traveling farther south along the Philadelphia Wagon Road into western North Carolina, accompanied by a slave named Julius Caesar, a gift from his father. Later, in search of even more remove, Parks and Caesar relocated to the red-dirt hills of North Georgia, to live among the Cherokee Indians.

Outsiders considered the isolated Appalachian mountain people to be "a fierce and uncouth race of men." Men like Benny Parks, living incomprehensibly at the very edge of American civilization, with wild Indians as neighbors, were viewed as "ignorant, mean, worthless, beggarly Irish Presbyterians, the scum of the Earth." But Parks found his neighbors in and around the towns of Dawsonville and Dahlonega (Cherokee for "golden color") to be just like him: proudly self-sufficient, uneducated yet bold, living off the land, distrustful of outsiders and authority, and crazy for deer hunting.

After considering wedlock to the daughter of a Cherokee chief— "dear me, how beautiful she was," Parks once said—he married the sensible Sally Henderson and embarked on a family of eleven children, ten of them boys. On his twenty-eighth birthday, October 27, 1828, Parks set off deer hunting with Becky and Long Susie. Wearing a birthday gift from his wife—a pair of new boots that were "not yet broke in"—he tripped on a rock. As he picked himself up, something about the color of the offending rock caught his eye. It looked, he later said, like "the yellow of an egg."

Word spread quickly of Uncle Benny's discovery, and the nation's first gold rush crashed upon the previously unspoiled land. Strangers came prospecting into North Georgia, "acting like crazy men," Parks observed. "It seemed within a few days as if the whole world must have heard of it, for men came from every state I ever heard of." The frenzy, combined with that fall's election of popular, anti-Indian Andrew Jackson, accelerated the displacement of the region's Cherokee tribe and put culpability for the region's rampant evolution squarely on Benny Parks's shoulders.

President Jackson, whose parents had emigrated from northern Ireland, supported treaties to remove the Cherokee—whom he considered "savage hunters"—from their land. That land would then be divvied up among a more "civilized population" of white settlers, who would plunder northern Georgia in search of more gold. Jackson's aggressive efforts to rid Georgia of its Native Americans were an insult to the Cherokee warriors who'd fought alongside U.S. soldiers and who had actually saved Jackson's life during an 1814 battle against Creek Indians. But in 1838, at gunpoint, the Cherokee of Georgia, Tennessee, North Carolina, and Alabama were shunted off to a settlement in Oklahoma. On the thousand-mile trek westward, one-third of the seventeen thousand natives died of disease, starvation, and exposure—including, quite possibly, Parks's former fiancée. That journey became known as the Trail of Tears. In later years, Parks would regret the role his golden discovery played in so many deaths.

Parks also hated that the gold frenzy displaced the quiet life he'd sought. And he was especially miffed that the profits eluded its own instigator. That's because Parks had impetuously sold his lease to the parcel where he'd discovered the gold, thinking it was a fair enough price at the time. The buyer—a South Carolina senator and future vice president, John Calhoun—went on to unearth many pounds of gold there (fortunes that later allowed his son-in-law, Thomas Clemson, to create Clemson University).

Parks lived to see his gold rush peak, then die, which plunged his homeland into economic depression. With its mountains, waterfalls, and forests, northern Georgia briefly reinvented itself as a tourist destination for wealthy travelers. But then came the Civil War, and the destructive wrath of Union general William Tecumseh Sherman, who marched down from Chattanooga on his way to Atlanta, trouncing and torching everything in his path. North Georgia devolved into an embittered land of impoverished people. It would take many years for the economy and its people to recover.

Thirty years after General Robert E. Lee surrendered at Appomattox Courthouse (not far from Parks's Virginia birthplace), Parks died facedown in a creek, not far from where he'd found gold. One of his sons found him there, Becky the mule by his side.

Uncle Benny was memorialized as a pioneering North Georgia settler and the man who established Parks as one of the region's founding family names. But his historical influence went beyond that. His discovery of gold created the false but lasting impression that salvation was just a happy accident away, that riches could come as easily as tripping over a yolk-colored rock. That attitude resonated among many Georgians: God, they believed, will provide. Many, including those of the extended Parks family, would spend a lifetime waiting for such a miracle, for a touch from the hand of God.

Twenty years after Benny Parks's death, his brother's great-grandson welcomed the first of his own sixteen children, a son. Raymond Parks grew into a tall, lean, handsome, and eager young man but had little in common with his great-great-uncle, Benny Parks.

Raymond may have inherited some of the attributes of the typical rural Georgian: conflicted by Civil War–inspired inferiority, distrusting of authority, confined by poverty to a narrow worldview, and shackled to the dusty acreage that provided his sustenance and income. But Raymond aspired to much more than befriending mules and shooting deer, and he had little patience for the quiet life of a struggling North Georgia farmer.

When Uncle Benny Parks and others had settled in the Cherokee's homeland, they assumed the tall pines and dense forests were signs of a fertile soil. They soon discovered the red, iron-rich clay earth was difficult to farm. In fact, it wasn't good for growing much, except cotton— and (thankfully, it would turn out) corn. In *Gone with the Wind*, Margaret Mitchell wrote of northern Georgia's "savagely red land" full of "savage red gulches." Savage also accurately described Raymond Parks's extended family and their desperately wanting lives.

Raymond was born just outside the gold-mining town of Dawsonville, into a clan whose drunk-and-dangerous factions contributed numerous misdeeds to the Dawson County Superior Court docket books, whose pages read like a William Faulkner novel.

The list of Parks family lawbreaking is long and, frequently, comical. They were fornicators, arsonists, assaulters, moonshine makers, moonshine drinkers, disturbers of the peace, and masters of using "opprobrious words" (that is, profanity and threats). Here's Leman Parks, drunkenly waving his pistol at Ola Martin, yelling, "By God, what will you take for a piece? I'll give you a dollar—a dollar and a half!" (The indictment helpfully explains: "meaning, would she allow him to have sexual intercourse with her.") Leman Parks was also known to set fire to the occasional storefront or church. Here's Rufus Parks threatening Clifton Burt's life: "I'll go get my gun and shoot your damn heart out, you goddam son of a bitch, you damn liar." That's the same Rufus Parks who "willfully and ridiculously" set fire to the Dawson County jailhouse; who once tried to "cut, stab and wound" a neighbor; who tried to "run over and squish" another; and who was regularly caught delivering whiskey in his old Dodge or driving said Dodge wildly through downtown Dawsonville "under the influence of intoxicating liquor."

And then there was the infamous 1924 murder of Dawson County's sheriff, Will Orr—"a man of violent character"—who was shot three times in the chest. Orr was Raymond Parks's maternal grandfather. The man who fired the fatal pistol shots (allegedly in self-defense, though a jury found otherwise) was a well-known Dawsonville moonshiner named Etna Parks, Raymond's paternal uncle.

Raymond's father, Alfred, was an educated man and, after a few years of farming, saved enough money to buy a small store, called the Five-Mile Store because it was five miles from town. When Raymond was ten, his mother, Leila, died of leukemia, and his father became a sloppy drunk and lost the store. Raymond and his siblings moved in with their grandparents, who raised sheep and mules and grew corn on a steep, rocky hillside.

As the oldest of six kids, most of the chores fell to Raymond, who hated shearing the sheep, tending the corn. Life only got worse when Raymond's father married his dead wife's sister, Ila, who soon gave birth to twin girls, followed a year later by another set of twin girls. She would eventually bear ten children, to join her dead sister's six children. All of them moved into a small farmhouse, but poverty forced the family to move every year to a smaller house, none of them with running water or electricity. Raymond didn't get along with his stepmother/aunt, and his father remained a beaten, drunken shell of a man. Parks had no interest in being part of such a household, tending to a flock of hungry siblings and a besotted father. Even as a young teen, Parks knew this much: "The mountains didn't have much to offer." Staying in North Georgia was as good as choosing death, for he almost surely would have ended up—like more than a few kin—drunk, imprisoned, or dead.

Like most southern farm boys, Parks rarely traveled more than a few miles from his farm. What he dreamed of most was making his way to the sparkling, automobile-filled city of Atlanta. So, in 1928, exactly one hundred years after Uncle Benny had tripped over gold, Parks did his usual predawn chores. He built the fire in the kitchen stove, milked the cows, and fed the other animals. Then he set off with a scythe over his shoulder, telling the family that he was going to cut briars down by the creek. When he was certain no one was watching or following, he ran across the cornfield to a waiting car and climbed inside. The man at the wheel would introduce him to a whole new world.

Parks had met Walter Day a few months earlier, after getting his first, bitter taste of the criminal's life. His father had sent him down the road to buy a bottle of whiskey from a family friend, as he'd done many times before. Parks fired up the family's beat-up 1926 Model T Ford, which he'd taught himself to drive. The repeal of Prohibition was still five years off, but the locals looked out for one another, and it was always possible to buy a jar of corn liquor. This time, though, a sheriff's deputy was watching and stopped Parks as he drove home. The judge, wanting to in-flict a strong message that teens and whiskey don't mix, sent Parks to the county jail, which had exactly the opposite effect than the judge had hoped. During his three months of incarceration, Parks met Walter Day, who'd been sentenced for making "illicit . . . untaxed whiskey." Day told Parks to come work for him after his release. The job—working at Day's backwoods moonshine stills, east of Atlanta—would pay far better than farmwork, Day told him.

The morning Parks jumped into the front seat of Day's Ford was his last on the farm. He was fourteen.

Raymond Parks's escape from his myopic, impoverished, farm-shackled life was not an uncommon route. Many southern boys were lured from their homes into the lucrative moonshining business. In time, that same desire to break free and see more of the world would inspire young southern men to enlist to fight overseas, in World War II, in far greater numbers than their northern counterparts. Such sentiments could be traced to a previous war. Southern culture had been deeply influenced by the lingering effects of the South's humiliating defeat and physical destruction in the Civil War.

General Sherman—"Uncle Billy" to his troops, a modern Atilla to the Confederates—ravaged and humiliated southern cities, burning homes and churches, freeing slaves, his troops gorging themselves on southern crops and livestock. As Rhett Butler says in *Gone with the Wind*, Sherman's March brought the South "to its knees—It'll never rise again." One in four Confederate men of military age died in that war. Among Federals, it was just one in ten. In other parts of the divided nation, people moved around more, migrating from town to town, and there was less of a connection to the land beneath their feet. In the South, families typically stayed in one place, sometimes for generations, so there was a deep, emotional connection to the land. "It's the only thing that lasts," Gerald O'Hara tells his daughter, Scarlett. "This is where you get your strength—the red earth. . . ."

But it was on that land, their home turf, that they'd lost the big fight. Afterward, the land continued to remind them, day after day, of defeat. Just like fistfights, a Civil War historian once observed, you remember most the ones you lost.

At the start, it wasn't even *their* war. Far north of Atlanta, few Georgians were slave owners or plantation barons. Like other Appalachian mountain people—in western North Carolina and eastern Tennessee—they had little in common with those in other parts of the Confederacy, especially the chief instigator, South Carolina. In towns such as Dawsonville, Georgia, loyalties were split between North and South. Some men, inspired by regional pride and an inborn distaste for government, volunteered for the Confederate States Army, believing (as one general told his men on the eve of battle) that northerners were "invaders of your country . . . agrarian mercenaries sent to subjugate you and to despoil you of your liberties, your property and your honor." But many other Dawsonville men and North Georgians enlisted with the Union Army, often firing against their southern brethren and aligning themselves with the reviled General Sherman.

"You are bound to fail," Sherman had taunted the South, and losing to Uncle Billy's mercenary invaders bred in southerners a bitter sense of tragedy. Subsequently living under the enemy's laws made them feel oppressed by the unwelcome government of another nation. Then came the equally tragic and humiliating era of Reconstruction, when carpetbaggers from the North took their land and their jobs. For the next decades, widespread illiteracy, terrible schools, limited railroad service and electricity afflicted the South, which came to hold a quarter of the nation's population but only a tenth of its wealth. President Roosevelt ultimately declared the South to be "the nation's number one economic problem." Even into the 1920s, the sting of loss remained so sharp that many towns refused to celebrate Memorial Day or Independence Day—those were *northern* holidays. Plus, July 4 was the day Vicksburg fell, and there was little to celebrate in that.

To distinguish themselves from the mannered, elitist North, rural southerners took pride in an earthy, homespun worldview. Men became masters of cars, machinery, and firearms—"all of which," one southern writer said, "can be operated stone drunk." Gun toting and whiskey drinking became the proud traits of southern men such as Raymond Parks's uncles. Southern-born writers such as Erskine Caldwell wrote of "lewd, crude, half-starved sharecroppers . . . hare-lipped jezebels slithering in the dust." And, as one Scots-Irish historian observed, "The barefoot, turnip devouring creatures of Erskine Caldwell's novels were only one click away from true reality." It troubled Caldwell that his homeland "purposely isolated itself from the world in retaliation for defeat, and [has] taken refuge in its feeling of inferiority." His wildly popular tales of unsophisticated Georgians earned him accusations as a traitor to the South. But Caldwell empathized with his homeland, which "has always been shoved around like a country cousin."

Outsiders, lacking such empathy, could be merciless. When the famous curmudgeon and *Baltimore Sun* columnist H. L. Mencken came to Tennessee in 1925 to cover the Scopes Monkey Trial (which pitted evolutionists against creationists), within twelve minutes of his arrival, he was offered a corn liquor cocktail. He later called the South "the bunghole of the United States, a cesspool of Baptists, a Miasma of Methodism, snakecharmers . . . and syphilitic evangelists."

Raymond Parks never considered his birthplace a cesspool. But neither was it a place to linger. When he left home at fourteen, he did so to take a step closer to the New South, the place that would soon bring riches and slowly lead him (and the nation) toward a southern salvation called NASCAR. He was just a stringy teen in overalls with a sixth-grade education. Then again, textbooks wouldn't help much for the next stage of his life. "Older men," as he called them, would teach him all he needed to know about snubbing Prohibition, the South's inferiority complex, and the so-called Great Depression.

As Walter Day's protégé, Parks became an apprentice in a craft that allowed him to quickly rise far above the rank of farmhand while still staying true to his southern, antiauthoritarian roots. Parks learned quickly that he was very, very good at moonshining.

His first job was working the well-hidden stills in the hills east of Atlanta, about forty miles from home back in Dawsonville. A still hand's job was like a sous-chef's—he'd procure and mix ingredients, tend to the cooking, making sure the recipe came out just right. He was also a grunt, chopping wood, carrying bags of sugar deep into the woods. Not accounting for the many regional variations, the recipe for southern moonshine basically involved two steps: cook the juice of rotting corn, then capture its potent steam. It speaks to the imagination of the South (and its Irish and/or Scotch forebears) that anyone figured out how to make one from the other.

Parks and his fellow still hands soaked corn kernels in water for a few days until the kernels germinated and sprouted. They dried the kernels and took them to a nearby mill to have them ground into "malt," which was again soaked in water for a few days, a process that changed the corn's starch into sugar. The resulting mush, called "sweet mash," was then mixed with water, sugar, and other grains and soaked inside large wooden vats until the corn's sugars mutated into an alcoholic sludge with the consistency of watery oatmeal. Parks and his coworkers set up planks across the tops of those square, wood-walled vats so they could stir the fermenting, bubbling, and stinky brew, now called "sour mash"—named for the dead-skunk odor it emitted. Parks then skimmed the solids off the top—the spent corn kernels and other grains—and transferred the liquid to large kettles called stills, or pot stills, set atop wood fires, where it was brought to a slow boil.

Because alcohol becomes vapor at a lower temperature than water, the mash had to be boiled at just the right temperature—about 176 degrees—so that the alcohol separated as steam from the rest of the liquid. This ancient process, called "distillation," had been created by the Babylonians and handed down over the centuries. Distilling took a practiced hand to keep the fire burning at just the right pace.

Alcoholic vapors would then snake up and out of the still and through a condenser—a curlicue copper tube attached to the top of the still, called the "worm," which passed through a vat of cool water that returned the spirituous steam back into a liquid. The result, clear and harsh, dribbled from a spout into a pail. That first batch, called "singlings," had to be distilled a second time, to remove excess water and toxins. The good stuff was the second distillation, or the "doublings."

However, even with the second batch, Parks had to make sure to toss away the first few quarts (the "heads") and the last few (the "tails"), which were both toxic, and to bottle only the pure and perfect "middlings." Moonshining was an exacting, meticulous process. With terms like *thumpers* and *slop, worm* and *bead, malt, mash,* and *middlings,* it had a lyrical language all its own. In able hands, the result was "corn squeezin's" or "white dog" or "tiger spit." In amateur or devious hands, such recipes could produce poison. Some unscrupulous moonshiners could get sloppy about disposing of their heads and tails, and their tainted whiskey sometimes caused illness, blindness, and even death.

At its best, the stuff had no smell at all. At its most potent, the stuff was 150 proof—75 percent alcohol. Parks's consumers could tell a potent brew by shaking the jar and assessing the stiff layer of bubbles atop, called the "bead." The stiffer the layer of bubbles, the stronger the alcohol content, or "proof." Some private liquor makers added peaches, pears, honey, or plums to mellow the taste. But the customers of Raymond Parks and his employer mostly preferred the bracing, knife-edged, explosive, and fiery jolt of straight-up, no-frills "white lightning."

Just a sip, and the Great Depression didn't seem so Great.

Parks—nearing sixteen in 1930—took seriously the backwoods schooling he received from Walter Day. He worked hard, saved his money, and never took a sip of the whiskey he helped make, determined not to live his father's life. He sometimes missed his siblings, but he never looked back, never regretted abandoning them.

Parks lived and ate meals with Day and his wife, who both considered Parks a reliable and responsible worker. As Day's trust grew, he allowed Parks to operate his own wooden mash-mixing box to brew his own whiskey. In time, profits from that side venture helped Parks buy his first car, a secondhand 1925 Model T Ford, the car that was nearing the end of its cultlike, twenty-year run as the most popular car in American history.

At six feet, with a handsome though slightly doleful face, Parks passed for much older than a teen and never aroused suspicions behind the wheel of his Ford. (In fact, many of NASCAR's early racers began driving well before their fifteenth birthday.) But Parks's Model T wasn't a luxury; it was a business decision. He was biding his time until his new car could carry him, geographically and financially, farther from his roots.

After two years of working for Day, Parks received a visit one day from his father's brother, who'd heard about his nephew's risky new job and managed to track him down. Uncle Miller asked Parks if he'd consider coming to live with him and his wife in Atlanta, to work a legitimate job at Miller's busy service station (called Hemphill Service Station) and adjacent garage (called Northside Auto Services). At the time, less than a quarter of a century into the age of mass-produced automobiles, service stations and mechanic businesses were mushrooming across the South to serve the needs of an increasingly mobile, car-obsessed nation. Atlantans had been buying fuel in buckets from street-side vendors or hardware stores and sloppily pouring it into their Model Ts.

But the convenience of a drive-through service station, with tidy pumps and nozzles, proved a financial boon to those who first pounced on the idea. Besides gas stations, the continued explosion of Fords during Parks's coming-of-age decade led to the creation of the first drive-in restaurants, motels, parking garages, and traffic lights. It was the golden age of the automobile, and each day brought new advances.

It wasn't just the idea of working at a service station that enticed Parks, nor was it solely the chance to finally live in Atlanta. Uncle Miller was a part-time bootlegger and needed Raymond's help to expand his whiskey business. So, one morning, Parks said good-bye to Walter Day, climbed into his Model T, and drove west into the big city, once again taking a chance on a better life, once again entrusting his future to moonshine.

Some southerners may have felt God would save them; others believed more fervently in themselves, and a church called Atlanta.

It had begun life as a railroad dead end named Terminus, which was later renamed Marthasville, a settlement with more saloons than churches. In 1845, it was renamed "Atlanta"—after a fleet-footed Greek goddess, which also happened to be the middle name of the governor's daughter. Twenty years later, Uncle Billy Sherman and his Union troops spent a full month burning the city to black ash. Afterward, Atlanta took the phoenix as its symbol and "Resurgens" as its motto. Unlike other large southern cities and colonial ports, Atlanta had relatively little history to preserve. So Atlanta started from scratch, re-creating itself as a southern city for the coming twentieth century. The boosterish newspaper editor Henry Grady helped by coining the phrase "The New South" in an effort to reconcile with the North and to lure northern investors.

Some hated what the Atlanta of Raymond Parks's day came to represent. "Every time I look at Atlanta, I see what a quarter million Confederate soldiers died to prevent," one southern writer famously bitched. Another remarked: "What is this place? Is this a place?" To others, Atlanta's gaudy rebirth was a justifiable response to the damage wrought by Sherman's torches and shells. For hungry young men such as Parks, who were tired of feeling second-rate, Atlanta was the place to make something of himself, a place where lying, cheating, and stealing—the Parks family way—could be very lucrative.

But first, he had to get there. Parks had never driven into Atlanta and didn't know how to find his uncle's garage, so Uncle Miller gave him careful directions to Ponce de Leon Avenue. They would meet there, near the Sears, Roebuck, at a designated time.

Parks's first drive into the teeming city was like seeing the ocean for the first time. He'd always heard about it and longed to see it for himself but could never have imagined how much bigger and louder and more thrilling it was in person. That first drive felt sumptuous and a bit dangerous, with streetcars clanging and kicking up sparks, and clacking noises coughing out from the textile mills, and all the well-dressed and important-looking strangers staring right through him. After all, back home was a sleepy and somber land of clapboard shacks propped atop stone pillars, scrappy dogs sleeping beneath wood porches, laundry flapping on a line. Atlanta was electricity and noisy newness. People hurried in and out of redbrick shops and waded through traffic, busy and determined. Except for the idled mill workers sulking on street corners, smoking and drinking, the men wore suits and ties, and the women wore pretty dresses cinched tight at the waist.

Occasionally, a shiny new Ford or Cadillac rolled past, the glints of chrome catching Parks's eye. As he rolled down Ponce de Leon, twisting his head from side to side at all the sights and signs, he saw up ahead the stolid brick exterior of the Ford Motor Company Assembly Plant, where his own car had likely been built. Ford automobiles and the city of Atlanta would soon have wondrous effects on his life. Like other adventurous men before him—like Henry Ford himself, who considered the farm-bound life of his youth to be "drudgery"—Parks knew instantly that city life was the life for him.

As he pulled over at the Sears department store and waited anxiously for his uncle to arrive, his Model T gurgling as it idled, Parks wondered what would become of him, now that he'd reached the shiny city of his dreams.

Prohibition has made nothing but trouble.
— AL CAPONE

3

Henry Ford "created a monster"

Moving to Atlanta gave Parks more than just immunity from the oncoming Depression. It was the next phase of a remarkable transformation from farm boy to businessman. And it was in Raymond Parks's circa-1930s Atlanta that NASCAR's seeds began to germinate. Fertilized, of course, by moonshine.

Soon after arriving, taking a cue from the fashionably dressed city men, Parks started wearing a suit, tie, and hat—even while working at his uncle's garage. He'd simply hang up his hat and jacket and zip protective coveralls over the shirt and tie. Sartorial flair symbolized putting the country boy behind, and Parks would continue to wear tailored suits and jaunty hats the rest of his days.

In the 1920s, only a third of southerners lived in cities such as Atlanta; most worked in agriculture, their incomes ranked far below the national average. But by the early 1930s, Atlanta was growing fast, on its way past three hundred thousand occupants. Parks's contributions to that metropolis began slowly, simply. He worked on cars—mostly Fords—at the garage and lived with Uncle Miller and his wife, Aunt Maude, in their small house on nearby Francis Street. Within two years of his first drive into Atlanta, however, and while still a teenager, Parks would own his uncle's business, his house, and most of the other houses on Francis Street. And he'd owe thanks largely to a man very much like himself, a man of Irish blood, undereducated, self-taught, and savvy in ways that teachers couldn't teach.

As a teenager, Henry Ford had also fled the farm for the city and, by the 1920s, was the richest man in the world, living proof that cars and cities were the means to success, not farms and tractors and mules.

Henry Ford, like corn whiskey, was one of Ireland's most influential by-products.

His father fled the Irish potato famine and came to America to start anew. He and his wife lost their first child as an infant, then welcomed a son they called Henry, born in 1863, the year of Emancipation and the Battle of Gettysburg. Like Raymond Parks, Henry's mother died when he was a child. As a curious, mechanically inclined boy raised on a rural Michigan farm, Henry was drawn to the nearby high-tech city of Detroit and the fascinating potential for the new machine there called the "horseless carriage." Detroit had become a magnet for inventors and in-novators, and by the late 1800s, the streets were filled with experimental motorized vehicles that some named "automobile" and others called "car," a derivation of the Gaelic word *carrus,* meaning cart or wagon.

At seventeen, nearly the same age at which Parks would journey to his own city of hope, Ford walked half a day into Detroit to begin working as a machinist. After a few years of apprenticeship, he began building his own horseless carriages. All his extra money went to buying parts and his free time into solving the problems of his prototypes. When Ford began driving his smoke-coughing "quadricycles" among the bicycles and horses of Detroit's dirt lanes, neighbors shook their heads and said, "there goes that crazy loon again. Some day he's going to blow himself up." On foot or bicycle, young boys chased behind Ford and his noisy contraptions. Other townsfolk yelled "get a horse" and denounced his "devil wagon."

From the start, Ford insisted—despite early investors' demands—

that his cars were not simply rich folks' playthings but for everyday use by "real people." It was as if Ford created his vehicles with the isolated, overworked farmer in mind—although even his own father the farmer at first refused a ride in one of his son's prototypes. Often working without sleep, once for two days straight, Ford would wake his wife, Clara, in the middle of the night so she could watch him drive down their cobblestone street in a pouring rain only to return, soaked to the skin, pushing his silenced vehicle.

By 1900, Ford's experiments had attracted the notice of the local press. A Detroit newsman wrote that the "chuck! chuck!" of Ford's gas-powered vehicle was the sound of a new era. "Not like any other sound ever heard in this world," the writer gushed. "It must be heard to be appreciated . . . civilization's latest lisp, its newest voice."

To distinguish his creations from those of the dozens of other Detroit automakers, Ford decided—with remarkable foresight—to start racing. In 1901, he entered a race at the fairgrounds in Grosse Point. Detroiters on their bicycles came by the thousands to watch Ford and one of his strange experimental models face off against Alexander Winton, an acclaimed racer, record holder, and one of America's first carmakers.

Winton, a "fiery Scotsman" and the odds-on favorite, roared ahead and into first place in his specially built "Bullet," and for most of the ten-mile race, Ford lagged behind, with Winton spraying dust and dirt into his face. But Ford slowly gained, and on the eighth of ten laps around the mile-long dirt oval, he passed Winton and crossed the finish line first. The seven thousand fans, having never seen anything travel so fast—forty-five miles an hour!—went wild. "Boy I'll never do that again," Ford said. "I was scared to death."

In 1902, Ford went looking for someone else to drive a ghastly looking prototype racer called the "999." He enlisted the roguish bicycle racer Barney Oldfield, who in his first-ever car race handily beat three other competitors in Ford's 999. Jubilant fans broke down fences and carried Oldfield from the suburban Detroit track on their shoulders.

Those victories helped attract financial backing for Ford to begin mass-producing his cars, and they taught him a lesson: fast cars are viewed—rightly or wrongly—as well-made, desirable machines. Racing therefore became the best way to advertise the Ford name. Ford hired Oldfield and others to race his cars on the hard-packed beaches of Daytona Beach, Florida, and atop frozen Michigan rivers, where in 1904 a Ford car set a world speed record of ninety-one miles an hour. A newspaper writer of the day chastised Ford for aligning himself and his company's future with "fast speed freaks."

In his heart, Ford concurred. He considered racing to be an improper use of the automobile. It offended his pragmatic nature. "I never really thought much of racing," he once said. But Ford also knew that "winning a race on a track told the public something about the merits of an automobile." This very same sentiment would one day lure Ford Motor Company and other carmakers to NASCAR. They'd coin a phrase for the quid pro quo of speed: *Win on Sunday, sell on Monday.*

And so, said Henry Ford, "if an automobile were going to be known for speed, then I was going to make an automobile that would be known wherever speed was known." These were prophetic words indeed, since the Fords of Raymond Parks's day would become very well known to those for whom speed was crucial.

Ford Motor Company was created in 1903 and quickly earned a reputation for quality that brought unprecedented profits, which Ford poured back into his factory. In time, Ford's passion became the art of mass production, a concept borrowed from the bicycle factories of his day. As his company passed its tenth anniversary and Ford handed the duties of car making over to a growing workforce, he would stalk the factory aisles, always carrying a notebook, scribbling notes and ideas on how to improve the production process. He memorized bons mots from Emerson's "Self-Reliance" and nudged workers to become "sober and honest and hardworking"—like him. He'd bark, "Get a move on" and "Get production!" But the workers didn't mind. To them, Ford's factory was "a wonderful place" where thousands of parts of all sizes and materials were assembled "to make a magical whole."

A job with Ford was like "being on hand at the creation of world," Upton Sinclair wrote. Love-struck factory workers named their kids Henry or Ford. The creation that inspired both worker and customer was the Model T, which Ford unveiled in 1908 and would continue to produce for two decades, and at increasingly unprecedented rates.

At first, cars were built like houses: in one place, with all materials delivered to that place. One of the many ways in which Ford revolutionized car making was to perfect the assembly-line concept, which had been introduced at General Motors but which Ford took to a new level. Instead of building the car in one spot, the assembly-line process was reversed, with the car chassis pulled by rope along a line of workers, who stayed put. Each worker had a sole responsibility—installing seats, tires, doors, and such—and the workers' materials were stacked beside them, within easy reach. With his stopwatch and notebook, Ford refined the process and slashed the time of assembling a car from twelve and a half hours to one and a half hours.

The southern novelist Erskine Caldwell once visited Detroit and dubbed it "Eight-Finger City," a place where workers were being maimed by Ford's machinery and where "fingers, hands, arms, legs and crushed bodies" were commonplace. Caldwell's obvious exaggeration was based on the realities of dangerous factory work. Still, Ford's unprecedented $5-per-day pay scale, unveiled to much mayhem in 1914— equivalent to a six-figure salary in 2005 dollars—seemed worth a few amputations, as did the revolutionary product that rolled by the tens of thousands from Ford's factory doors.

The stately Model T, looking like a top hat on wheels, was sold for about $850 at bicycle shops and hardware stores and was an instant rage: a tough, affordable car that could manhandle the dirt roads of a prepaved nation. Ford found that each time he dropped the price, sales rose wildly. By 1914, the year of Raymond Parks's birth, Ford was churning out two hundred thousand Model Ts a year, selling each for $500 or less. Heavy sales in the South prompted Ford to open a massive plant on Ponce de Leon Avenue in downtown Atlanta. The car earned affectionate nicknames such as "flivver" and "tin lizzy," and by the 1920s, two-thirds of America's cars were Model Ts. *Ford* and *car* had become synonyms.

John Steinbeck wrote that the Model T "was not a car . . . it was a person—crotchety and mean, frolicsome and full of jokes." But some people weren't laughing and instead warned about the dark side of this new age of mechanized mobility. An Atlanta newspaper editor complained that by putting the automobile "within easy reach of everybody," Henry Ford had "inadvertently created a monster that has caused more trouble in the larger cities than bootleggers, speakeasies and alley bandits." Indeed, Ford cars became wonderful tools for a new generation of criminals.

For southern moonshiners, the mass manufacturing of Fords came just in time, colliding as it did with an antialcohol campaign that, after simmering for a century, had finally erupted.

Efforts to prohibit alcoholic consumption in America gained a strong following through the 1800s. Puritans such as Frances Willard, founder of the Women's Christian Temperance Union, pushed schools to teach that alcohol was "a colorless liquid poison." Abraham Lincoln spoke out against such prohibition efforts, saying that such a law "strikes at the very principal upon which our Government was founded." But as America matured into the twentieth century, the forces of abstinence had become an army. Its soldiers included the Anti-Saloon League, Bible-thumping Baptists, and firebrands such as Billy Sunday, Lemonade Lucy, and hatchet-wielding, tavern-smashing Carry Nation. The American Medical Association denounced alcohol, as did Georgia baseball great Ty Cobb, and even the Ku Klux Klan, which stoked southerners' fears by claiming that alcohol fueled the lasciviousness of southern blacks. Throughout 1918, state after state voted in favor of Prohibition, which became law once Nebraska finally voted on January 16, 1919, becoming the thirty-sixth state to say no to liquor and providing the required three-fourths consensus.

Prohibition banned "the manufacture, sale or transportation of intoxicating liquors." A year later, with passage of the Volstead Act, violations became punishable by imprisonment. Billy Sunday sang praise that "the reign of tears is over." He predicted that without mind-addling alcohol, the jails and prisons would actually be closed and turned into factories, and "the slums will soon be a memory."

"Goodbye forever to my old friend booze," satirist Ring Lardner lamented, and W. C. Fields fretted that he'd be "forced to live for days on nothing but food and water." But they needn't have worried. The nation's police departments were hardly prepared to fight America's ingrained thirst for alcohol. And proponents of Prohibition did not anticipate Henry Ford's unintended complicity with southern moonshiners.

Although Ford was known to despise alcohol and tobacco—even blaming booze as the real cause of World War I, with "the beer-drinking German taking after the wine-drinking Frenchman"—he would profit nicely, if ironically, from the popularity of his vehicles among bootleggers such as Raymond Parks.

Southern bootleggers—initially named for the practice of hiding liquor in a boot, but also known as whiskey trippers, rumrunners, transporters, and blockaders—adored Henry Ford and his no-nonsense workhorse vehicles. Beginning around the 1920s, bootleggers became folk heroes as they stealthily drove jars of whiskey out from the mountain hollows and down into the thirsty cities of Atlanta, Asheville, Memphis, Greenville, Knoxville, and Charlotte. They punished Ford's cars as no one had, and the cars rarely failed them; like a loyal dog, a Ford Model T eagerly complied with its master's orders. In the black of night, across rutted and muddy lanes, through cornfields and down switchbacked mountain roads, bootleggers drove as fast as Ford's engines would take them. And, like Robert Mitchum in the film *Thunder Road*, they did it all with a heedless calm, driving one-handed with a cigarette dangling from their lips.

Henry Ford's plan to use speed and racing victories to sell cars certainly made an impression on the speed demons of Dixie. But it must have galled him to learn that his cars had become the primary method of delivering whiskey to the Prohibition-era South.

Ford's well-known revulsion for alcohol was possibly inspired by his Irish father's destructive love of whiskey, or maybe it was just prejudice against those who didn't share his views on abstinence. When his wife, Clara, and son, Edsel, visited relatives in the South, he wrote to them, "Do they carry whiskey jugs in their blouses in Kentucky?" Ford was known to smash the liquor bottles of his son and enforced sobriety among his workers. When he was ceremoniously handed a jar of moonshine while visiting Asheville, North Carolina, Ford huffily refused even a sip.

If Ford was aware of the symbiotic relationship between his cars and whiskey tripping, it did not affect his efforts to rid America of what he called "addictive poisons." In fact, in his own small way, Ford helped instigate the national ban on alcohol. Andrew Carnegie, Pierre du Pont, John Rockefeller, and other superpowers of the day also supported Prohibition, largely because they thought a ban on alcohol would lead to a safer, more productive workforce. But Ford's distaste for spirits went beyond that. He presciently claimed that the increasing speed of automobiles and growing intricacy of modern machinery could be dangerous when combined with the numbing effects of liquor. In time, he became a prominent supporter of the Anti-Saloon League.

Started in 1893 by an Ohio minister, the ASL had gained power through the early 1900s with aggressive lobbying campaigns and moralistic slogans such as "You can't drink liquor and have strong babies" or "Can you imagine a cocktail party in heaven?" The league's spokesman was Wayne Wheeler, a savvy Washington lobbyist who amassed large financial donations from Ford and other industrialists.

Ford could afford such investments. Prohibition and the 1920s coincided with enormous growth and financial success at Ford Motor Company. As Ford continued to perfect his assembly-line process, he became obsessed with time-and-motion studies, feeling that any slight tweak in the production process might lead to increased productivity and profit. As production increased, allowing him to keep dropping prices, Ford's sales and revenues boomed. A $2,500 investment placed in the company in 1903 was worth $29 million by 1920.

Ford didn't want liquor to muck up that successful formula and had long banned drinking by his workers, both on and off the job. He demanded that employees be "living wholesomely," and he fired unrepentant drinkers. To regulate workers' morals, he created a nest of spies, euphemistically named the "sociological department" and later the "service department," which sought out not only drinkers but union agitators. Ford even once suggested that the U.S. military enforce Prohibition. He also occasionally let slip darker, weirder concerns about liquor, once claiming that American Jews conspired to prevent Prohibition "because they wanted America drunk." In Ford's paranoid, anti-Semitic mind, whiskey was part of a Jewish plot to take over the world, a scheme to disseminate "liquor to befuddle the brains of Christian leaders."

In truth, despite his best efforts, it was Ford who indirectly enabled the spread of liquor.

Through the 1920s, cultural upheaval transformed the nation. People listened to jazz, danced strange new dances, watched Hollywood stars kiss on the big screen. Women could now vote. Prohibition was ignored by drinkers such as F. Scott Fitzgerald, who declared "all Gods dead." The country was becoming so *modern*. Its tastes in cars changed, too, and this troubled Henry Ford, who had come to distrust too much modernization and pined for an earlier, simpler America. As Upton Sinclair said in his book *The Flivver King,* "There were so many things in the world that were not to Henry's tastes." Ford complained often about the degeneration of society, something he blamed largely on Jews, Hollywood, whiskey, and also on machines. Yet Ford was doing more than any man alive to replace old America with a new, high-speed, mechanical America.

Despite Ford's oft-repeated, stubborn refusal to change anything on the Model T, or consider a new model, he finally realized in the mid-1920s that "the modern world wanted pep, zip, chic." Ford acknowledged that to compete with other carmakers, chiefly Chevy and its lithe and sensual designs, he'd have to make cars that weren't just boxy and utilitarian. So in 1927, at the height of Prohibition, Ford unveiled the Model A, unwittingly helping the cause of the southern moonshiner, who found it an even better delivery tool than the Model T. Revenue agents had to wonder whose side Ford was on.

Five years later, with his aging company losing about $120 million a year, Ford created another new model: the first affordable V-8. Ford had previously named all his cars "models," such as Model T, Model A, Model K, and so on. When he introduced the first Ford with a V-8 engine inside, he named the car simply the "V-8."

Ford initially resisted the trend toward anything with more juice than a four-cylinder. On his Model K, Ford tried a six-cylinder engine but didn't like it and complained that "a car should not have any more cylinders than a cow has teats." But when other carmakers threatened Ford's dominance in the industry, he reversed himself to introduce not a six-, but an eight-cylinder engine. If the Model T was a reliable old mule and, as one writer once put it, the Model A was "like a friendly farm dog," the V-8 coupes of the 1930s were sexy, growling panthers.

Most car engines, like the Model T's, were four-cylinder "in-line" engines, with four pistons working in a straight line, perpendicular to the ground, churning the crankshaft and powering the wheels like a row of marching soldiers. V-8 engines crammed twice as many pistons into a "V" shape, with a set of four cylinders on either side. The balanced design created more torque, more horsepower, and more stability at high speeds. The V-8 beast and the coupe it powered seemed tailor-made for bootlegging. Incredibly, a V-8 coupe seemed to handle more nimbly the faster it went. In the South, powerful V-8s left many sheriff's deputies in the dust. And once whiskey mechanics added extra carburetors to the engine and heavy tires and stronger suspensions to the chassis, a Ford V-8 could fly at a hundred miles an hour across jagged mountain roads.

Criminals elsewhere in the country also found Ford's cars to be useful to their careers. Bank robbers such as John Dillinger and Pretty Boy

Floyd preferred Ford V-8s as their getaway cars. Even full of bullet holes, the V-8 could carry a gangster to safety. Two months before he was killed in 1934, Dillinger wrote to thank Henry Ford for his "wonderful car. . . . I can make any other car take a Ford's dust." Clyde Barrow (of Bonnie and Clyde) also wrote to tell Ford "even if my business hasn't been strictly legal it don't hurt anything to tell you what a fine car you got in the V-8." One newspaper crime writer of the day denounced "powerful V-8 engines" as "the greatest impetus" on Depression-era crime; "75% of all crimes now are perpetrated with the aid of the automobile." Just weeks after writing to Ford, Clyde and his murderous sidekick, Bonnie Parker, were driving a stolen 1934 Ford V-8 when they were ambushed and pumped full of bullets.

In the South, Ford V-8s were the literal and symbolic engine behind an unprecedented period of American criminal ingenuity. The era created two new professions: the sly and resourceful car mechanic and the reviled yet relentless tax agent.

One worked to assist the bootlegger, the other to nail him.

Raymond Parks, with his 1925 Model T Ford, soon found himself allied with the former and an avowed foe of the latter.

Parks's days of working for Uncle Miller occurred at a time of great change for northern Georgia. Boll weevils had decimated the region's cotton crops, leaving many farmhands in need of work. The Depression was about to decimate the South even further. Despite the national ban on spirits, hard times meant people wanted hard drink at day's end. Parks had arrived at just the right time, with just the right set of skills.

At the garage by day, Parks learned to tear apart and rebuild cars. Most were Fords, but Parks also began learning the nuances of up-and-coming carmakers such as Buick, Cadillac, Oldsmobile, Lincoln, Packard, and Ford's nemesis, Chevrolet. It was hard, grimy work, but it was honest work, and the pay was good.

There was even better money to be had, Parks found, after hours and in the dark of night. In addition to the service station, Uncle Miller and his wife owned a small restaurant on Luckie Street in Atlanta, and many of their customers came for more than just food. Uncle Miller sold them pint-size "mason" jars of white lightning. Raymond's job a couple of nights a week was to drive to the country and buy a few dozen gallon-size tins of corn whiskey—sometimes from Walter Day, sometimes from family and friends back home in Dawsonville. He'd deliver the load to his uncle, who transferred the liquor to the pint jars. Parks began earning much more delivering whiskey than he would have made working solely as his uncle's mechanic. He also watched and learned.

If Walter Day taught Parks about the art of distillation, Uncle Miller taught him the business side of buying and reselling moonshine. And in time, Parks decided to go into business for himself. On one of his trips to Dawsonville, he negotiated with some family members, who agreed to sell him gallons of corn liquor at 90 cents apiece. Then, on nights when Uncle Miller didn't need him, he drove to Dawsonville and back to Atlanta with a Ford full of liquor. He solicited customers in his northwest Atlanta neighborhood, offering a gallon for $1.20 to $1.30. Like a milkman, he drove around taking orders—ten gallons here, twenty there. Some customers were restaurant owners who wanted to keep a few jars of something special behind the counter. Some were retailers, who bought in bulk, then decanted the liquor into more manageable jars.

Parks's entrée into big-time whiskey selling coincided with the mass migration of the descendants of southern slaves, many thousands of blacks fleeing the poverty of the farmland. Unemployed black farmhands were migrating from idled farms into cities—some to Atlanta, others traveling the "Hillbilly Highways" toward the Midwest, especially to Ford's Detroit. Whiskey's formerly rural consumers—white and black—were seeking factory work, starting new lives in the city, and taking with them a taste for moonshine. That diaspora created the need for subversive new transportation systems for illegal whiskey. Parks, with a canny eye for opportunity, catered largely to those black customers who had settled near his uncle's service station in the grittier, less developed northwest corner of Atlanta.

Parks delivered to rough, illicit watering holes such as the Bucket of

Blood and Club Martinique, to makeshift joints in people's homes, such as Peg's Inn and Mountain Breeze. As many of his customers were un-welcome at white establishments, they created their own illegal bars called "nip joints" or "nip houses," where drinkers came to buy one-dollar shots of Parks's high-proof white whiskey. One famous joint tried to fool any snooping revenuers by hiding tanks of whiskey in the ceiling and piping it directly to the kitchen faucet.

Customers usually paid up front, and Parks filled their orders within a few days. Yet, while the enterprise allowed Parks to put more distance between himself and the poverty and violence of his rural Georgia birth-place, the threat of arrest lurked constantly.

After working for Uncle Miller during the day, Parks would drive his Model T up to Dawsonville, load it with sixty to a hundred one-gallon tin cans of liquor, arranging it all tightly in the trunk of his Model T and in the space created by the yanked-out backseats, over which he tossed a blanket. He'd drive back down Highway 9 toward Atlanta, or west along Highway 53, taking the winding dirt lanes slowly so as not to at-tract the law's attention. He'd stop and park on a dirt path or behind a barn and sleep until dawn, then continue down from the mountains, stopping where the dirt road became blacktop. There, he'd pull over and, using a bucket he kept hidden beneath a bridge, dip water from a creek and wash the red dirt off his wheels and fenders. Then he'd roll through Marietta and on into Atlanta, nonchalantly blending in with the other morning commuters. He'd deliver the whiskey to his customers, or stow the car at a public parking garage for delivery later that day, then start another workday fixing Fords at his uncle's garage.

Parks was just sixteen at this point, but the fortuitous duality of his profession—daytime mechanic, nighttime moonshiner—brought income the likes of which he'd never seen. In addition to his pay from Uncle Miller, for both his day job and night job, Parks was netting 30 cents per gallon in his own moonshining enterprise. That meant Parks, on top of his regular pay, was making an extra $30 for each night of tripping. His hunger for more profits had him delivering whiskey nearly every night of the week, either for himself or for his uncle. With the extra $150 to $200 a week in moonshine profits, Parks bought a second, slightly more luxurious personal car, a '29 Chevy convertible. He kept the heavy-duty, workhorse Model T as his delivery car. But each night of tripping increased that chance that his car would end up in the wrong hands.

One morning, he drove carefully, though slightly above the speed limit, on the Canton Highway toward Atlanta, with a load of whiskey stacked behind him. At the city's outskirts, an unmarked deputy's car roared up from behind, passed, and then cut in front of him. Parks stomped on the brakes and swerved off the highway. He instinctively jumped out of his whiskey-crammed Ford and bolted across a newly plowed cornfield toward the dense woods on the other side. The deputy fired a warning shot in the air, but Parks's long legs just pumped faster. Fit and muscular from all the mash mixing and trudging through the woods carrying sugar sacks to Walter Day's stills, Parks was "fast as a rabbit," a childhood friend once said.

When he reached the far side of the field, with the flabby deputy lagging behind, Parks plunged into a thicket of brambles. When the thorny branches became too thick to proceed, he dropped to the dirt and slithered. Finally, he found a low spot in the ground, curled into a ball, and waited. The deputy shouted and cursed, but hesitated to tangle with thorn-covered briars. He finally stalked off back to his patrol car. Parks was scared, and not about to take any chances, even after the deputy drove off. So he waited, and waited.

Later that day, he heard the growl of a wrecking truck towing away his Ford.

Still he waited.

As dusk turned to dark, he finally crawled from his hiding spot, brushed himself off, walked to the nearest streetcar stop, and rode back into Atlanta. He laid low at home for a few days, while an attorney—a sharp named Swift Tyler, who would serve him well in the coming years—agreed to take on his case and tried to get his car back. Incredibly, Tyler was able to successfully argue that Parks wasn't in his own vehicle that day and managed to get the cops to return the Model T. The case was dropped due to lack of evidence, and Parks was back in business. But the experience taught him a lesson: don't take chances, don't be stupid, and consider every other car on the road as the enemy.

A few months later, while driving through the downtown intersection called Five Points, Parks got spooked by a car that came up fast behind him and rode his tail. Parks's backseat was stacked so high with liquor, he couldn't get a good look at the driver. He decided, same as before, to stop and run, and turned onto Marietta Street looking for a place to pull off. Then he noticed the other car was no longer behind him—it had continued straight. Parks drove off to make his delivery (he called it "doing the work") and then stopped at a west side restaurant for lunch with a friend. In the parking lot, Parks saw the very car that had tailed him, and Parks's friend knew who owned it—a boy named Ralph, who was inside the restaurant, sitting at a booth with three girlfriends.

Parks's friend went back to his car to get a tire iron to fight with, but Parks just strutted into the restaurant, right up to Ralph's table. Before Ralph could open his mouth, Parks punched him square in the face. The girls screamed and the boy tried to get up, but Parks popped him again and then fled before anyone could call the cops.

Word of Parks's reputation began to spread. And he was soon on his way to becoming the new force in North Georgia moonshine.

As the number of Fords and other cars began choking downtown Atlanta's streets, a new type of structure began to rise into the skyline: the multilevel parking garage. Those structures became very useful for Parks's growing moonshine business.

Parks purchased more vehicles and began hiring others to help him with deliveries. He started keeping his cars in the city garages, rotating them in and out for delivery jobs to avoid drawing the law's attention to one particular car. He also used the parking garages as transfer spots. He called it "setting off"—a large load of a hundred gallons would be "set off" into smaller deliveries of ten to twenty gallons, the parsing-out of which was done in the garages at the Terminal Railway Station, near the Fox Theater, at the famed Varsity Drive-In, and around Georgia Tech University.

One day, Parks was setting off some five-gallon sacks of liquor on the top deck of the Ivy Street Garage. He had driven to the garage with the load, and he and a coworker were sorting it into other delivery cars when a police car screeched up behind them. Parks and the other boy ran. One of the cops caught his coworker, but Parks made it to the top of the stairs just a few steps ahead of the other officer. He ran and fell and rolled down three flights until he reached Ivy Street. Parks waited in a crouch at the bottom of the stairwell, catching his breath and making sure no one was hiding outside to nab him. Then he heard the cop's voice echo down through the stairwell, "Let the son of a bitch go. I ain't gonna break my neck for him." Parks took off through the exit and sprinted right through Five Points. He didn't stop until he got home to Francis Street, a couple of miles away.

His whiskey cars became property of the city of Atlanta, but Parks would rather buy new cars than strive for heroics trying to retrieve them and end up shackled before a judge. At the time, it was common for moonshiners to sacrifice the occasional car, even one full of whiskey.

Parks tried to avoid more close calls by getting his hands on one of the new two-way radios the police had begun using. He listened in to keep up with roadblocks and such, and if he overheard talk of busy police activity, he'd call it quits. One afternoon, he got spooked when he heard his own name repeated over and over on the radio ("Be on the lookout for a Raymond Parks . . ."). He simply pulled over on the spot and walked away from his liquor car.

As business improved, he decided to stop buying whiskey from a middleman and to start making his own. The thirty-cent-per-gallon profit was nice, but he figured he could make even more. So he borrowed money to purchase a few pot stills, copper tubing, sacks of sugar. He scouted the backwoods of Dawsonville for clean creeks and the right amount of protective cover. Then he hired still hands to do the work he'd recently done for Walter Day. For this new venture, he sought help from the owner of a parking deck near the Spring Street train station, a moon-shiner-turned-businessman named Henry Penson. Parks's Uncle Miller had worked for Penson before buying the service station and had introduced Parks to the man. When Parks first told Penson about his whiskey-making enterprise, Penson told him to meet him on the third floor of his parking garage, where he kept a huge stash of used tires, stacked taller than a man. Hidden deep inside the tire stacks was a small safe where Penson kept extra cash. He pulled out a wad of bills and loaned Parks $2,000 with no interest. Whenever Parks needed more money, Penson would tell him, "Meet me at the tires."

Parks never quite considered himself a criminal. With a wealthy patron behind him, though, Parks could easily have ventured into darker enterprises—loan-sharking, prostitution, or robbery. Many infamous criminals of the late 1920s and early 1930s—murderous bank robbers such as Machine Gun Kelley and Baby Face Nelson—got their start in the crime trade as bootleggers. It was just a short step from moonshiner to bank robber.

But Parks had no plans to start cleaning out banks or toting a machine gun, though he did start a lucrative new venture: his own private three-number lottery, which he called "the numbers" and which others called "the bug."

Parks's bug worked like a legit, state-run lottery, with customers paying a dime for each three-number pick. Whoever picked the correct combination won five dollars. Parks oversaw the whole operation like a maestro. He was the "banker" and hired "pick-up men," most of them black, to drive around collecting customers' tickets (usually restaurant cashiers' checks), which were sold on the streets by scores of "runners." Each night, at an office at Uncle Miller's garage, the tickets were sorted and the money counted. The pick-up men would stop by to see if any of their customers won and would deliver their winnings the next day. Pick-up men received 10 percent of all they sold, and the runners received fifty cents for each "hit." To avoid accusations of cheating, the day's winning number was determined arbitrarily—Parks took the middle three numbers from that day's butter and egg futures close on Wall

Street. The operation grew so quickly that Parks soon had forty-three pick-up men working for him. In time, he bought most of them a used car to help with pick-ups and payoffs. Parks even brought one of his sisters to Atlanta to work for him counting all the cash.

Parks's lottery became so popular, he was soon collecting thousands of dollars a day. Some days, hundreds of customers would guess correctly, and he'd have to shell out five dollars for each winning "hit." But there were far more days of profit than loss.

Parks wasn't the only numbers man. At the time, Atlanta's "bug racket" was growing so fast that the mayor and police chief announced plans to more aggressively investigate "numbers big shots" and to "stamp out the lottery evil." Parks considered the bug just a friendly little neighborhood game and, like moonshining, hardly a crime. But the law didn't see it that way. Just like robbing banks, running numbers and liquor was illegal and deserved incarceration. And just like any dangerous profession, the longer you did it, the greater the risk. Parks knew that a moonshining racketeer's luck is short-lived, and he began to worry that he'd grown too big too fast. If he wasn't careful, he'd end up dead or in prison, like more than a few of his friends and relatives.

Parks began offering donations to a few neighborhood street cops. Atlanta's men in blue didn't receive a paycheck, exactly. But they sure appreciated the occasional jars of white lightning, especially at Christmastime, and repaid the favor by looking the other way when one of Parks's delivery boys rolled past in a low-slung Ford. As the lottery business grew, more and more police held out their hands. With his moonshine and lottery profits, Parks could afford such wise investments. At a time when most men his age were earning less than five dollars a day, Parks was raking in twenty times that on his moonshining alone, and he was just getting started. He had even earned himself a title. They called him the "moonshine baron."

Trouble was, the detectives and the chief downtown had another name for him: mobster. And they were watching him more closely each day.

By the early 1930s, Prohibition had become a joke. Even Al Capone mocked the hypocrisy: "When I sell liquor, it's bootlegging. When my patrons serve it on a silver tray . . . it's hospitality." H. L. Mencken observed that drinking had actually increased during Prohibition but that people were drinking more bad, illegal whiskey than the good, legal whiskey they'd drunk before Prohibition. Among those fighting to keep Prohibition intact was Henry Ford, who once threatened to shut down his assembly lines if the Eighteenth Amendment was overturned. But the majority of the nation had grown weary of the experiment with abstinence, and in 1933, Prohibition was repealed, thirteen years after it began. Franklin Roosevelt celebrated with a cocktail at the White House, and Mencken slugged back a tall glass of water, wiped his lips, and declared it "my first in 13 years."

Even Henry Ford quickly gave in to the new reality of liquor in America. The day after repeal, at a luncheon at the Dearborn Inn, he served his guests flagons of beer.

Parks wondered what the legalization of liquor would do to his moonshining empire. But he wouldn't have to wait long for an answer.

Prohibition's repeal in 1933 made it legal once again for most Americans to buy, sell, and drink alcohol. However, the end of a federal ban hardly put an end to the forces of abstinence. For starters, repealing Prohibition meant that local governments controlled the sale of alcohol in their regions. Large, primarily Baptist swaths of northern Georgia, eastern Tennessee, and western North Carolina voluntarily remained "dry," meaning: alcohol was still illegal there and therefore in much demand. Furthermore, in regions where alcohol *was* permitted, there remained the issue of the fine print.

The only legal alcohol was now the stuff brewed in legitimate, taxpaying distilleries. Bottles emerging from those distilleries carried a stamped label to prove that the appropriate tax had been paid to Uncle Sam—roughly two dollars a gallon by 1934. Citizens could brew small batches of beer and wine for their personal use but were not allowed to make even small amounts of liquor. Selling untaxed, homemade whiskey—aka moonshine—was still very illegal.

For many southerners, illegal moonshine remained preferable to legally taxed and "bonded" whiskey. During Prohibition, folks had developed a strong taste for backwoods white lightning, which offered the added pleasure of thumbing a nose at the federal government up north. The repeal of Prohibition, therefore, instead of slowing the flow, actually kicked off a heyday for southern moonshine that would last until World War II, a period in which a complex, emotional game of cat and mouse was played out between bootleggers and their pursuers.

By Prohibition's demise, Parks had earned enough from bootlegging and the bug to buy out his Uncle Miller and take over Hemphill Service Station. Parks saved money obsessively, rarely attending dances and nightclubs like others his age. For him, it was all about the work. He began investing his money, first by buying his uncle's house, then buying others along Francis Street and renting them out. On one of his moonshining runs, he met a beautiful woman named Lois. They married and were soon expecting a child. Parks also made plans to open one of northwest Atlanta's first legal liquor stores.

Now nineteen and just barely a man, he had transformed himself from the dirt-poor son of a sot into a successful if semilegitimate businessman. Parks remained wary of the country twang in his voice and his lack of education, though. In social settings, he spoke little, for fear of giving away his farmer's pedigree. But his laconic and taciturn pose only added to the impression others had of him as intense, moody, thoughtful, and powerful. "The biggest introvert I've ever known," one friend called him. "The most secretive, private human being."

Parks developed a practice of remaining in the background of his businesses. He gave others his instructions, then kept his distance. Some workers tried to befriend him, but he had never learned the art of small talk and didn't tolerate idleness. A worker named Ralph "Bad Eye" Shirley—who lost his eye on a barbed-wire fence as a kid—finally gave up trying to talk to Parks, and it took half a year before Parks initiated a conversation.

(Shirley eventually became one of Parks's closest friends, would one day marry his sister Lucille, and worked for Parks for nearly seventy-five years.)

"Raymond was all business, even though he was just a little boy," Lucille Shirley recalled. "But I don't know what we would have done without him."

With his rising fortunes, Parks bought a large farm south of Atlanta, in a town called Moultrie, and moved a few brothers and sisters there. He bought them new clothes and food. It was partly a selfless effort to rescue them from Dawsonville, but with the added benefit of putting loyal kinfolk in charge of some moonshine stills he'd set up nearby. Parks moved his father to the new farm, too, though the arrangement had its complications. Parks bought farm equipment, a plow and tractor, and then helped his family plant crops. But his father pawned the family tractor and was twice arrested, once when police found shelves of whiskey jars behind the false wall of a clothes closet, and once when they found a stash inside a secret compartment beneath a windowsill. Parks was often apprehensive about visiting. "Every time I go down there I've got a new brother or sister," he told a friend. Even so, he paid the family's bills, visited now and then, and even began hiring siblings to work with him in Atlanta.*

By the mid-1930s, Parks had completed the transformation into a self-made and—on the outside, anyway—respectable denizen in the new world order of Atlanta, where he was surrounded by the money, cars, women, and nice clothes he craved. In business, he was sneaky and effective. The city of Atlanta placed a limit on how many liquor stores some-

---

*Two of Parks's brothers were still working for him seventy years later, as were two brothers-in-law; "Bad Eye" Shirley was still working for Parks at the time of his death in late 2004. He was ninety-three.

one could own and operate. The limit was two. Parks managed to own six, and briefly eight, usually by putting the stores in other people's names, such as friends or family. Still, he needed the county commissioners to approve those liquor stores. So, to be safe, each commissioner who voted "yes" received a $3,000 "favor" from Parks—along with a steady supply of some good corn liquor.

Although he had married, and in 1934 had welcomed a son, Raymond Jr., Parks found that married life wasn't for him and divorced. Parks developed an impressive reputation with beautiful women and would marry again and again.

In other strategic ways, Parks sought to stand out a little, to be a bit different, even if it meant spending some of his hard-earned money. He had no interest in a mansion; the small house on Francis Street was sufficient. Nice cars, on the other hand, sent a message to customers and competitors. When he purchased a gorgeous new yellow Chevy convertible, he had it decked out with extra lights and gadgets. When he later treated himself to a new Cadillac, he went to Montgomery Ward to buy four whitewall tires that cost $100 apiece—almost as much as a new Ford. Like the suit and tie, it was a statement: *I'm not a poor country boy, I'm a rich city boy.* Atlanta newspapers in subsequent years would regularly praise Parks as a man of "probity and reliability" and "a gentleman of inestimable character and honorable instincts." Said one writer, "Few men have exceeded him in contributing of their time, energy and finances to the development of Atlanta."

In business matters, Parks took risks and sometimes failed, but he treated employees and customers fairly. He expected honesty and loyalty in return. If someone crossed him, he'd cut them out of his life without blinking and was notorious for never again speaking to those who wronged him. Some friends and employees were terrified of getting on his bad side and dreaded being subjected to his silent, probing stare.

In time, Parks's reputation in certain Atlanta circles exceeded even his considerable talents. A rumor spread that if you wanted someone killed, Raymond Parks was the man to talk to. Not that he did the killing, they'd whisper—but he knew the right people for the job. In truth, Parks knew no such people. But neither did he deny it, which only added to the mystery and mystique of this southern gangster-child. He was like a micro–Al Capone, without the machine guns or thugs. Still, a clock was ticking on his freedom.

By 1935, the Atlanta police had built up a mound of criminal evidence against Parks.

They had never caught him in the act of moonshining or racketeering, and that frustrated them. But after arresting many of his number runners and whiskey drivers, the police and the city prosecutor finally felt they had enough evidence to charge Parks with conspiracy. The case was heard in the district court in Atlanta. This time, Parks's attorney, Swift Tyler, wasn't able to protect him. "Bad Eye" Shirley was charged as well, and both he and Parks pleaded guilty in exchange for a lenient sentence.

They were sent to the federal penitentiary in Chillicothe, Ohio, on the grounds of Camp Sherman, a former World War I army training base named for General William Tecumseh Sherman. The sentence was a year and a day. Shirley was talkative and made friends quickly, but Parks was shy and nervous, and Shirley tried to look out for him. When Shirley was assigned to the mess hall, he sneaked extra food to Parks. And when Shirley—a stellar pitcher, despite the missing eye—was recruited to play baseball for the guards' team, he convinced one of the guards to move Parks to a better cell.

The two were finally released in 1937. In Park's absence, one of his sisters had kept the moonshine and lottery businesses alive. During his nine months of incarceration, Parks had taken a few math classes and learned a few things he'd missed by skipping high school. Far from rehabilitating him, these new skills gave him a few new tricks to take back home to Atlanta. He'd later call his prison term "going to school."

Many southern boys—and future NASCAR pioneers—had childhoods similar to Parks's, and they, too, considered moonshining a noble profession and only illegal on a technicality. Few achieved his level of crime-tainted success, but they possessed a similar desire for a better life. Just as Uncle Benny's gold had called out to men of the gold rush era a century before, the clear-liquid gold of corn liquor held the promise of a better future.

Southerners over time have been described as hardworking, God-fearing people or bootlegging, delinquent "rednecks"—or both. Men such as Parks wanted desperately to be known for something more. In the South, following the Depression, it was becoming increasingly apparent that cars and speed—in particular, a Ford V-8—were tickets to a better life. A V-8 released a man from the ties to the land that had been his heritage. Parks and his kind needed the land, of course. They needed the corn and the spring water and a secret creek beside which to set their pot stills. But the automobile helped crack open new worlds to them, introducing them to a thrilling, magical, and dangerous new language of twentieth-century words: *cams, cylinders, valves, magnetos, flywheels, rocker arms, push rods, crankshafts,* and *dipsticks.*

A new generation of Ford fans was on the rise. After introducing an improved new V-8 in 1935, Ford sought to create an even better model, to be unveiled in late 1938. It would become the greatest V-8 of all, and the first car of NASCAR.

It was into this era of collusion between crime and car that two of Raymond Parks's cousins—Lloyd Seay and "Reckless Roy" Hall—came of age. The three were never exactly sure how they were related. Family histories in the South are tangled and complex, and most folks in Dawsonville knew they were all, in some way, tied by blood. And by moonshine.

Parks, after his release from prison, had not decided to quit the moonshining business, but he did feel it was time to let others handle even more of the driving. So he turned to those he trusted, to his closest friends and "cousins." Parks handed the delivery duties over to "Bad Eye" Shirley and another friend (and distant relative) named "Legs"

Law. In time, cousins Seay and Hall came aboard as well. In addition to the tutelage of their older, wiser cousin, Seay and Hall soon received help from a redheaded, ill-tempered mechanic named Red Vogt. Together, that cabal of southern moonshiners began to do something unexpected and remarkable with Ford V-8s.

Most moonshiners weren't criminals at all.
They were violating a law, of course, but . . .
how else could you make a living up there?
— ERNIE PYLE

4

The bootlegger turn

From Dawsonville to Atlanta lay sixty treacherous miles. Long before a four-lane highway made the trip more mundane, driving from the foothills of the Appalachians down into the city required an indirect and jagged route. Culturally, the two locales were even further apart, with dirt-poor Dawsonville lagging decades behind big-city Atlanta. But Dawsonville had something Atlanta needed. And on a good night, Lloyd Seay could cover those sixty crooked miles, and satisfy Atlanta's cravings, in less than an hour.

Since the automobile's infancy, the advice of every driving instructor had been to keep one's hands at the ten o'clock and two o'clock positions on the steering wheel. But Seay had his own clock: hands at the bottom of the wheel, palms up, left hand at roughly 7:30, right hand at about 4:30. "When I have to turn," he told a friend who was riding along one night, "I can bring the steering wheel all the way around in one motion."

Newsmen would one day describe Seay as "devil-may-care" and remark on his "angel face." Seay was indeed a good-hearted, laid-back country boy, with a shy face that was handsome bordering on pretty. He was physically lean and slight but had the same simmering confidence of his older cousin Raymond and sometimes boasted that he could make a Ford V-8 coupe "climb a pine tree."

That's an important skill when you're traveling one hundred miles an hour down Georgia State Highway 9 toward Atlanta, with a hundred gallons of corn liquor sloshing around in the trunk and the angry lights of a roadblock flashing suddenly up ahead.

It plays out like this: Seay hits the brake pedal and slows to sixty, then fifty. He releases the brake pedal and spins the wheel, then reaches down with one hand to tug on the emergency brake, which locks the rear wheels. The car twists violently, spinning precisely 180 degrees as it switches from fifty miles an hour forward to fifty miles an hour backward. With his car now pointed in the opposite direction, away from the roadblock, he releases the emergency brake and jams the accelerator. The car slows its backward slide, comes to a barely perceptible stop, unleashes a rocket plume of dirt and gravel behind it, finds a grip on the rocky red road, and shoots forward again, showering the cops with a fusillade of flying roadbed. In less than ten seconds, Seay is traveling sixty miles an hour, then eighty, on his way back to one hundred or more. Before the law has even shifted into gear, he's a mile ahead. In no time, he's out of reach and headed back toward Dawsonville.

Seay's buddy is sitting beside him, trembling, but Seay just grins. He drapes an arm out the window, asks for a smoke. His days are numbered, but he doesn't know it then and might not care if he did. His buddy is thinking (and would declare as much to a newsman sixty years later): *You're the coolest feller I've ever seen.*

They make it back to Dawsonville and ditch the Ford. Maybe they'll try again at dawn. After all, Atlantans are counting on their daily delivery of Dawsonville's finest.

Dawsonville. The hub of American moonshining in the 1930s. The moonshining capital of the world. And in many ways the taproot of NASCAR's lineage. A town of hard and violent men and their hardworking women, who raised the kids and ran the farm while their men played with cars and booze and rotated in and out of prison.

Dawsonville, where the water of life brought both riches and death, where the career path of choice was littered with whiskey widows.

To understand the deep emotions beneath whiskey makers' life-risking disdain for the laws governing their product, it's helpful to follow the route whiskey took to reach Dawsonville.

That journey begins in the ancient region now known as Iraq, where Mesopotamians learned to distill rotting grain juice into a miraculous, mind-altering liquid they called *al kohl*—the spirit. From there, the recipe for *al kohl* migrated across to Northern Africa, where the Moors grabbed on to it and took it with them north into Spain and France, where *al kohl* became *alcohol* and then *aqua vitae*—literally, the "water of life." The Celts then took over, delivering the secrets of alcohol across the North Sea to Ireland and the Irish-founded land of Scotland, where aqua vitae, in the Gaelic language of the Irish, became *uisque breatha*. In time, Brits anglicized the pronunciation of the Irish drink, and the moniker stuck: *whiskey*.

Scotland and Ireland are where the complicated recipes for whiskey—using barley, rye, or potatoes—were perfected. Future generations of Scotch drinkers, Manhattan drinkers, and bourbon drinkers would owe an enormous debt to the dedicated whiskey artisans of the British Isles, the land where the modern history of moonshine began.

Whiskey became more than an intoxicating liquid, and America herself would owe great thanks to the Irish and Scotch and their hand-crafted drink, without which the young United States would not have survived. Whiskey not only provided a source of tax revenue during America's creation (helping, for example, to pay down the debts incurred during the Revolutionary War) but was also the very force behind some of the antiauthority sentiments that caused the Scots-Irish to flee Britain in the first place, men who then helped the United States break its ties with the motherland.

In 1610, three years after creating the Jamestown plantation in America, England's King James I—son of Mary Queen of Scots—attempted to create a new plantation in northern Ireland. He supplanted pesky citizens of Ireland's Ulster region with presumably more docile subjects from his homeland of Scotland. The Scottish newcomers swapped whiskey-making recipes with their new Irish neighbors, and the two like-minded tribes intermarried to create a new breed. The British crown came to view the so-called Scots-Irish, just like the Irish, as an undisciplined and inferior race—"the dreamers and daredevils of their lot . . . an openly sensual people." When Oliver Cromwell dethroned and then beheaded James's son, King Charles I, Cromwell initiated a brutal campaign in 1649 to quash Ireland's independence, in which thousands of Irish were slaughtered and/or forced to turn their lands over to England (a terror that the Scots-Irish of the American South would relive two centuries later during Sherman's March to the Sea).

Subsequent British laws sought to quash any uprisings among Ulster's "problem children." The English crown prevented Irish and Scots-Irish from holding office. It discouraged Catholicism and Presbyterianism and chipped away at their culture, religion, and civil rights. Adding insult to all that, it began taxing their homemade whiskey, claiming that the only legal whiskey would be that which carried an English seal.

After a century of mingling together in Ireland, and together withstanding the brutal treatment of England, the native Irish and the Scottish transplants felt orphaned and abused. In the early 1700s, beaten down by the poverty, drought, famine, and oppressive British rule, they began fleeing Ireland for America.

Upon arrival in the new land, however, the newcomers were again spurned, this time by the prissy Puritans and elitist Yankees of the northeastern coastal cities of Philadelphia, Boston, and New York. "Communities in New England and New York wanted nothing to do with them," writes James Webb in *Born Fighting: How the Scots-Irish Shaped America*. Many of them trekked inland to central Pennsylvania and its cold winters. They fought hard against England in the war for American independence, comprising at least a third of George Washington's army. Those same loyalists then responded with anger and violence to Alexander Hamilton's post–Revolutionary War excise tax on alcohol, which in 1794 inspired an uprising called the Whiskey Rebellion. Washington quashed the rebellion with federal troops—led by "Light-Horse" Harry Lee, father of future Confederate general Robert E. Lee—but not before a few tax agents were tarred and feathered. In disgust, the Scots-Irish migrated south, away from the power hubs, toward warmer, hillier, lonelier climes.

As Webb writes, "Nonconformity as well as mistrust of central power was now in their blood." Toward the rococo ridges of the unwelcoming and remote Appalachian mountain range, they traveled down the Ohio River, or along Daniel Boone's Wilderness Trail, far from the snooty and superior leaders in Philadelphia and New York, bringing their whiskey recipes to the hills and hollows of lands whose misty green folds, rocky slopes, cool air, and clear rivers reminded them of their Irish homeland.

It was America's first and largest mass migration. Among those in the mule-pulled wagons clogging the Great Philadelphia Wagon Road were the ancestors of Raymond Parks, Lloyd Seay, and Roy Hall. They traveled south into Indian regions that later became the states of Virginia, Georgia, North Carolina, Tennessee, and Kentucky. In particular, it was the rough, knobby, higher-altitude regions that called loudest to these migrants, and they settled in areas where the Blue Ridge and Smoky mountains merged, rippling across western North Carolina, eastern Tennessee, and northern Georgia, the land where Uncle Benny Parks had found gold.

The Scots-Irish also found that the soft, cool limestone spring water of the southern Appalachians brewed an excellent product, which helped establish the region as the future home of most U.S.-made whiskey. Thanks to America's natives—such as North Georgia's Cherokee, whom the settlers subsequently slaughtered or displaced—the Scots-Irish also discovered a surprising new ingredient for their whiskey.

Corn was a purely American grain. Cherokee Indians taught the Scots-Irish how to grow it and how it could thrive in otherwise unyielding red soils. Settlers began using this newfound grain—instead of barley, rye, or potatoes—to make their whiskey. In ways they could not have imagined, distilled corn juice became the perfect antidote to the impoverished frontier lives they'd chosen. Instead of hauling bulky baskets of corn or sacks of grain to sell at distant markets, they could distill a bushel of corn down into a few portable gallons of white whiskey. They'd then sell or trade it, either locally or in the larger cities and towns, just as Seay and his bootlegger buddies would do 150 years later with a Ford instead of a mule.

At the time of America's birth, a bushel of corn worth fifty cents at the market could instead produce three gallons of corn liquor worth an incredible two dollars apiece. Not only were the profits greater, but it was light, easy to transport, and didn't spoil, actually improving with age instead. Along the way, southern whiskey makers discovered that aging corn whiskey inside charred oak barrels further mellowed the taste, from bitter to smoky, which put Kentucky and its bourbon (named for the county in which it was made) on the map.* By the late 1700s, a third of America's settlers were Scots-Irish, and most kept a still in the backyard or behind the barn, where they magically turned corn into whiskey.

Corn whiskey was much more than a cocktail.

In eighteenth-century southern America, whiskey truly became aqua vitae, the water of life, as sustaining a staple as bread. It helped fuel the new nation's growth, and not only in the South. A vital cog in the young economy, whiskey (and, in the North, rum) was often used as currency.

---

*Jack Daniels, Jim Beam, Wild Turkey, and most of the better-known American bourbons and whiskeys are still made in Kentucky or Tennessee.

George Washington built a large whiskey distillery at Mount Vernon and often paid his gardener, doctor, and seamstress with corn and rye whiskey. Thomas Jefferson was known to brew some potent whiskey at Monticello, even though he and Washington both played a role in enacting America's first tax on liquor.

In remote hollows where potable water was scarce, or in cities where it was dirty, whiskey and other spirits were among the few drinkable liquids. In the Revolutionary War, Washington's soldiers received daily rations of whiskey. Those who were injured in battle sucked on a bottle for anesthetic. As America's first medication, whiskey was used to treat ailments from snake bites to fever. Mothers rubbed whiskey on a teething child's gums. It fueled social life, too, at taverns, barn raisings, and weddings. Campaigning politicians always carried a bottle to share, and flasks were passed from mouth to mouth at church meetings as the preacher shouted and thumped from a backwoods pulpit.

By the 1800s, corn whiskey sustained southern life. In the North, rum had long been the preferred drink. Rum's production owed much to the triangular trade between England, Africa, and America. That trade route brought slaves from Africa to the British islands of the Caribbean. In the Caribbean, the slave ships picked up sugar cane, which was delivered to America and distilled into rum; some of the African slaves were delivered to southern cotton plantations. When the slave trade was disrupted in the 1800s, the availability of sugar cane and rum declined. Southern-made whiskey took up the slack.

Scots-Irish settlers also introduced to southern America their melancholy fiddle music, set and step dancing (predecessors to square dancing), whimsical storytelling, vigorous independence, strong family values, and, as a result of the shabby treatment they'd received in Northern Ireland and in New England, a xenophobic distrust of authority and outsiders. Scots-Irish aspect and attitude distilled into a southern culture that would influence the entire culture of the new nation.

Four of the first five U.S. presidents came from the South, their character shaped by the land of moonshine. For forty-nine of the nation's first seventy-two years, a slaveholding southerner was president.

Southerners wrote the Declaration of Independence and the Constitution. They dominated Congress and the Supreme Court. The land of moonshine helped form not only the U.S. political and justice systems but the ideas behind it all: gritty self-rule and independence, free thinking and free speech.

"Booze was food, medicine, and companionship in the early days of America," Eric Burns writes in *Spirits of America: A Social History of Alcohol.* "Alcoholic beverages . . . would serve as an almost indispensable accompaniment to liberty: sparking the urge to separate from the motherland, igniting patriotism, stoking the passion for growth and prosperity . . . as if freedom were an engine and spirits the fuel."

Such passions were personified in men such as Amos Owens, a hard-drinking Scots-Irish outdoorsman from western North Carolina. "Uncle Amos" became widely known for his whiskey flavored with sourwood honey and cherries, which he called "cherry bounce." When the Civil War slashed the nation in two, Amos fought with Jeb Stuart and the Rebel army, was captured, and served many months near starvation in a Union stockade. To pay off war debts, the government reinstated a tax on whiskey* and created the Internal Revenue Service to collect it, along with income taxes.

Amos returned home to Cherry Mountain, vowing never to pay a cent of tax on his moonshine, especially not to the enemy government that had defeated his people. Like many southerners, Amos was mad—mad that his side lost the war, mad that a foreign government was now trying to profit from his cherry juice. "Amos believed it was his God-given right to make Cherry Bounce," one southern writer later said. "That's why God put cherry trees on his mountain in the first place."

Tax collectors and federal agents repeatedly visited Amos's place. He used a telescope to keep an eye out for them. At one point, he wrote to a Charlotte newspaper announcing that his mountain was seceding from the United States. Such antics kept federal judge Robert Dick busy and

---

*The first liquor tax, which paid for the Revolution, was rescinded in 1802, then briefly reinstated for three years to pay the debts of the War of 1812.

amused, as Amos made frequent appearances in Dick's courtroom, taunting the judge in his whiskey-tinged, falsetto voice. When Judge Dick scolded Amos, telling him that *he'd* never even *touched* a drop of whiskey, Amos told Dick he'd "missed a durned lotsa fun." The judge sent Amos to federal prison three times for a total of nine years, but incarceration never seemed to rehabilitate the man. With his ever-present beaver hat, Amos would preside over goose-pulling contests and nude dancing at his famous annual Cherry Bounce Festival. If he was arrested, he would sell whiskey to the folks who came to town for court week, right out of the back of his wagon, right outside the courthouse.

Many southerners came to share Amos's belief that the northern government had no business regulating their God-given right to make, drink, sell, and deliver whiskey. They deeply, almost religiously, felt that not only was there nothing illegal or immoral about moonshining, it was a proud and noble tradition. American moonshine and its clean-shaven cousin, bourbon, would indeed become true American originals, along with other products of the South, such as peanut butter, grits, bluegrass music, and the blues.

Soon to be added to that list of southern creations: stock car racing.

Like Raymond Parks, Lloyd Seay was born into a dark, angry, embittered family of drunken, felonious recidivists, men who taunted the law, their women, and one another. Often, they died violent deaths involving cars, liquor, guns, or all three.

Poor and desperate, the men of the Seay family sometimes broke into neighbors' homes just to steal clothing. More than once, they stole Ford coupes. At the courthouse, they signed court papers with an "X," because they had never learned to read or write. Through the 1920s and '30s, Seay men were caught fornicating with neighbors' wives, assaulting unwilling sexual partners, and, of course, running and drinking corn liquor.

For Lloyd, there was little choice but to become part of that world. His parents were dead-tired and dirt-poor by the time he came along, the baby of the family. Parental guidance, such as it was, came from reckless, moonshine-swilling uncles who helped raise Lloyd. Seay's name appeared plenty in the pages of court docket books, beside the "X" he scratched to indicate that he understood the charges against him, just like his uncles. His were usually minor offenses: stealing a thirty-cent quart of motor oil from Harben Brothers Service Station, speeding, reckless driving. He was once charged with "operating a Ford automobile on the Dawsonville-Tate public highway in the night time without having any lights thereon." Moonshiners often drove without their lights to elude the law. Still, Seay—like his elder cousin Raymond—seemed to find ways to make peace with his violent, genetic instincts, or at least keep them largely in check.

Seay's other cousin, Roy Hall, discovered no such balance in his life. There seemed to be no moral regulator built into his psyche. For Roy Hall, life had to be full speed or not at all. He was obscenely handsome and absurdly cocky. Everyone around him assumed Hall's life would be cut short by violence.

Hall's father had left home before he was born and died of illness ten days after his birth. When Hall was ten, his mother also died, just like Raymond Parks's mother.* An uncle came and took Hall out of his Dawsonville school—for good. He was separated from his only sister, Eula May, and went to live with the uncle in Atlanta, where he began a streetwise life of crime. Before he was even a teenager, Roy was working as a numbers runner for "the bug." First, he worked for his uncle and later for cousin Raymond. From the bug, it was just a baby step toward the life of high-speed moonshining.

In the mid-1930s, unskilled laborers in and around Atlanta might earn as little as forty cents an hour, less than twenty dollars a week. A tripper

---

*. . . and Henry Ford's mother and future NASCAR racer Red Byron's.

could earn twice that for a single Dawsonville-to-Atlanta run. In just one week of moonshining, with two or three nightly trips, Seay and Hall could make enough to buy a new Model A Ford. As Jess Carr put it in his book *The Second Oldest Profession,* "It was a thousand-dollar-a-week job if the driver worked every night—and lived through it." For many, the risk of jail or death was worth the reward. Better to live boldly than die of boredom in a factory.

Before Prohibition, moonshining had been largely a family business and a mostly harmless local one. During Prohibition, moonshiners became sophisticated, commercial mass producers. After Prohibition, the production of corn liquor continued its maturity from quaint, backwoods artisanal hobby to profitable and dangerous enterprise, which one writer likened to "a gentle home pet that grew to become a devouring monster." More than anywhere else, that monster prowled the roads between Atlanta and Dawsonville. Of an estimated thirty-five million gallons of moonshine produced nationwide in 1934, nearly a million gallons a year came from the foothills surrounding Dawsonville. One famous backwoods distillery, in an emptied-out chicken house, pumped out seven hundred gallons of corn liquor a day. "Virtually everyone in Dawson County was associated with the whiskey business in some way," one retired Dawsonville bootlegger said.

Across the thirteen years of Prohibition, the price of liquor had risen tenfold, to $20 or more per gallon. But even after the Eighteenth Amendment was repealed by the ratification of the Twenty-first Amendment (giving whiskey the distinction of being the only target of two constitutional amendments), the price remained high—partly because the two hundred or so legal distilleries that had existed before Prohibition took a few years to rebuild, but also because the government was collecting a whopping $2-per-gallon tax. For many, the decision was simple: Why buy legal whiskey when moonshine was far cheaper? And why work for $20 a week when you can make $400 delivering that moonshine?

Of course, it wasn't *just* Dawsonville. All across Appalachia, entrepreneurial farm boys made small fortunes in Martinsville, Virginia;

Wilkes County, North Carolina; Asheville, North Carolina; Greenville, South Carolina; eastern Kentucky; and so on. In the culture of the South, fathers thought little of sending their twelve- and fourteen-year-old sons out to deliver a load of moonshine. It was a rite of passage, like bagging your first deer, your first woman. Also, in the minds of many southern farmers, moonshining was just an extension of agriculture, and bootlegging no more than delivering a farm product to market. They saw no reason the IRS should take a cut.

NASCAR legend Curtis Turner claimed to have delivered his first load of whiskey in 1934, at age ten. A few miles from home, with one hundred gallons in his father's Oldsmobile, Curtis approached a slow-moving mail truck but couldn't remember, *Do I pass on the left or the right?* He chose the right and slid off the road into a fence. Years later, to show off his well-honed "bootlegger turn" to a fellow moonshiner, Turner lined up two rows of whiskey jars on the road, ten feet apart. He then sped toward the jars, spun 180 degrees, and slid backward between the two rows, without touching a jar.

"It was easy," he said. "I couldn't waste all the good liquor."

In 1935, police and IRS agents pounced on the village of Ingle Hollow, in North Carolina's notorious Wilkes County, another moon-shining hub, to make the biggest moonshine bust in U.S. history. Officials found the tiny Johnson house crammed to the ceiling with 7,100 gallons of liquor, and agents hauled Robert Johnson Sr. off to prison. Again. Four-year-old Robert Glenn "Junior" Johnson, barefoot and in overalls, waved good-bye to his daddy, while his mother poured coffee and served pie to the tax agents, whose names she'd come to know. Junior's father would spend a third of his sixty-three years behind bars. At age fourteen, Junior followed his father's path, treating bootlegging like a full-time job, driving back roads by day to learn which escape routes to take at night. Johnson, like Curtis Turner, would also become a major player in NASCAR's first quarter century and in many minds is considered NASCAR's best driver of all time.

"Moonshiners put more time, energy, thought and love into their cars than any racers ever will," Johnson said later in life. "Lose on the

track and you go home. Lose with a load of whiskey and you go to jail."
Johnson knew what he was talking about. He spent a year inside Chillicothe, the same Ohio prison that had been the temporary home to a
number of Dawsonville moonshiners, including Raymond Parks.

Other racers would later claim they had little choice in the matter. "If
it hadn't been for bootlegging and racing, we'd have starved to death,"
said Tim Flock, one of three moonshining brothers who would each become a NASCAR legend.

In the rural South, such young men grew fast. And with practice, the
smart ones—those who didn't get killed or arrested—learned how to
transfer their moonshining skills to the racetrack. Racing ahead of the
law on snaky dirt roads honed in Lloyd Seay, Roy Hall, and their con-
temporaries instincts that would transfer perfectly to racing.

But first, the job of the North Georgia bootlegger grew more complicated.

Until Seay and Hall joined the ranks in the mid-1930s, policing moonshiners had mostly been a job for local sheriffs and their deputies, who
were often outmanned or easily paid off with a hundred-dollar bill. In
1934, the IRS created a new Alcohol Tax Unit, which leveled the playing
field a bit by recruiting state troopers, college athletes, and ex-soldiers as
its first agents, whose job was to mercilessly quash the bootleg whiskey
business.

In Chicago, Elliot Ness and his "Untouchables" had tangled with
mobster Al Capone's liquor boys. But in the South, "revenuers"—so
named because they sought to collect whiskey revenues—prowled the
back roads of southern states alone, in search of untaxed whiskey and its
makers. The era produced men such as Kentucky's famous, gun-toting
William "Big Six" Henderson—"the Elliot Ness of moonshiners"—
a lanky revenuer who arrested five thousand moonshiners in his decades-
long career. Suspects rarely gave up their real names, instead claiming
to be Franklin Roosevelt, Daniel Boone, Abraham Lincoln, Charles
Lindbergh, George Washington, or Henry Ford. Revenuers considered

moonshiners their prey, likening their job to deer hunting at an extreme level.

"It was a game, you against them," said one tax agent.

Some bootleggers tried to elude their pursuers by being coy. They hid whiskey inside truckloads of lumber, sacks of cotton, stacks of tires, even crates of chickens. But trucks were slow and obvious targets for a savvy revenuer, so most moonshiners delivered their loads by car, usually a V-8–powered Ford.

Among the early lessons learned was how to carefully pack a load of glass jars into a Ford so they didn't crack when jostled by a rutted road. Some trippers covered their load with an army blanket, then doused the blanket with bleach, to mask the smell of alcohol, just in case they got pulled over. Some posed as traveling salesmen or, like Raymond Parks, wore a suit and tie and blended in with morning commuters. One moonshiner, when he sensed revenuers might be nearby, added to that morning-commute tactic an extra touch: "I'd start picking my nose because nobody is going to keep staring at you if you start picking your nose." But even an empty whiskey car attracted revenuers' attentions. Larger springs were added to the rear suspension of a whiskey car, to help it carry a hundred gallons of liquor. When it wasn't loaded down, an empty whiskey car bounced, and the heavy-duty springs caused its rear end to ride high, "like a cat in heat."

A bouncing, butt-in-the-air Ford could be easily spotted by a revenue agent. Although sometimes it did no good to catch an empty whiskey car. One night, a North Georgia tripper hit a rut and smashed a few of his jars. Even after he'd delivered the unbroken jars, the car reeked like a distillery. On his way home, a revenue agent pulled him over. The agent searched the car, looking for evidence beyond the powerful odor.

"Where are you from?" he finally asked.

"Dawsonville."

"What do you do there?"

"I'm a farmer," the bootlegger lied.

Eventually, the agent had no choice but to let him and his reeking whiskey car go.

To catch trippers in the act of delivering a full load of corn liquor, revenuers designed a pincer device attached to the front of their cars that could snag the rear fender of a fleeing Ford. This would usually be used in pursuit up a hill, where the whiskey-laden car lost some of its speed. The bootleggers' response was to use wire coat hangers to attach their fenders loosely to the car's rear end. If a revenuer pinched it, the fender would snap off and tangle beneath the revenuer's wheels. Revenuers took the fight up a notch and began welding steel battering rams to the front of their cars. They'd try to catch a bootlegger in a curve and hit him at an angle, so he'd spin out. But the bootleggers learned to slow down just a notch, wait for the revenuer to get close, then gun it, which often sent the lesser-skilled revenuer spinning off the road.

Some bootleggers attached canisters to their cars that, with the press of a button, spewed smoke screens, laid down oil slicks, or dropped buckets of tire-shredding tacks. Revenuers fought back angrily by shooting out radiators or tires, or just blasting the car full of holes. That's when whiskey mechanics started welding steel plates in front of the radiators or relocated the radiator to the trunk.

Bootleggers sometimes traveled with a "blocker"—another driver who'd run interference between the whiskey car and the revenuer. (That tactic would later come in handy on the racetrack.) Or, in tight-knit communities, a moonshiner's neighbor would warn of approaching revenuers by firing a gun or setting off a stick of dynamite. One revenuer complained that "the moonshiners found out I was in the mountains before I knew the fact myself."

In time, Lloyd Seay and Roy Hall joined the select group of elite bootleggers who came to realize the obvious: the best way to elude a revenuer wasn't to outsmart him but to outrun him. Speed, not guile, became the most effective means of whiskey tripping. If revenuers blocked the road, the best drivers learned to hit the brakes, tug the emergency brake, spin the wheel, and slide into the 180-degree bootlegger turn.

In downtown Dawsonville, there was just one public pay phone, and it was attached to Harben Brothers Service Station, a squat, white building with a "PURE" oil sign above the gas pumps. It stayed open twenty-four hours a day, and that's where Lloyd Seay could be found loitering most nights, waiting for a customer to call.

Sometimes they asked coyly if Seay had any "apples," or "You got any stuff today?" Often, they ordered in code, requesting a certain "bead" or proof by asking for "flash speed" (jars that, when shaken, produced a layer of bubbles that disappeared quickly—about 85 proof) or "hoss eyes" (bigger bubbles that signified the good stuff: 160 proof).

Because Harben's was near Dawsonville's crossroads, Seay could easily hop onto Route 53 toward Gainesville or onto Route 9 toward Atlanta to deliver his load. His pals, most of them fellow whiskey trippers, would hang around and listen for Seay's return, the sound of his engine slowing and then accelerating as it crossed Gold Creek or climbed Gober Hill, some three to four miles away. If a couple of the trippers were out on deliveries, those still hanging around Harben's would place bets on whose engine they were hearing approach from the east. Seay? Roy Hall? If it was a slow night, the trippers might have some fun right there in town. They'd call the sheriff's office and report a bogus crime somewhere outside of town, then dump used motor oil around the downtown square and take turns spinning donuts around the courthouse.

In short, Harben's is where Seay became a man, or at least by local definition. He learned to work on car engines, make a buck, survive. Roy Hall was learning the same game down in Atlanta, where Raymond Parks one day introduced both Seay and Hall to an up-and-coming whiskey mechanic named Red, the man who would help them both survive the deadly game they were playing.

Across Prohibition's thirteen years, federal agents had seized 340,000 stills and arrested just shy of one million men. Even after Prohibition, the aggressive pursuit of untaxed whiskey led to the imprisonment of many a captured bootlegger. Through the 1920s and 1930s, leading every other state in numbers of seized stills and arrests was Georgia. Though Al Capone's machine-gunning exploits received the news ink, more bootleg whiskey ran through Atlanta than any other city in the nation.

And more than a little blood was shed. During Prohibition, 126 federal agents were killed. Some were gunned down during still raids. At least one was pushed from a moving car by a moonshiner. A few died freakishly, scalded to death after falling into a vat of boiling mash or asphyxiated by the fumes of fermenting corn. One agent was maimed by a bootlegger whose brakes failed and who slammed into a roadblock.

Moonshiners also sustained horrific injuries or died violent deaths. One South Carolina sheriff was known to fire point-blank into the skulls of captured bootleggers. Untold numbers of whiskey trippers burned to death when their cars rolled and their whiskey load ignited after a failed attempt at a bootlegger turn. As Robert Mitchum sings in the theme song he cowrote for the classic moonshining flick *Thunder Road*:

> *He left the road at 90; that's all there is to say.*
> *The devil got the moonshine and the mountain boy that day.*

And yet, in certain communities, there was a brotherly aspect to the grim battles. When famed columnist Ernie Pyle spent a day with a Tennessee revenuer, he wrote of the surprising "mutual respect" the two sides had for each other. Revenuers and moonshiners came to know one another's names and families. A federal agent might arrest a man and send him to prison for two years, then help him find a job, a home, or a girlfriend when he got out. Some moonshiners named their kids after revenuers they had feared and fled, but whom they secretly admired. The familial rivalry even influenced children's games. Instead of cowboys and Indians, the children of Dawsonville and other moonshining communities played bootleggers and revenuers. Sometimes they flipped coins to decide who played whiskey trippers such as Lloyd Seay or Roy Hall and who played the feds.

"The losers had to play the law," one Dawsonville youth-cum-bootlegger said.

As Sherwood Anderson noted in an article about a famous 1935 moonshining trial in rural Virginia, southern moonshiners were "mostly kids who liked the excitement . . . the kick of it."

The late 1930s then saw a number of developments occur in accidental co-operation, which changed the rules of the moonshining game: the ranks of revenue agents grew larger and smarter, forcing whiskey mechanics to get craftier. Cars got much, much faster, and the whiskey trippers grew more skillful. The Great Depression weakened, and southerners found a little extra money in their pockets. They wanted a place to spend it and to have some fun. These developments all happened in Dawsonville or Atlanta, or on the byways that connected the two, and began to clear the way for the sport of stock car racing to bloom. The period in history, starting around 1938, was like a trough of calm between two swells. The Depression was ebbing, and World War II would soon rise up and consume the nation.

But first, for three thrilling years, southerners lucky enough to live near a fairgrounds or a homemade racetrack enjoyed the entertaining by-product of moonshine and its sidekick, the Ford. Leading the way were two bootlegging cousins from Dawsonville named Roy and Lloyd, men skilled enough to drive like the devil and live to brag about it.

NASCAR pioneers later concurred that Seay was absolutely fearless and, as a respectful revenuer once confirmed, "without a doubt the best automobile driver of [his] time." One revenue agent later claimed to have caught Seay eight times during his career but admitted that he had only done so by shooting holes in Seay's tires. A popular story about Seay describes him being pulled over by police. There was no whiskey aboard, so the officer fined him ten dollars for speeding. Seay handed over twenty dollars, explaining that he was paying in advance for his return trip. "Maybe you could let me go on through?" he said.

Revenuers tolerated Seay because he was mostly respectful, polite, and even shy. He seemed like a good kid caught up in a dangerous game for which he had a genetic talent. If it had been football instead of bootlegging, Seay was like the quiet kid in class who suddenly found himself with the talents to become quarterback. Roy Hall, on the other hand, was a born linebacker, bolder and more reckless than angel-faced Lloyd.

Revenue agents came to admire Hall's driving talents as well, one of them going so far as to call him a driving "genius." But they were also scared to death of the man.

For Hall, the trick was to make sure the whiskey was packed tightly in the back. The way he drove, too much sloshing and banging around and he might roll his top-heavy Ford into a ditch. For that very reason, glass fruit jars were not good containers for guys like Hall. Some trippers wrapped the jars tightly in netting or butcher paper, but the way Hall drove, there was still too much risk of splintered glass and loosed liquor. He preferred the tougher gallon-size tin cans, packed six per canvas sleeve—an official six-gallon "case." Hall could stack at least twenty cases into his Ford's trunk and backseat.

From Dawsonville south to Cumming was an especially dangerous route. State Highway 9 was all dirt, twisted like a roadkill snake, and was "hot with law every night," one ex-tripper recalled. Drainage gulches of angry red dirt skulked beside the road; during heavy rains, they filled with water and became rivers of orangey chocolate. Tall pines loomed on either side of switchbacks that cut jagged, dark-copper gouges into hillsides.

Hall's tactic was the straight-ahead, no-bullshit approach. At the outskirts of town, he mashed the accelerator and avoided the brake pedal. When the curves began, Hall chopped them in half. If a curve bore to the left, he first veered far to the right, just inches from where the roadway dropped off into the pines, then cut hard to the left, hugging tight against the inner arc. That's when the physics got tricky.

A gallon of whiskey, depending on its proof, weighed six pounds; the tin can another pound or two. Hauling 120 gallons was like having four fat guys crammed in the backseat. Do the math: a half ton of booze plus a three thousand–pound Ford plus eighty miles an hour on a ninety-degree arcing road, banking left and down, *plus* an unstable surface of red dirt beneath four wheels . . . well, it equaled a Ford that was going to slide into a ditch and explode, unless you knew what you were doing. But that's when Hall shined, and why moonshiners would soon prove themselves to be natural, intuitive racers.

With his hands on the bottom of the steering wheel, Hall would throw himself into the turn, spinning the wheel in toward the curve. When he felt the car begin to slip, he would hit the gas, not the brake, actually *accelerating* through the turn, with the car moving forward and sideways at the same time. When the rear end began to slide too far, he would torque the wheel in the same direction; to the right in a left-hand curve, for example—otherwise, he'd spin out. If his split-second timing was dead-on, just before he reached the road's edge and the steep embankment beyond it, the mechanics and geometry and gravity of the moment converged in perfect synchronicity. Tires somehow found purchase on the dirt, the momentum of the slide yielded to the forward urging of the engine, and Hall and Ford and whiskey all straightened out and rocketed forward.

Until the next curve. Hall burned through many sets of tires in this manner. Said one thirties-era Atlanta mechanic, "He never knew what a brake was." The revenuers simply couldn't keep up. And when they tried, they sometimes wished they hadn't.

One night, two revenue agents spotted a loaded '39 Ford coupe heading south from the town of Tate, toward Atlanta. The agents sped after the coupe, following it through the tight curves of Highway 5. It was a dark night, and the coupe was beginning to pull away from the revenuers. The agent behind the wheel wasn't familiar enough with the road and took a sharp curve too fast and spun off the road. The car plowed into a jagged pile of scrap marble that'd been dumped there. One agent was thrown from the car and landed amid the sharp rocks, one of which struck his head and knocked him out. The other agent was

injured, too, but managed to radio for help, then waited beside his unconscious partner. When backup agents arrived, they said their colleagues were so scratched, bloodied, and scabbed that it "looked like
they'd been sortin' wildcats."

The coupe, meanwhile, crested a hill and then plunged down the
other side. As it entered more "esses," the driver cranked the wheel left-
right, left-right. Only after a couple of rolling straightaways gave way to
a few road swizzles that dropped into the paved metropolitan reaches of
Atlanta did the driver ease up on the throttle, making sure he'd lost all
pursuers, before catching his breath and driving more humanely.

The injured revenue agent lay unconscious in a hospital bed for the
next two days. On the second day, a huge bouquet of flowers arrived, accompanied by a card simply signed "The Coupe." They learned later
that the flowers had come from their prey.

Roy Hall.

Pavement and paved speedways were still years away; stock car racing
on asphalt wouldn't begin until in 1950, three years after NASCAR's
birth. In the late 1930s, the racetracks of the South—like the roads
north of Atlanta—were red dirt.

Not the loamy, coffee-colored soil typically thought of as "dirt."
North Georgia soil was as unique as its citizens. It shined like the color
of a new penny; ancient, Martian stuff, thick with clay and tinted deep
orangey red by iron deposits. Racetracks that would soon become
moonshiners' stomping grounds were ovals of such redness: two red-dirt
straightaways enclosed by four red-dirt turns, each a far lesser version of
a Dawsonville-to-Cumming curve, which, of course, was handled only at
night, with half a ton of liquor, and often a gun-toting revenuer close behind. Future NASCAR racers who, like Hall and Seay, honed their driving skills as whiskey trippers, would later admit that high-speed races on
paved ovals were fairly simple feats compared to midnight moonshine
runs, that no racetrack could scare them like screaming at 120 miles an
hour into the vortex of a red-rutted lane barely wider than a Ford.

Men such as Hall and Seay found peace on such lanes. But for all their innate skills, talent alone couldn't carry them into the racing world. For that, they needed machinery to match their driving abilities. They needed their Fords to perform as flawlessly as themselves. And for that, they needed a wizard.

The South produced statesmen and soldiers, planters and doctors and
lawyers and poets, but certainly no engineers and mechanics.
Let Yankees adopt such low callings.
— MARGARET MITCHELL

5

An "orgy of dust, liquor and noise"

Across its first decades, the automobile's effect on American culture and productivity was akin to the computer's effect on everyday life many decades later: it changed people's lives, but no one knew how the hell it worked.

And so, the auto mechanic—like a shaman, who could reveal, interpret, and manipulate the car's grimy inner secrets—became a minor deity. Car-smitten teenagers would loiter outside garages, smoking and talking of overhead cams and piston displacement. At those garages, moonshine culture and car culture merged and, like a chemical reaction, sizzled into something altogether new. It happened right there in Atlanta, right there on Spring Street, where chain-smoking Red Vogt seemed always to be bent at the waist, his buzz-cut red head and his broad shoulders buried deep in the engine cavity of a Ford, with Seay, Hall, and other teens awaiting their sage's prognosis.

Louis Jerome "Red" Vogt was born in Washington, D.C., in 1904. At age twelve, he got his first job with a local Cadillac dealership, where he fell in love with the mysteries of the internal combustion engine. Vogt also loved the workplace, the solidity of concrete floors and steel-grip tools, and found he had a knack for the job. By sixteen, he was named shop foreman, which sometimes required the burly youngster to fight off older mechanics who didn't like taking orders from a freckle-faced teen.

Vogt's father, Charles, whom everyone called "Louie," worked for the government printing office in D.C., and young Red—whose orange hair came from his strict, Victorian mother, Caroline—took pains to veer far from his father's dull career path. Vogt's parents were friends with a Mr. and Mrs. France, and during a visit to the France house, five-year-old Red asked why Mrs. France's belly looked so fat. Red's dad explained that she'd swallowed a watermelon seed and that a melon was growing inside her. When baby Bill France was born, Red took to calling him "watermelon." And a complicated but important friendship began—one that would last eighty years and would eventually bring one man riches, the other heartache.

As teens, Bill France worked as a mechanic at a local Ford dealership while Red worked at the Cadillac dealership. France and Vogt both traveled on the weekends in search of races, most often to the wooden board racetracks in Laurel, Maryland; Altoona, Pennsylvania; and Atlantic City, New Jersey. Sometimes France secretly raced his dad's Model T, and his father began wondering why the tires wore out so fast.

Vogt preferred motorcycles, especially the classic beasts manufactured by Indian. Racing them on the steeply banked board tracks was like racing inside a large wooden mixing bowl. The speeds were incredible, as were the spills. At one such race, Vogt lost control of his bike, flew face-first into a fence post, and lost all but a few of his teeth. He'd wear dentures the rest of his life. Another tumbling wipeout on the pitted planks shredded Vogt's leather riding outfit; when he finally came to a stop, he was wearing little more than his helmet and boots. Vogt rotated in and out of the hospital for three months and would forever after carry splinters in his flesh.

During his rehabilitation, he met a medical volunteer named Ruth, who nursed him back to health. She came from a wealthy family, spoke fluent French, and had begun studying for a career in the growing cosmetics industry. At the time, the muscle-bound, leather-clad biker seemed the man of her dreams. And when Red said he was moving to Atlanta, she agreed to go with him.

In 1927, Red and his bride-to-be drove south and moved into an Atlanta hotel. Arriving at the height of Prohibition was a fortunate bit of timing for Vogt. Atlanta's illegal liquor industry desperately needed a forward-thinking mechanic. That first week, Vogt met with various bankers until he finally convinced one to loan him one hundred dollars so he could buy tools and rent a garage. He also met with a well-known Atlanta bootlegger named Peachtree Williams, who wanted Vogt to fix some of the cars that his employees used to deliver their product.

Vogt's hero and lifelong role model—like Bill France's—was Henry Ford. At his downtown garage, Vogt developed a Ford-like reputation as an obsessive, meticulous, strong-willed mechanic but also a capricious and demanding employer. A distinction for quality workmanship lured North Georgia's whiskey trippers to the corner of Spring Street and Linden Avenue, where Vogt became a most trusted ally.

Sheriff's deputies and federal revenue agents dropped their cars at the garage as well, but Vogt had a saying that he'd use the rest of his life: *Money equals speed.* "Bootleggers paid better than public servants," Vogt would say. So it's not hard to guess whose cars received his keenest attentions. "We had the money and the know-how, and the sheriffs didn't," a famous moonshiner-turned-NASCAR-racer once boasted.

Creative whiskey mechanics elsewhere focused their attention on guise and guile. They yanked out the backseats of cars and installed 250-gallon tanks. Others transformed hearses into whiskey haulers, which led processions of a dozen black cars full of moonshine, a so-called wet funeral. Vogt felt his job was more straightforward than that, and he focused simply on making Henry Ford's cars strong enough to carry 200 gallons of liquor and fast enough to evade the growing ranks of federal agents.

He also became very wealthy. Vogt made so much whiskey-soaked money in those first few years that he moved his family—Ruth and two boys, born in 1932 and 1934—to a huge house in a suburb called East

Lake, where he and Ruth employed a small staff of servants. Word of Vogt's mechanical prowess spread well beyond moonshining circles. Competitors in the annual five hundred–mile race at Indianapolis wanted his help, and he'd leave Ruth at home to attend the Memorial Day Classic.

With his massive arms and chest and a huge handshake—with which he challenged other men, sometimes bringing them to their knees—Vogt seemed always to be fighting, sometimes openly, sometimes subtly. He demanded precision and respect from his employees, many of whom were black, a rarity in segregated Atlanta. He sometimes treated his workers—men named Deacon and Half-Pint, nicknamed for the half pint of whiskey he kept in his pocket—like dogs, but he paid them well and they were loyal to him. Vogt took pride in his German heritage, considering Germans the world's most brilliant engineers. But he also voiced racist and anti-Semitic sentiments, even sympathy for Hitler—sentiments that would similarly forever tarnish the image of Henry Ford, whom Hitler once called a "leader" of the Fascist movement in the United States.

Vogt, like Ford, had left school at a young age and was both proud of and sensitive about his lack of education. As Upton Sinclair once said of Ford, "Henry remained what he had been born: a supermechanic with the mind of a stubborn peasant." The same could be said of Vogt, who was also intensely proud to be a Confederate: "I'm a southerner," he'd say. "And don't you ever call me a goddam Yankee."

He didn't have a sharp mind for business, though, and was lucky to have his wife handling their finances, collecting money from the bootlegger clients, and hiring and paying the employees. The bootleggers called her Mom, but if they failed to pay on time, they'd meet her wrath and muttered to one another what a "tyrannical bitch" she could be.

Vogt was also a violent and unpredictable man—taut and quiet, like a spring tensed for release. He could be polite and gentlemanly with women but was socially awkward, defensive about his limited education and social skills, and in general, didn't like people and had few friends. As a parent, he was "terrible, just awful . . . dysfunctional," recalls Vogt's son Tom. He spent little time with his sons and sent them off to Georgia Military Academy when they were just four and six. "In private he was a mean, angry, beligerent, violent man," Tom Vogt said.

After Raymond Parks got to know Vogt, he would wince at how Vogt treated his wife and kids. Others stopped even asking about the children, assuming that, since Vogt never mentioned them, they must have died. But Parks saw something in Vogt. As his only real friend, Parks was able to overlook his many flaws and accept him for that one brilliant gift, the reason Parks found Vogt in the first place, and possibly the one reason Vogt was put on earth. Like an idiot savant, Vogt was oblivious to most human matters. But he knew all about one thing and knew it better than anyone in Atlanta.

He knew speed.

Speed became a valuable commodity in Atlanta during the 1930s. Mainly, it took the form of Ford coupes and sedans powered by V-8 engines. Those cars were built right in downtown Atlanta and comprised the bulk of Red Vogt's business through that decade.

Ford's V-8s earned him the loyalty of many bootleggers, and those loyalists gathered daily outside Red Vogt's shop, swapping tales of federal agents as they passed around a flask of whiskey and talked of engines and tires, speed and tactics. Southern whiskey boys loitered outside the legend's workplace the way northern or midwestern boys hung around basketball courts or sandlot baseball fields. Inside, Vogt tore apart engines, tweaked the stock parts, added hot-rod parts he ordered from California or Philadelphia, or homemade parts he machined himself, and pieced it all together again.

Among Vogt's truest acolytes were Lloyd Seay and Roy Hall. Other moonshining clients (and future NASCAR racers) found their way to Vogt's shop, too. Vogt would ask them, "What roads are you driving?" and "How many gallons are you hauling?" He then tailored his modifications to a specific route and weight load. Just as the trippers' delivery skills would translate into dirt-track racing skills, Vogt's ability to make

Ford engines perform above and beyond their mechanical limitations helped establish him as one of the nation's first and best racing mechanics, and one of the sport's driving forces.

Word of Vogt's mechanical prowess had already reached Atlanta's moonshine kingpin, Raymond Parks, who entrusted Vogt with his whiskey cars. Parks paid Vogt once every week or two to keep his whiskey cars in peak condition. Vogt's wife, Ruth, angrily nagged Parks if he was even a day late with a payment. Some suspected that Vogt's wife was among the reasons he spent so many hours at the garage, and the couple would indeed soon divorce. Vogt's garage stayed "Open 24 hours," as the neon sign above the front bay declared. He sometimes worked days at a time, catching catnaps here and there on a cot or simply passing out, flat on his back beneath a car on one of his wheeled crawlers. If an employee kicked one of Vogt's outstretched legs and asked, "You asleep, Red?" he'd snap awake and bark at him.

"Hell no I ain't asleep—get back to work."

When exhaustion threatened to drop him, Vogt would go home and sleep fifteen hours straight, then come back to the garage and work another three days in a row. He combated fatigue with a steady diet of coffee, chocolate, cigarettes, and Coke. Chain-smoking had stained the two fingers of his right hand a permanent yellow. In winter, he warmed the unheated garage with buckets of burning coal and an old kettle stove he rigged with a stopcock that dribbled used motor oil into the fire. The sides of the stove sometimes glowed red, and on top sat a pot of strong, thickening coffee. Vogt's snarling, snaggly toothed boxer dog, named Buddy, often slept near the burning stove.

In time, Vogt built a secret room at the far back of the garage, behind a false wall, where he experimented on bootleggers' engines. Vogt knew the feds watched his garage, and he didn't want a revenuer walking in one day to find him tinkering on a Roy Hall or Lloyd Seay whiskey car.

While his personality and social graces were something of a mess, Vogt's personal appearance and his garage were incredibly pristine. He wore the same uniform, day after day: white pants, white T-shirt, and white socks. With his neatly combed red hair and sparkling white clothes, he always looked impossibly clean. The only physical signs that he was a mechanic were dark smudges around the pants pockets and the permanent black beneath his fingernails. The white uniform was a gimmicky display of Vogt's arrogance and obsessiveness. So was the meticulous organization of his tools, which lay neatly in drawers and on shelves, as if part of a museum display. He made workers polish his tools and sweep the floors; except for the occasional cigarette butt, the garage floor was always spotless. He even made his employees change uniforms if they got a bit too dirty.

Vogt's paranoia and obsession with cleanliness were more than a fixation. They were his secret weapon and would be copied by future generations of racing mechanics. It turned out that a fastidiously clean engine lasted longer and ran faster. Vogt wouldn't even allow workers to use rags in certain areas of his shop, for fear that errant pieces of microscopic lint would enter one of his engines and shave a sliver off a V-8's top speed. As usual, Vogt was way ahead of his time. And in the chronology of America's racing history, his timing was absolutely perfect.

Car racing in America in the 1930s was still largely a sport of the Northeast, the Midwest, and the West—and a sport of the rich. It had been that way from the start. Future NASCAR legend Richard Petty said that car racing began when the second automobile rolled from the factory, which is practically the truth. As early as the 1890s, men on steam-powered "quadricycles" raced one another in comical, five-mile-an-hour duels a pedestrian could have won. The first official gasoline-powered race was held in Chicago in 1895, a fifty-two-mile contest that was won by a one-cylinder car in ten hours.

The inaugural organized races of America were playgrounds for wealthy playboys and their specially made race cars. Henry Ford had proved with his racing victory in 1901 that gas-powered vehicles were the speedsters of the future and that winning was a proven sales tactic. Ford had therefore built special racing cars for that sole purpose of winning races and attracting attention to his brand. His regular, factory-built cars, meanwhile—the Model Ts and Model As—were built for everyday use. Through the early 1900s, then, there were two types of cars: built-from-scratch racing cars and mass-manufactured "stock" cars, such as the Model T and its descendants.

Racing cars first found a home in the Northeast, where the first American automobiles had been manufactured in the early 1890s by the Duryea brothers of Springfield, Massachusetts. Race cars then migrated west to cities such as Detroit and Indianapolis, and south to Daytona Beach, which was prized for its hard-packed sand.

In Daytona, the first races were straight-ahead sprints down the smooth surface of the flat beach. Alexander Winton, whom Henry Ford had beaten in his only race in 1901, was among the nation's first speed demons, beating Ransom Olds (namesake of the Oldsmobile) in a 60-mile-an-hour duel at Daytona Beach in 1903. Both cars were one-of-a-kind prototypes. Three years later, a sleek canvas-and-wood experimental vehicle sped to an amazing 127 miles an hour there. Four years after that, Barney Oldfield reached 131 miles an hour on Daytona's sands in a powerful, German-built experimental model and declared that he had achieved "the absolute limit of speed as humanity will ever travel." Such speeds, he said, felt like "riding a rocket through space."

Elsewhere in the United States, specialized race cars used public roads as racetracks, following the European "Grand Prix" model. Millionaire racer W. K. Vanderbilt began hosting wildly popular, absurdly dangerous Vanderbilt Cup races along Long Island's roadways in 1904. Many of those early road races suffered from the problem of spectatorship. On Long Island, a quarter million spectators might line up along the route. So eager were they to see drivers that the crowds would close in tight beside the road, creating a human wall of potential carnage; one driver said he "brushed at least a dozen coats while making the turn."

The issue of heedless spectators on public-roadway racetracks was partially solved by the creation of circular tracks, around which spectators gathered in grandstands. One such oval speedway was built in Indianapolis in 1909. Barney Oldfield took the first spin and averaged eighty-four miles an hour on a dangerous surface of crushed stone and tar. But the problem of casualties lingered: during the first three-day Indianapolis meet, two spectators, a driver, and two mechanics were killed. The track was resurfaced with 3.2 million bricks, and in 1911, the brick-paved speedway began hosting annual 500-mile races. The Indianapolis 500 was soon declared "the greatest race in the world" and "the greatest spectacle in sport." One early observer called it "a transcendent event that dwells in the very bloodstream of America—a virus of velocity."

During the first two decades of American auto racing, a variety of diverse racing styles, cars, and governing organizations competed for fans' attentions. Nagging questions associated with the young sport included: *How do we harness the public's interest?* and *Who should oversee it all?* In baseball, football, and basketball, a single league eventually emerged to oversee the rules and regulations, with the nation's top teams gathering obediently beneath that umbrella organization. But in racing, unity was elusive. A fierce battle would be waged for many decades to come. The difficulty was partly due to the evolution of so many species of car racing, such as drag races, dirt-track racing, board-track racing, road rallies, hill climbs, time trials, endurance races, demolition derbies, and many more. Also, bigger-than-life racing personalities such as Oldfield resisted efforts to bring too much structure and rule making to racing.

After a successful bicycle-racing career and a not-so-successful boxing career, Bernd Eli "Barney" Oldfield drove Henry Ford's first race car to victory in 1902 and quickly went on to become the first legend of auto racing and a household name.

Born poor on an Ohio farm, he made a perfect transition from bikes to cars, learning to slide his race cars through the turns of dirt tracks, just as he did when racing bicycles. Oldfield made history by driving a mile a minute in a gas-powered car in 1903 and a year later beat Henry Ford and others in a one-mile race at Daytona Beach.

He liked racing on dirt more than pavement or bricks, a preference that would recur among many subsequent racers. In 1915, he became the first person to race up the dirt road leading to the 14,110-foot summit of Pike's Peak. But Oldfield was at his best on the small-town dirt ovals. Oldfield's trademarks were a scarf around his neck and a chewed-up cigar that he kept clamped in his jaw during races, to keep his teeth from chattering on the rutted dirt tracks. His cross-country barnstorming trips to hundreds of fairground racetracks became hugely popular, even if many of his victories were fixed.

Oldfield's notoriety contributed to auto racing's rise to prominence, and his pudgy, cigar-stuck face personified the popularity of the "open-wheel" race car that dominated the contests of the first quarter century of automobile racing in America.

Open-wheel cars were shaped like stubby baguettes, or two bullet slugs attached end to end, with the wheels sticking out from the fuselage—hence, the term *open-wheel*. These cars would go by many names and come in many different sizes—big cars, dirt cars, champ cars, sprints, midgets—but the premier version was the high-powered Indy car, capable by the mid-1930s of reaching 140 miles an hour at its namesake track. It wasn't just wheels jutting from the body that distinguished the cars from regular, everyday Fords. Racers' torsos also stuck partway out of the shell, exposing them to all sorts of horrific injuries.

Many of the top open-wheel auto races of the first third of the twentieth century were governed by AAA—the American Automobile Association. Though it later became solely a road-service and travel organization, AAA started life as a support group for motorists and local motor clubs, which mostly consisted of wealthy men and their expensive playthings. When it became clear that the increasingly popular sport of auto racing needed some rules and organization, AAA took on the responsibility with great relish, beginning around 1909 with the creation of its Contest Board, which quickly earned a reputation as a stuffy, arrogant, and capricious governing group.

AAA endorsed or "sanctioned" races and established itself as an ironfisted patron. If a race wasn't officially sanctioned by AAA's Contest Board, it was considered an "outlaw" race, and that term would be used in future years to disparage racing events considered to be less than legitimate. Even the most famous racer of his day, Barney Oldfield, was occasionally fined by or barred by AAA for racing in outlaw events.

Oldfield would win just two national-level races in his career and would fail three times in a row at the Indianapolis Speedway—in 1914 (finishing fifth), 1915 (failing to qualify), and 1916 (again finishing fifth). Oldfield's infamy on the racetrack was rivaled by his renown as a notorious drinker, a "barroom brawler, dirt-track daredevil, a man without fear"—all of them apt descriptors for many of the pioneers of stock car racing to follow in his wake. He bristled against AAA's efforts to regulate racing and control drivers, and his retirement in 1918 was largely a result of his many conflicts with AAA's tetchy Contest Board.

Various other racing organizations tried to compete with AAA, but as the sponsor of the greatest race of all—the Indy 500—AAA easily kept upstart groups in line. Most racers of the day aspired to compete at Indy and were reluctant to incur the Contest Board's wrath by racing in events run by AAA's competitors.

Through the 1920s and 1930s, therefore, most of America's official races remained exclusive, elitist events, often in the North (AAA was headquartered in New York) or the Midwest, with well-paid professional drivers in their costly, specially made cars circling specially made tracks. A Kentucky Derby–like air of aristocracy hung over most races. Fans were typically men, wearing suits and bowlers, smoking pipes. Bands sometimes performed, and catered lunches were served. Even famed evangelist and prohibitionist Billy Sunday was known to attend such highbrow events, although some of the more adventurous fans considered them "rather dull and colorless affairs."

In the mid-1930s, a colorful new style of racing began to gain credibility, and fans. Rather than pro drivers in the open-wheel vehicles of Indy and AAA, these new races featured amateur racers in off-the-lot "stock" cars. Most of them were Fords, and many of them were modified for whiskey tripping. At first, AAA could afford to ignore such races, since they mostly occurred in the South. But not for long.

It's impossible to pinpoint the exact origins of stock car racing. At first, it was a gimmick. As early as 1914, short stock car events were tacked on as entertaining sideshow acts to legitimate open-wheel races. In the 1930s, stock cars began attracting a loyal following of their own. Before NASCAR came along, however, regional organizations overseeing such races were either spurious or nonexistent. The sport was entirely home-made and didn't so much emerge with fanfare as evolve in grungy little baby steps.

But there were two crux points—twin birthplaces, if you will—where stock cars were raced more often than elsewhere: Daytona Beach and Atlanta. In those two geographic regions, two distinct groups of men hammered the upstart sport into refinement. Those men ground down the rough, outlaw edges a bit, and in time, some semblance of structure and legitimacy was slowly, sometimes painfully imposed.

Racing had first come to Daytona and adjacent Ormond Beach with speed-record attempts in 1902. During low tide, the recession of the Atlantic created a two hundred–yard–wide swath of sand that was baked hard and flat by the sun. The straightaway stretched twenty miles and—at a time when paved and straight roads were but a distant dream—was considered the nation's premier speed-racing surface. Henry Ford came to Daytona and Ormond Beach a few times to try one of his experimental vehicles on the beach. Ford's driver was often that "rogue, rule breaker, braggart" Barney Oldfield.

In 1935, Sir Malcolm Campbell set a new world speed record of 276.8 miles per hour at Daytona. Soon after, the annual International World Speed Trials left Daytona and moved to the more reliable surface of the Bonneville Salt Flats in Utah, where G.E.T. Eyston would shatter Campbell's record by reaching 357 miles an hour in 1938.

Fearing the loss of tourism dollars to Utah, Daytona's town fathers decided to replace the speed trials with a new type of race in 1936. They used the hard-packed beach as one of two straightaways in what became known as the Beach-and-Road course, an elongated, 3.2-mile oval that would come to rival the mythic status of Indianapolis Speedway. Part of the appeal among fans was the proximity to sea life—one straightaway ran along the sand, just feet from the Atlantic surf. The other straightaway was Daytona's main street, Highway A1A, which ran parallel to the beach. City fathers plowed two paths through the dunes to connect the two straightaways. Those new paths became the north and south turns, tight arcs where most of the spectators lined up to watch the inaugural 250-mile contest, sponsored by Daytona City and AAA, on March 8, 1936.

Instead of inviting open-wheel race cars, promoters decided to gamble on stock cars and only allowed American-made, "strictly stock" automobiles to enter. AAA had experimented with a similar stock car event ten years earlier; its 1926 advertisement had lured fans with the promise of seeing the very same cars driven by them and their neighbors: "Will the Car Like You Drive Win Over the Kind Driven by Your Friend?" Fans hadn't seemed too wild for stock car racing in the late 1920s, but AAA agreed to give it another chance in 1936 at Daytona and officially "sanction" the race.

Although the terms *strictly stock* and *stock car race* had been around for years, no one could yet claim to be a professional stock car racer. After AAA's event in 1926, there had been too few "stock" races anywhere in the United States to create racers who called themselves "stock car" drivers. Most of the competitors in the March 8 race were transplants from dirt-track, midget, board-track, and Indy racing, including 1934's Indy 500 champ, Wild Bill Cummings. For many drivers, it was their first attempt at stock car racing. For many fans, it was also their first taste of stocks, and everything about the first stock car race at Daytona Beach carried a whiff of experimentation—and danger. Wary newspapers warned spectators to "KEEP OFF THE COURSE, for your own safety."

Of the twenty-seven starters, twenty were Fords, which proved to be the only cars capable of handling the Beach-and-Road course. The final laps devolved into a jumbled mess. The north and south turns became rutted "hog wallows," and nearly every racer had to be pulled from the thick sand by tow trucks. So many disabled cars clogged the course that organizers cut the race short by ten miles. Only ten cars—all but one of them Fords—finished the race. But spectators loved it, having been treated to such sights as one racer getting flung out of his tumbling convertible and others rolling into the Atlantic surf.

Milt Marion, in a Ford, was declared the winner, and Red Vogt's childhood friend from D.C., Bill France, came in fifth, though he'd later claim that he had actually lapped Milt Marion twice. With imperfect rules and lap-counting systems, such disputes would become a common affliction across the early years of stock car racing.

Ford V-8s took the top five spots, and the top finishers split the five thousand–dollar winners' purse. The sponsors—the city of Daytona and AAA—were the only losers, coming out of the weekend twenty thousand dollars short. The organizers had poured money into the event but accidentally allowed thousands of fans to enter without paying. It was AAA's first and last race at Daytona Beach. Factory-built stock cars, AAA decided, were simply not meant to race, and the organization returned to more reliable open-wheel race venues.

A local Elks club hosted a similar stock car race on the Beach-and-Road course, on Labor Day in 1937, but also lost money. It wasn't until the summer of 1938 that stock car racing in Daytona began to truly catch fire. That's when twenty-nine-year-old Bill France took over as chief sponsor and promoter, as well as part-time racer, pursuits to which he would dedicate the rest of his life.

Tired of the cold and snow up north, France had left his mechanic's job in Washington, D.C., and headed for Florida with his wife and son. When he arrived at Daytona Beach in 1934, he thought it was "the prettiest place I'd ever seen."

The Frances moved into a fifteen-dollar-a-month one-bedroom house. France found a fifteen-dollar-a-week job as a mechanic but spent most weekends working on racing cars or driving to and from races. The three hundred dollars he won for fifth place in the 1936 Beach-and-

Road race convinced him that racing was not just fun but potentially profitable.

In 1938, at the request of the Chamber of Commerce, France and another local businessman—Charlie Reese, the owner of Charlie's Grill and Cocktail Bar—agreed to sponsor two races that summer. The first, held on July 10, netted France, as the contest's cosponsor and its runner-up, a tidy little one hundred–dollar profit. The next race, scheduled for Labor Day, foreshadowed many of the complications that would confound stock car racing a decade later, when France took charge of the entire sport.

On September 5, 1938, five thousand spectators paid fifty cents apiece to attend France's Labor Day race, featuring fourteen cars, all but one of them a 1937 or 1938 Ford V-8. To funnel fans through the ticket turnstiles and prevent unpaid crashers, France posted signs through the surrounding dunes, "Careful—Rattlesnakes."

A leather-faced, pistol-carrying moonshiner/gambler from Georgia named Smokey Purser took the checkered flag at the end of the 160-mile race, just as he had a year earlier, when he won the 1937 Elks Club's Labor Day race. The 1938 winner was to receive not only a $240 purse but also a case of beer, a bottle of rum, a box of cigars, and a case of motor oil; Purser was especially looking forward to the beer and rum. But instead of pulling into the pits to claim his trophy and winnings, Purser drove straight up the beach and out of sight.

France had instituted prerace and postrace engine inspections, to make sure racers didn't tweak their "stock" cars with illegal modifications. At the time, inspections weren't too strict—mechanics were typically free to tweak and soup their cars at will—and some race organizers didn't even bother to inspect cars. France's inspection was a rarity in an otherwise free-for-all culture.

Purser returned for a 4:00 p.m. postrace inspection, but France—assuming that Purser had fled to remove evidence of illegal modifications from his '38 Ford V-8—disqualified him.

Born to a family of North Georgia moonshiners, Purser had left home as a teen and landed in Florida, where he became street-smart and slick. During Prohibition, he delivered liquor to southern waterfront cities by boat, sometimes traveling up the Mississippi River to St. Louis. He also delivered whiskey in a van labeled "Florida Fresh Fish," and his favorite disguise was as a Roman Catholic priest. A notorious gambler, Purser was once tied to a tree and left for dead by an angry gang to which he owned money. By 1938, Purser had become wealthy and philanthropic, often donating Thanksgiving turkeys to a local orphanage. Now in his forties, and mostly retired from moonshining, except for the corn liquor he sometimes served to trusted patrons of his tavern, the New Yorker Bar & Grill, he took to stock car racing with ease—and relish. Taking a cue from Barney Oldfield, Purser was a vigorous self-promoter and aggressively averse to rules and restrictions. He had won just $43 for his victory in the Elks Club's 1937 Labor Day race. But this time, with $240 *plus* the Ballantine beer, rum, and cigars on the line, he was not about to yield quietly to France's authority.

"I am entitled to my winnings," Purser complained after being informed of his disqualification. He argued that his car had been inspected before the race, that he was told to come back for a postrace inspection by 4:00 p.m., and had arrived ten minutes early.

"The time to disqualify a car is before and not after a race," Purser told the race officials. "My car is strictly stock. I don't feel I've been given a fair deal."

It was no use. France declared that he would give the victory to the second-place finisher: *himself*. France's partner, Charlie Reese, realized that awarding the winner's purse to the race promoter on a technicality would look bad. So, while France was given credit for the victory, they bumped the third-place driver, Lloyd Moody, into second place and gave him the $240 winner's purse. Purser was given fourteenth place.

Purser's frustrations foreshadowed the many disputes that would arise between Big Bill France and the crafty, rule-breaking moonshiner/racers with their mechanical ingenuity. Paul Hemphill speaks of a stock car truism in his book *Wheels*: "The surest way to get a 'hillbilly' to do something was to tell him it was against the law."

France would never quite learn that lesson and would continue to battle against wily racers such as Purser the rest of his life. He would mature into a tireless, intuitive salesman and promoter, the P. T. Barnum of the racing world. But he would also develop a reputation as a cutthroat, imperious, domineering, pistol-toting bully.

Still, he was smart enough to know there was something to this new kind of racing, and he decided right then, in 1938, to dedicate himself to stock cars. No one, not even a friend, could stop him now.

Meanwhile, in stock car racing's other birthplace, Atlanta's moonshiners improvised. They may not have had Daytona's packed sands. But they had cow pastures.

It turns out the thick, iron-rich red soil of North Georgia was a poor host to most living things—except corn (and its by-product, moonshine). But the red clay found just beneath the thin layer of topsoil made the perfect racing surface. That's why most of the first southern stock car racing promoters were farmers. They found that a tractor and some chicken fencing could turn a cow pasture into a racetrack in no time. Some farmers confounded racers by spraying water on the track, turning it slick, thick and syrupy, like a spilled can of ocher-colored paint. In part, it was an effort to prevent dust on dry summer days, but it also treated the crowds to a more entertaining, slip-sliding spectacle. Racers came home with orange clothes and scalps, ears and mouths full of red grit.

In truth, there were many such pasture tracks around Atlanta and North Georgia, so trying to narrow down a single starting point is futile. Still, some moonshiners-cum-racers insist it all started outside the town of Stockbridge, just south of Atlanta, where bootleggers sought bragging rights as having the fastest car in their chosen profession. Thirty or forty of them would gather there, speeding around a cow field, spinning their wheels to etch a half-mile racing oval into the same "savagely red land" described in the book all Atlantans were reading at that time, Margaret Mitchell's *Gone with the Wind*.

The transition from participatory sport to spectator sport progressed fairly quickly. At first, a few dozen neighbors might show up, wondering what was happening beneath the cloud of dust. The next week, a hundred people might show. Word spread, and soon it was three hundred, then four. In the beginning, such races were virtual free-for-alls, and attendance was also free. Money only entered the picture when racers started passing around one of the leather football helmets they wore, collecting nickels and dimes from the fans and putting the cash into a pot that the winner would take home.

Once small-time entrepreneurs realized there was money to be made, they hosted stock car races at horse tracks and county fairgrounds, which began to attract paying crowds in the thousands. Fairground races had an innocent, homemade feel, almost naïve despite all the noise and brawn of the V-8s. Money for the racers was hard to come by at first, and fraud and theft were rampant. Without a AAA-type umbrella organization, races were usually sponsored by local slicksters, who'd collect sponsorship dollars from the local gas station, grocery store, or tavern. Winners might bring home seventy-five dollars for their life-threatening victory— just enough money to pay for their tires and gas. Unless a sleazy promoter took off with the purse.

In contrast to AAA events and their traveling bands of professionals, stock car races were often filled with amateur local drivers in local cars, which erased the elitist taint from auto racing and, in the South, multiplied the thrills. A peanut farmer with dreams of speed and victory might come in from his fields, hand-paint a number on his family sedan, and race his heart out, bumping fenders with other farmers, mill workers, mechanics, and moonshiners, until his face was caked and his throat clogged with dust. Moonshiners had their own weekend routine. They'd come down from the hills with a carload of moonshine on Friday or Saturday night, then party all night in Atlanta's nightclubs and honky-tonks. They'd race on Saturday or Sunday afternoon, then pick up sacks of sugar for the stills and deliver them back home on Sunday night.

To cut costs, some racers in those early days would try to get Sears, Roebuck to share the tab. They'd buy Sears tires from the Atlanta showroom on Ponce de Leon Avenue and then, after racing on them on a Sunday, try to return the chewed-up tires on Monday, innocently claiming, "I don't know how they got wore out so fast."

Partnered with the lawbreaking moonshiner in such early stock car races were, of course, the law-bending whiskey mechanics. As they bored out the cylinders of whiskey cars, and added dual manifolds and carburetors, men such as Red Vogt were in effect learning how to build race cars. Vogt's reputation even earned him an invitation to the 1938 Indy 500, where he worked on the car of Floyd Roberts, the victor. Vogt's wizardry and hard-to-detect machining tactics would attract controversy throughout his entire career and lead to infamous run-ins with lifelong friend Bill France.

The year 1938 was both the year that Bill France began promoting stock car races at Daytona and the year of Atlanta's first big stock car event, which ignited a competition between the two cities as the hub of stock car racing.

Two months after France's first big Labor Day race at Daytona, Atlanta scheduled its own stock car race for Armistice Day, November 11, 1938. Despite the recent march of German troops into Czechoslovakia, and of Japanese troops into China, war seemed a faraway notion. The twentieth anniversary of the armistice that ended World War I seemed as good an excuse as any for a car race at Lakewood Speedway, which the Atlanta papers had dubbed "Dixie's greatest track."

Lakewood Speedway was about to offer southerners, on an enormous scale, a new kind of racing altogether. The track had begun life as a horse track encircling a lake and was part of south-side Atlanta's amusement park and fairgrounds complex. It had been converted to a one-mile car track in 1915, to compete with the popular Atlanta Speedway, a short-lived, two-mile track created in 1909 by Coca-Cola magnate Asa Candler.

Barney Oldfield himself had been a favorite at Lakewood, where he once narrowly escaped death when an acrobatic pilot hired to entertain crowds during a race crashed his plane onto the racetrack. Through the 1920s and '30s, Lakewood became a regular stop for open-wheel racers, the so-called big cars, and other AAA-sponsored contests. By the mid-1930s, Lakewood was considered the "Indy of the South," and AAA sponsored hugely popular Indy-style races on July 4 and Labor Day in 1938.

But never before had Lakewood sponsored a stock car race, and the instant success of the November 11 race shocked all who were there, racers and fans alike.

Having graduated from the makeshift cow pasture racetracks, the biggest names in southern racing gathered that Friday in late 1938, along with twenty thousand enthusiastic fans. The two previous races at Daytona Beach had each drawn fewer than five thousand spectators, making Lakewood's race—with four times as many fans—the South's first true big-time "stock car" race, and one of the largest stock car races anywhere in the United States.

It was Vogt's first big stock car race, as well as Lloyd Seay's, Roy Hall's, and Raymond Parks's. It would also be the first time that Parks crossed paths with Bill France, who entered the race at the last minute, at the urging of Red Vogt. In fact, many of the men who would create "NASCAR" ten years later were there, including Red Byron, a recent transplant to the South from Colorado.

Even before the 150-mile event began, Red Vogt and Lloyd Seay were stirring up the kind of trouble that would become commonplace at nearly every subsequent race. As with France's Daytona races, this race was supposed to include only "strictly stock" cars—no tweaking of any kind was allowed, and certainly none of the performance-enhancing tricks that men such as Vogt regularly added to their whiskey cars. But folks knew of Vogt's reputation with engines, and rumors of illicit modifications began to fly. One racer complained that one of Vogt's cars—a 1926 Chrysler being driven by another redheaded Atlantan, the hotheaded Red Singleton—contained illegally milled cylinder heads.

"Plus," complained one protester, "it doesn't have fenders on it."

Vogt, who chaired the race's technical committee, denied violating his own rules. When the promoter threatened to replace him as technical chairman, he snapped. "My car has not been modified!" Vogt insisted. He offered to donate one thousand dollars to the "community chest fund" if anyone could prove that he was cheating.

Prerace jitters and backbiting led another racer to publicly claim that Lloyd Seay—who had recently broken his arm, which now rested in a sling—"would be a hazard to the other drivers." Seay countered that he was quite capable of driving his Ford one-handed, thank you.

As it would turn out, one-handed driving was hardly the most hazardous threat amid a gathering of thirty V-8s on a mile-long converted horse track. Before the big race even began, one of the favorites—Bert "The Flying Dutchman" Hellmueller—was lying in a hospital bed. On a qualifying run a few days earlier, Hellmueller's front tire had blown and his car rolled into the grandstands. If fans had been sitting there, many would have been killed. But such risks didn't stanch the flow of eager fans on race day.

At the time, only Indianapolis had been able to consistently draw thousands of Americans to a single racing stadium for an automobile race. Far more popular were baseball and horse racing. Ten days earlier, an overflow crowd of fifty thousand had watched Seabiscuit dethrone War Admiral at Pimlico racetrack in Baltimore. The 1938 baseball season drew more than ten million people to the games of the nation's sixteen, mostly northern teams. In the former Confederacy, word had just begun to spread about these so-called stock car races in Alabama, North and South Carolina, Tennessee, and Virginia.

Leading up to the Armistice Day race, city officials had the foresight to offer special bus, streetcar, and taxi service to the track, to avoid clogged roads and a parking nightmare. Newspapers called it "a sporting event that is churning up the most interest since back in 1909," referring to a popular open-wheel race held that year. Newsmen also touted the chance for potential carnage at Lakewood. "They'll spill speed and maybe some gore," one newsman teased. It was not an empty promise.

Racers considered Lakewood a treacherous track. Unlike most racetracks, it was flat, not banked, which made it difficult for cars to grip dirt in the turns. As a result, more than a few racers had lost their lives there over the years. A few slid off the track and into the lake, where they drowned still strapped in their cars. A few burned to death. Sometimes, they flipped into the grandstands, injuring or killing not only themselves but spectators.

Nonetheless, the gates opened at 9:00 a.m., and while the main race wouldn't start until 2:00 p.m., fans poured into the grandstands from all over North Georgia. All morning there were warm-up races, preliminary heats, a consolation race, and stunt driving. The racetrack became an instant carnival, with fans picnicking on fried chicken and biscuits, drinking from flasks of corn liquor, hooting and hollering, and occasionally fighting.

During the previous week's qualifying trials, two female racers had failed to qualify for the main race but were allowed to entertain the crowd with some prerace stunts. After "Captain" Frank performed some spins and what the newspaper called "hell driving," Buddy Evans and his wife took turns plowing through a burning wall and the shapely Miss Birdie Draper drove her car through sixteen sticks of exploding dynamite.

As the 2:00 p.m. main event approached, fans spilled out of the grandstands and stood alongside the flimsy rail fence surrounding the track. A field of thirty cars began rolling into their starting positions. Among the better-known drivers was Mexican movie star Ramon Cortez and a full-blooded Cherokee Indian stunt driver nicknamed "Chief Ride in the Storm." A descendant of the tribe that had been shoved out of Georgia during the gold rush a century earlier, the Oklahoman raced with his pet fox terrier sitting in the passenger seat. A few rows back from the front, starting side by side, were the cars of Roy Hall, Lloyd Seay, and the stoic Alabama newcomer Red Byron, making his stock car racing debut. Hall and Seay were driving whiskey cars that had been "wrenched" by Red Vogt. Two rows behind them sat the car of Bill France. All four men—and all but two of the day's racers—were driving Fords.

On a holiday intended to celebrate peace, the roar of thirty V-8 engines simultaneously accelerating was a sound unlike anything Atlantans had ever heard, as if hell itself had opened up and released the howls of its angry souls. Awesome and frightening sound waves pounded into the chest and head. It almost *hurt*. A tornado of red dirt immediately rose and swirled above the track. Racers at the rear of the pack found themselves in a sandstorm of red silt, barely able to see a car length in front of them. The smart ones wore glasses or goggles; others squinted to find the turns.

Seay, in a '38 Ford coupe, drove with his broken left arm propped in the window. Beneath the hood, the V-8 rumbled with who-knows-what kind of Red Vogt magic. Like Seay, many of the day's racers were driving whiskey cars, or at least cars that had been modified to perform beyond their factory-tuned abilities, and they weren't about to complain of the nonstock engines of others. In fact, Red Byron's car consisted of a ten-year-old Model A chassis, while under the hood purred a V-8 engine with so many aftermarket parts, including a Crager head, that his car could just barely be called a Ford.

Complaints about Vogt's allegedly modified Chrysler were the exception that proved the rule, and the defining line between a "modified" stock car and a "strictly stock" car would remain squiggly and faint for many years to come.

After a few laps, as the field spread out and the dust settled a bit, the real fun began. In the first turn, two racers (one from Atlanta and a Yankee from New Jersey) collided. The race proceeded slowly under a yellow caution flag while one of the damaged cars was driven away and the other, number 52, was shoved off to the side of the track.

When the race resumed—as indicated by the wave of a green flag— an Atlanta moonshiner named Harley Taylor took the lead. Ernest Bush, behind him, then flipped in the first turn and slammed into the previously wrecked number 52 car, causing both cars to block part of the racetrack. As drivers swerved to avoid those two wrecked cars, Bush's car burst into flames. He was still trapped inside. Members of various pit crews sprinted across the track to try to rescue him. A crewman named Blackie Black got to Bush first and reached into the car to pull the injured man free. Bush and Black then ran arm in arm away from the wreckage just as the flames hit the gas tank, which exploded behind them—"just like the movies," the next day's headline would declare.

Harley Taylor held the lead for nearly seventy miles, until his car's steering arm cracked, and he was sidelined, along with growing numbers of others. Racers slipped in and out of first place as Seay, Hall, Byron, and France slowly worked their way through the field. Seay was twice forced to pull into the pits to change flat tires, but as cars continued to crash, burn, or pull off with mechanical woes, he was able to return to the race and continue picking off the slower drivers until he finally found himself leading.

As darkness began to shroud the track, the weary, worried promoters decided to cut the race short. At the 135-mile mark, after nearly two and a half hours, Seay raced past the checkered flag and was declared "the world's stock car auto race champion."

Seay pocketed one hundred dollars—less than he'd earn in a typical night of whiskey tripping. His dark blond hair was pocked with red-dirt clumps, his white coveralls, teeth, ears, and corners of his smile all tinted red-orange. In all the confusion, scorers lost track of how many laps each driver had completed, so they fudged it: "Chief Ride in the Storm" was given second place; Dan Murphy (a Floridian who'd won at Daytona that summer) took third. Bill France took fourth and Roy Hall fifth. Debut racer Red Byron earned no mention in the next day's papers. He later insisted that he and his '29 Model A roadster had really won. By his count, he only stopped once, for water, and had actually *lapped* Lloyd Seay. But scoring officials, either mixed-up or maybe biased in favor of a local driver, seemed to have overlooked Byron's allegedly winning performance.

Byron would get another chance and would soon find himself part of a duel that would continue for the next ten years as stock car racing experienced the complicated merging of two distinct influences: the authoritarian and puritanical Bill France crowd from Daytona Beach, and the lawless, moonshining men of Atlanta. France was intent on making Daytona Beach the home of stock car racing. Lloyd Seay and the other whiskey boys of Atlanta, along with their mechanics, were obstacles to France's goal. France would one day seek to kick bootleggers out of *his* sport, but in the beginning, the two factions needed each other. There weren't enough stock car races or drivers to sustain the sport together, let alone in factions. So it became a marriage of opposites: moralistic hucksters such as France and lawbreaking rednecks such as Seay, Parks, and Hall. It would take a few more years, plus a world war, for one man—Byron—to bring the two groups more closely together.

Races such as Lakewood's Armistice Day contest immediately drew cult-like followings in the sport-starved South. In other small southern towns, at Saturday night jamborees or on Sunday afternoons after church, clouds of dust rose skyward above the booming roar of Ford V-8s kicking up rooster tails of copper-colored dirt, smashing and crunching into one another and, occasionally, into the crowds. Safety features such as hard-shell helmets and seat belts were for sissies. Real racers, when the windshield got mud-covered, just stuck their heads out the side window and chewed dirt.

Of course, dirt and danger were part of the appeal. Southern stock car racing grew quickly into a rough sport that attracted tough, dangerous, lascivious men who bashed one another's cars on the track, then settled scores afterward. Some carried pistols; others wielded tire irons. After just a dozen races, these men were hardened veterans, wearing signs of their longevity with pride: missing teeth, scars and burns, unseen aches and pains, broken bones that healed into crooked limbs. One longtime racer chugged milk before each race to soothe bleeding stomach ulcers. Another was missing a kneecap. Many began to lose at least their hearing, if not their lives.

And the fans loved it, the audacity of it all, sometimes displaying their revved-up emotions by hurling beer bottles onto the track. On one infamous Sunday afternoon at Lakewood, the father of six children was killed by a car that flipped into the grandstands. A short time later, policemen tried to arrest a rowdy fan, but as they dragged him out of the stands, they were pummeled by scores of rocks thrown by the crowd, which pinged off their squad cars and their heads. Such lawlessness prompted a letter of complaint to an Atlanta newspaper: "Automobile racing at the Lakewood track should be stopped. . . . [It] was never built for automobile racing in the first place." And because many of the racers had criminal records, the writer argued, "the odor of the races has never been too good."

That, too, was part of the appeal. Fans considered stock car racing the cutting edge of the wild side to which they aspired, or at least admired. As Pete Daniel says in *Lost Revolutions,* "The fiercely competitive racing culture was characterized by a disrespect for authority that had been the underpinning of the bootlegger culture and of the worldview of the working class." The racetrack was their place, their bacchanal, and fans "happily lost themselves in the orgy of dust, liquor and noise."

As 1938 came to a close, newspaper summaries of the year's sporting events included not only baseball, football, and basketball but also yacht races, speed skating, bait casting, bowling, polo, English Channel swimming, bicycle races, horseshoe pitching, tennis, archery, golf, billiards, even cricket. Seabiscuit's wild run that summer and Joe Louis's KO of Max Schmeling were the sports headlines of the year. Even the fifteen-foot, ten-inch record-breaking jump by "Zip" at the annual Calaveras County frog-jumping contest received more ink than did racing, Lakewood, or Lloyd Seay.

If car racing was mentioned at all, it was the prestigious Vanderbilt Cup road race on Long Island or the Indianapolis 500 or the latest world speed record. Despite its growing southern fan base, stock car racing simply wasn't considered worthy of sports writers' attentions. Even the local press was inconsistent at best in its coverage of stock car races. That would begin to change in the thrilling and awful summer of 1941.

Following his release from prison in 1937, Raymond Parks had delegated most of his moonshining operations to family members or trusted employees, and the "baron" began investing in relatively legitimate (though hardly wholesome) businesses, such as cigarette machines, jukeboxes, pinball and slot machines. As with his moonshine sales, Parks catered mostly to black customers in northwest Atlanta. He had even opened his new *legal* liquor store, the first of many stores he'd own throughout Atlanta.

Not everything was legit. Parks was still making whiskey and still heavily involved in the illegal lottery business. The slot machines weren't quite legal, either. Atlanta police once staged a raid on an illegal gambling site and discovered that most of the machines belonged to Parks, who rented them out to the proprietor. They called Parks and said he could have the confiscated machines back if he came down to headquarters to pick them up. "I'm no fool," he said, ignoring their kind offer. "I guess they melted 'em."

Still, the legitimate half of Parks Novelty Machine Co. was very profitable. Feeling good about all his financial success, Parks was ready for yet another investment.

Lakewood's Armistice Day race had given Parks his first glimpse of Fords doing something more interesting and exciting than delivering whiskey and fleeing cops. Watching from the stands that day as Seay took the checkered flag gave Parks an idea. The race—and its twenty thousand spectators—seemed proof that stock cars promised more thrills than even the snooty, conservative, law-abiding open-wheel racers from places outside of Dixie. He was smitten by the noise and dust and danger of Lakewood. And, like France, he smelled opportunity.

"I've got the fever," Parks told Seay.

Seay and cousin Roy Hall stoked his fever, pestering Parks to buy them each one of the new 1939 Ford V-8 models that were just rolling off the assembly line at downtown Atlanta's Ford factory and, at the time, were designed to be one of the fastest passenger cars ever produced. Parks finally agreed and came up with a plan: he would buy and finance the cars and cover travel costs and mechanical expenses for "the team." Seay and Hall would give him two-thirds of all their winnings. Parks's scheme for "sponsoring" Seay and Hall meant painting the name of his legitimate business interests on the sides of their cars: "Hemphill Service Station," "Northside Auto Service," and "Parks Novelty Machine Co., Atlanta, Ga." Parks asked Vogt to be his official mechanic, in exchange for free advertising, an occasional "Red Vogt Garage" on a race car's roof.

When Parks's younger cousins hungrily agreed to the plan, he drove down to Beaudry Ford Co. in downtown Atlanta to purchase two shiny black 1939 Ford coupes from the back lot. Thus began Parks's career as owner of a racing team, considered the first such team in stock car racing. In time, other racers would join Parks's team, including other whiskey trippers and even Big Bill France.

Parks's investment satisfied his cousins, but Parks primarily had moneymaking in mind. Profit was the whole point of the thing. Just good for business. Free advertising.

At least that's what he told himself at the start of 1939.

If Henry Ford's unveiling of the first V-8 in 1932 had endeared him to southern moonshiners, the 1939 model, with a V-8 engine crammed inside the light, small frame of a coupe, made him a bootlegger's hero. The '39 Ford would become the most famous whiskey car of all, and quite possibly the best stock car racing machine ever.

It's doubtful that Ford—now an aging eccentric—knew much about how southerners used his cars.* It's a good thing, for he surely would have been horrified.

Red Vogt, for one, was more impressed than ever. He became even more singularly focused on Ford V-8s—and more dysfunctionally

---

*According to Red Vogt's son, Tom, Vogt's renown and his specialization in Fords did reach Detroit and the offices of Henry Ford, who reportedly sent emissaries to meet with Vogt. Henry Ford himself allegedly once paid a brief visit to Vogt's garage, a story recounted in a diary kept by Tom's mother, Ruth, discovered after her death in 1994. Researchers at the Benton Ford Research Center at the Henry Ford Museum in Detroit, however, have no record of such a visit.

antisocial—after losing one of his few friends. His sister's husband, Joe, died one afternoon while driving a motorcycle out of Vogt's shop. He flew so fast out the garage doors, he failed to turn onto Spring Street and slammed into a brick wall. Vogt began to spend most of his days and nights at the shop, casting spells on Ford V-8s in his secret back room. His marriage to his first wife, Ruth, already an embittered, accusatory shambles, devolved even further. But Ruth did offer a prescient warning. As the brains behind the business side of Vogt's twenty-four-hour garage, she had an extra sense when it came to matters of finance—and bullshit.

"I don't trust that man," she told her husband one night, speaking of Bill France.

Vogt dismissed Ruth with a wave of his hand.

"I know Bill," he snarled. "And I trust him."

He should have listened to his wife.

It has been my experience that folks who have no vices have very few virtues.
— ABRAHAM LINCOLN

6

"All the women screamin' Roy Hall"

Typically, when a speed-minded southern boy caught the racing bug, his first stop was the junkyard, where he'd hunt down an orphaned, mid-1930s Ford body and offer the junkman, say, fifty dollars. He'd then tear out the seats, maybe weld shut the doors. Next, he'd return to the junkyard for a rusty old V-8, preferably a 1932 or 1934, which he'd get for another fifty dollars. Back home, he'd bore out the cylinders and, if he had a little extra cash, splurge on a new cylinder head, an extra carburetor or two, and some good tires.

The finished product was as ugly and mean as a junkyard dog, but far cheaper than an open-wheel racer—and *damn,* it could fly. Such mashed-together vehicles, called "modified stock" cars, would hardly be allowed in a "strictly stock" race, which restricted excessive modifications and aftermarket parts. But strictly stock races were rarities in the late 1930s. Most races were for beat-up, secondhand, ingeniously *modified* stock cars. No one bought *new* cars for racing. No need to when, for a total investment of less than five hundred dollars, you could become a race car driver.

Then again, if you'd earned a small fortune off moonshine, why not race a couple of new 1939 Ford V-8s, which, in Raymond Parks's mind, were "the pick of the litter"?

The '39 Fords had hydraulic brakes and a gear shifter on the floor, which moonshiners loved. The cars were built right there at the Ford factory on Ponce de Leon Avenue, with cast-iron heads, high-compression cylinders, and dual manifolds. They were also fairly cheap and, with a bit of voodoo, could be made to go *very* fast.

Parks's first step as stock car racing's first team owner was to deliver his two new '39 Fords to the twenty-four-hour-a-day garage on Spring Street. No need to call ahead. Red Vogt was always there, and he immediately started dismantling both cars. In no time, Parks's new Fords had their guts ripped out and lay in pieces on Vogt's clean floor.

Vogt had long dabbled in all forms of racing. He went to Indianapolis every year and often worked on racing machines of the AAA world, such as midget and sprint cars, both smaller versions of the larger cars that ran at Indy. But the appeal of this new stock car sport was particularly strong, especially the challenge of taking Henry Ford's passenger vehicles and transforming them into racing vehicles. His work on whiskey cars had been satisfying and lucrative, but the results were elusive—he couldn't be there to watch Roy Hall outrun a revenuer on Highway 9. But he could be there to observe his workmanship on the racetrack.

At the time, Ford V-8s and other Detroit-made vehicles were already fast, solid cars. Some amateur racers simply fine-tuned them, adjusted the timing, taped up or removed the headlights (so they wouldn't smash on the racetrack), put special bolts on the right-side wheels (so they wouldn't tear off), and then drove them right onto the track, a true "stock" car with a white shoe-polish number on its sides. The smart ones also tacked on any number of aftermarket modifications, such as a mesh cage bolted to the front end, a so-called shaker that would catch mud kicked up by other cars and shake it off, preventing it from reaching and clogging the radiator.

Vogt went way beyond those minimums. No one was quite sure

where he got his ideas, or his enormous talents. His formal schooling had ended before high school, and, except for some on-the-job training at the Cadillac dealership back in Washington, everything he knew was self-taught and experimental. But he had a deep curiosity that led him to seek out engineers and other experts, especially those at Atlanta's Ford assembly plant, whose brains he picked incessantly. Vogt also seemed to have some innate understanding of engines, like some sort of horse whisperer fluent in the secret language of metals and machinery. In a rare father-son moment, Vogt once explained to his son, Tom, that engines were simple if you knew how to view them from the right perspective. "An engine is nothing more than an air machine," he said. "It sucks air in, and it pushes air out." If a mechanic could find ways to get more air sucking into and blowing out of the engine, he could nearly double an engine's horsepower.

In addition to adding extra carburetors, which helped the car inhale more fuel and air, Vogt added extra pipes to the exhaust manifold, to help the engine exhale. He bored out the cylinders to accommodate wider pistons, then shaved down the bottom lip of each piston to save weight. He also shaved away portions of the engine block to make it lighter and installed aftermarket aluminum cylinder heads, which were lighter than the factory heads that gave the "flathead" V-8 its name. He widened the intake and exhaust ports (called porting) to increase the engine's breathability (called volumetric efficiency) and lengthened the stroke of the pistons (called stroking). He adjusted the transmission gears to achieve maximum torque and ground down the camshafts to help the engine more efficiently inhale its fuel-air mixture and exhale its exhaust.

Vogt admired some of Ford's factory-made parts but felt a few things needed improving, primarily the valves and cams. So Vogt ordered hand-machined cams from a shop in Philadelphia. Cams are oblong metal parts attached to a cylindrical "camshaft," which spins and is responsible for opening and closing the engine valves—key to the air-in, air-out process. Most cams are factory-built, but Vogt felt the precision of those particular parts was crucial to an air-sucking engine and worth the extra cost. At the time, not many racers could tell the difference between handmade or factory-made cams or camshafts. Vogt was in a league of his own and, in the beginning, was able to slip many of his creations into allegedly "stock" cars and their engines. Still, he wanted the work done out of town, so no spies could leak word about how he used specially made cams.

Vogt also made some parts himself, with a lathe and other equipment kept in the secret room of his garage. The back room became the perfect place to experiment with strange and crafty modifications to Ford's engines.

Neighborhood kids liked to hang around Vogt's shop after school and on weekends. Vogt and the moonshiners kept an eye on one boy, a curious fast-talker named Billy Watson, whose parents owned a nearby bakery. Roy Hall even taught Watson how to drive. Up around Dawsonville, Hall would let Watson take the wheel, and every time he made a mistake, Hall punched the kid's thigh. "The right side of the road is the Atlantic, the left is the Pacific," Hall would tell Watson. "One mistake, you drown."

Watson became a mascot of sorts at Red Vogt's shop, eventually dropping out of school. The moonshiners all teased him and treated him like their pet, but he worshipped them, especially Hall. "I didn't want to be a steelworker or a laborer like the other people in my neighborhood," Watson recalled. "I wanted to be like him."

Watson brewed moonshine in the woods for Legs Law, sleeping in a tent for weeks at a time. Another of Raymond Parks's drivers, Norman Wrigley, took Watson along on deliveries. Wrigley always stopped at church before a moonshine delivery, making Watson wait in the car, tending the whiskey. Watson started hauling liquor himself at age fourteen but would never make a successful transition to the racetrack.*

---

*Facing liquor and conspiracy charges against him in 1948, Watson refused to testify against Wrigley but agreed to join the Marine Corps to avoid indictment.

In time, Red Vogt took Watson under his wing, and he became one of the few whom Vogt let into the secret room; Vogt's own sons rarely went back there. One day, Vogt had a Ford V-8 engine cracked open and asked Watson, whom he called "kid," for two pennies. Using the round end of a ball-peen hammer, Vogt tapped the pennies into two cooling holes in the block; they fit perfectly. He pieced the engine back together and fired it up. Billy thought it sounded "mean." Vogt explained that the cooling holes were extraneous, and that blocking them up would help the engine heat up quicker and run faster, without harming its overall ability to cool itself. To be safe, he drilled a few minuscule holes around the exterior of the engine block to help cool air reach the engine.

Many of Vogt's modifications would eventually become illegal under the ever-changing rules of stock racing, particularly after NASCAR became the officiating entity. But that was still nearly a decade away. During the anything-goes racing seasons of 1939, 1940, and 1941, the main rule was that there are no rules. A saying that would later be adopted by other pioneering NASCAR mechanics was: *It's not cheating if you don't get caught.* That was Vogt's motto right from the start.

Vogt was a cranky loner and misfit, working at night, often until dawn, forgetting to sleep, incessantly smoking and drinking coffee, nurturing an obsessive-compulsive disorder that had him constantly washing his hands, cleaning car parts, and neatly aligning tools on shelves. Yet, as with the German engineering he admired, a Vogt-built motor ran like a German watch. "I had some great drivers," Parks liked to say. "But none of it would have happened without the abilities of car builder Red Vogt."

And none of it would have happened without Parks's whiskey money.

Until they started racing together in 1939, Lloyd Seay and Roy Hall had been the best of friends. They delivered whiskey together, though neither drank much themselves. In many ways, they were more like brothers than cousins. They both knew what it was like to emerge intact from a family of drunken, thieving, lying, cheating men—men with chips on their shoulders, mad at the world, out to avenge the lousy hand they'd been dealt.

In adulthood, the two deeply admired their dapper, successful older cousin, whom folks in Atlanta now called "Mr. Parks" or "sir." Parks knew what his younger cousins wanted: "They knew I had money," he'd say. "And I worked with Red." But Parks also knew that they needed a father figure, just as he had. Someone to keep them from veering too far toward the darker side, which constantly lurked.

This wasn't too difficult with Seay. He was thoughtful and, except on the racetrack, gentle. Seay took eagerly to Parks's subtle tutelage. And in time, Parks would come to think of Seay as more son than cousin. Parks and Seay even looked alike. A newspaper reporter once said, "The look-alikes could pass for brothers." Seay was six feet tall and had a narrow face and squinted eyes that avoided your gaze. A "bashful young Atlantan" with a "baby face"—that's how some newspapers described him.

Hall, on the other hand, was sultry, smoky. The more alpha of the two, he loomed above Seay—more handsome, more eloquent, more dangerous. He wore jaunty fedoras, flowery shirts, and matching ties beneath herringbone-plaid jackets. He had the look of a movie star playing a criminal. With a full face, broad nose, bushy brows above dark eyes, and a hardened, unafraid "I'll kill you" smirk, Hall's was the kind of look a young Marlon Brando—whom he resembled—likely practiced in the mirror. Across the next decade, Hall hammered that demeanor at the federal agents who arrested him, the judges who sentenced him, and the prison guards who came to know him by name.

In a picture taken in those days, Hall and Seay are kneeling beside a car, a black puppy sitting on the running board between them. Seay looks lovingly at the precious little dog. Hall, barefoot, looks as if he could eat it.

They called themselves "the team," but the 1939 racing season quickly became the Roy Hall Show. Seay's lone victory at Atlanta's Lakewood Speedway in late 1938 would soon seem quaint.

Although Seay and Hall had the same new '39 Fords, wrenched the same way by Vogt, something deep inside Hall exploded on the dirt tracks of Fort Wayne, Indiana; Salisbury, North Carolina; Langhorne, Pennsylvania; and Atlanta's own Lakewood. He was scary to watch, and Parks feared that, in no time, Hall would push too far.

Hall never denied it, either. He once told a reporter that he lived hard and, in truth, would likely die young. "Until then, I have nothing to lose," Hall said, before sticking a wad of bills from that day's victory into a hip pocket and stalking off.

As bootleggers, Seay and Hall were both fast and fearless. But Hall seemed to race with more anger, as if he had something to prove, taking it out on the accelerator. Because his rap sheet was growing longer and he knew the police and revenuers were always looking for him, Hall sometimes raced in disguise or under a false name. He was a bit of a goofball, too. As it turned out, Hall's entertaining showboat qualities were exactly what racing fans wanted to see. He went on a tear that summer of 1939.

Seay, meanwhile, seemed to be biding his time, on the racetrack and in life. During the first half of a race, he'd lag back and let the other racers knock one another out and burn up their engines. Then he'd begin weaving through the thinned-out field until he was in striking distance of the lead. It was a wise tactic and one that would soon pay off for Seay and be copied by many others. But in the short term, Hall was *always* out front.

Take Fort Wayne's quarter-mile, steeply banked track. In the tight turns, racers would drive right at the top edge of the bank, then shoot down into a short straightaway. Seay handled those turns smoothly, consistently. But in early 1939, Hall raced like a wild man at Fort Wayne, cutting jagged turns and sliding and fishtailing, flirting with the top of the bank as if he were about to sail right over the top edge of the track. That's exactly what happened to drivers who got in Hall's way. Just a small bump from behind, and they'd be airborne. And Hall would never look back.

In the words of the press, Seay was a smoother, more likable driver: "youthful Lloyd . . . the Atlanta speedster." Hall was more like a demented clown: a "dirt-smeared, wind-burned Georgian" who learned to drive by "piloting hooch." But during the nation's first two semilegitimate stock car racing seasons—1938 and 1939—there was no denying Hall's skills, nor his unabating disdain for the law.

Seay finally beat his cousin at the 1939 Fourth of July contest at Lakewood. But Hall racked up many more victories than Seay that summer, including Lakewood's Labor Day contest. Hall's luck off the racetrack was not as strong and actually ran out weeks before that Labor Day victory. Police from Atlanta and two nearby counties cornered him on the highway and dragged him into court. After two years of chasing him, federal agents and sheriff's deputies had compiled a long list of charges, from running liquor to speeding to reckless driving.

Hall was released after Parks paid the $2,300 bond, but his driver's license was suspended and he was ordered to return later for sentencing—an order he would ignore. Following his Labor Day victory, the newspapers stoked the flames of Hall's rising fame by reporting for the first time how "Reckless" Roy's racing career often conflicted with his moonshining career. "For two years, Hall gave chase to Atlanta police, being charged with running liquor, but proved to be a veritable will o' wisp, always outspeeding the law," said the *Atlanta Journal*. The paper even quoted an unnamed cop who called Hall "a genius at the wheel."

Hall's arrest only bolstered his renegade appeal among Atlantans, who loved such underdog stories. As Rhett Butler said in *Gone with the Wind*, that summer's blockbuster movie, "Southerners can never resist a losing cause." Still, none of Hall's brushes with the law stopped him from continuing to ramble across the South to races.

At that time, and for many years to come, most racers were free agents. In an era long before financial support flowed from national sponsors that would advertise their company name on a race car's flanks, driving stock cars was a bit like joining a pickup basketball game. You show up, you play. You race your own car, work on your own car, and drive to and from races yourself, maybe with the wife beside you, the kids in the back. If you're lucky, you can pay for gas and tires with a few bucks pitched in by a local garage or tavern, in exchange for painting its name on your car door.

Parks and Vogt created a more sophisticated three-way collaboration: owner, mechanic, racer. In the latter months of 1939, the Georgia Gang—Seay, Hall, Vogt, and Parks—caravanned to races in two-man teams, each towing a race car. They usually left Vogt's place around midnight and raced each other along two-lane roads at one hundred miles an hour, driving through the night and arriving groggy and twitchy at dawn. After competing in that day's race, they drove straight home that night, or on to the next race.

Sometimes the team was joined by young racers Bob Flock—the "wild-eyed Atlantan"—or his loony brother, Fonty, both moonshiners who delivered for their older brother and who had gotten to know Parks while hanging around Red Vogt's garage. Bill France even raced for Parks when, for example, Roy Hall was in a courtroom or behind bars.

But Parks's star was still Hall, and across the last months of 1939, he won four races in a row, including the year's finale, a one hundred–miler at Salisbury, North Carolina, where he edged out the leader, Bill France. Sportswriters called Hall a "nerveless, don't-give-a-damn young man" and said the "young Atlantan has no respect for life or limb."

A few auto magazines and newspapers named Hall 1939's national stock car racing champ, more of an honorary title than an official one, since there was no official stock car association. An informal system had developed in which racers accumulated points for victories and top-ten finishes. The crude system, agreed upon by various regional stock car clubs, is what led to Seay's "championship" in 1938 and Hall's in 1939.

Even France conceded at the time, "Hall had the best of me." However, France was determined not to let that happen again in 1940. The first big race of the 1940 season would be one of France's own races, at Daytona Beach. "If I can't beat him here, I never will," France said as that contest approached. "But I think I'm going to beat him."

When Hall arrived in Daytona Beach the morning of March 5, 1940, he boasted to a reporter—with no mention of his suspended license, of course—"I left the Cracker City [Atlanta] seven hours ago and averaged 62 miles per hour." This was before interstates existed along the 450-mile route of winding two-lanes through small towns. Five days later, ten thousand fans watched in disbelief as Hall put on a new kind of driving show.

Most racers at the Beach-and-Road course accelerated down the two straightaways but drove conservatively through the soft sand of the tricky north and south turns, where it was too easy to roll over, sometimes into the crowd, which always gathered too close to the track. But Hall had a different approach. He simply kept his foot mashed on the accelerator. At one point early in the 160-mile race, Hall was running second and, in an effort to overtake the leader, drove wide around the north turn. The left side of his Ford lifted into the air as the right-side tires dug into the sand. It looked as if Hall's car was going to flip right into the lap of Daytona's mayor, Ucal Cunningham. At the outer edge of the turn, just feet from the grandstands, Hall dropped back to four wheels and spun toward the leader, spraying sand all over the mayor and his guests.

Hall amazed fans and competitors alike with his two-wheeled move. Another driver, Larry Grant, tried the move but flipped and rolled his car, coming to a stop beside Mayor Cunningham, unconscious. As he was being loaded into an ambulance, Grant awoke and yelled, "What's going on here?" The ambulance crew told Grant he needed a checkup at the hospital. "'Fraid not," Grant said. "Lemme outa here." He stumbled to his car and asked two nearby National Guardsmen to help get his upside-down Ford rolled back onto its wheels so he could rejoin the race. But there was no catching Roy Hall.

At the time, a normal pit stop took about two minutes. Crews had to jack up the car, unscrew the lug nuts, remove the old tire, slap on a new one, then replace the lug nuts and tighten them with a lug wrench. Red Vogt used specialized air-powered equipment that he had brought—precursors to the pneumatic drills used today—and managed to change Hall's tires and refuel in an incredible forty seconds.

Hall held the lead for the entire second half of the race, finishing more than a mile ahead of the nearest competitor. France finished fourth, getting spanked in his own backyard. Hall decided to rub France's nose in it. "I feel like going another 160 miles," he said, boasting that Vogt's workmanship kept his Ford averaging ninety-five miles an hour. When asked if he'd return for the next race, Hall said, "Sure . . . if I'm still alive."

Despite all efforts to the contrary, Hall was indeed still alive for the July 7, 1940, race at Daytona. But he had a previous engagement that kept him from racing that day. Daytona's newspapers helpfully explained his absence: "The foot-loose and fancy-free daredevil . . . is now serving a short sentence on a prohibition charge."

Lloyd Seay also missed that race. Without Hall or Seay in the field, Bill France managed to jump into the lead and never looked back. With Hall in jail, and Seay missing the Daytona race and a few other races that summer of 1940, France saw an opportunity to insinuate himself, not only to the top of the year's points standings but into the hearts of southern racing fans. He knew how much the fans loved Hall and Seay, and it galled him. So France traveled to every race he could find and won an impressive majority of them—a couple of times with Red Vogt as his mechanic.

But fans would never cheer for France the way they would for Seay and Hall. In fact, the two twenty-one-year-olds had come to symbolize everything a poor Georgia boy aspired to be. They were folk heroes at the fairgrounds and makeshift racing ovals of the rural South. On Sunday afternoons, tearing around the red dirt, arms dangling out the window as if it were just a Sunday-go-to-meeting drive, Seay and Hall gave people a break from their farm-bound routines. Fans crammed into rickety grandstands to watch the famous two-wheeled "bicycle" move. Like Hall, Seay was also learning to lurch his car up onto the two right wheels and squeeze between two competitors. Just as NASCAR legend Dale Earnhardt would many years later, Seay and Hall oozed a fearlessness and insouciant cool that gave people something to dream of, to hope for.

An Atlanta bluesman even put such admiration to music. The drunken, spider-fingered guitarist Blind Willie McTell (rumored to have been blinded by bad corn whiskey) strolled through the parking lot of the Blue Lantern on Ponce de Leon Avenue, singing and playing for tips. If someone gave him a bottle, he'd cackle, "Just throw away the cap." Among Blind Willie's most-requested songs was the one about Roy Hall.

> *He's trouble in a Cadillac, He's a mess in a Ford V-8.*
> *I got to repeat, he don't never retreat, he's the runninest guy to hit*
> *this state.*
> *Don't get funny, wait and save your money. All the women*
> *screamin' Roy Hall.*

For Bill France, the growing legend of Seay and Hall was a mixed blessing. It was great for the sport of stock car racing, of course, but maddening for every other racer, himself included. And it frustrated France that a small group of southern moonshiners was monopolizing *his* sport. But then a North-versus-South battle erupted among rival racing groups, which created a temporary peace in the growing Daytona-versus-Atlanta scrum by putting France and the moonshiners on the same side of a fight. For a while.

Ever since stock cars had roared onto the motorsports scene two years earlier, they had been competing with other forms of auto racing, particularly AAA-sponsored Indy-style races and their open-wheel, open-cockpit racing machines.

In an effort to slap down the upstart stock cars, a AAA promoter in Langhorne, Pennsylvania—one of the North's racing capitals, along with Paterson, New Jersey—announced that summer that he was banning all "southern" racers from his track. The promoter, Ralph Hankinson, considered stock car racing an unruly southern sport and its drivers "outlaws." Not only would he not allow stock cars at his track, but he wouldn't allow known stock car drivers to compete in any of his AAA races there, either. Hankinson then visited his onetime friend Bill France's hometown and tried to convince Daytona's city officials to allow him to promote AAA-sponsored Indy races at Daytona, to replace France and his stock cars with more sophisticated *real* racing cars. After listening to Hankinson's pitch, the city decided to stick with France, the local boy, and his increasingly popular stock cars.

With the momentum of stock cars working against him, Hankinson grudgingly rescinded the ban he'd enacted against southern drivers in July of 1940, allowing stock cars to begin spreading into AAA-controlled territory up north. Daytona's newspaper gloated, claiming that by letting stocks onto his track, Hankinson "is admitting that some of the country's better speed demons come from our section of the good ol' USA. . . . The cracker boys do a pretty good job of showing in the first 10 when the final flag is finished."

Indeed, most of the stock car races in 1940 (and more than a few open-wheel races) were won by a southerner. Seay won at Allentown, Pennsylvania; High Point and Greensboro, North Carolina; and twice at a dirt track in Deland, Florida. Hall won at Daytona and Lakewood, although legal troubles kept him from racing during the latter half of the season. The Flock brothers, Bob and Fonty, each won a couple of races. And France, after finishing second at a late-summer race on Hankinson's track in Langhorne, by season's end had won enough races to be declared the 1940 national champion.

All of which established 1941 as stock car racing's breakout year.

That's when a three-way contest would be waged among the champions of the three previous years: France, Seay, and Hall, who would be released from prison just in time for the 1941 season. Fans looked forward to witnessing a season of racing that would prove who was better: Georgia's whiskey boys or Daytona's beach boy.

For three years, the partnership of Hall and Seay the racers, Vogt the mechanic, and Parks the moneyman had been wildly successful. With dozens of victories between 1939 and 1941, Seay and Hall became celebrities throughout the South. But could Hall and Seay become folk heroes beyond the relatively small stock car racing regions of North

Georgia, Florida, and North and South Carolina? With continued resistance from AAA promoters and open-wheel Indy racing tracks in other states, could stock car racing succeed beyond the South?

When stock cars first came to Daytona in 1936, an Indy racer from Philadelphia presciently called it the sport of the future. "Every car owner in the country wants to see how the automobile of his choice will stand up under the competition," said the driver, Doc Mackenzie, who added—again, with remarkable foresight—that stock car races at Daytona would benefit the automotive industry more than "any other race in history."

Mackenzie also claimed to know a bit more than his southern counterparts about how to tame tracks such as the Beach-and-Road course, although in that regard, he proved less insightful. "The guy who uses his head more than his foot is the man who's going to win," he said. "Getting in a car and just keeping the accelerator jammed to the floor won't be what is needed." During his cautious first attempt at qualifying at Daytona, Mackenzie skidded into the Atlantic. His theory on cautious driving was soon loudly debunked by the success of accelerator-jamming bootleggers such as Roy Hall and Lloyd Seay.

Hall proved with his Daytona wins in 1939 and 1940 that using more foot than head was his ticket to the winner's circle. He intended to prove more of the same in 1941.

Seay was ready to prove that his 1938 championship hadn't been pure luck.

And Bill France desperately wanted to show Atlanta's whiskey boys that he was just as fast as they were, that his championship the previous year was no fluke.

Since taking over as promoter of the Daytona races three years earlier, in 1938, France had installed more grandstands and a scoreboard. He got local businesses to pitch in with prize money, in exchange for advertising. He fine-tuned some of the rules, which had been largely lacking, even though France's "rules" were applied or ignored at will.

In addition to prerace engine inspections, France appointed a "technical inspector" to tear apart the engines of top finishers, in search of illegal modifications. This practice often pitted him against his cunning friend Red Vogt. A little bribe could sometimes encourage an inspector to overlook, say, two pennies stuck in a cooling vent. Then again, an inspector might decide to overturn a racer's victory if, say, the number two finisher was a friend. Still, little by little, France was attempting to legitimize the new sport, and that legitimacy was beginning to turn him a bit more profit.

France's take from his 1938 races had been about two thousand dollars. Not much, but neither was it the twenty thousand–dollar loss that Daytona city officials sustained when they'd sponsored their race in 1936. The crowds grew larger in 1939 and again in 1940, and so did the winner's purse, which attracted more racers and began putting more money in France's pocket.

Thousands of fans would pay a dollar apiece to watch the sport's rising stars. When the bleachers filled, many fans simply stood alongside the track, just feet from where forty cars raced by at one hundred miles an hour. On race day, the newspapers would implore fans to "stay off the track today. . . . A fatal accident might be caused by a foolhardy decision." Public address announcers also pleaded with fans to move back, but the fans ignored such requests—sometimes to their regret. Errant cars regularly tumbled into the naïvely incautious crowds, and more than a few lives were spared by quick-thinking drivers who would cut a hard-right turn into the Atlantic rather than mow down an ignorant fan walking across the racetrack. At one race, an elderly woman stumbled into the sand, face-first, and a driver coming full speed at her had to swerve into a sand dune to save her life. Afterward, the driver furiously complained that the old woman never even apologized.

Still, stock car racing was on the rise, and the best drivers planned to kick off the 1941 season at France's 160-mile Daytona event, on March 2. In addition to France, Hall, and Seay, other notable racers included the ex-Georgian, ex–whiskey tripper Smokey Purser, who now lived in Daytona and often helped France with his races; a few moonshiner/racers from the Carolinas; and Atlanta's moonshining Fonty Flock. The newspapers claimed that half of the forty-one starters were "champions" of some title or another. They made no mention that half were also probable bootleggers.

At midnight on March 1, Red Vogt dialed the number of Bill France's garage and Amoco service station on Main Street in Daytona.

"We're on our way," Vogt told his friend.

He said they'd see him by 7:00 a.m., at which France scoffed. The 450-mile drive could take a normal driver twelve hours.

Roy Hall had been released from prison just days earlier and joined the Georgia Gang's high-speed caravan down from Atlanta. Racing along narrow roads, through small towns, at two or three times the speed limit, they stopped for gas three times and a quick bite for breakfast but still managed to reach Daytona before seven o'clock, a new record.

That Saturday, during a qualification race for the next day's main event, Seay flipped his Ford in the north turn, landing upside-down in a sand dune. Later, Hall smashed his car, too. Parks was furious. "Two cars and they're both wrecked before the race even begins," he complained. "This is my last race."

Before their wrecks, Seay and Hall had driven fast enough to qualify for Sunday's race, but Vogt had to work through the night to repair the cars in time. The next afternoon, ten thousand eager fans crowded around the track. Most of the racers were southern—Georgia boys, Carolina boys, Florida boys—except for skinny, bald, cigar-chomping Red Byron, who had made his stock car debut at Lakewood's 1938 race but had then switched back to mostly open-wheel racing. Byron had recently moved from Colorado to Alabama and drove a Ford that had been wrenched by a one-legged Alabama mechanic. Looking like a scrawny Barney Oldfield—white coveralls, dark goggles, an unlit cigar clamped in his jaw—Byron lined up at the start and watched as Bill France jumped ahead of him and into an early lead.

On the paved straightaway, Roy Hall roared from the pack and caught up with France. In the south turn, he cut inside France and broadsided him. As the two battled for the lead, sometimes bumping and scraping against each other, a driver named Joe Littlejohn lost control in the north turn, skidded over the lip of the embankment, and rolled straight into the crowd. Fans ran and dove for cover as a local carpenter and a schoolteacher were struck by the tumbling Ford and had to be rushed to the hospital.

The track announcer again begged fans to step back off the track, but as usual, they paid no heed. A South Carolina driver named Massey Atkins then tumbled into the imprudent crowd. Incredibly, no one was hurt, except for one woman who fainted and had to be carried away.

For the next fifty miles, racers flipped and spun into sand or surf. Every few laps, another racer was taken to the hospital. After rolling into the grandstands, Massey Atkins rejoined the race only to lose control again on the paved straightaway. Massey was driving a convertible and wasn't wearing a seat belt. As his car flipped into the palmettos, he flew into the air and landed, amazingly, on his back in a soft sand dune. He stood up, brushed himself off, and walked back to the pits, but that was the end of his race.

A few laps later, Atkins's brother, Elbert, took the south turn too wide and roared straight at a fan standing alone at the edge of the track. It must have dawned on the fan in that instant why no one else was standing with him. He tried to jump clear, but Atkins's right fender caught his trousers and ripped off one of the pants legs, which clung to the fender for another three laps. Even the public address announcer had to drop his mike and "run like hell to the bushes" more than once when cars careened too close to his booth.

A hundred miles into the race, with Hall having nudged France aside and vaulted into the lead, Seay began to pick his way through the now depleted field. A few times, he took the north turn so fast that his left wheels lifted off the sand and he managed to squeeze between two other cars on just two wheels. When Hall came into the pits to refuel, his cousin shot ahead and into the lead. But four laps later, when Seay again lifted his Ford up onto two wheels, the right front tire caught a rut and he flipped. Hall retook the lead, while Seay and a few helpful fans rolled his V-8 back onto its wheels. Seay rejoined the race, flipped again a few laps later, and still managed to finish seventh.

Hall won the race, and $475, which he accepted with a bloody right hand that he'd gashed on his gear shifter. "It's nothing," he said. "Just part of the game." The local papers dubbed him "Reckless Roy . . . the 20-year-old Atlanta madman who drives a stock car as though he were operating a tank with wings." Daytona had never seen anyone like Hall, "a boy with speed on his mind and a reckless devil spurring him on."

Later that same month, on March 30, the Georgia Gang returned to Daytona. Seay's car fell victim to uncharacteristic mechanical trouble, and Hall seemed headed for another victory until his engine began to overheat on the final lap and died on the homestretch. Hall was beaten by a local favorite, the colorful ex-tripper Smokey Purser. "That old man drove a hell of a race," Hall said of Purser, who was twice his age.

On July 27, the Georgia boys returned to Daytona once more, the third time in four months; 1941 was on its way to becoming the biggest stock car racing year ever, with dozens of new tracks competing against one another to lure racers to their town. France's efforts to hold as many races as possible in Daytona were part of a plan to wrest away from Atlanta and Lakewood Speedway the title of "home to stock car racing," to establish Daytona Beach as the sport's headquarters. This time, Bill France also intended to finally win in his own backyard. He'd been having great financial success promoting the summer's races, but he was anxious to get back to victory lane.

Fifty cars entered the race, but France decided to limit the field to thirty-three. So, the day before the race, drivers had to drive qualifying laps. The top thirty-three qualifiers were entered in the next day's race, with the fastest qualifier assigned the enviable first, or "pole," position. France, however, drove one of the slowest qualifying laps and failed to qualify for his own race. So did Daytona's other star, Smokey Purser, and it looked as if France would have to sit and watch Atlantans dominate his race once more.

But in a move that presaged the self-serving decision-making style of the future NASCAR, France broke his own rules and allowed Purser—and himself—to join the race. At the time, no other racer was willing to challenge France, which in subsequent years only heightened his willingness to bend and break the rules.*

The July 27 Beach-and-Road race started with two bootlegging Atlantans, Roy Hall and Fonty Flock, fighting ahead of the pack, with Flock slightly out front. In the south turn of the first lap, Hall bumped Flock hard to the right, and Flock's car sped up the embankment and right over the edge. His '39 Ford flipped end over end while also spinning, finally landing on its roof in the palmettos. The roof collapsed, and Flock was crushed inside. He was taken to the hospital with a broken pelvis; bruised kidneys, lungs, and back; as well as severe shock. Doctors couldn't even x-ray him for two days, for fear the procedure would kill him. He remained in Florida for weeks, bandaged practically from head to toe.

He wouldn't return to racing for six years.

Meanwhile, Lloyd Seay had been working his way toward the lead but, in the north turn, caught a rut and flipped and rolled. The Ford incredibly landed back on all four wheels, and Seay jammed it into gear and took off. A few laps later, he was again up on two wheels in the north turn. The crowd gasped as he wobbled, but then managed to drop softly back onto four wheels and tore down the paved straightaway.

Seay tried the two-wheeler move a few laps later, but just as he'd done in two previous races that summer, he flipped and lost valuable time. He managed to turn his badly crumpled Ford back over and rejoin the race, though his efforts were only good enough for fourth place.

---

*France was later known to carry a pistol with him to enforce his ever-shifting rules. At a race twenty years later, he bullied racers into signing a pledge to reject a unionization drive, threatening to blackball those who didn't sign. "If you don't sign this form . . . I'll use a pistol to enforce it. I have a pistol, and I know how to use it."

Hall, after his crack-up with Fonty Flock, had another crash later in the race and finished eighth. A Dawsonville moonshiner named Bernard Long, in only the second (and final) race of his career, celebrated his win with a cold Coca-Cola.

A reporter asked Seay afterward, "Was it a hard race?"

"It feels a lot harder to me when I don't win," Seay replied.

The biggest year ever for racing at Daytona Beach continued seven weeks later, when the Georgia Gang returned to Florida for yet another 160-miler, the final beach race of the season. This time, Seay intended to get the best of his cousin, and Bill France.

Seay had always been a modest young man, and he was proud to consider cousin Hall part of what he called "the racing team"—but he hated to lose, especially to Hall.

"Seay and Hall have a bitter rivalry on the track," a reporter once said.

All summer long, Seay had been winning, fulfilling the promise of his championship performance three years earlier, in 1938. He won at Lakewood in May; in Allentown, Pennsylvania, on Memorial Day; in High Point, North Carolina, in June; in Greensboro in July. With so many wins, a Philadelphia newspaper called Seay "the hottest stock car driver in the land." And yet, while it was satisfying to regularly trounce his cousin Roy, the big prize for a stock car racer in 1941 (and to this day) was to take the checkered flag at Daytona, something that had eluded Seay. By his count, Seay had won races at every other track in the South, and a few up North, too. Seay had raced at Daytona nearly a dozen times during the previous two seasons. But, as he told a reporter prior to the August 24 race, "something would always keep me from winning."

This time, he planned to scrap his cautious approach and go for victory right from the start. Before twelve thousand fans, Seay shot out to the front to take an early lead. It was an aggressive Roy Hall–style tactic that Lloyd had previously deemed too risky.

It was riskier still on August 24 because, with all the activity on the Beach-and-Road course that summer, the northbound straightaway along the beach had become seriously corrugated. To avoid those wash-board ruts, Seay drove at the hard-packed outer edge of the course, the narrow strip where the ocean kissed the sand. Drivers had tried that technique many times over the years, with mixed results. The slightest turn too far right, or an errant wave that washed higher than the others, and Seay's right wheels would be sucked into the softer, waterlogged sand, pulling his car into the surf.

In the treacherous north turn, Seay never let up on the gas and arced through on two wheels with "alarming regularity," a sportswriter said afterward. France tried to keep pace but got stuck once in the north turn and lost valuable minutes. Hall also took the north turn on two wheels, twice, but late in the race cracked the frame and had to pull out.

Which left Seay all alone up front. He never slowed and never looked back. Seay drove so fast and so cleanly that he lapped many of the slower racers. His bicycle move worked perfectly—no flips or rolls this time. In fact, he led the entire fifty laps, start to finish, averaging between seventy-eight and eighty-five miles an hour, a new course record.* Seay took the checkered flag a full lap ahead of the rest—3.5 miles from the number two driver. One reporter called it "one of the finest exhibitions of driving ever witnessed on a race track."

"It's about time I won here," Seay said afterward.

Hall's cracked car frame and failure to finish were enormously grati-fying to Seay, whose other rival, France, ended his summer of bad luck in seventh place. Though he would compete in a few more races, France's days as a winner were mostly over. That summer of 1941 marked the ac-celeration of his transition from racer to promoter.

In the pits after the race, Seay was giddy. So was Parks, the two of them giggling, as one sportswriter noted, "as tickled as a couple kids with a stick of candy."

It would forever gall France that Atlanta's moonshiners got the best of him that summer of 1941; he would subsequently lash out at

---

*Reports varied on Seay's actual speed. The Daytona paper said it was 78.5; the Atlanta paper said it was 80; another report called it 85.

moonshiners with increasing frequency, in subtle and not-so-subtle ways. Then again, France knew that if he was to attract the crowds and make stock car racing the success he believed it could be, he needed entertaining drivers, the best drivers, and that included bootleggers.

Late in life, when asked about the best NASCAR drivers of all time, France often put Lloyd Seay on his list, even though Seay never competed in a single NASCAR race.

He never got the chance.

Death, that cruel leveller of all distinctions . . .
— DAVY CROCKETT

7

"Yesterday his luck ran out"

A week after his stunning victory at Daytona in late August of 1941, Seay faced off against Bill France and twenty others at a dirt track in High Point, North Carolina. A year earlier, Seay and France had collided on the same track, and France's car flipped seven times. He was lucky to survive. This time, France hoped to repay Seay. Retribution was a common tactic, and some successful drivers even earned bounties—payoffs to a driver, from gamblers or pissed-off racers, to put the favorite into the wall.

Earlier that summer, a driver from Macon, Georgia, had vowed to put Seay into the lake at Lakewood, but Seay heard about the bounty and halfway into the race sneaked up behind him and bashed repeatedly into his left rear fender. Seay disabled the driver's car, but then his own car slid off the track and into the lake. Fellow Dawsonville moonshiner Gober Sosebee knew Seay couldn't swim and pulled off the track to save Seay from his slowly sinking car. After the race, the two went looking for the driver from Macon, but he had disappeared, and they never saw him at another race.

At the High Point race of August 29, Seay managed to stay clear of trouble and finished just ahead of France for his seventh victory of the year. "Lloyd Seay looks like a timid choir boy, but on the speedway he's a hell-bent-for-election dare devil," one newspaper declared. Seay had finally found his place on the racetrack, emerging from cousin Hall's substantial shadow, and France's.

Three days later, on September 1, 1941, Seay lined up at the start of the annual one hundred–mile Labor Day race at Lakewood, his hometown track, where his career had begun.

Atlanta's road superintendent spread forty thousand pounds of calcium chloride on the track, "to guarantee a dustless track for Labor Day." Speedway officials had also added a new scoreboard and extra grandstands and had groomed the dirt track to perfection, anticipating "the greatest stock car race ever held here."

The day's lineup was among the strongest in stock car racing's short history. In addition to Seay, the field included Eddie Samples and Gober Sosebee, both products of the Dawsonville-to-Atlanta school of whiskey driving, and other well-known Atlanta racers such as Bob Flock, Carson Dyer, Jap Brogdon, and Harley Taylor, who would race with two broken ribs sustained in an earlier accident. France even decided to join up, to try to beat the Atlanta boys on their own track. The only one missing was Roy Hall, who was in Alabama trying to avoid an arrest warrant with his name on it. Sportswriters speculated over whether Seay could compete in his hometown against one of the strongest fields of the year. Said one reporter, "Seay has an outstanding reputation in other parts, but in a town of hot, lead-footed stock car drivers, he's just one of the boys."

For reasons he would never get a chance to explain, Seay chose to race a convertible instead of a hardtop and—odder still—changed his car number from 7 to 13. Racers are a wildly superstitious bunch. A green car, women in the pits, even peanuts were all considered bad luck. Racers spited their enemies by tossing peanut shells into their cars. But number thirteen was considered the unluckiest of all. Racers dreaded having to start in the thirteenth position, and no one willingly drove a car numbered 13.*

As fifteen thousand fans rose to their feet, Ed Samples and Harley Taylor, despite his broken ribs, raced to the lead, scraping and nudging each other so much, their cars became locked together in the first turn. The two cars threatened to choke off the entire field, but they finally veered off in tandem and into the rails, allowing the rest of the field to pass.

Carson Dyer led the first half of the race but then pulled into the pits with a flat tire and an oil leak. Seay, Bob Flock, and Skimp Hersey raced bumper to bumper for a few laps until Seay pulled away and into the lead. He lost a lap during a much-needed pit stop, and Red Singleton enjoyed a short-lived lead. France then took a stab at the lead and in one turn tried to duplicate the two-wheel "bicycle" move that Seay and Hall had perfected. He twitched too far right and flipped over.

After his pit stop, Seay proved that his unlucky number 13 had no effect on his driving. By the eightieth lap, only twelve cars remained on the track, and Seay pulled away from them all. His tactic of driving carefully, letting the other racers peeter and putter out, worked brilliantly. Then, on lap ninety-five out of one hundred, Seay's motor began hissing and spewing, and it looked as if it might betray his significant lead. The field began to gain on Seay's slowing car, but the Vogt-built engine had just enough life in it. Seay sputtered across the finish line, just barely victorious, his engine dying with a final cough.

Seay spoke briefly to the crowd, thanking Parks and Vogt. Despite the calcium chloride, the red dust had still swirled wildly and now covered every available surface. Seay's white overalls were tinged red, and sportswriters described how "the parked cars were red-topped and the dust-draped crowd was rust-colored."

---

*The next person to drive Seay's number 13 car, popular "Cannonball" Bob Baker from Daytona Beach, would wreck on the final lap of a race and sustain injuries that would leave him crippled. Years later, a pugnacious racer named "Little" Joe Weatherly would be killed on the thirteenth lap, in thirteenth place—they'd find thirteen dollars in his pocket.

Seay pocketed one-third of the $450 winner's purse, gave the other $300 to Parks, and climbed into his personal car—a shiny maroon rag-top Ford with six spotlights. As the sun began to set, he drove the curved dirt roads back toward Dawsonville, skipping the fireworks display that would shower over Lakewood that night.

Seay spent the night at his brother's place on the road north of Dawsonville, a few hundred yards from the house where Raymond Parks had been born. Seay was stiff and sore from the previous week's racing. He had blisters on his hands, a crick in his neck, and bruises all over. He had hoped to sleep late. But early the next morning—September 2—he was awakened by a knock at the door.

Seay's cousin, Woodrow Anderson, was a short, wide bulldog of a man. After knocking on the door of the Seay household that morning, he nodded solemnly to Lloyd's brother, Jim, and Jim's wife, then walked back to where Lloyd slept and roused his groggy and sore cousin, demanding to go for a ride and "settle up."

Despite his success on the racetrack that summer, Seay had never distanced himself from his chief source of income. And what happened next would continue to reverberate through NASCAR's creation and infancy, as if to prove Bill France's belief that moonshining and stock car racing don't, can't, shouldn't mix.

About a week earlier, before heading to Daytona, Seay had purchased a few fifty-pound sacks of sugar for the family stills that he, brother Jim, and cousin Woodrow operated in the dense hills outside Dawsonville. Instead of paying for the sugar on the spot, he asked the grocer to tack the cost onto Woodrow's credit account.

Woodrow was a well-known moonshiner, part of a notorious family of Dawsonville-area lawbreakers. He and his uncle—named Ford— were once charged with beating a neighbor to the brink of death simply because his cows had gotten loose and wandered into the Andersons' yard. A friend of Woodrow's once went hunting with him and watched him shoot his own dog. Woodrow had also served two prior prison sentences for manufacturing illegal whiskey. He was a mean, bitter, and dangerous young man, and Lloyd and Jim Seay knew to be careful around him. But driving race cars was no way to earn a living. Not yet. To make money, Lloyd Seay did what he'd learned to do as a child. He ran moonshine, often in wary alliance with some unhinged kin.

A three-way business partnership had begun earlier that summer: Jim Seay and Woodrow made the stuff, and Lloyd delivered it. They were supposed to split all costs.

Lloyd and Woodrow had recently bought a load of sugar together, but Woodrow was short of cash so Lloyd paid for it with his own cash. To balance out the transaction, Woodrow told Lloyd to get the next batch of sugar at a different store to and charge it to a credit account Woodrow had there. But when Woodrow checked that account later, it seemed to him as though someone had charged an extra $120 to the account—over and above the amount that Woodrow owed Lloyd for the previous transaction. Woodrow accused Lloyd of taking advantage of him and using his credit account to buy extra sugar.

This is the matter that Woodrow now wanted to "settle up." But Lloyd's brother didn't like how Woodrow was acting and insisted on coming along. Lloyd and Jim started walking toward Lloyd's maroon Ford convertible, but Woodrow suspiciously insisted they all ride in his car, a beat-up Model A.

"How will me and Jim get back home?" Lloyd asked.

"I'll bring you back," Woodrow said.

They got into Woodrow's car—Jim up front, Lloyd in back—and headed north toward the town of Dahlonega. Jim suggested they stop at their Aunt Monie's and have her act as impartial mediator. "She's aunt to all three of us. Let her do the figuring," he said. But they'd never make it to Aunt Monie's.

On the drive up Highway 9, Woodrow asked Lloyd if he still thought 13, the number of his winning race car, was lucky.

"I reckon so," Lloyd said. "Why?"

"Don't be too sure of that," Woodrow replied, then swerved off Highway 9 into the driveway of his father's house, claiming he needed to add water to his radiator.

When the car came to a stop, Woodrow turned around and laid into Lloyd, badgering Lloyd to pay him for the sugar and accusing Lloyd of stealing from him. Lloyd argued that he had already delivered to Woodrow all the sugar he'd charged to the account and didn't owe him a goddamn thing. What happened next depends on which version of the story is true. According to Woodrow's version, all three men started arguing and fussing. Lloyd slapped him, so Woodrow ran into his father's bedroom and grabbed a pistol from under the pillow. When he got back outside, Lloyd and Jim were waiting for him. They jumped him and wrestled him to the ground, Woodrow claimed.

Jim's version—the story a jury would later accept as true—unfolded like this . . .

After pulling into his father's driveway, Woodrow got out of the car, walked to the front, and opened the hood, then pretended to unscrew the radiator cap. He then reached into the engine compartment and grabbed something. Jim couldn't see what it was, but he saw Woodrow stick it into the front pocket of his overalls. Woodrow then walked around to the passenger side and told Jim to get out of the car.

"If you don't want to get mixed up in anything," Woodrow muttered.

When Jim refused, Woodrow yanked a .32 pistol from his overalls, waved it over his head, and yelled, "By God, get out!" Jim slowly opened the door and got out.

Woodrow then reached into the backseat and began slapping Lloyd in the face and head. He shoved the gun in Lloyd's face, yelling and cussing about the money he felt he was owed, then pistol-whipped his cousin across the face. Lloyd stumbled out of the car, but before he could run clear, Woodrow punched him again, and again.

Jim stepped between the two men, screaming at Woodrow to "Put the gun up!"

"You black son of a bitch," Woodrow yelled. "I'll shoot you first."

He lifted the gun and fired. Jim screamed as the bullet burrowed into his neck, nicking his jugular vein, and passed through his right lung. He dropped to the dirt, grabbing his neck with both hands as blood spurted through his fingers.

A split second later, Woodrow turned the gun on Lloyd, and without another word, he fired. The bullet slammed into Lloyd's chest, just under his arm, and pierced his heart. Lloyd fell backward, flat on his back, with Woodrow looming over him, still cursing.

Clutching his chest, Lloyd looked up at his cousin and whispered, "*Why?*" Woodrow finally stopped yelling and grew suddenly quiet, as if emerging from a dream.

Lloyd asked again, this time in a soft, gurgling rasp, "Why'd . . . you . . . shoot me?"

"Goddamn you," Woodrow growled. "You know what I shot you for."

As Lloyd lay dying in the dusty driveway, he asked for water. Woodrow acted as if he didn't understand him, the words were mere whispers. Lloyd asked again, and this time Woodrow heard him but callously refused. Finally, Seay lifted his head, looked over at his wounded, bleeding brother, and said his last words.

"Tell Raymond . . . ," he began.

Before he could finish the thought or whisper another word, Lloyd lost all strength, breathed one last breath, then laid his head back down and died.

Woodrow reached into Lloyd's pocket and found the money Lloyd had won the previous day at Lakewood—$217 in one-dollar bills, plus a silver dollar that Lloyd carried for luck. Woodrow counted out $120 and put the blood-covered bills in his own overalls, giving the rest to Jim, who lay beside his dead brother.

Lloyd's older brother and another cousin arrived to find Lloyd still lying on the ground. They carried his body inside Woodrow's father's house and laid him on a cot.

After his arrest, Woodrow peddled his version, even claiming that Lloyd's dying words were, "Woodrow, I done you wrong, and I'm sorry." He told newsmen that Lloyd and Jim attacked him and he shot in self-defense. "It looked like they were about to give me a whuppin' so I started shootin'," he said. "The first thing I knew we were quarrelling, then I was runnin', then I was shootin'. That's all there was to it."

A jury later convened in the Dahlonega courthouse—not far from where Raymond Parks's great-great uncle Benny had found gold—and decided there *was* more to it than that.* They sentenced Woodrow to life in prison. (Woodrow was released ten years later, after working on a prison road crew that repaired Dawsonville-area highways. In an ironic twist, he later worked at Ford's new postwar factory outside Atlanta.)

At almost the precise moment that Seay's corpse was loaded into the county coroner's van and the scrawny sheriff, Joe Davis, carried the still-warm murder weapon to his car, the huge loving cup for Seay's victory at Lakewood arrived at Parks's office at the Northside Auto Service Station on Hemphill Avenue in downtown Atlanta.

Parks learned that afternoon that Lloyd had died.

The next day's newspaper showed a photo of Seay's Ford convertible sputtering across the finish line two days earlier. The cutline said "Unlucky 13" in boldface, and beneath that read, "At Lakewood, it brought him luck. Yesterday his luck ran out."

The *Atlanta Journal* story continued:

> Lloyd Seay, lead-footed mountain boy who didn't care whether he was outrunning revenuers or race-drivers just so long as he was riding fast. . . . Lanky blond and youthful, he was well known in Atlanta and all along the highways and in the mountains. Federal, state and county law enforcement officers knew him as the most daring of all the daredevil crew that hauled liquor from mountain stills

---

*Neither cousin was very good with numbers, and the subsequent trial revealed that the dispute actually came down to a difference of five cents. At that trial, witnesses and attorneys also speculated that the sugar story was concocted afterward, and that the whole argument may have been over a woman.

into Atlanta. They had many a wild chase when they hit his trail, but they had caught him only rarely, for he hurled his car down the twisting black-top hill-country roads at a pace few of them cared to follow. He will be missed by racetrack fans as well.

A caravan of cars surrounded Seay's funeral—"liquor haulers and race fans and thrill seekers and reporters." As one southern writer said, you'd have thought ex–Dixie president Jefferson Davis himself was in the coffin. Seay's story captured the imagination of Georgians in need of inspiration. The drums of world war had begun beating louder and louder. Atlantans knew, as the nation knew, that it was just a matter of time before they started sending their boys overseas. But Seay had given them a brilliant distraction, a poignant, folk hero story line of triumph and tragedy, a tale with a bloody ending that would have made Erskine Caldwell blush.

Standing among the hundreds of mourners were a few revenue agents and sheriff's deputies, men who had tried so hard to put Seay behind bars but who respected—envied, even—the young man's driving skills.

None of the mourners was more distraught than Raymond Parks. He looked dignified and serene in his fedora and brown suit. On the inside, he was devastated. He'd nursed such high hopes for Seay, whom he considered a better racer than his other cousin, Roy. Better than Bill France or the Flock brothers, too. If Seay had lived, Parks felt he would have become "one of the great drivers."

The cemetery sat three blocks from Dawsonville's town square. A few weeks after the funeral, a four-foot-high granite monument was installed at Seay's grave. It read, "Winner National Stock Car Championship, Sept. 1, 1941, Lakewood Speedway." A bas-relief '39 Ford was etched into the granite and a glass-encased photo of Seay glued into the driver's side window. For many decades to come, Lloyd Seay's photograph would peer out onto nearby Highway 9, the "Whiskey Trail" he helped blaze.

The headstone was ordered and paid for by Parks, who kept asking himself, *What the hell am I going to do now?*

I would rather be a superb meteor, every atom of me in a
significant glow, than a sleepy and permanent planet.
The proper function of man is to live, not to exist. . . .
— JACK LONDON

8

"MIRACULOUS DEATH ESCAPE"

Seay's death left a gaping hole in Raymond Parks's young racing team and threatened to derail the fast-growing popularity of a sport whose rules and rituals Seay himself had helped define. How would the shaky-legged new sport survive without its first star? Parks knew that Roy Hall, who spent more time fleeing police than leading races, was no successor to Lloyd Seay, regardless of his ample driving skills.

While Parks, Vogt, France, and the other pioneers of stock car racing mourned the loss of Seay, another intrepid racer was positioning himself to fill Seay's shoes. The man who would take up the flag of southern stock car racing would turn out to be a sullen, brainy, prematurely bald cigar chewer born in the South, raised out West, and now settled back South where he belonged. Another man named Red.

Robert Nold Byron had been a soft-spoken, curious, happy little red-head. Born in 1916 to Scots-Irish parents, he would live a hard-luck life, a life darkened—in eerie similarity to Raymond Parks, Roy Hall, and Henry Ford—by the death of a parent.

At first, home was a company town in southwest Virginia called Plasterco, where Byron's father, Jack, worked as a mining engineer for the U.S. Gypsum Co.,* creator of wallboards and ceiling tiles. The family lived in employee housing, which at that time consisted of large tents. Jack, who as a child had worked the mines in his hometown in Ohio following the death of his own father, would return from the gypsum mine to his canvas-walled home at night, hacking and wheezing, spitting up blood and thick white globs of coagulated gypsum. After many months of this, the company doctors diagnosed pulmonary tuberculosis and suggested that the Byrons move west to the cleaner air of Colorado, Arizona, or California. Jack chose Colorado. Bob was just a toddler.

Jack spent his first months in Colorado at a sanatorium until he recovered from his TB and was hired again by the Colorado branch of U.S. Gypsum. The jagged peaks and pinnacles, the red-rock cliffs and lush pine forests full of wildlife made an idyllic boy's playground. Bob, as Red was known as a child, now eight and adventurous, attracted a gaggle of friends. They played war games and hide-and-seek, explored caves and rock formations. One boy's pet pig followed them everywhere.

The Byrons moved to Boulder in 1924, and for a while, life was good. Jack got a better job. His wife, Elizabeth, gave birth to a daughter, Virginia. Bob was well behaved, mechanically inclined, and bookish, although starting to show signs of increasing energy and daring. He joined the Boy Scouts, played football, and in summertime disappeared into the mountains, rock climbing among the sheer-faced Flatirons. In winter, he waxed the steel runners of his sled and flew down snow-covered streets, sometimes at night.

Bob was an industrious boy, too, delivering newspapers and shoveling snow from neighbors' driveways. At night, the family gathered in the den, in front of a fire, to read books and listen to phonographs or *Amos and Andy* on the radio. Jack was a college-educated man and had filled the house with books. Bob loved the boyhood adventure stories of Jack

---

*Now an avid sponsor of NASCAR race cars and trucks.

London and Ernest Thompson Seton, especially Seton's *Rolf in the Woods* series about a boy who escapes a drunken aunt and uncle to join an Indian tribe.

In time, Bob's daredevil side began to emerge more boldly. Hand-drawn pictures and clipped-out photos of automobiles began to cover his bedroom walls. He maintained a growing stack of *Popular Mechanics* magazines. Teachers noticed that Bob was scribbling sketches of racing cars into his notebooks and textbooks. They warned his parents that Bob "wasn't applying himself." For Christmas one year, Bob received a mechanical drawing set and drafting table, which became his pride and joy. He kept the drawing instruments neatly lined up in the proper slots of a blue velvet-lined box. He also built a ham radio and took up Hawaiian guitar. Then, through Boy Scouts, Bob was introduced to "soapbox" derby car racing. That's when trouble really began.

Not content to create simple rectangles on wheels, Bob spent many hours crafting streamlined, meticulously painted boy-sized racing machines. Pieces from his sister's toys began to disappear, particularly the wheels, "borrowed" from her tricycle, baby buggy, or wagon. Bob won many soapbox derbies in his little homemade racing cars.

In high school, Bob got his driver's license, which led to further trouble. He and his friends, after school or after Saturday football games, gathered on the outskirts of town and raced one another on dirt roads or in a cow field. Bob was already one of the more popular kids at school. He dated one of the prettiest girls, and everyone knew about his musical group, which played Hawaiian songs at church parties and school dances. His car-racing prowess raised his social stock even higher.

One Saturday, a farmer complained about kids racing recklessly and without permission in his field. The police were called, and Bob was arrested. His parents took away his driving privileges. Bob responded by pooling money with his friends to buy a secondhand Model T, which he kept in the backyard. If he couldn't drive a car, he could at least play with one. Bob spent many hours dismantling and rebuilding the Ford. He stripped off the fenders, stiffened the suspension, and beefed up the engine, with plans to start racing other boys once again in a nearby cow pasture. Every now and then, he'd get the engine running, only to have it splurt, sputter, and die. He became obsessed with the uncooperative Ford. He'd absentmindedly leave his father's tools in the rain and snow, where they'd rust. Grease and oil covered his clothes, hands, and face. His parents, frustrated by Bob's sudden irresponsibility, finally told him to get rid of the car.

The household grew edgy with the tense rift that was developing between father and son. Bob's mother, Elizabeth, and sister, Virginia, tried to act as buffers between the two headstrong men. Life in the Byron household grew tenser yet when the Depression forced Bob to leave school and start earning money. He got a job with the Civilian Conservation Corps. Potato soup became a family staple.

Then, in the winter of 1934, Elizabeth came down with the flu, which devolved into pneumonia. She was rushed one night to the hospital, but it was too late. Her death plunged the family into a fog of confusion and grief. Jack remarried a year later, and Bob knew he would have to leave home soon.

Jack Byron was a stern, devout Catholic; he and his new wife did not want a rule-breaking, thrill-seeking gearhead for a son. Jack felt Bob should be focusing on his education—pursuing college, not cars. His mother had been his advocate and confidante, but Bob openly shunned his father's conservative advice. When the elder Byron threatened to disown him, Bob decided, like Rolf in the boyhood tales of his youth, it was time to seek out his dream of a robust life built around cars and speed. Bob was seventeen, the same age at which Henry Ford had left home. Like Raymond Parks, he latched onto Ford's Model T as his vehicle for escape, catching the bug that infected many young men his age.

Bob moved out and got a job working in a coal mine south of Denver. His coworkers thought he was so laid-back they once bought him a leather whip as a gag. But on the weekends, he hooked up with a rowdy gang of teens who sometimes delivered moonshine, drag-raced, and bob-sledded in the mountains, a dangerous sport that killed two of his friends. Bob lived in the shadow of Pike's Peak, which hosted the annual hill-climbing races he'd read about as a child. Those races had been inspired by Henry Ford's former driver, Barney Oldfield.

During the earliest days of American racing, Oldfield had been the first daredevil showman, but also a natural, gut-level driver who felt more at home on small-town dirt tracks than on paved speedways such as Indy (where he never won). Among Oldfield's many feats and firsts was, in 1915, becoming the first man to race up the new 12.5-mile dirt road leading to the top of Pike's Peak, a feat that led to annual races there.

Pike's Peak lured a band of racing groupies who turned the region into a small community of Oldfield wannabes. Oldfield always drove with an unlit cigar clamped in his jaw, a cushion of tobacco that prevented the ruts of a racetrack from chipping his teeth. That cigar and his dark-tinted goggles, to keep dust out of his eyes, had been the notorious speed demon's trademarks. Bob Byron decided they'd be his trademarks, too.

After spending a year or so in and around Pike's Peak, Byron decided to follow a hunch. He'd heard that some of the best racing of the day was happening down South. A friend's cousin had recently moved to Alabama, and Byron decided to join him, in a little town called Talladega. He found a job as a mechanic at a Chevrolet dealer and on weekends sought out other race-minded young men at the scrappy, unruly little dirt tracks of Alabama and nearby Georgia. He was a bit of an outsider—a *westerner* among southerners—but his enthusiasm for racing quickly earned him a group of pals.

Byron befriended a jittery, chatty dude named Shorty, who soon became his infamous sidekick. He also frequently visited nearby Anniston and the shop of an eccentric, one-legged mechanic named A. J. Weldon, who'd lost his leg to cancer. His disability had no effect on his renown for supplying souped-up flathead Ford V-8 engines to many of the top Alabama racers of the 1930s and 1940s. Weldon had an immaculate room full of spare parts on the second floor above his shop and an obsession for cleanliness and tidiness to rival Red Vogt's. Unlike Vogt,

Weldon's expertise was mainly in creating open-wheel cars, the specially built racers that competed in the AAA circuit, including full-sized Indy cars and the smaller "dirt" and "midget" versions.

Outside the South, AAA's championship circuit was the pinnacle of motorsports, as Major League Baseball is to Little League or stickball. Stock car racing was still an unproven novelty. As with most racers of the day, Byron's goal was Indy. He drove made-from-scratch, bullet-shaped, open-wheel racers known as big cars or three-quarter cars. The number painted on his first racer was "99"—a tribute to the Barney Oldfield / Henry Ford creation, the "999," which Oldfield had raced into the history books in 1902. Through the mid- to late 1930s, Byron and his pal Shorty became regulars at dozens of dirt racetracks, traveling all across northern Alabama and into Georgia in search of races. Those tracks were part of an informal AAA minor-league network, whose racers dreamed of reaching the big leagues. Byron clipped out news articles about his occasional victories and mailed them home to his family.

By 1937, Byron—now known as Red—had aligned himself with other drivers and mechanics, who together founded the Alabama Racing Association. But car racing in Old South Alabama wasn't as welcome as it was at that time in New South Atlanta, and Byron's racing club had a hard time finding a home. The group hosted a few open-wheel races in 1937 at a track in Oxford but was soon chased out by a court injunction, due to the noise and unruly crowds. Occasional races at the Birmingham Fairgrounds attracted as many as eight thousand, but other tracks—such as the half-mile track in Gadsen called Melrose Park, near Byron's home—attracted more controversy than fans.

In 1938, after a few Sunday-afternoon races, northern Alabama church leaders began to complain that the Melrose Park races were, in short, sinful—and "a disturbance of their peace." The religious leaders brought their complaints to county officials and other elected leaders who, preferring not to alienate their churchgoing voters, asked Sheriff P. W. Cotton to look into the matter. Sheriff Cotton had no problem threatening to arrest anyone racing on a Sunday. After all, many of the racers were well known to Cotton as whiskey trippers. A local judge upheld the sheriff's threat, citing the state's "blue law," which prohibited any business activities on the Lord's day that weren't necessary for "life and health." Byron worried about the blow to his club's nascent racing program, which had already begun advertising its races and stood to lose money. "You might as well write our obituary," he said. Byron was then warned by the sheriff's office: *Call off the races or face arrest.* "We haven't made anything off racing here yet," Byron complained to a reporter. "We had hoped to keep at it until we built up a following."

Byron and his association then tried racing on Wednesday nights instead of Sundays, but the crowds were paltry. So he and the other Alabama racers began looking for new racing venues. On July 3, 1938, Byron and three other Alabamans drove eighty miles east into southside Atlanta for Byron's first-ever race at Lakewood Speedway.

Lakewood had not yet hosted a stock car race but offered a highly publicized series of AAA-sponsored Fourth of July races in 1938, featuring open-wheel big cars and some of the nation's best-known racers. The July 4 races taught Byron that he still had a lot to learn.

After finishing second and third in two ancillary "heat" races, Byron qualified to start in the main twenty-mile event, which attracted twenty-five thousand fans, the biggest crowd Byron had ever seen at a racetrack. An Atlanta racer named Crash lived up to his reputation and kicked off the race by smashing dramatically through the fence and rolling his car onto himself, one of a handful of thrilling collisions that inspired the newspapers to call it "easily the greatest race meet ever conducted in Atlanta." Byron watched it all from the pits with an engine that died a few miles into the race.

He returned to Lakewood for another AAA-sponsored open-wheel race on Labor Day, competing against other big-car racers, but none of the South's beloved stock car drivers. Byron's luck was no better there, and he again failed to finish the race.

Two months later, on Armistice Day, Byron returned to Lakewood in a beat-up 1926 Model A Ford roadster that one sportswriter said "was a little rough in appearance and sounded as if the engine would come apart any time."

The 1938 Armistice Day race was Atlanta's and Byron's first stock car race. Though he longed to race at Indianapolis, Byron enjoyed all kinds of racing, and the wild stories he'd heard about this new style of racing in his adopted South had aroused Byron's curiosity. For the first time, Byron found himself at the same track with Lloyd Seay, Roy Hall, Bill France, Raymond Parks, and Red Vogt. Byron had heard about them all, especially Vogt, whom Byron knew had worked on the winning car at the Indianapolis 500 earlier that year. Byron considered himself a pretty good mechanic, but he could tell from just the *sound* of Vogt's engines—a steady, machine-gun thrumping—that they were potent.

Byron's engine, meanwhile, sounded "blappity" and sick. His car looked like a regular, if raggedy, Model A "stock" Ford, but under the hood grumbled the engine from his open-wheel car. Still, not even his blatantly nonstock car was enough to beat some of the whiskey drivers at their game. Byron placed third in an eight-mile heat race. He then qualified for the 150-mile main event, and when he crossed the finish line, he thought he had just won his first stock car race. But race officials gave the victory to Lloyd Seay, claiming that Byron was a lap behind Seay. Byron complained, but the ruling stood.

For the next three years, Byron focused mainly on AAA-sponsored open-wheel races while occasionally trying his luck at stock car races. In 1939, at a July Fourth AAA race at Lakewood, Byron "gave the crowded grandstands one of Lakewood's greatest thrills," according to the *Atlanta Journal*. Lakewood's notorious dust blinded Byron in the first turn on the first lap, and he gouged a hundred-yard hole in the fencing as he flipped his car end over end and was thrown clear. A photograph in the next day's paper shows Byron standing beside his mangled scrap heap of a car, with a look on his face as if he was wondering how he'd emerged alive.

"MIRACULOUS DEATH ESCAPE," the headline blared.

Byron returned to Lakewood for a stock car race on Labor Day of that year, 1939, but again lost to the best southern stock car racers of the day—Roy Hall and Fonty and Bob Flock finished 1-2-3. Byron's path had begun to intersect more and more with Raymond Parks's. But every time he competed against Parks's team—Seay, Hall, or the Flock brothers—he finished well behind at least one of the moonshining racers.

Byron felt he was as good a driver as Seay and Hall, and a strong mechanic, but he couldn't beat the stock car boys at their game. And he never seemed able to beat the top dogs of AAA racing, either. He knew of Red Vogt's genius, and that made a huge difference—that and thousands of dollars from Parks. As Vogt said, "money equals speed," and Parks's patronage paid the substantial bill for Vogt's speed-boosting parts and labor. Whenever he was in Atlanta for a race, Byron would enviously visit Vogt's garage.

He thought, *If I could just hook up with a team like that . . .*

Byron's introduction to Parks, Seay, Vogt, and the others marked the start of his dual loyalties to open-wheel cars and stock cars. Open-wheelers were expensive, usually premade by expert race car builders, and, culturally, very *northern*. Stock cars could be made on the cheap from an orphaned Ford from a junkyard and transformed into a race car in the backyard. They were very *southern*. Byron, at the start of his career, placed himself between those two racing genres and their divergent cultures. But before he could declare loyalty to one or the other, the course of history led him in another direction.

In the summer of 1941, Byron returned to Colorado for a rare visit with his father and stepmother. His younger sister laughed at the southern accent he'd picked up; he sounded more southern than even the Alabama-born friends he brought with him. Byron was soft-spoken but seemed confident, well-dressed, and charming. He told funny stories about the southern boys and their wild ways. He spoke of his "miraculous death escape" in Atlanta. Jack Byron noticed that his rebellious son had become a handsome and dignified young man, his dapper appearance giving no sign that he was a race car driver.

Father and son felt more relaxed around each other than they'd been in years, and one night during a game of bridge, Byron told his father that he was happy doing the thing he'd always dreamed of: driving faster than most men could ever imagine. He wasn't having the success he'd hoped for, though, he explained.

So he had decided to join the army.

Byron's first steps toward one of the lesser-known battlegrounds of World War II began when he walked into an army recruiting office in Montgomery, Alabama, in mid-1941. Sensing that war was imminent, Byron hoped to join early and become a pilot with the Army Air Corps, predecessor of the U.S. Air Force. He was devastated to learn he had imperfect eyesight and could not qualify to fly planes. Instead, the army wanted him to become a navigator and tail gunner. He agreed and was assigned to a Louisiana air base. Soon after reporting for duty, Byron was given two days of liberty and drove to Atlanta for one last race before getting swallowed up by his military obligations.

The July 13, 1941, event featured an open-wheel race and stock car races of five, ten, and twenty-five miles. Early in the twenty-five-mile stock car race, Lloyd Seay, driving his convertible, flipped and was tossed out of his car. He tumbled through the air and seemed headed right for the lake, which was not a good place for Seay. He couldn't swim. Seay splash-landed right at the water's edge, uninjured, but unable to rejoin the race. With just three laps to go, Byron found himself vying for the lead with three other racers, until a group of slower cars up ahead became entangled in the first turn. The yellow caution flag came out, warning drivers to slow down, but many of them were blinded by a swirl of dust that shrouded the tangled cars. Byron and the other co-leaders, unaware of the yellow flag or the wrecked cars ahead of them, barreled straight ahead toward the "mass of spilled vehicles and drivers." At the last second, all four drivers finally saw the wreckage in front of them and veered hard to the right, crashing into the wall, side by side. Byron's face slammed into his steering wheel, breaking his nose and splitting a deep gash into his lip and mouth. The race was stopped, and race officials decided to give one of the co-leaders who had been racing beside Byron the victory.

Byron was angry. Determined to achieve victory that day, he declined medical attention so he could race his banged-up car in the ten-mile race. With blood dribbling down his chin and neck, and a blood-soaked cigar in the uninjured half of his mouth, he finished second. Finally, he lined up for the last event of the day, the five-mile stock car race. His face was a painful, blood-caked pulp. Dust was glued to his face, and blood from his injury had dribbled down his neck and turned his white coveralls crimson. Each rut of the beat-up track sent a jolt of pain to his cracked nose. Byron kept his foot mashed on the accelerator and never dropped below sixty miles an hour. He finished the five-miler in four minutes and two seconds, just a car length ahead of three Atlanta drivers.

Byron celebrated his first-ever stock car victory, and the Atlanta boys were clearly impressed. But it would be Byron's last race for five years.

Afterward, he had a doctor look at his face. They straightened his cracked nose, but it took fourteen stitches to close the tear in his mouth, which he then had to explain to the U.S. Army back in Louisiana on Monday morning.

Following the nightmare of Lloyd Seay's death, Raymond Parks realized he was far from ready to relinquish his own dreams of greatness in the still untested world of stock cars. By late 1941, he had spent seven thousand dollars on his cars and on Vogt's bills and travel expenses. With his two-thirds share of Seay's and Hall's victories, he barely broke even. Still, he had that fever. And he wanted to stoke it. He wanted to win.

When Parks first met Byron, he seemed too quiet and aloof, especially compared to loudmouthed, pistol-toting racers such as Roy Hall. Parks thought Byron had "a face you can't read." Indeed, his face was usually hidden behind round sunglasses, shaded by a helmet visor, his mouth clamped tight around an unlit cigar, which seemed to hold back any conversation. His jumpy sidekick, Shorty, did most of the talking.

Parks would never have guessed at the time that mysterious Red

Byron would, a decade later, take his racing team—and the entire sport—to new heights.

After Lloyd Seay's death, on a recommendation from Red Vogt, Parks had briefly considered asking Byron to join his fractured team, but he would not get the chance.

World War II interrupted the entire sport of stock car racing. Parks would soon be crouched in a foxhole during one of the coldest, bloodiest battles in the history of modern warfare, while Byron would find himself with a shard of hot metal burning into his thigh as his shredded airplane plummeted toward apparent doom. Surviving the horrific physical and psychological damages of war would make their eventual return to stock cars all the more remarkable.

PART II

War suits them. They are splendid riders,
first rate shots and utterly reckless.
—UNION GENERAL WILLIAM T. SHERMAN

9

Body bags and B-24 bombers

World War II would accidentally play a significant role in the evolution of stock car racing. Many of the creators of the sport would see far corners of the earth during wartime, places they'd never imagined. Afterward, they would return to the South dramatically altered by war. The experience gave southern men an even deeper sense of adventure, a respect for fear, a taste for freedom.

As the nation prepared for that war in late 1941, dark days followed the death of Lloyd Seay, whose killer was convicted and sentenced to life in prison. A jury declared that Woodrow Anderson "shot the Seays while their hands were raised and they were begging him not to shoot." The same day as his sentencing, a U.S. Navy destroyer was torpedoed off the coast of Greenland, and nearly a hundred men sank to their deaths. President Roosevelt was getting fed up and had recently promised Hitler that American men were ready to "stand up as free men and fight." Three days later, the nation's best-known stunt driver, Lucky Teeter, who had started his career at Lakewood in 1933, was killed at Indianapolis in a failed attempt to jump his car over a bus. That same afternoon,

November 2, 1941, the Lloyd Seay Memorial Race gunned to a start at Lakewood.

Seay's parents had become quite reliant on their son's moonshining income and were struggling desperately without his help. So the managers of Lakewood Speedway allowed Raymond Parks, Red Vogt, Bill France, and a handful of other racers to host a race in Seay's memory. Their intent was to donate the winner's purse to Seay's family.

Among the racers listed at the start was Parks's bootlegger friend Ralph "Bad Eye" Shirley. In truth, it was Roy Hall sitting behind the wheel in disguise, hiding once more from the law. Bill France joined the race, as did Fonty and Bob Flock, both driving Red Vogt cars. Except for Red Byron, who was back at his army training camp, all of stock car racing's stars were there. Racers named Tip, Crash, Red, Buster, and Speed.

The Lloyd Seay Memorial turned out to be the last southern stock car race before World War II, which would suspend racing for five years. An envelope with the race proceeds—$831.32—was afterward handed to Seay's father, Robert, who had never once seen his own son race. The winner was a veteran Georgia racer, nicknamed "Jap"—and Roy Hall was awarded the 1941 championship, which would have been Seay's, had he lived.

Five Sundays later, Japanese warplanes bombarded an unsuspecting U.S. Navy fleet on an otherwise quiet Hawaiian morning. The attack on Pearl Harbor finally pulled the country into war, and the National Office of Defense Transportation immediately banned all sporting events. America's men, women, and machines prepared to focus the nation's brainpower and firepower on the Pacific and in Europe, where U.S. troops would soon engage once more in visceral Tom-versus-Jerry battle against German foes.

In the South, young men lined up outside recruiting offices, enlisting in far greater numbers than their northern peers. Those who didn't enlist were soon drafted.

At thirty-seven, Red Vogt was too old to be drafted and would remain stateside. His father had served overseas in World War I, but Vogt would now serve in a different capacity. His reputation as a mechanical wizard earned him a "critical to the war effort" classification and a job as an army mechanic. Because he stayed open twenty-four hours, the army sent a steady supply of trucks in need of repair from various military bases.*

Bill France, now thirty-two, also remained stateside, working as foreman of an engine-installation crew at the Daytona Beach Boat Works, which built submarine chasers and other light ships for the navy and army.

Red Byron, twenty-six, was headed to one of the coldest U.S. military bases to prepare for the only battle of World War II to be waged near American soil. A few of the Aleutian Islands off the Alaskan coast had been taken over by the Japanese, and the Army Air Corps, recently renamed the Army Air Force, was determined to reclaim them. Byron had finished his training and was now an engineer and tail gunner in the largest American airplane ever built, one of the most difficult planes to fly, but also a remarkably resilient aircraft capable of taking a beating and remaining airborne. Its co-creator happened to be Henry Ford.

Twenty-seven-year-old Raymond Parks, meanwhile, was drafted in 1942 and trained with a U.S. Army division headed for the famously brutal and wintry Battle of the Bulge in the Ardennes region of Belgium. There, Parks would face unfamiliar snows and the men and machines of Hitler's feared Panzer divisions—terrifying examples of the German work ethic and engineering Red Vogt so admired.

Parks had tried hard to avoid the war. With a wife and a son at home, two ex-wives counting on his financial support, his liquor stores and

---

*In an awkward display of his apparently dual loyalties — to his German heritage and American existence — Red Vogt had named his sons Tom and Jerry.

numbers racket, his growing real estate holdings, and a dirt-poor family and drunken father depending on him, Parks felt he had more to lose than most. At first, he tried to act a little crazy so the draft board people would declare him 4-F and unfit to serve. When that failed, he managed to get a noncombat job at nearby Dobbins Air Base, which gave him a deferment from overseas military service. But he and a coworker were one day caught driving a fire truck down the runway.

Parks was fired and then reassigned—to the U.S. Army's Ninety-ninth Infantry Division. After a brief stay at Fort Benning, Georgia, he was shipped to Camp Van Dorn in Mississippi for thirteen weeks of training designed to turn regular citizens into soldiers.

Parks's first lesson was that, even in the army, moonshine was currency. He managed to have jars delivered to his sergeant, a guy from Ohio named Parkhill. During the endless and grueling marching sessions, Parkhill allowed Parks to slip off to the motor pool and hang out with the mechanics while the other trainees marched for miles. Sergeant Parkhill also gave Parks a German pistol, a Luger, in exchange for a jar of corn liquor. Parks and the rest of his unit—the 394th Infantry—next spent months at Camp Maxey, near Paris, Texas, training for and awaiting their call-up to war.

Parks's third marriage was already on the rocks. He met another woman in nearby Paris and rented an apartment there. At night, he'd sneak out of the barracks and stay in town, then slip back to base before dawn. The other soldiers noticed how Parks's bed always seemed to be made, and how he'd be up and mopping floors when they awoke.

One day, he received a telegram from his sister, who had taken over his lottery operations. Due to a strange accident of luck (or possibly cheating), hundreds of people had picked the correct numbers, and Parks lost twenty thousand dollars. He asked his sergeant for a few days of liberty so he could go home and clean up the mess. Before he even got on the bus, he got another telegram: another loss, this time ten thousand dollars. Parks decided it was finally time to get out of the lottery business. In Atlanta, he sold some property to a colleague and put the cash in a suitcase and the suitcase in his trunk. He then drove around Atlanta, paying off his lottery customers and telling them he was done with the bug.

Parks's embarkation orders came a few weeks later, in the summer of 1944. Allied troops had already stormed the beaches of Normandy and begun fighting east toward Germany. Parks's regiment and the entire Ninety-ninth Infantry Division were scheduled to catch up with that fight in Belgium.

In late September of 1944, Parks left Boston aboard the "Liberty ship" *Excelsior,* which for him and many of his southern colleagues was their first time at sea. While crossing the rough and stormy Atlantic, the men were allowed on the top deck only two hours a day. Parks spent most of his time in the crowded troop holds below, where the air quickly became stale with the smells of body odor, cigarette smoke, and seasickness.

After stopping in Scotland, the Ninety-ninth traveled to the French coast, where troops unloaded and began their long trek eastward. By November, they reached the hills of eastern Belgium. As they continued toward the German border, rain turned to snow, and Parks was soon glad he had brought extra socks and sturdier civilian boots.

Days began early with hot coffee and warm bread and, after many miles of marching or riding in the back of a transport truck, ended with a shivering night inside a two-man pup tent. One night, a foot of snow fell on their tents, and a major wrote in his diary, "I hate the cold. Men are miserable, too. Am afraid this is only the beginning."

Eastern Belgium had been overrun by Germany in World War I but regained its independence after Germany's defeat in that war. In 1940, Hitler reclaimed eastern Belgium as part of his "Third Reich." After the success of D-day and the U.S. Army's invasion of mainland Europe, the Allies began closing in on Germany's western front, in preparation for a full-scale offensive. Hitler, meanwhile, was making plans to blast through the Allied lines—thereby splitting the coalition in two—then to plow west into Antwerp and negotiate peace from a position of strength. But Hitler didn't expect the fierce Ninety-ninth Infantry, nor the brutal winter and its waist-high snows, nor the turning-point Battle of the Bulge, which signaled the beginning of the end for the Third Reich.

Parks entered that historic standoff in mid-November of 1944. Because Parks's 394th Infantry Regiment, and much of the 99th Infantry Division, lacked combat experience, they were assigned to a region far south of the point where military officials expected the Germans to attack. But within days of arriving in the Ardennes region, Parks's regiment suffered its first fatalities. The leader of a reconnaissance patrol was "ripped from head to groin" by enemy machine-gun fire. Two of the men sent to recover the body were also killed—just a tepid prelude to one of the toughest battles ever fought by the U.S. Army.

On December 12, 1944, Parks and the others were told to stuff all their personal possessions into duffle bags, stack them up, and begin moving farther east toward the enemy. They'd never see those duffle bags again. The men knew their war was about to get serious, even though creeping through the pine trees with fingers on the triggers of their army-issue M-1 rifles felt "melodramatic and unreal," as one soldier put it.

After three days of eerie quiet, the riflemen of Parks's D Company (a subset of the 394th Infantry) continued to advance through the snow, followed by the rest of the company's machine guns and mortars. Up ahead, the earth suddenly exploded. As one soldier described it, "Mortar bomb explosions ripped the air with hot metal, dirt, snow, and rocks . . . thousands of bullets snapped, crackled, and whined, all searching for yielding flesh and fragile bone."

Hitler's generals had taken the U.S. Army by surprise, and the four-day battle that began December 16 would determine the course of the war in Europe. Parks's regiment was among the few in a position to stop the German armored divisions from cutting deep into Allied territory and achieving Hitler's goal of bisecting his enemy's defenses.

At first, Parks and the others tried digging into the ground to hide from the fusillade, but the frozen ground was unyielding and their fingers quickly became bloody and frozen. Then came the "sssst-WHUMP" of artillery fire and the plop-plop-plop of incoming mortar rounds, followed by their concussive explosions and the whizzing release of shrapnel. Rockets called screaming meemies, which "sounded like howling wolves," tore into pine trees and the limbs rained down on the soldiers. Then came the buzzing of bullets and the "BLA-A-AP" of German machine pistols called burp guns.

Through it all keened the shrieks of the wounded and dying. By the end of that first day of battle, Parks learned that most of his company's rifle platoon had been slaughtered.

Parks had by now been promoted to technical sergeant, under orders to oversee and maintain the company's trucks and armored vehicles. His job as a "T-sergeant"—Parks joked he was a "Model T" sergeant—kept him back from the front lines, stationed with the vehicles in his care. Still, German bombs dropped all around, day and night.

For the next four seemingly endless days, Parks and the Ninety-ninth Infantry were attacked again and again by screaming platoons of German soldiers dressed in white camouflage suits, who emerged like ghosts from the thick mist. Some advances were so thick, U.S. soldiers just aimed forward and began firing, their bullets cutting down enemies like scythes mowing tall grass. One night, Parks's company was pummeled for ninety minutes by heavy German mortar and artillery fire. When the bombing ceased, German patrols suddenly appeared from the rear, where Parks's trucks and jeeps were parked. They had outflanked Parks's company, which fought back with mortar and machine-gun fire. They successfully repelled the German attack, and Parks's company sought a better position farther away from the front. After a mile-long sprint to higher ground, Parks ate his bland K rations but would not get another meal for three days.

The Americans were wildly outnumbered. Some platoons were wiped out entirely, their soldiers killed or captured, while many other platoons lost half their men. Scores of young men had their arms and legs blown off, and during the hasty retreat, their dead or dying bodies were often left behind, crushed into muddy roads by advancing German tanks and trucks. U.S. Army commanders finally decided to pull even farther back, to a high ridge called Elsenborn. Parks and the others fled along slushy, muddy roads, fighting their way through dangerous villages. Officers urged the men on toward the hot coffee up ahead, but there was no coffee. At night, they marched single file, dejected at having been forced to flee, disgusted by the ruined roadside bodies of comrades. "They couldn't bag us fast enough," Parks would recall years later.

One of Parks's duties during that time was tending to the dead. He and his men would occasionally stop and bury American soldiers. More than once they stacked frozen German corpses in a barn. On December 19, Parks reached the hilltop of Elsenborn Ridge. He and the others were told this was their new home and to start digging foxholes. It took most of the night to dig a hole six feet square and five feet deep, and over the next twenty-four hours, wounded soldiers continued straggling into the encampments that would become the U.S. Army's final stand.

Parks's men now had the chance to notice a transformation. They had remembered how, back in training, he had escaped the marching sessions with his bribes of moonshine, how he'd disappear at night to sleep with his girlfriend in their Texas love nest. But on Elsenborn Ridge, Parks seemed all business and, for the first time in his two years with the regiment, seemed willing to be part of their war.

"How come you decided to start working?" one of Parks's platoon mates asked.

Parks was now thirty years old, a decade older than most of the others. Back home, he'd left behind lucrative businesses, his son, and a passion for racing cars. Parks never thought the war would drag on this long. He thought he'd be back in Atlanta by now. But the past few horrific days proved otherwise. His shaky nerves had become hardened. He was angry and now felt he had no choice but to fight.

"I'll do anything to get this damn war over with," Parks said.

The very next day, the Germans attacked from behind a hedgerow down the hill. Parks's platoon leader and platoon sergeant were killed when a shell exploded in their foxhole. But Hitler's troops were quickly mowed down by U.S. machine gunners atop the ridge, and many of the Germans subsequently surrendered. It was the first of many hard-won victories against a larger, better-armed, and persistent German opponent.

During a brief lull in the fighting five days later, on a crisp, clear Christmas Day, Parks and his men shared cookies and cakes from home, melted caramel candy bars into their coffee, curled up with letters from home, and listened to the ringing of the church bells in the nearby village, now occupied by Germans. After that brief respite, Parks and the rest of the Ninety-ninth Infantry would spend the next five weeks repelling unpredictable German efforts to cut through their depleted lines of defense.

Immediately after that crystalline Christmas, the snows came. Almost nightly, snow blanketed the ridge and packed the openings of the foxholes. Dawn then bloomed with soldiers, one by one, popping out of their snow-covered foxholes—"like some oversized gopher," one man later wrote, "like a deranged garden sprouting mushrooms." The men's faces were blackened with soot from the makeshift lanterns they'd devised, using bottles or cans and, as wicks, strips of sock or blankets soaked in gasoline.

During the day, Parks occasionally got sent on patrols to strike against German positions. His olive-drab uniform was an easy target against the backdrop of snowdrifts. The Germans in their white camouflage suits would loom suddenly out of thick fog and snow. Day after day, Parks's luck held, as he watched others get shot by those ghosts.

At night, Parks curled into his corner of the two-man foxhole but slept fitfully. He and his foxhole mate were supposed to take turns on watch. But when it came to such crucial matters as his life, Parks wasn't comfortable trusting others. Most nights, Parks stayed awake, too, fearful that the other guy would fall asleep on watch.

Rations were delivered every few days. Parks melted snow in his helmet to wash his hands and face but went weeks without bathing. Many of those who survived that terrible January got frostbite, and Parks was again glad that he'd swapped his army-issue boots for heavier civilian boots and that he'd brought extra pairs of wool socks.

On January 30, the standoff finally came to an end. Parks and his regiment were ordered to attack through waist-deep snow against the entrenched Germans. "Move out," came the order. An drab olive hulk of men marched straight ahead into the invisible enemy's machine-gun fire.

Those who weren't immediately cut down couldn't believe they were still alive, still walking. But the first attack ended in an exhausted, demoralizing retreat. Then came another order. "Get ready, boys. We attack again in twenty minutes. HQ wants those woods."

It would take two more attacks to finally reach those woods, on January 31, when the snow turned suddenly to rain. The Germans were finally in retreat, but the U.S. Army had paid dearly. Parks helped stack frozen American corpses like firewood.

Through February and March, the Ninety-ninth Infantry pushed the German army farther east, out of Belgium and into its homeland. The Battle of the Bulge and the terrible winter at Elsenborn Ridge were over. The United States was now on the offensive, and Parks's optimistic commanders allowed him a three-day pass to Paris, where Parks and his colleagues ate like wolves and drank champagne and spoke broken French with pretty young women—a surreal escape from the ungodly carnage. When Parks rejoined the 394th Infantry, they kept pushing east against the retreating Germans, past signs that read in English, "You are entering Germany, there will be no fraternization with any German."

On March 10, Parks was among the first U.S. soldiers to cross the Rhine River. At the town of Remagen, German regiments fired ceaselessly onto the railroad bridge below them, trying to destroy the U.S. Army's prime means of entry into their heartland.

Parks led his trucks and jeeps across the bridge, past the crumpled bodies of dead soldiers, feeling exposed and terrified. Other troops marched single file, jumping across holes in the bridge. The crossing seemed to last forever. Some men, their hunger outweighing their fear of German bullets, stopped to grab K rations from the packs of their dead comrades.

Fierce fighting continued on the hard-won east bank of the Rhine, where Parks and his fellow soldiers—many of them from the South—were surprised to be joined by the black faces of newly arrived troops. Due to a shortage of infantry, and the desires of African American soldiers to swap kitchen and laundry duty for battle, General Eisenhower had ordered the integration of black platoons, which now fought side by side with white soldiers and helped drive the German army back toward Berlin. The soldiers of Company K joined the 394th in mid-March, making it the first fully integrated U.S. Army regiment since the Revolutionary War.

For the next month, the 394th and Company K pushed deeper into Germany. Parks drove through town after town, surveying the heartbreaking destruction of once-beautiful villages, where German children with pails begged for food. Photos that he and his colleagues snapped captured the woe of their melancholy task. In some photos, Parks's company mates are clowning around, pretending to chug from empty champagne bottles. Behind them are scenes of carnage: debris-choked streets, twisted train tracks, smoke rising from crumbled stone homes and churches. One photograph shows cold-looking German soldiers crouched behind the wire fence of a POW camp.

In photographs of that period, Parks appears somber, subdued. When the men found stashes of wine or champagne in a cellar, he never got drunk like the others. He had never developed a taste for drink. Not the champagne in Paris nor the moonshine back home. There was nothing to celebrate about pilfering hooch from a beaten village.

At one town, soldiers stopped at the rural home of a German farmer, his wife, and their beautiful eighteen-year-old daughter, a farm that could have fit into the hills of northern Georgia. In the tree-shaded yard, surrounded by a privet hedge, sat a 1937 Ford. The Americans took turns driving it up and down the rutted lane, until the transmission seized and the car ground to a halt. The soldiers apologized and left. Parks just shook his head, watching the German family stand helplessly in their yard.

Through April of 1945, as springtime flowers bloomed on trees and in fields, Parks and his regiment continued to plow across Germany's industrial heartland, attacking the retreating pockets of German resistance. On April 12, President Roosevelt died at his retreat in Warm Springs, Georgia, south of Atlanta.

A few weeks later, after crossing the Danube, the Ninety-ninth Infantry received orders from headquarters to "cease active operations."

At first, there were no cheers of jubilation. Troops refused to believe their war could be ending. Later, another message relayed a more explicit message—the "unconditional surrender" of Germany—and smiles blossomed across the faces of T-Sergeant Parks and his weary men.

Parks sailed home from Marseille, but instead of being delivered to Georgia, a paperwork snafu landed him in Florida. He had to ask one of his workers in Atlanta to pick him up and drive him back home to Georgia. On September 27, 1945, Parks was officially relieved of duty. More than eleven hundred of his colleagues in the Ninety-ninth Infantry had been killed and more than four thousand injured. Parks, amazingly, sustained hardly a scratch.

Parks and the entire 394th Infantry were officially honored by General George Marshall for repelling the enemy attacks at the Battle of the Bulge. The 394th, said Marshall, had been outnumbered six to one; was repeatedly attacked from the front, sides, and rear; but held their ground without allowing the enemy to breach the Allied line of defense. In a strongly worded letter of commendation, Marshall wrote of the "tenacious stand," "the unflinching courage," and the "overwhelming odds."

Parks was personally awarded a Good Conduct Medal and a Distinguished Unit Badge, both of which he put into a safe-deposit box, and then got back to work. He considered himself "one of the lucky ones," even though the chatter of gunfire and the screams of dying young men would remain inside his head for many years.

Parks would soon learn that he'd been fortunate compared to Red Byron.

Byron's introduction to his own battlefield began with a slow, aerial descent toward the jagged, volcanic, snow-blanketed Aleutian Islands, which stretched in a crooked chain off the southwest corner of the U.S. territory of Alaska (to be named the forty-ninth state in 1959). The islands created an east-to-west barrier of sorts between the north Pacific and, above that, the Bering Sea. The strategic military value of the islands lay in the fact that they were among the closest U.S. territories to the Japanese mainland. And, for the Japanese, these islands presented an enticing stepping-stone toward the U.S. mainland.

The Japanese struck first, taking hold of the virtually uninhabited westernmost Aleutian islands of Attu and Kiska in 1942, while the U.S. Army created an air base and headquarters of its own on the island of Umnak, roughly five hundred miles east of Kiska.

Despite terrible weather, relentless snows, hurricane-force winds, and gauze-thick fog that caused navy ships to grope gingerly and sometimes clunk into one another, U.S. troops managed to build another, larger airstrip on the island of Adak, just 210 miles east of Kiska, in late 1942. That's where T-Sergeant Robert Nold Byron reported for duty as part of a massive deployment preparing to attack Kiska in the spring of 1943. Soon after Byron's arrival came the big, lumbering U.S. airplanes. Lots of them.

Despite Henry Ford's unseemly admiration of Adolf Hitler, and his oft-repeated claims to be a pacifist, Ford had largely ceased production of passenger cars in 1941 and set about becoming the nation's third-largest defense contractor.

Back in World War I, Ford had experimented with the role of peacemaker. In 1915, he'd sailed to Europe on a so-called Peace Ship, seeking to "get the boys out of the trenches by Christmas." But Ford's stab at international diplomacy ended with embarrassing failure when European leaders declined to even meet with him and the press ridiculed his efforts. Afterward, he turned his attentions back to what he knew best: building things and making money. Ford profited handsomely from the First World War. Despite a famous prewar vow to burn down his factory rather than turn it into a tool of war, beginning in 1917, Ford began manufacturing tractors, airplane engines, ambulance chassis, armor plating, soldiers' helmets, and gas masks.

He had publicly vowed not to keep a single penny of war profits, but he kept it a mystery where those World War I earnings ended up. Ford similarly found a profitable role for his factories as World War II began. Ford churned out jeeps, trucks, airplane engines, and tank engines. But his main contribution to the war was the result of Ford's obsessive efforts to build a bomber airplane called the B-24, nicknamed the "Liberator."

In early March of 1941, on a day when Lloyd Seay and Roy Hall had been racing at Daytona, Ford had unveiled his plans to build the world's largest factory at a rural site south of Detroit. To be called Willow Run, the mile-long factory was designed to turn out a B-24 every hour. Ford later called his B-24 manufacturing days "the biggest challenge of my life," days that likely contributed to the stroke he suffered that same year; Ford spent many weeks resting and recovering at his Georgia retreat during 1941.

Due to a shortage of Detroit-area workers, many B-24 laborers came from the South, so much so that the Michigan town of Ypsilanti became known as "Ypsitucky." When the plant was up and running in 1942, the Detroit newspapers gushed that Willow Run held "a promise of revenge for Pearl Harbor."

"Look out, Hitler. Here comes the flood!" one headline blared, oblivious to the unintended irony of pitting Ford—a Jew baiter with sympathies for Hitler—as the Nazis' foe. For this war, Ford spoke not of peace. As a subcontractor for Consolidated Aircraft Corp., Ford built nearly half of the war's eighteen thousand B-24s, with help from such assembly-line workers as tomboy Rose Monroe of Kentucky (a.k.a. "Rosie the Riveter") and a crew of midgets hired to crawl into tight spaces.

At the time, the B-24 was hailed as one of the largest, ugliest, and most effective military planes ever built. A four-engine, propeller-driven aircraft with an incredible wingspan of 110 feet, the B-24 could travel three hundred miles an hour. Due to its huge fuel capacity, it could fly across the United States and partway back again without refueling. It had a stubby fuselage, its nose encased in glass, an odd-looking tail also encased in glass, a glass dome on top, and an udderlike bubble beneath. The crew of six to ten men was stuffed into ridiculously small spaces to make room for four to six *tons* of bombs.

Charles Lindbergh, who worked briefly as a Willow Run test pilot, complained of the B-24's "mediocrity." But in Germany, B-24 crews praised the workhorse that could fly even when slashed and pocked by enemy bullets and flak. The Army Air Force launched a propaganda campaign that touted B-24s as "the greatest flying machines ever made." The army air force even hired John Steinbeck to write stories of proud, patriotic, and free-spirited B-24 pilots, whom Steinbeck called a mix of "Daniel Boone and Henry Ford."

Jimmy Stewart and Clark Gable were among those assigned to B-24 crews; so were future newsman Walter Cronkite, future *Catch 22* author Joseph Heller, and future presidential candidate George McGovern, who later said that flying in a B-24 "literally exhausted every resource of mind and body and spirit I had."

When Red Byron completed his training and transferred to Adak as part of the Eleventh Air Force, he joined the ranks of those who had— or would soon develop—a love-hate relationship with Ford's B-24. The aircraft had no windshield wipers; during rains, the pilot had to stick his head out the side window to see. There was no heat and no bathroom. On flights that lasted eight to ten hours, the crew had to peel off the many layers of insulating clothing to urinate into small tubes. At higher altitudes, dizziness and nausea were common symptoms because the aircraft wasn't pressurized, and the crew had to breathe with the help of cold, clammy oxygen masks that often froze to their face.

Many pilots complained that the Liberator was incredibly difficult to fly. With no power steering, pilots had to use their left hand to turn the huge steering wheel while constantly adjusting the throttle and fuel mixture with their right hand. The seats were cramped and unpadded, and in the frigid temperatures of twenty thousand to thirty thousand feet above the earth, more men were injured by frostbite than enemy fire. As at the Battle of the Bulge, men wore every stitch of clothing they owned. Back on the ground, they lived in frigid, metal-sided Quonset huts, a war village amid a "gaunt and majestic" landscape that, one soldier wrote in his diary, seemed "out of place in a world that belongs so little to man." Byron's younger sister sent care packages of warm socks, cookies, and books, and Byron sent home long letters about the native Inuit tribes who came to sell handmade crafts to the soldiers.

Now twenty-eight, Byron was five to ten years older than most of the others, and they often called him "old man." The average age of a B-24 pilot was twenty-one, and one airman observed that the younger ones were "not smart enough to be afraid."

Byron served as a navigator, flight engineer, tail gunner, and occasional bombardier, depending on which job was needed on that particular flight. Each job carried different duties, and dangers. Just getting into position was a chore in itself. Byron wore a layer of long underwear, then his woolen uniform, then a pair of pants and a heavy coat lined with sheepskin. Thick boots came last, and Byron had to waddle along narrow catwalks into the plane's bowels, then squeeze himself into a cramped seat in the nose, tail, or belly. Byron's career as an automobile racer likely helped him withstand many hours seated uncomfortably in one spot inside a noisy machine.

As flight engineer, Byron's job was to start the B-24's engines. The roar on takeoff was deafening, and every piece of equipment rattled as the plane gained speed and finally, oh-so-slowly, rose into the sky. Above ten thousand feet, Byron would keep chattering into the radio, making sure none of the crewmen had passed out from the lack of oxygen.

If Byron's job of the day was tail gunner, he'd man one of the ten .50-caliber machine guns that bristled off the B-24. But he knew, as did every B-24 crewman, that his bullets were no match for a well-timed barrage of flak from an enemy far below. *Flak* was the term for antiaircraft artillery shells fired into the sky and timed to explode at, say, twenty thousand feet. When the shells exploded, hundreds of pieces of shrapnel could handily penetrate a B-24's aluminum skin. A flak jacket, with a steel plate stitched over Byron's chest, might protect his heart, but flak could also take off a man's head. Often, as one airman wrote, "the flak was so thick you could walk on it."

One particular B-24 battle sent ripples of fear through the air corps. In an effort to cripple Germany's main oil supply line, a squadron of U.S. B-24s was sent in 1943 to attack oil refineries in Ploesti, Romania. Fifty-four planes—nearly a third of the squadron—never returned, and 532 men were killed or taken prisoner. Until that time, many B-24 crewmen had felt a romantic separation from the grisly, bodily risks taken by ground-based soldiers and ship-bound sailors. But the Ploesti disaster was a humbling reminder that B-24s were hardly impervious to enemy flak. It reverberated throughout the air corps, and Byron realized, *I could die—or worse.*

George McGovern would later say that flying into the angry black cloud of a flak barrage is what he imagined hell looked like. Soon after Ploesti, Red Byron found himself in the middle of that hell, and he would not escape unscathed.

Japan had feared that the buildup of American (and some Canadian) troops in the Aleutians meant the Allies were planning to use the Aleutians as a staging ground for attacks on the Japanese mainland. That's why Japan had established bases on Kiska and Attu in the first place. In February of 1943, Japan's military headquarters issued orders to the troops occupying those islands to "hold the western Aleutians at all cost."

Soon after, U.S. troops launched a ground attack on Attu. The Japanese soldiers, seriously outnumbered, made banzai charges, screaming maniacally as they ran headlong into U.S. gunfire. Finally, the Japanese realized they were outmanned. Instead of surrendering, hundreds killed themselves, many with their own hand grenades.

That left Kiska Island as the last Japanese stronghold, and Byron's crew was sent repeatedly over the island as part of a continuous bombing campaign. The Kiska raids were considered very risky, because of the island's jagged volcanic mountains, strong winds and snows, unpredictable weather changes, and the constant, pea-soup fog.

The bombing campaign demoralized the entrenched Japanese troops; one wrote in his diary that the U.S. attacks were "most furious." Japanese headquarters finally ordered an evacuation, and five thousand Japanese soldiers left Kiska one morning under the cover of a thick fog, setting the U.S. Army up for an embarrassing fiasco.

Due to reports of phantom flak attacks, American B-24s continued bombing the vacant island for another *three weeks*. Planes even dropped propaganda pamphlets calling on the Japanese to surrender. The U.S. Army wouldn't learn that the Japanese were gone until it launched a ground attack. When that attack began, edgy American soldiers fired on one another, and twenty-five men died; seventy more died when their boats sank—one hundred men dead at the hands of an absent enemy. Soldiers searched caves and huts but found only mongrel dogs. A song about the failed battle of Kiska went:

> *It took three days before we learnt,*
> *That more than dogs there simply weren't.*

Still, removing a Japanese foothold from so close to U.S. soil was a huge tactical and moral victory—one that Red Byron would not be around to enjoy for long. Byron had managed to survive dozens of successful missions, many more than the Army Air Force required. The army typically sent its flyers home after thirty-five missions, but Byron—whether by choice or by force is unclear—had by now flown more than fifty missions. He must have felt assured that he was nearing the end of his service time. But one day, Byron volunteered to replace a fellow flight engineer whose wife was expecting the couple's first child. It was his fifty-eighth mission, and it would finally be his last.

Although the Japanese had been chased from Kiska, to deter them from regrouping and attacking the Aleutians once more, U.S. B-24s were sent on long missions west across the Pacific to the Japanese air base at Paramushiro, northernmost of the Kuril Islands, which stretched northeast from Japan toward Russia's eastern extremes. The fifteen hundred–mile round-trip Paramushiro raids were among the longest over-water night missions conducted by the United States. Still, it was considered relatively light duty compared to the previous risks above Kiska and Attu. And in the early stages of bombing Paramushiro, not a single U.S. plane was lost. Byron's spirits were high as he and his crewman looked forward to easier duty in the coming months, and maybe even orders to go home.

Unfortunately, the enemy was still on the offensive. While dropping a load of bombs on Paramushiro, Byron's B-24 and its thin aluminum skin were shredded by antiaircraft fire. It was one of the only U.S. planes damaged in that campaign. Hot shards of shrapnel plunged a jagged course deep into the Ford-built aircraft, and at least two hunks of razor-sharp hot metal sliced into Byron's left thigh. Byron let loose a terrible howl as blood began to gush from the wound. The pilot turned the damaged bomber toward home, an unbearably long and painful journey for Byron. The wounded plane and its 4,800-horsepower engines had barely enough power left to reach the nearest runway, and the pilot crash-landed on the too-short, crater-pocked runway at Kiska.

At a makeshift army hospital, a doctor took a quick look at Byron's injuries and immediately suggested amputation. One shrapnel fragment had burrowed too deep into Byron's hip for the doctors to extract it. If Byron didn't bleed to death first, he'd surely die of infection. Byron was furious, refusing to let the doctors saw off his leg. Back home, he made his *livelihood* with that leg. He implored them to find another doctor for a second opinion.

Byron was stabilized, then evacuated to an army hospital in Seattle, where his father came to visit. Jack Byron was shocked at how terrible his son looked. He learned from doctors that Byron had lost all use of his leg, from the hip down. The leg was dying.

At one point, his 160-pound frame had shrunk down to half its size. Byron knew he was likely dying, too. One night, he asked a Red Cross worker for a pencil and paper, so he could write a farewell letter to his family. The Red Cross worker refused, in a gesture intended to prevent Byron from giving up. Byron was as angry as he could be in his weakened state and vowed to bad-mouth the Red Cross ever after—if he survived.

The army, expecting the worst, relocated Byron to Fitzsimmons Army Hospital in Denver,* to be nearer his family. On Sunday

---

*During Byron's time at Fitzsimmons, U.S. Senator and 2004 presidential candidate John Kerry was born there — on December 11, 1943. Kerry's father, an Army Air Force pilot, was receiving treatment there for tuberculosis.

afternoons, former high school friends and his ex-girlfriend would visit from Boulder, cringing at the sprawling but cramped ward full of wounded men. Byron's friends helped him walk around on crutches; he'd lost so much weight, it was hard to walk without help. A few months later, the doctors told him his best chance for survival was to amputate the withered leg. Again, Byron refused.

Finally, after two years of shuttling to and from various military hospitals for tests, second opinions, and unsuccessful attempts to rebuild and rehabilitate the leg, doctors told Byron they had done all they could. If he wouldn't let them amputate, his recovery was as complete as it was ever going to be. As World War II came to a close in late 1945, they sent him home to his father's house, with a bottle of painkillers and a brace that attached to his hip, ran down the length of his leg, and was bolted to an orthopedic shoe. Despite the jagged break in their relationship ten years earlier, Byron and his father repaired their relationship as Red moved into the downstairs family room. Byron began receiving monthly disability checks—small recompense for a dead leg. His father then watched in amazement as his son forced his withered body back to health.

With growing determination, Red would rise early each day and maneuver the four steps up into the bathroom. After showering, he'd attach his leg brace and practice walking back and forth across the family room, day after day. Thanks to a family doctor's prescription of iron pills, an infection that had developed at the army hospital began to clear up. That doctor also prescribed painkillers, but Red found they made him drowsy and unfocused; he only took them on days when the pain was especially piercing.

His stepmother, Peg, prepared hearty meals that helped him gain back most of his weight. Two army nurses visited every other week to change his bandages and clean the fluids and blood that constantly oozed from the wound. His ex-girlfriend, Laura, visited often, bringing books and magazines for him to read. He developed an affinity for ro-

mance novels, especially the sexy ones. In the evenings, he began drawing sketches of hand-operated clutches he hoped to build if he ever got
well enough to drive.

One day, Laura and Red's sister, Virginia, suggested it was time for
Red to really get out and about. Why not take some of your soldier's pay
and buy yourself a car? Maybe even a convertible? At first, it was just a
joke among them. In time, the idea found a comfortable place in Byron's
mind. He found a well-priced, secondhand Ford with a sporty red paint
job and had it taken to a local mechanic, where he unfolded the sketches
he'd drawn of a clutch he could operate with his hand.

"Can you make this?" Byron asked the guy.

When the car was ready a few weeks later, Byron started spending
his afternoons touring all over central Colorado, in the mountains west
of Boulder and east across the endless yellow plains. He drove to visit
relatives in Fort Collins and old friends at Pike's Peak. He was free once
again, and his morale began improving along with his strength.

One day, he announced to his father that he was headed back
to Dixie.

"I'm going to try to get back into racing," he said.

The muscular coordination, satanic humor and split-second timing. . . .
Sugar Boy couldn't talk but he could express himself when
he got his foot on the accelerator.
— ROBERT PENN WARREN, *ALL THE KING'S MEN*, 1946

10

"It's too late now to bring this crowd under control"

Until the 1940s, many rural-born southerners had been exposed largely to a male-dominated culture defined by geographic isolation and an inferiority complex born of the Civil War. In that war's wake, a majority of southerners grew up poor, on a farm, with little access to transportation, public or otherwise, except maybe the family tractor. Up North, trains and buses allowed people to see many cities and states beyond their hometowns. In the Deep South, a man's world view took in a five-mile radius of the farm.

At the onset of World War II, southerners had eagerly surged into recruiting offices. On the battlefield, emboldened by patriotism and a zeal for adventure, they took home a greater share of Purple Hearts than northerners. During the initial four-day fight of the monthlong Battle of the Bulge, the actions of six men merited the Medal of Honor; four of them were southerners. Hard-fighting, hard-living southerners had always admired the Daniel Boone lifestyle. Despite the gore, pain, and heartache, World War II gave them a chance to live it. They saw wild corners of the planet, places that bore no resemblance to the red-clay fields they knew. In the ridges of the Belgian Ardennes, in the skies above the Arctic, in the steamy jungles, and on the Pacific, they were tested.

As James Webb writes in *Born Fighting*, the largely Scots-Irish citizens of the former Confederacy had always been hunters, competitors, and agitators—"probably the most antiauthoritarian culture in America . . . naturally rebellious . . . filled with wanderlust." They were also "the most intensely patriotic segment of the country."

World War II gave soldiers, sailors, and flyers from the South the chance to live heroically in places where killing the other guy wasn't a crime but a ticket to a medal of goddamn *honor*. The war had placed a gun in their able hands, shown them an enemy worth dying for, and told them to swallow any fears and to attack, and attack again.

When soldiers returned to the South from their far-off and exotic killing fields, few were ready for the same old life. Some men returned home bruised and battered, ready for nothing more exciting than a steady job, a wife and kid, a dog, and a two-bedroom split-level. Many others came home itching for more adventure, and they weren't about to let, say, a crippling leg injury force them into a desk job.

Turns out, there was plenty of adventure to be had in the postwar South. Revenue agents were still a dangerous adversary for those who returned to moonshining. And for those eager to return to racing, the red-dirt ovals and hard-packed sands would soon become the new battlefields.

For moonshiners and racers alike, Ford Motor Company was there waiting with the artillery.

By the time war ended in 1945, Henry Ford was a sick, sad, lonely man of eighty-two. His only son, Edsel, after serving half his life as president of his overbearing father's company, had developed stomach ulcers that became cancerous. Henry blamed his son's "high flying lifestyle," at times calling him "dilettante" and "dandy." He told Edsel that if he simply lived healthier, and gave up drinking, he'd recover.

In 1942, doctors removed half of Edsel's stomach, and in May of the following year, he was diagnosed with "undulant fever," the result of drinking unpasteurized milk from his father's farm. He died a few days later at the age of forty-nine. That same year, Ford's grandson—Edsel's eldest son, Henry II—took over as company president and began to repair much of the damage the company had lately sustained under its stubborn founder. Henry II set about turning Ford back into a modern corporation with a singular goal. "Beat Chevrolet," Henry II told anyone who asked. When Ford and the other carmakers resumed production in 1946, cars sold faster in the South than anywhere else. Henry II responded to the South's renewed hunger by replacing the old Ponce de Leon Avenue factory in downtown Atlanta with a new assembly plant on the city's outskirts.

With his soldier's pay or a job in the war-boosted economy, even a poor country boy could now buy his first car, something to baby and call his own, something that offered speed, power, escape. "People will pay any price for motion," William Faulkner wrote of the era when a man washed his car so often that friends warned he'd "soak all the paint off of it." With a car, a man could scorch the dusty back roads, roll proudly through town, spin a donut in the Tastee-Freez parking lot, and take his girl to a romantic hilltop. The car was, as John Updike once said, a "sheath for the knife of himself." Freed from wartime rationing and restrictions, southerners were hungrier than ever for fun and entertainment. Awaiting them was a sport with their very own cars on the track.

Rather than being stanched by war, the adventures abroad and the sweetness of victory had stirred anew the passions of stock car racing's pioneers and fans, becoming nothing short of a new religion. Men back from war, and women reunited with their men, became its zealots. The delicious metal-on-metal crackups, like mechanized cockfights, attracted hordes of new devotees who displayed what one sportswriter called "worship of a newfound power—and freedom." Stock car racers and their fans were "rude, violent, uncouth, and proud of it . . . attending races reaffirmed their status as outsiders, outlaws."

But the sport's outlaw creators and fans would quickly be challenged by puritans trying to whitewash their sport. A battle between the sport's

two factions—dirty and clean, drunk and sober, naughty and nice—
would rage for years to come.

In August of 1945, just days after Japan's surrender, the Office of
Defense Transportation officially lifted its wartime ban on sporting
events. The South wasted no time, and the first postwar stock car race
was immediately scheduled for Labor Day, at the same site that had
hosted the last notable prewar race, and Lloyd Seay's final victory.

At Atlanta's Lakewood Speedway, a record crowd of more than
thirty thousand piled inside, swarming over the five thousand–seat
grandstands and jostling for a spot around the track. As race time approached, eager fans anticipating Atlanta's largest sporting event of any
kind since the war—described by one reporter as "a sweating, howling
crowd"—whipped themselves into a near riotous frenzy.

Then they heard an unexpected announcement over the public address system.

In the days leading up to the race, Atlanta's Methodist and Baptist
ministers had teamed up to publicly denounce a race that had "acknowledged criminals cast in roles of heroes" and convinced Atlanta's mayor
Hartsfield that he was allowing the city to host a "rat race." The *Atlanta
Journal* then picked up the flag. Its editorial writers viscerally denounced
city and Lakewood officials for allowing "some of the more notorious
racketeers of liquor running" to compete, calling it "a shocking display
of bad taste."

"To permit them brazenly to race in public is too much for us to
stomach."

Such admonitions reached the offices of the city police and Mayor
Hartsfield, who then leaked to the newspapers the names of five "un-
derworld rats." Hartsfield's chief of police then decided to ban those
men from the Labor Day race. His last-minute announcement at
Lakewood—*Five drivers have been barred from this race, by order of
Atlanta mayor William B. Hartsfield, because of liquor-hauling violations*—elicited the seething rancor of fans who came specifically to see
those rats race.

Three of them were Raymond Parks's drivers: Roy Hall, Bob Flock, and noted Dawsonville moonshiner Glenn "Legs" Law, who had married one of Parks's sisters. Another "rat" was Jack Cantrell of Dawsonville, Lloyd Seay's cousin and Hall's half brother.* Cantrell was wanted in connection with the death of a young girl. Police had chased Cantrell's speeding car full of liquor down Ponce de Leon Avenue, but Cantrell lost control and flipped his car onto the sidewalk, killing the girl, then fled on foot. Bob Flock—known to police by various aliases, such as Frankie Johns and Robert Clark—was barred because of a lengthy record of speeding and liquor violations dating to 1936. He'd spent a year in jail on earlier charges of hit-and-run and carrying a concealed weapon.

Flock and Cantrell wisely decided not to show for the race, for fear of arrest. But Hall arrived in his 1939 Ford, unbowed and ready to pick up where he'd left off in 1941. Hall's obsession with racing had never ebbed. In fact, one reason he was on the police list of rats was his role in an illegal drag race among moonshiners back in March.

Police called it a "bootlegger sweepstakes," and it had drawn a handful of Atlanta's best-known whiskey trippers. Red Vogt even showed up, to see firsthand how his workmanship on Hall's Ford performed. During the one-hundred-mile-an-hour contest down the unpaved Buford highway east of Atlanta, one driver lost control, crashed, and was killed. Everyone disappeared before police got there, but investigators learned that Hall had been among the ringleaders that night—that he had, in fact, won the deadly race.

Over the past eight years, starting at age seventeen, Roy Hall had been arrested at least sixteen times by police in and around Atlanta—on liquor charges, lottery charges, driving charges—and had cumulatively spent more than a year behind bars. His driver's license had been revoked for years. Police were fed up with him, tired of hearing his

---

*Cantrell would later be shot and killed in a moonshining argument at Red Vogt's garage, one of two liquor-fueled gunfights at Vogt's garage that year. The other shoot-out was witnessed by Bill France and a racer named Frank Mundy, who both dived under a car when the shooting started.

name, and saw no reason why a criminal should be allowed to continue racing.

For all his good looks and street savvy, his movie star cool, his nice clothes, hats, and shiny shoes, Hall had become nothing more than a thug. With cousin Parks off at war, with cousin Seay dead, with no father figure to try to keep him straight, Hall became addicted to trouble and during the war hooked up with the wrong crowd. When Parks had left for war, he agreed to keep a friend's fancy, custom-built Ford roadster locked up in his garage. Hall would break into the garage and take the roadster out for a cruise, usually ending up at the Varsity Drive-in, where a gaggle of pretty Georgia peaches would flock to the cherry red car and its handsome driver. For Parks, Hall was a constant disappointment. He tried again and again to help Hall stay straight, as he did with many family members and friends. Parks wasn't one to give second chances to those who abused his trust. But for some reason, he kept giving Hall chances, which Hall kept blowing.*

Atlanta's police wanted to prevent Hall from reestablishing the outlaws' stranglehold on a sport that had been created by and for southern lawbreakers. Parks was, at that moment, on a westbound ship crossing the Atlantic, on his way back from the war, and unable to intervene this time on Hall's behalf. The newspaper campaign against Hall continued with another editorial questioning why Hall and the others "made no contribution to the war. Why were they not in the Army?"† Trouble was, regardless of Hall's unexplained avoidance of military service, most of the Lakewood fans arrived on Labor Day 1945 dying to see Reckless Roy drive to victory once again.

The fuming crowd began chanting, "We want Hall! We want Hall!" Race officials quickly gathered for a tense meeting with Police Chief

---

*Parks's brother-in-law, Legs Law, also drove him crazy. He'd set Law up with a business — a fruit stand or service station — only to learn Law had lost it in a card game. Like Hall, Law revolved in and out of prison on liquor and driving charges. When Law died, at age seventy, he'd spent a total of thirty years behind bars.

†Billy Watson, a longtime friend of Parks, said Hall's police record kept him out of the armed services.

Marion Hornsby, who finally, to avert a riot, agreed to let the race continue, bootleggers and all. Hornsby claimed that he hadn't received the mayor's orders until that morning, so he did not have enough time to enforce the ban. "It's too late now to bring this crowd under control," Hornsby said over the loudspeakers, to the wild cheers of the increasingly impatient fans.

The decision likely saved a few lives.

Lakewood's 1945 Labor Day race finally began—two hours later than expected and exactly four years after Lloyd Seay's murder. Police efforts to bar Roy Hall meant he didn't have a chance to properly qualify before the race, but officials allowed him to compete anyway, giving him the second-to-last position among fourteen starters.

Hall would race from the dreaded number thirteen spot. Bill France, meanwhile, had qualified earlier with the fastest time and started up front on the pole.

Starting in thirteenth place brought Hall no bad luck at all. For fifty miles, he averaged a mile a minute—"a speed far tamer than police say he has set up in liquor chases," the newspaper sniffed the next day. Hall passed the dozen drivers who'd started ahead of him, including France, who lurked on Hall's tail the rest of the race.

Despite France's disgust over the stink of moonshine at his first postwar race, he simply couldn't catch Hall and settled for second place—a position that would become frustratingly familiar to the onetime champ. France had been a popular figure at southern racetracks before the war. He traveled far and wide and often finished in the top five. But he was usually kept out of victory lane by moonshiners such as Seay and Hall. Now, even with Seay gone, France was settling for second behind a moonshiner from Dawsonville.

The newspaper expressed its own disgust again the next day, excoriating "shameful" city officials for caving in and allowing Hall not only to race but to win. The race was evidence that bootleggers "have more authority than the police force." The writer suggested sarcastically that the police might as well stop chasing the bootleggers and allow them to deliver their liquor "free of molestation"—as long as they painted their cars red "so that innocent pedestrians give them a wide berth." Then, like a poke in the writer's eye, Roy Hall refused to turn himself in to court officials for his scheduled hearing later that month. In his absence, Hall was sentenced to a year in prison.

Clearly, postwar Atlanta was going to have a complicated relationship with stock car racing and its lawless star drivers. Chief Hornsby vowed to uphold Mayor Hartsfield's ban at all future Lakewood races, which sent drivers looking for newer venues.

About that time, Sergeant Robert "Red" Byron was slowly working his way east across the country, driving his red Ford ragtop with the makeshift hand clutch. Byron's entire body had withstood harsh aftereffects of the injury—the loss of blood, the loss of half his body weight. Doctors had warned that, by not allowing them to amputate his useless leg, Byron would always walk with a pronounced limp, would often be in pain, and should expect to treat the leg and his health gingerly.

They advised him: *Take it easy, son. Take a desk job. Ease into life.* That wasn't Red's style. A desk job was inconceivable and would surely have been a death sentence.

When he finally reached Alabama, he briefly reconnected with his friends and his one-legged mechanic, A. J. Weldon, who must have sympathized with Byron's leg injury. Weldon, surely more than the rest, understood Byron's determination to avoid amputation, which would have ended his racing career. Still, they were all surprised to hear of Byron's plan to start racing again. Byron shocked his friends further when he told them he would not be staying long in Alabama. He would be racing elsewhere.

Before the war, Byron's group of racing pals had mostly belonged to the world of open-wheel cars. That's what Weldon built, and that's what Byron had mostly raced—three-quarter-sized Indy-style sprint cars and smaller midget cars. Stock cars hadn't proliferated in his part of Alabama the way they had across Georgia and the Carolinas. Yet, while Byron knew he didn't exactly fit the mold of a Roy Hall–style outlaw stock car racer, he had decided to restart his racing career not on the open-wheel circuit but on the stock car circuit to which he'd been introduced before the war. For that reason, he was headed to a city that appreciated racing as much as he did, a city where stock cars reigned—Atlanta.

Byron never fully explained his decision to switch to stock cars, although his obvious disability played a factor. In open-wheel cars, a driver's torso stuck up out of the open cockpit, and drivers rarely wore seat belts. If the car rolled, a driver ducked, jumped, or sometimes died. With his bad leg, Byron couldn't jump free of a tumbling "big car." Stock cars, with a hard roof overhead, seemed a safer bet for Byron and his handicap.

It wasn't just safety he had in mind. The idea to relocate to Atlanta to pursue stock car racing sprouted during his many months in the hospital and, during the long drive east, had taken firm root. It was absurd to think he'd be able to race again—in stocks or open-wheelers—but he knew he had to at least try. And to give himself an edge, he decided to position himself in the same hometown as the impressive team of Parks and Vogt.

Byron found a hotel room to stash his meager belongings in, then stopped at Vogt's garage, where he learned that the nearest available race was a seventy-five-miler scheduled for late October in Charlotte. Unlike Atlanta, Charlotte hadn't banned criminals from its stock car races, and Roy Hall, Bob Flock, and other moonshiners were headed there, along with an eager lineup of war veterans, mechanics, farmers, and mill workers.

Take it easy, the doctor had said. Take a desk job. Instead, on October 27, 1945, a cool Saturday afternoon, Byron returned to the workplace he'd dreamed of so often during those agonizing months of recovery. With his leg still clamped into a metal brace, and with his strange-looking hand clutch, Byron reunited with men he hadn't seen for four years. At the Southern States Fairgrounds track, a dustbowl of a

raceway, forty-five hundred spectators arrived early for a contest sponsored by a local veterans' group—and Bill France.

As soon as the war had officially ended, and France was relieved of his
duties at the Daytona Beach Boat Works, he began making plans for a
race. The Beach-and-Road course was in terrible shape, the grandstands
rotted and crumbling after four years of neglect. So France called around
to others in his rejuvenated fraternity, searching for a racetrack. He
found willing partners at the Southern States Fairgrounds and immediately called the *Charlotte Observer*'s sports editor, begging for some
publicity. France even told the editor, Wilton Garrison, to call it a
"National Championship Race."

"Who's going to be in this race of yours?" Garrison asked.

France rattled off a few names, including Roy Hall, Skimp Hersey,
and Buddy Shuman, all of them southern boys and more than a few of
them known moonshiners.

"How can you call it a national championship with local boys like
that running?" Garrison asked. "Maybe you could call it a southern
championship, but there's no way it's a national championship race."

Garrison proceeded to give France some harsh words of advice that
would guide him through the next few bumpy years. If France wanted to
make something of stock cars, Garrison said, he'd have to create structure and uniformity. He needed rules and a consistent system of tallying
points to determine the "champion." He could do that by allying himself
with AAA—which was mainly sanctioning open-wheel events—or by
creating his own AAA-type organization specifically for stock cars.

France had in fact approached AAA, seeking a partnership, but was
rejected. "We're only interested in big races," they told him, and France
knew he was on his own.

That first postwar race at Charlotte reminded him that stock car racing was still popular and potentially profitable, still worthy of his life's
work. It also reminded him that, while he might not need AAA, he still
needed the moonshiners.

Roy Hall whipped around the tight turns of the red-clay oval that afternoon, averaging eighty miles an hour and seemingly destined for yet another victory—his second in a row since war's end. But on the final lap, a swirl of dust on the backstretch blinded him, he lost his bearings, then lost control and flipped. Bob Flock swept past and took the checkered flag. Fonty Flock rushed over and scooped brother Bob out of his Ford, hoisted him onto his shoulders, and paraded him before the screaming crowd. Red Byron finished back in the pack, in desperate need of a pile of aspirin for his ravaged left leg and a canteen of water to rinse the dust from his mouth.

Fans streamed off into the cool autumn evening, content with what they'd gotten for their fifty-cent admission fee. A sportswriter said that, due to the swirling red dust, "the spectators had a reddish color at the end." And Bill France had the greenish hue of crisp cash in his pocket.

With bootlegging racers chased from Lakewood by Atlanta's new ban on drivers with criminal records, racetracks in other southern states seized the opportunity. A group of inventors just outside Orlando, Florida, built a one-mile dirt oval called Seminole Speedway, which hosted its first race in December of 1945. Once again, Roy Hall—still on the lam, despite recently being sentenced to a year in prison—beat out Bill France for his second victory of the abbreviated 1945 season.

Hall was awarded the title of national champ—his third. As in previous years, the title was a questionable achievement. With no AAA-like body governing stock car racing, Hall's title wasn't so much an official designation as an informal agreement among various stock car racing clubs that he was the year's best racer. Mainly, Hall's 1945 title was a victory of bragging rights. Such was the second-tier status of stock cars, and another reminder to France of the need for validity.

A full slate of stock car races was scheduled for 1946.

France planned to take his first stab at bringing a more viable structure to the sport by unveiling his own AAA-like sanctioning body for stock cars, to be called the National Championship Stock Car

Circuit (NCSCC). Red Byron planned to race as often as possible in 1946, for France and anyone else offering a decent winner's purse. First, Byron realized he needed some help. Turns out, someone needed his help, too.

Having moved to Atlanta after the war, Byron became a regular visitor to Red Vogt's garage on Spring Street. He and Vogt found they had a similar passion for Ford V-8s and spoke a similar language, both of them interested in various open-wheel cars as well as stocks. Byron spent much of his free time there and eventually told Vogt that he wanted to race one of Parks's stock cars for the 1946 season. Secretly Byron wondered how his damaged and withered left leg would hold up, but he kept that to himself.

Vogt saw something in Byron that he hadn't seen in Hall or Parks's other occasional racers, such as Legs Law or the "kid," Billy Watson. For them, racing was all about gut instinct, which in Law's case was askew—he was a great moonshine runner but a terrible racer. Recklessness frustrated Vogt. After all, he'd have to repair cars wrecked due to a bad decision on the track. In Byron, Vogt sensed a deeper understanding of the tactics and strategy of racing. So, in late 1945, Vogt decided to formally introduce Byron to Raymond Parks, which led to a few meetings at Vogt's garage. Byron's timing turned out to be perfect, and by January of 1946, a historic new partnership had formed.

Parks had been getting increasingly nervous about Roy Hall's unresolved problems with the law and his pending jail sentence. Parks knew time was running out on his cousin's freedom. If he wanted to keep his racing team alive, he'd need a new driver. Parks remembered Byron from a few races before the war—the quiet redhead with the nervous and chatty sidekick, Shorty. But Parks also recalled Byron's steady, solid driving. There were qualities in Byron's driving and personality that reminded Parks of Lloyd Seay. He was more human, had a modest confidence, seemed a bit smarter than most of the other drivers, and was certainly more reliable than Roy Hall.

Parks may have wavered a bit when he first witnessed Byron's pronounced limp and learned the extent of his one-legged condition. But Parks told Byron he'd bring him onto his team. If Vogt was willing to vouch for him, that was enough for Parks. And after Byron's acceptable finish at Charlotte back in October, Parks was willing to take a chance on the crippled vet. In fact, Parks respected Byron's gritty fight back from his World War II ordeal, which was even more horrific than Parks's. That respect allowed Byron to become one of the few members of Parks's inner circle who wasn't a criminal or kin.

Parks then asked Vogt to come up with a better contraption to replace Byron's risky hand clutch. Through January of 1946, Vogt worked many late nights, like a mad scientist in his lab, chewing his chocolate bars and drinking syrupy black coffee from a tin cup. The potbellied stove that he'd converted into a heater gave off foul-smelling fumes. He occasionally stopped to pet Buddy, his dog. One day, Vogt emerged from his lab with a new device that he felt would help Byron compete with the sport's best racers. Vogt's solution was a new clutch pedal with what he called "fatigue pins" welded onto it.

Because Byron had regained some feeling and strength in the left leg, Vogt figured he could at least depress the clutch pedal, as long as he didn't have to lift his foot up onto the pedal each time he shifted gears. With the stirruplike fatigue pins—two steel posts welded a few inches apart at the bottom of the pedal—Byron could rest the heel of his orthopedic shoe between those pins, keeping his foot cradled atop the clutch pedal. Then, because his shoe was attached to a leg brace that ran all the way up to his hip, Byron could lift and depress the clutch by shifting his lower body—literally twisting his left side so that his left hip pulled and pushed the half-dead leg and the clutch pedal beneath it.

It was a ridiculously primitive and risky setup. With Byron's foot resting right on the clutch pedal, he had to keep his body at a slight angle so his leg didn't accidentally push the clutch. After some prerace practice runs at Lakewood, he seemed to get the hang of it, though he still worried about operating the clutch rig for a hundred high-speed laps, and he worried about bumps and ruts knocking his leg off the pedal.

The first race of 1946, cosponsored by France, was scheduled for mid-February, again at the new Seminole Speedway outside Orlando, Florida.

Roy Hall and Bill France were again the favorites, and fans looked forward to another chapter in the ongoing rivalry between the two. Up in Atlanta, where fans were steeped in the moonshining culture that created men such as Hall, Hall was clearly the favorite. But France had plenty of fans in his home state of Florida and was itching for a chance to beat Hall in his backyard. "I hate to win a race I'm sponsoring," France told a newsman before the race. "But I'm afraid I'll have to do it."

Qualifying runs began on Saturday, February 23. Veteran racer and unrepentant North Carolina moonshiner Buddy Shuman won the pole position, followed by Hall, France, Bob Flock, and then Red Byron. Fans paid $1.04 to attend Sunday's main event, but instead of watching Hall or France take the checkered flag, a little-known, handicapped war vet eked out his first major stock car victory.

Biting as usual on an unlit cigar, like biting a bullet against the pain in his leg, Byron drove a steady race despite the ruts jackhammering his body and the Japanese metal twisting and poking deep inside his hip. Byron outlasted France, who spun out in a turn, and Hall, who finished second. In victory lane, Byron had to be helped from his car, where he took off his helmet and smiled a tight smile. "This racing game is still fun," Byron said, though the pained look on his face spoke otherwise.

One sportswriter called the victory "heartwarming" but added that when Byron removed his helmet and goggles, "it appeared as though the man was twice his 30 years." Writers and fans considered it quaint that a cripple could win a race against men such as Hall and France. When Byron sat down with one reporter, he explained that he didn't intend for the day's victory to be a one-off, that he was a serious racer, not a sideshow freak. He wanted Bill France and Roy Hall and all the other racers to know he was now in the game for good, bad leg and all.

"I never gave up hope of racing again, even when I was laying in the hospital and the doctors didn't know whether I'd ever walk again," Byron said.

Byron immediately began looking ahead to the next big race, in April, on the famed Beach-and-Road course of Daytona Beach, which France still controlled.

The spring of 1946 saw stock car racing regain all its momentum. Bill France replaced the rotted wood of the grandstands in preparation for a 160-mile race on the Beach-and-Road course, the first at Daytona since Lloyd Seay's remarkable 1941 victory.

France promised the race would include "all of the top-name gasoline jockeys in the South." France publicly invited "anyone in the country who owns a stock car and who likes to step on the gas pedal," but the favorites were beach-driving veterans such as himself, as well as Roy Hall, semiretired Smokey Purser, Joe Littlejohn, and Dawsonville's own Gober Sosebee and Ed Samples.

Byron had raced at Daytona only once, in 1939, and was considered an underdog. His recent victory at Seminole Speedway was viewed by many as a fluke. After all, the skinny redhead was *disabled,* for God's sake.

Before the April 14 race at Daytona Beach, South Carolina driver Joe Littlejohn boasted that his 1941 Buick would handily beat the prewar Fords that comprised all but three of the starters' cars. Roy Hall countered that he and his Ford would be "hard to beat in this one." Byron steered clear of any boasts and said simply that the race would be won not by speed alone but by the guy who drove a strategic, calculated race. Instead of battling Hall for the lead, Byron started the race carefully, avoiding all the early wrecks. Once he felt he had a feel for the sandy north and south turns, he began to cut into Hall's lead and, after a few laps, was right on Hall's tail, hanging a hundred yards behind, waiting . . .

For the first third of the fifty-lap race, Byron chased Hall but refused to get drawn into a dangerous tussle for the lead. Not yet. Hall was driving balls-out, but every time he looked back, Byron's number 11 car was right there. The ocean's tide began to rise at around lap sixteen, and Hall, knowing that the firmer sand was right at the water's edge, drove with his right tires slightly in the water. The saltwater spray caked Byron's windshield, forcing him to stick his head out the side window to see where he was going.

On lap nineteen, as Hall approached the north turn, his right tire got caught in a rut of softer sand. His car was pulled off course and veered straight toward a row of fans standing too close to the track. To avoid plowing into the crowd, Hall reacted quickly, spinning the wheel sharply to the right as spectators dove for cover. Hall narrowly missed a few of the airborne fans and drove his Ford a few yards into the surf. Within moments, he was able to reverse out of the Atlantic and rejoin the race.

Byron had passed him, but his lead was brief. Hall pulled ahead six laps later. Byron continued with the same patient tactic, driving a few dozen yards behind Hall, hoping for another mistake, until he got his wish. In an overly aggressive attack on the south turn, Hall got caught in another rut and his right wheel was shorn off. Once again, Hall had to spin away from the fans standing right beside the track. He catapulted over an embankment and plowed into the palmettos, bouncing and crunching and gouging a deep trough through the sand, but amazingly emerged with only minor injuries.

Byron held the lead unchallenged and finished nearly three miles, a full lap, ahead of Joe Littlejohn.* In keeping with his unintended streak of top-five finishes, France—who had flipped early in the race—finished fourth.

Now there was no denying it. Byron was no fluke. "It was a tough race to win," he said afterward. "But they're all tough when you have to bear down all the way for 160 miles." The eight thousand fans went wild, and the next day's newspapers called Byron's performance a "one-man extravaganza" and "a championship display of skill and

---

*Littlejohn had also finished second behind Lloyd Seay in 1941 and would go on to take more second-place finishes than any racer of the 1940s.

endurance." Only eleven of twenty-eight cars finished the race, and one writer praised Byron for his "consistency and persistence." Byron had raced exactly as planned, and the fatigue pins helped greatly. But he was physically spent. In fact, despite his earlier declaration that the racing game was "still fun," Byron wondered about his ability to compete over the long haul in such grueling stock car races.

But he perked up that night. While leaning against the bar and sipping a beer at a Daytona Beach nightclub, he spotted a beautiful, dark-haired woman in a tight, bright pantsuit walking toward him, a sultry smile on her face.

For a one-legged racer, it was easier to drive the Indy-style race cars of the AAA circuit, which required less shifting than a stock car. Byron told Parks he wanted to take a break and try competing in a few shorter races in the AAA circuit, which was also getting back on its feet after the war. Even though he'd decided to race mostly in stock cars, Byron knew the survival of stock car racing was far from a sure thing.

Stock car racing—disorganized and motley and full of outlaws—was scoffed at by the cleaner, more organized AAA with its gorgeous open-wheel cars and nationally recognized stars such as Ted Horn, Mauri Rose, and Bill Holland. No one yet knew whether stock car racing was a trend or a fad. So, as a racing gourmand, interested in all styles of motorsports, Byron courted stock cars while still courting Indy cars—like dating two cousins at the same time. It just seemed safer—not to mention easier for a wounded racer, and potentially more lucrative, too—to straddle both worlds until he was sure of stock cars' future. He was wisely hedging his bets and, for the next two years, would bounce back and forth between stocks and AAA.

In AAA races, Byron drove a car partially built by a famed Indy car-builder named Pop Dreyer and seriously modified by Red Vogt. By mid-1946, after just a handful of AAA-sanctioned open-wheel races, Byron was suddenly ranked twentieth on AAA's list of the year's top points leaders, ranked incredibly among the best Indy-style racers of the day.

He was also ranked second in the informal stock car standings, although, in a sure sign that stock car racing wasn't yet a legitimate sport, some newspapers couldn't get his name right, referring to him as Red Bryan, Bed Byron, or Rey Byron. Byron's top AAA ranking would not last long, but it emboldened his longtime dream of reaching auto racing's mecca, Indianapolis, which seemed finally within reach.

Roy Hall, meanwhile, pursued the same dream, with disappointing results.

Through the first half of 1946, Reckless Roy was poised to become stock car racing's winningest postwar champ, its brightest star, and potential successor to cousin Lloyd as the fan favorite. Despite continued financial support from Parks and emotional support from the fans, Hall seemed determined to sabotage his promising career.

Parks expected loyalty in return for his generous financial sustenance. But Hall continued to cross the unspoken line, going beyond the harmless sins of moonshine into darker territory. Hall and Billy Watson—the neighborhood kid whom he'd taught to drive and who now worked for Parks—would drive around Atlanta looking for cops to taunt. Hall loved luring them into a chase, which he always won. Parks wouldn't learn until late 1946 just how far Hall had veered into even darker territory.

On the rare occasions when Parks tried to talk to him about his recklessness, Hall just laughed and told him not to worry. "You're too wild," Parks told Hall one day. It was like talking to a junkyard dog—undisciplined, wild, and angry. Lately, Parks had quit talking. And Hall knew from the cold stares and steely silence that he'd let his cousin down. In an apparent effort to reconcile with Parks, in early May of 1946, Hall walked into the offices of the *Atlanta Constitution* and asked to speak with a reporter.

Columnist Jack Troy sat with Hall, who explained that he wanted to "tell my story," including the announcement that he'd soon be racing at the upcoming Indianapolis 500, in a car financed by Parks and with a crew headed by Red Vogt. Hall said he was trying to prove to Atlantans "that I am worthy" of racing with AAA's best.

"I have two fine backers in Red Vogt and Raymond Parks and I intend to give them the best I have. I intend to stick strictly to auto racing in the future," Hall said in a conciliatory statement aimed at Parks as well as Atlanta's mayor and police chief.

"I realize I did some things that went against me, but that's all over now. I'm just asking for a fair chance," he said. "I've seen the error of my ways. I want to make good in big-time racing."

Hall practically pleaded for "a helping hand" but seemed incapable of helping himself. It only worsened his fragile emotional state when his attempt at Indianapolis in late May ended in smoky failure. In an open-wheel Maserati racer honed by Vogt, Hall whipped around the famous Brickyard track during his qualifying laps at speeds he'd never before reached—one-twenty, then one-thirty. But Hall's engine began to smoke and cough, and he had to pull out. The car was scratched at the last minute, and Hall missed his shot at Indy, which would turn out to be the only chance of his career.

Bill France was there that day, serving on the pit crew for racer George Robson. France must have felt some satisfaction at seeing his rival experience failure, a feeling that was stoked further as France celebrated Robson's eventual victory.

After his washout at Indianapolis, Hall returned to more familiar territory—a June 30 stock car race at Daytona, and a jail cell. In his typical, hotdogging fashion, he roared into town at 4:00 a.m. and announced his arrival by speeding down Main Street and spinning a few screeching, tire-smoking donuts in the otherwise quiet intersections.

Police immediately arrested Hall, who joked with them that Daytona's hotel rates were too high and all he really wanted was a place to sleep. They led him to his cell and shut the barred door. "What, no sheets?" Hall complained. "I've just driven non-stop from Virginia and I need a good day's rest. I would sure appreciate some sheets."

Hall was released from the Daytona jailhouse in time for his race, which he handily won with a record-breaking performance in which he averaged ninety-two miles an hour. He finished six *miles* ahead of the second-place finisher. It seemed as if the more emotionally unhinged Hall became, the better he raced. Afterward, even Bill France praised Hall's driving as well as his mechanical prowess. "Give that boy a set of tools and he could make a covered wagon do sixty," France said.

Through 1946, Bill France continued wearing two hats, as racer and promoter. Parks still considered France a good driver, and when France raced, Parks often allowed him to drive one of his cars. But France hadn't won a race in years, and he was beginning to think it was time to quit. France's promoting duties were taking up more and more of his time. He had begun to make plans for another annual Labor Day race at Daytona later that summer and had signed on to promote a July Fourth event at the Greenville-Pickens Speedway, just west of downtown Greenville, in South Carolina.

With his wife, Anne, France arrived a few days before that race. They stayed at Greenville's Ponsett Hotel, and France drove over to the racetrack on Friday to see how preparations were coming. Two days of horse racing had been scheduled before Sunday's stock car race, but when France arrived on Friday, he saw a pathetic smattering of people in the stands to watch the horses. He grew very nervous. Even if a crowd twice that size showed up on Sunday, he'd lose money. And France hated to lose money.

The next morning, he told Anne that he was abandoning the race and they were going home. The turnout would be bad, he said, and he wouldn't take in enough at the ticket booth to pay drivers their winnings. Better to bail out now than face a bunch of angry racers with their palms out on Sunday. Anne tried to talk him into staying, but he refused. "I ain't going back there," he said, and they began driving back home to Florida.

About an hour south of Greenville, Anne finally convinced him to turn back. The next day, as they drove from their hotel toward the track, they saw an enormous swirl of dust in the distance. France quickly learned that it was no tornado; the dust was caused by early arrivals, part of a crowd that would swell to twenty thousand by race time, which sportswriters declared was the largest crowd ever to attend a South Carolina sporting event. Choking traffic jams forced police to turn away another five thousand or so fans.

Dawsonville's Ed Samples won the race, but the big winner was France. Instead of losing money, he took in thirty-six hundred dollars— one of his best days to date as a promoter and proof that stock car racing could be a moneymaker in places other than Daytona.

He later told friends, "That was the start of NASCAR."

France followed his profitable success in South Carolina with a series of business maneuvers and short-lived partnerships that turned the rest of the 1946 season into a confusing mess that vexed drivers and set the stage for some future showdowns.

For starters, the civic leaders and citizens of Daytona Beach—especially those with beachfront homes—began complaining about the crowds and noise of France's increasingly popular races, whose many wrecks and injuries inspired some to call them "undertaker's races." They wanted France, or the city, to build a new racetrack that didn't include a straightaway that ran through downtown. Because France only leased the land for his racetrack (from the city and a few private landowners), and because that lease could easily be revoked, pressure from the townsfolk forced him to cancel his upcoming Labor Day race, which sent stock car racers looking for venues in more welcoming states.

Atlanta was not one of those welcoming locations. The mayor and police chief refused to rescind their ban on liquor-running race drivers, so stock car racing bypassed its two most famous venues late that summer, Daytona and Lakewood. France teamed up with promoters at other racetracks and cohosted a few races in North Carolina, South Carolina, Pennsylvania, and Connecticut. AAA remained the dominant sanctioning body of the day for auto racing, and France had bills to pay. He had a family and finally decided he had no choice but to befriend—albeit briefly—the notoriously imperious AAA.

AAA's home base was in Paterson, New Jersey, otherwise known as Gasoline Alley. AAA controlled many of the racetracks up and down the east and west coasts, and in parts of the Midwest. Since 1909, AAA's primary focus had been open-wheel racing, though after World War II, it expanded into similar types of racing, such as sprint and midget cars, which weren't quite Indy machines but still hand-built racers and as different from "stock" cars as corn liquor was from fine brandy.

But AAA had decided in 1946 to again dip a tentative toe into southern racing and to experiment with a few stock car events, just as it had occasionally done before the war. And because France needed to earn a living, he swallowed his considerable pride and promoted a few stock car races as AAA's partner. The partnership wouldn't last long.

France had been scheming to cut into AAA's increasing dominance of auto racing by creating his own organization to oversee stock car racing. In late summer of 1946, he abruptly split with AAA and unveiled his new group, the NCSCC. In no time, a bitter rivalry would develop, with AAA declaring France's stock car races to be "outlaw" races and forbidding its drivers to compete in such contests. France would respond by similarly banning his stock car drivers from AAA races. In time, he'd also call anyone who dared race in events other than his *outlaws*.

That situation would cause problems for dual-minded racers such as Byron. The luxury of calling himself both an open-wheel racer and a stock car racer, with a ranking among the top-twenty AAA drivers and the top-ten stock car drivers, would not last long.

One day soon, he'd have to choose.

Red Byron's hero, Barney Oldfield, died that October at age sixty-eight. If Byron had been a religious man, he might have viewed the death as a sign from above.

Oldfield had come to the realization, after his failed attempts at Indy, that he was simply a better driver on dirt tracks. Byron, though not quite ready to abandon his dream of racing at Indy, was beginning to accept the same reality. By late 1946, Byron had slid back in the AAA points standings. But he suddenly found himself the top points earner in Bill France's new stock car organization, the NCSCC.

France quickly pulled together five NCSCC races for the fall of 1946. Bob Flock, driving Raymond Parks's car in place of Roy Hall, incredibly won them all, shoving Byron off his perch as the new league's best driver. But when the season came to an end, Dawsonville's Ed Samples—who had won France's July 4 race at Greenville, South Carolina, among others—was named the so-called national stock car champion.

Once again, the term *champion* was an imprecise one. Because France's new group emerged late in the year, he couldn't legitimately award an NCSCC championship. He conferred with the heads of a few other stock car groups—including the National Stock Car Racing Association, or NSCRA, which had been created in Atlanta earlier that year, and the U.S. Stock Car Drivers Association—and together they added up drivers' victories in various races that year and determined that Samples had the best record.

Still, Byron finished tenth in the points standing for the year's stock car championship race and nineteenth in AAA, making him the only driver in history to finish in the top twenty of both AAA/Indy racing and stock car racing.

Bill France finished a distant fourteenth in the stock car standings and announced his retirement from racing. France joked that he decided to give up driving and take up flying, "because it's not so dangerous." In truth, he admitted, he'd been dividing his time between driving and promoting and "haven't got time to do both."

Roy Hall finished second in the stock car standings, followed by Bob Flock, who had been driving Hall's number 14 car. But by the end of 1946, Hall was no longer racing. In the aftermath of his desperate plea to the Atlanta newspaper back in May, his failure to qualify at Indy in

June, and his arrest in Daytona Beach in July, the twenty-five-year-old moonshiner was showing signs of a losing grip on reality, on life. He had to know his days of freedom were dwindling down, that his luck was finally about to run dry, especially after an incident in Greensboro, North Carolina, in August of 1946.

Following a race outside Greensboro, Hall was staying at a local hotel with another racer from Atlanta named J. R. Walden, along with Walden's friend Walter Leonard, whom the newspapers later described as an "Atlanta produce dealer."

The night after the race, police arrived at the King Cotton Hotel with plans to pick up Hall and deliver him to Atlanta. It seems the cops were investigating a recent forty thousand–dollar bank robbery outside Atlanta—and Hall was a suspect. They knocked on Hall's hotel room door around 1:00 a.m. He and his friends were still awake, having a fun night after the afternoon race. Police began questioning him and his two friends. When Hall claimed not to know the other two men, his lack of cooperation led the cops to arrest all three on the spot. As the three were led toward the patrol cars, one of them, Walden, took off running.

An officer opened fire, and Walden appeared to have been hit, but after stutter-stepping down a side street, he turned the corner and got away. The police later discovered that Walden had recently escaped from a Georgia prison, and they issued a description of the escaped prisoner, who was "bearing the appearance of a 'hillbilly.' "

The authorities charged Hall with abetting the "desperate criminal." Hall was then returned to Atlanta to face charges in connection with the forty thousand–dollar robbery.

Weeks later, Hall was sentenced to six years in prison for his role in the bank robbery and other pent-up charges. He said good-bye to Margaret, his wife of three years, and their son, Ronnie, born earlier that year. Hall wrote letters to Ronnie, always telling his son, "Take care of your momma."

Roy Hall had been a wanted criminal for most of his adult life. Despite his promises to clean up, he never displayed serious intentions of making amends. Instead of turning himself in and confronting the many charges against him, Hall always gambled and stayed mobile, hoping he could outrun the law long enough for the past to just disappear. Hall became practiced in the art of evasion, staying with friends and relatives, rarely settling down in one place for too long, even after the birth of his son.

Hall often received help from other whiskey trippers, such as "Bad Eye" Shirley. Through the late 1930s and into the postwar years of stock car racing, Shirley's name appeared often on racing programs. On the racetrack, he would drive behind the wheel of a '39 Ford owned by Parks and tuned up by Red Vogt. His driving style, not to mention his physical appearance, was remarkably similar to Roy Hall's. He even had the same number—"14"—painted on the car's door. It would take fifty years for Bad Eye to finally confess: "I never raced a day in my life. But I helped out Roy Hall quite a bit."*

The start of his long-coming prison sentence in late 1946 only added to Hall's mythic, southern stock car racer story. He'd hauled liquor and carried a pistol. He was incredibly handsome, smooth-talking, sharply dressed, sexy as hell, and a flat-out badass. He'd survived in dual professions—moonshining and racing—that had killed his cousin and many peers. In addition to the song penned years earlier by Blind Willie McTell, another songwriter would one day put Hall's big, fast, audacious life to music. Jim Croce's musical homage to Hall would one day go like this:

> Oh Rapid Roy that stock car boy
> He too much to believe
> You know he always got an extra pack of cigarettes
> Rolled up in his t-shirt sleeve
> He got a tattoo on his arm that say Baby
> He got another one that just say Hey

---

*Shirley, who died in 2005, "raced" for others, too, starting in 1941 at Daytona, when an Atlanta driver named Carson Dyer was on probation and not allowed to leave the state of Georgia. Shirley let Carson, and later Hall, borrow his name.

Oh Rapid Roy that stock car boy
He's the best driver in the land
He say that he learned to race a stock car
By runnin' shine outta Alabam'
And Sunday afternoon he is a dirt track demon in a '57 Chevrolet
Yeah Roy so cool that racin' fool he don't know what fear's about
He do a hundred thirty mile an hour, smilin' at the camera,
With a toothpick in his mouth
He got a girl back home, name of Dixie Dawn
But he got honeys all along the way
And you oughta hear 'em screamin'
For that dirt track demon in a '57 Chevrolet*

And so, stock car racing lost another great driver, and Parks lost his top star. Again. There was an odd sense of relief, at least, that Hall reached the end of his career alive, unlike Seay. But losing drivers was becoming a theme of Parks's stock car career.

---

*Of course, Hall only drove Fords, not Chevys—although, late in life and years after his release from prison, Hall ironically would work as a Chevy salesman.

I never really thought much of racing.
— HENRY FORD

11

Henry Ford is dead

Before each race, she'd coach him.

"Be careful, Red," she'd say. "Be careful, but win the race."

That's what she said when he left home in late January of 1947 for the year's first race in Daytona Beach—the town where they'd met—where Bill France's "Battle of the Champions" would kick off the first full year of his new NCSCC governing body.

Her name was Eva Nellis Davis, but everyone called her Nell. She was raised on a farm east of Atlanta, a farm she'd been scheming to escape since childhood. Nell was half Cherokee, with dark skin, a stunning figure, bold dark eyes, and high cheekbones. She reminded Byron of the exotic squaws he'd read about in his favorite childhood series Rolf in the Woods: "silent, reserved, and shy . . . but very human." Her innocence, restraint, and self-determination also reminded Byron of the native Inuit women he'd met selling their primitive crafts on the Aleutian Islands. During the war, Nell took a job at a railroad office in Atlanta. She rode the bus into the city on Monday, stayed at a boardinghouse all week, and returned home to her family on weekends.

One weekend in 1946, her coworkers planned a trip to Daytona

Beach to see a stock car race. Nell said she said she couldn't afford to join them, but her boss loaned her forty dollars, and the women piled into a car and drove to Florida. It was Nell's first race, and she quickly discovered she wasn't all that interested in stock cars. Nearby fans, however, were very interested in her. She was buxom and shapely; she wore a tight pantsuit, and men worked hard to strike up a conversation. But she barely spoke to anyone—"I was so shy." Then, after the race, she and her girlfriends went to a nearby nightclub, where she saw the same racer she'd spotted in victory lane—Red Byron. She was instantly smitten by the smoldering war vet with the brave limp. She told her sister it was "love at first sight." He thought she was spectacular and back in Atlanta began visiting her at the railroad office where she worked.

"Where do you want to live?" Red finally asked her. "I'll build you a house."

"That'll work," she told him.

They'd soon marry and begin a new life in an apartment in downtown Atlanta. But she told him right from the start: *I want to see the ocean, to live at the beach. Take me to Florida.* In January of 1947, he drove south to Florida without her. He couldn't show her the ocean, but he promised to return a few short days later with a trophy—and some cash.

One of the frustrations of being a stock car racer in the 1940s was trying to understand the sloppy, complicated, ever-changing rules and rulers of the sport. The postwar racing culture was so convoluted—the complex relationships among racetrack owners, race promoters, and race-sanctioning bodies, with their alphabet soup of acronyms—it could have comprised an entire college course. With the lack of uniform guiding principles, and the risk of losing large amounts of cash, it's amazing that anyone willingly chose to dabble in the business side of stock car races in the 1940s.

The three-tiered hierarchy went something like this: someone owned the track; someone else hosted and promoted the race; someone else authorized or "sanctioned" the races of a particular region or racetrack.

The tracks were typically owned by local entrepreneurs or, in the case of public fairgrounds such as Lakewood, by the city; Daytona's Beach-and-Road course consisted of a mix of public and private parcels that Bill France leased.

The races were often, but not always, organized by someone other than the track owner. In fact, a race could be "promoted" by just about any risk taker with a knack for numbers who was willing to rent a track from its owner, advertise the race, lure the drivers, hire folks to sell concessions and programs, charge admission, then choreograph the qualifying heats and the race itself. Promoters were sometimes local businessmen, or racers such as Bill France, or affiliates of larger organizations such as AAA. The promoter was also responsible for paying the drivers their winnings. The winner's purse was typically a portion of that day's ticket sales—40 percent was becoming the standard—but a local franchise might also donate a case of beer or motor oil to the winner.

Finally, there was the race sanctioner, an overseeing entity that gave its stamp of approval to events and controlled the tallying of points and the naming of champions. Sanctioning organizations emerged to provide stability and constancy in a world that resisted both. The sanctioner's role was twofold. First, its presence told a racer there was a legitimate organization lording over the race. Second, sanctioners doled out championships. Without a sanctioning group's stamp of approval, a race wouldn't necessarily count toward a "championship" of any sort. While most drivers of the day competed primarily to win each individual race and its winner's purse, many were also interested in earning themselves a "championship" title.

Making heads or tails of the often cutthroat and byzantine machinations of sanctioning could induce some serious head-spinning, which is why Bill France struggled so messily to enforce some semblance of governance.

In the Indy racing world of expensive open-wheel cars, AAA's racing arm, the Contest Board, "sanctioned" races such as the Indy 500. That meant AAA tracked each driver's performance through the year, tallied the drivers' points, then awarded a year-end championship to the driver with the most points. Back in 1941, AAA also tallied numbers for the handful of semilegitimate stock car races. Roy Hall's championship that year was more or less a AAA-sanctioned championship.

By the end of 1946, however, AAA had stopped sanctioning stock car races and, in fact, wanted little to do with them. After its few stock car experiments that year, AAA's Contest Board announced at the end of the '46 season that it would no longer affiliate itself with Bill France or his stock cars: "The Contest Board is bitterly opposed to what it calls 'junk car' events and believes the fad . . . is dying out." Scores of small sanctioning groups arose throughout the South to fill that void, each competing to become the premier stock car–sanctioning entity. The problem for drivers was that the rules and point-tallying systems varied from group to group, often in conflict with one another.

Three dominant groups emerged by 1947: the National Championship Stock Racing Association (NCSRA); the Atlanta-based National Stock Car Racing Association (known as the NSCRA and sometimes the NSRA); and France's NCSCC, the National Championship Stock Car Circuit.

Because the NCSCC didn't begin sanctioning races until halfway through 1946, the NSCRA—with France's concurrence—christened Ed Samples as champion, based on his performance in races sanctioned by various organizations. The consensus choice of Ed Samples as champion had been a rare display of cooperation among sanctioning bodies. Such cooperation would not exist in 1947. Nor ever again. In many ways, 1947 would be the turning point for a sport soon to be governed by one group, one man.

The face of the sport was changing, too. Many of stock car racing's first stars were dead, retired, or coming to their senses. Many who'd raced before the war were now in their thirties and dropping out, looking for real jobs, starting families. Lloyd Seay was dead; Roy Hall behind bars. Bill France had stopped racing, though he was involved more than ever as a promoter and sanctioner.

In the early postwar days, stock car events were filled with eager, greenhorn young men just back from battle, looking for adventure on the racetrack. Some veteran racers, including the bootleggers, grumbled about the inexperienced new drivers and how racetracks were being littered with the wrecked carcasses of amateurs' cars. Furthermore, the cars themselves contributed to the increasingly downtrodden look of stock car racing. Because no new postwar car models had rolled out of the factories yet, racers still competed in beat-up, ragged-looking late-1930s Fords. And at six or eight years old, a Ford V-8 coupe looked as if it had been through a war itself.

Into this uncertain era roared a promising new batch of speed demons. As had been the case from the beginning, many were whiskey drivers, and more than a few hailed from Dawsonville, Georgia. Notable among the liquor trippers were Gober Sosebee and the 1946 champ, Ed Samples, both of whom as teens a decade earlier had been inspired by Seay and Hall. One night just before the war, Samples was shot three times in a moonshining argument. He recovered, but later, after watching one of Seay's final races, he told a friend, "I gotta try something safer than moonshine. I think I'll try racing."

The newcomers didn't exactly know what to make of Red Byron. They knew that he could race, that he was a good mechanic, that he was affiliated with two of the sport's most potent forces, Parks and Vogt. But he was also something of an anomaly. He didn't drink the way they did. He didn't run moonshine the way they did. He didn't talk the way they did. He smoked cigars instead of cigarettes, wore nice shirts and slacks instead of overalls. Sometimes he even raced fancy open-wheel cars way up *north*. He may have been born in Virginia, but his childhood was certainly nothing like their own Dixie youths. And why was he so damn quiet? Instead of lingering after a race to sip whiskey, clown around, and chase women, he'd get back in the car with his sultry wife and just disappear.

Byron was wary of them as well. He may have been relieved to have competitors such as Roy Hall and Bill France out of the racing picture. But the new boys were clearly an ornery, aggressive bunch, ready to challenge any edge that Hall's absence might have given Byron. Of particular concern to Byron were the Flock brothers, Bob and Fonty, a veritable

Mutt and Jeff team. In nearly every picture of the Flock brothers through the 1940s, Fonty is smiling; Bob is not.

Bob had served with an army infantry unit during the war but was discharged in 1943 with a "nervous condition" and "bad stomach," for which he continued to collect disability. He would drive Roy Hall's car for the Parks team throughout 1947.

Fonty had vowed never to race again after his terrible wreck at Daytona Beach in 1941, when his seat belt snapped and he was tossed around like a puppy in a clothes dryer. But after recovering from his injuries and serving stateside with the army, he couldn't stay away and had found a car and a sponsor for the 1947 season. And if two Flocks wasn't bad enough, before year's end the youngest brother, Tim, would join the sport as well—a triple threat of moonshining Flock boys.

Byron had reason to feel like an outsider in a world jammed so full of bootleggers, both active and retired. He belonged to that minority of stock car drivers who'd never had a revenuer on his tail, who'd never felt the cool touch of prison bars in his hands.

Daytona Beach and its warm February weather had become host to the traditional first race of the season. The first race of 1947 would also kick off the first full year of Bill France's promising new NCSCC organization.

On January 26, Red Byron thankfully had just one Flock to contend with: nervous, blue-eyed, superstitious Bob, who always dipped his knuckles into the dirt before each race and tasted the grit for luck. Lined up with Byron and Flock were Sosebee, Samples, and two dozen other threats, every last one of them in a prewar Ford.

Adding to the day's drama was the presence of camera crews from Universal and Paramount studios, which planned to include highlights of the fifty-lap, 160-mile race* with their newsreels shown in movie

---

*Most racetracks were a mile or a half mile in length, and races were even-numbered events of 25, 50, 100, or 150 miles. Because Daytona's Beach-and-Road course was 3.2 miles long, races were often 160 miles—or fifty 3.2-mile laps.

theaters. Apparently, word of the steel-crunching contests had reached Hollywood, and these would become the first nationally broadcast images of the South's homemade, decade-old racing style.

Before the race, sportswriters wondered in print whether Byron, now thirty-one, was still capable of handling the Beach-and-Road course—*and* his much-younger competitors. Raymond Parks wondered the same. He knew Byron's health wasn't what should be for such grueling races. Byron's upper body was now strong, his arms ropy and taut, to compensate for his battered lower half. As such, steering wasn't the problem. It was that clutch pedal. Even with the fatigue pins, the clutch proved a challenge. Byron's damaged leg would have to depress the pedal dozens of times over the 160 miles.

As race time approached, Red Vogt skittered around the car, parked behind pit road.* He had made small adjustments to his makeshift clutch pedal, searching for just the right spacing of the two pins so Byron's boot would fit snugly between them, tight enough so the rutted track wouldn't shake his foot off the pedal during the two-hour ride.

Byron's pit crew—which included a new crew chief named "Fat" Russell—helped him get into the car, while Parks, well dressed as usual, wished Byron luck. As the green flag was dropped, Ed Samples rocketed ahead of the twenty-seven others, as if they had all forgotten to put their cars into gear. By the time the rest of the field had reached full speed, Samples was already half a mile ahead. Within five laps around the 3.2-mile course, he was a full lap ahead of the others, averaging ninety-three miles an hour.

Byron never understood such Roy Hall–like showboating. The ten thousand fans loved to watch Ford V-8s pushed to their maximum limits. But no car, no matter how well tuned, could withstand such a pace for 160 miles. In no time, Samples's impetuous, full-speed assault began

---

*In the early days, a trench was dug beside the start-finish line at most racetracks, where each car's backup crew kept gas cans and extra tires. That trench, or "pit," was later replaced with a ground-level area that came to be called "pit road."

to do terrible things to his overworked engine, which finally exploded in a plume of smoke. As usual, Byron had gambled on a high attrition rate and held back as other racers blew engines or tires and, one by one, did themselves in.

After Samples dropped out, Jack Etheridge built up a three-mile lead until his engine also seized, allowing Byron to take the lead at lap number thirty. Leading a race just past the halfway point was a bit too soon for Byron, and it made him uneasy to be alone out front with twenty more laps looming ahead—especially with Bob Flock now stalking menacingly behind his trunk. Flock decided to make his move on the forty-fifth lap, at the approach to the north turn. Driving a Ford that also had Red Vogt's magic inside, Flock accelerated into the turn and tried to pass Byron on the outside. The north turn had long been the spot where a Daytona Beach race was won or lost. This time, the thick sand of the turn's outer edge grabbed hold of Flock's right rear wheel, which violently snapped off its hub and spun crazily toward the grandstands.

Despite repeated warnings from announcers to back away, fans were standing on the apron of the track and Flock's whirligigging wheel slammed into the group like a bowling ball into pins. Once again, the fans were lucky. Only three men were taken to the local hospital, the worst of them with a snapped leg. Flock tried to keep driving on three wheels, but his Ford soon collapsed, and Byron sped on ahead toward the checkered flag. With no challengers within striking distance, Byron wisely eased up and drove cautiously over the last fifteen miles.

By the time Byron crossed the finish line, just twelve of the twenty-eight starters were still running. Even driving tentatively through the last laps, Byron pulled into victory lane four miles ahead of the second-place finisher. He earned one thousand dollars and praise from the noted but fickle sportswriter Bernard Kahn, who called him "steady driving Byron . . . a bespectacled, balding wounded war veteran who wears a steel brace and drives with a special clutch to offset the handicap of a lame left leg." Kahn praised Byron for "plugging away to cash in on a nice job of driving, endurance and mechanical efficiency."

It was Byron's second win in three starts at Daytona, and in the weeks to come, his story would begin to spread. Sportswriters praised this "redhead with a flaming spirit to match." The story tumbled domino-like across the South, whose writers latched onto the hard-luck tale of an unlikely, underdog hero with "a war injury that rendered his left leg almost useless." Some writers puffed up the story and hyperbolized that Byron's withered and paralyzed left leg—"filled with Jap shrapnel!"—was actually bolted directly onto the clutch pedal. A few said it was bolted to the accelerator. Others said variously that his foot had been shot off or that the left leg was missing altogether.

The leg. It's what distinguished him, and that troubled Byron. Already something of an outsider in his field, he wanted to be known as a racer, not a *crippled* racer. When asked about his success, Byron preferred to discuss the technical details of his engines and, always humble, to give credit to his team of Parks and Vogt. But when pressed, he would admit that racing with only one good leg was tougher than it had been with two.

"I get tired a little," he told one writer. "But it doesn't bother me otherwise."

Byron would return to Daytona Beach six weeks later, on March 9, for a one hundred–mile race in unseasonably chilly weather. This time, he wasn't as grateful to his benefactors.

Despite Nell's parting words—"*Be careful, but win . . .*"—Byron found himself a spectator. During a practice session, his engine overheated and cracked. The prerace favorite, Byron was scratched from the main event. There just wasn't enough time for Vogt to repair or replace the engine, especially since Vogt was still perfecting Bob Flock's red and white number 14 car, which was about to make history. As Byron watched from pit road, Flock quickly sloughed off the pack and stayed there for more than an hour.

Unlike Byron, Flock had no qualms about holding on to first place, start to finish. His average speed of eighty-five miles an hour set a new record for a one hundred–mile race, previously held by Lloyd Seay, at seventy-eight miles an hour.*

For Byron, driving seven hours to a race and then sitting in the pits with a busted engine was unacceptable. He decided, partly out of frustration, to cut back on his stock car–racing schedule to prepare for the event that was still the biggest show in auto racing.

The five hundred–mile Indianapolis Classic, traditionally held on Memorial Day weekend, had been Byron's obsession ever since Barney Oldfield lured him into racing as a teen. Byron dreamed of whipping around the famed Brickyard, where racers were reaching 180 miles an hour along each of the two four thousand–foot straightaways.

Despite a few disappointing second-place finishes and overheated engines in the early months of 1947, Byron still felt confident heading toward the thirty-first annual Memorial Day race at Indianapolis. Unlike the fairground races and the sloppy half-mile, red-dirt ovals of the South, Indy was a regal, sophisticated event. Marching bands kicked off a week of activity, and a parade of sleek, sexy cars arrived early so their strong young professional drivers could take practice laps and confer with their mechanics.

The initial open-wheel racers of Indy were often built by European companies such as Peugeot or Duesenberg, and by the 1930s and 1940s, some Maseratis, Mercedes, and Alfa Romeos cost as much as thirty-five thousand dollars. The 1920s and 1930s saw American carmakers such as Miller begin to succeed with cheaper Indy cars. Engines made in the United States by Offenhauser, known as Offys, dominated the late 1930s at Indianapolis. But by 1947, the fastest open-wheel cars could still cost more than a house. By comparison, a Ford stock car, even with

---

*Actually, Roy Hall averaged an incredible ninety-two miles an hour in a 1946 Daytona race, in the same Vogt-tuned car. But that wasn't considered an "official" race, and therefore, his feat was not entered into any record books — among many examples of sloppy record keeping *and* the need for an official organization to oversee stock cars.

a slew of power-enhancing modifications, might be worth two thousand dollars.

In recent months, Byron and Red Vogt had worked together, often all night, to cobble together a loaf-shaped, open-wheel car for Byron to take to Indy. Without thirty-five thousand dollars to spare, they had decided to try something new: a Frankensteinian merger of stock car and Indy car. The odd-looking vehicle consisted of a homemade chassis, with sheet metal molded around a steel-pipe frame. Vogt then installed a Ford V-8 inside, creating one of just three cars at Indy that year with a Ford engine—two of which would not qualify.

Qualifying laps began a full week before the big race. Red and Nell drove out of Atlanta in late May in Red's Ford convertible. Vogt decided to loan Byron one of his mechanics, the hard-drinking Fat Russell, who followed behind the Byrons, towing the red and blue number 22 car northward toward Indiana.*

Though Vogt would have felt out of place—like a thrift-store-clothed kid at a black-tie ball—Byron loved the upscale, celebrity feel of the event, with movie stars in the grandstands among well-dressed fans. Byron's would-be competitors ranked among the biggest names in motorsports: Mauri Rose, Bill Holland, Rex Mays, and Ted Horn.

Despite the glitter and glamour, Indy was still a dangerous event and could be as potentially violent, deadly, and bizarre as any stock car race. Years earlier, a wheel flew off a car, over the racetrack fence, and into an adjacent backyard, where it landed on a twelve-year-old boy, killing him. Indy drivers competed in other AAA-sanctioned races, in their same open-cockpit cars, and despite the regularity with which they were flung from those cars—sometimes to be run over by peers—racers rarely wore

---

*Number 22 had been assigned to Byron by AAA, based on his finish in the AAA standings the previous year. AAA's champ always put 1 on his car the following year; the runner-up was assigned car 2, and so on—except for unlucky 13, which was skipped. Byron initially finished twenty-first in AAA's 1946 standings, which gave him number 22 for the 1947 season. Byron was then bumped up to nineteenth place when two drivers who had finished ahead of him in the standings were killed in late 1946.

seat belts and only recently had begun wearing hard-shell helmets. Some drivers kept them refrigerated the night before a race, to cool their heads during the miles of hard driving.

Still, AAA events such as the Indy 500 were considered a "gentleman's" sport. Car owners were typically industrialists or heirs, often referred to as "sportsmen," who had earned or inherited fortunes in beer, beef, or steel. Racing was their weekend hobby, just as racehorses occupied the spare time of other millionaires. Byron had to feel like an odd man out among such men, at a race called Decoration Day.*

To qualify at Indy in 1947, drivers had to average 115 miles an hour for four laps. Ted Horn, the 1946 AAA champ, qualified for the pole position at 126 miles an hour in his beautiful Maserati. Although Horn had raced a Ford V-8 at Indianapolis back in 1935, Fords were now a rarity at Indy, even as they had come to dominate the dirt tracks of the stock car–racing circuit. It became clear during qualifications for the 1947 Indy 500 that Byron's Ford engine was out of its element and in the wrong league at the Brickyard.

During practice laps, Byron bumped and bucked along the brick-paved macadam of the 2.5-mile track, a cigar locked in his jaw. But Byron's homemade racer—not nearly as sensual as a Maserati or an Alfa Romeo, nor as powerful as an Offy-powered car—strained to find enough zoom. The car wasn't hugging tightly to the surface the way it should. The suspension felt soft, and Byron phoned Vogt back in Atlanta and told him the car kept slewing to the right. "It's wanting to spin out," he growled into the phone.

Byron and Fat Russell kept making adjustments, and Byron returned to the track for his final shot at qualifying. After driving a few warm-up laps, he gave the timing official the thumbs-up, to indicate he was ready to start his four official qualification laps. Byron took his first lap at 114

---

*Decoration Day was the holiday created to honor Union soldiers who died in the Civil War. People would decorate soldiers' graves on that day. It was later renamed Memorial Day, but many southerners still considered it a Yankee holiday.

miles an hour, then pushed his car to 114.85 on the second lap. He knew he'd have to do much better than that for the final two laps.

Byron pushed the car just above 115 for the next two laps, but he could tell they hadn't worked out all the bugs. At the end of his four-lap attempt, he pulled into the pits and waited nervously for his results to be announced over the public address system. Finally, he learned that he was a hair too slow. His average speed was announced as 114.69 miles—close, but not enough to qualify.* He'd missed his chance by a split second. Heartbroken, Byron reluctantly called Vogt again and told him the bad news.

"Well," Vogt said, "just put it on the trailer and bring it home."

Byron and Nell stayed to watch the main event. Amid sixty-five thousand others, Byron watched with envy as fan favorite Bill Holland held the lead for the first hundred miles. Holland then unexpectedly skidded sideways in front of the oncoming car of Shorty Cantlon, who unintentionally nudged Holland back into a forward position but whose car then drove headfirst into the concrete barrier. Cantlon was instantly killed.

When drivers died on a racetrack, in both AAA/Indy races and stock car races, the protocol depended on the severity and gore. If the body was still intact—and many racers did die of head wounds or internal injuries, neither of which resulted in much blood or gore—race officials waved the yellow "caution" flag, which told drivers to slow to a crawl and stay in the same order; for bigger, bloodier wrecks, they waved a red flag, which brought racers to a temporary stop. Either way, the wreckage was cleaned up, the dead racer's body removed by ambulance, and the race restarted—the deceased would have wanted it that way being the assumption. Sportswriters would later euphemistically

---

*In a sign of the spurious motorsports journalism of the day, one North Carolina columnist wrote a story about a bird, allegedly a starling, flying into Byron's path, cracking his windshield and glancing off Byron's goggles, cracking the glass. Race officials were said to have waved a red flag, a signal for Byron to pull out because he couldn't legally qualify with a broken windshield. The story was apparently false.

explain that the driver was "fatally injured" or his "injuries proved to be fatal."

After Cantlon's body and wreckage were cleared and the race restarted, Holland's teammate, Mauri Rose, took the lead with less than twenty miles to go and kept it. In another stark difference between the poor man's world of stock car racing and the "gentleman's" sport of Indy, Rose's winning purse totaled more than thirty-one thousand dollars. Even the day's last-place finisher won more than the first-place finisher of most stock car races.

But Byron was not destined to partake of those riches. He thought about his lousy Indy weekend during the quiet drive home to Georgia. Despite his lifelong dream of an Indianapolis victory, he knew he was just as much an outsider in that world as in the world of stock car racing, if not more so. And the Ford V-8 seemed better suited for dirt tracks than such elite contests as Indy, whose open-wheelers were skittish greyhounds compared to Fords, old reliable hunting hounds. Sleek speed mattered more than reliability at Indy. Maybe, Byron pondered, the hound could be taught some new tricks.

But just weeks earlier, the hound's master had died.

In early 1947, with his only son, Edsel, now dead and his company in the hands of a grandson, Henry Ford seemed rootless and lost. For all his many faults, he had always been, maybe above all else, a productive, industrious self-starter. Without a company to run, or a son to nag, Ford grew bored. As grandson Henry II later put it, "He gave up."

"The unhappiest man on earth is the one who has nothing to do," Ford once said. And it appeared that he had done all he could do in life. In his eighties, he began spending winters far from his Detroit factories, meandering around the thousands of acres of his Georgia estate, called Richmond Hill.

Henry Ford's life had spanned the Civil War and two world wars. He had lived through—and, in fact, personally *symbolized*—the evolution from rural farm life to mechanized city life, an era now driven by electricity and gas-powered automobiles. But in his dotage, Ford seemed to regret those dramatic changes. At his southern estate, Ford would drive around the countryside, stopping to talk with farmers, scooping up handfuls of red dirt, sitting on tree stumps and whittling sticks of wood with his pocket knife—"like a character in a Willa Cather novel," Douglas Brinkley wrote in *Wheels for the World*. It was as if he were suddenly saddened by, maybe frightened by, all he had created. "The plants have grown so big," he once said to a friend visiting him in Georgia, referring to the Ford factories back home in Detroit. As Brinkley put it, "He was the master of the modern world—but he longed for the nineteenth century way of life."

Ford still showed signs of his spunky, puritanical distaste for liquor. He may have lost his fight to keep Prohibition intact, but untaxed whiskey was still illegal. So, whenever he found a moonshine still on his property—which was often, this being Georgia, after all—he would have someone on his staff destroy it. Such outbursts of energy were rare, though, and his zeal for life was on the wane.

In January of 1947, Ford and his wife, Clara, left their suburban Detroit home and drove south to Georgia, fleeing a brutal Michigan winter that had left Ford feeling ill. Two months later, in early April, they returned home to Dearborn, whose streets had been flooded by heavy rains and swollen rivers. On April 7, a day after Easter Sunday, Ford and a chauffeur took a ride around the city—in a Ford V-8—to survey the flooding, which had knocked out the power to Ford's homestead and was threatening to overtake his factories. On the way back home, Ford asked his driver, Robert Rankin, to stop at the cemetery on Joy Road, where his family had been interred.

"Rankin," said Ford, who was wearing bedroom slippers and stayed in the car, "this is where I'm going to be buried when I die. . . . Will you take care of that?"

That night, Ford drank a glass of milk and went to bed. He awoke a short time later, gasping for air. Clara sent Rankin to fetch a doctor and sat stroking her husband's head as he breathed his last, labored breaths. Ford died just before midnight, April 7, 1947, of a cerebral hemorrhage. He was eighty-three.

Two days later, one hundred thousand people lined up to pay their respects, parading past Ford's open coffin. The day after that, all of Detroit's carmakers stopped their assembly lines at 2:30 p.m. for a few eerie, silent moments of homage to the man who had started it all. At that very moment, said *Time* magazine, "They lowered the coffin into the wet, clayey mud. . . . The cars rushed past, filling the night with the smell of gasoline."

Ford had openly proclaimed his belief in reincarnation and once said he always felt his soul had previously belonged to a Union soldier killed at Gettysburg, the terrible Civil War battle that had raged four weeks before Ford was born in 1863. It's doubtful that Ford, with all his disdain for moonshiners and their stock car races, would have liked to see his own soul reincarnated into anything or anyone involved in such unwholesome pursuits. But it is at least an interesting coincidence of automotive history that the year of Henry Ford's death was also the year of NASCAR's birth.

Bill France may not have been an exemplary racer, nor an ingenious mechanic, though he was surely above average in both regards, having won a number of races and the 1940 championship. Mostly, he was a shrewd, savvy salesman who had also become a natural showman, comfortable with microphones, crowds, and newsmen. Across his nearly ten years as a racing promoter, France had learned to borrow the best ideas from other promoters, including his AAA rivals. He had decided from the start that stock car races should be more than just speed contests, they should be *shows*.

Having given up on his racing career, France focused more than ever on being the P. T. Barnum of stock car racing, intent on creating events that were part circus, part race. For that, he needed the best drivers. "Better drivers mean better races and larger crowds," France told a magazine writer in mid-1947. To lure those drivers and those crowds, France studied other promoters of the day, particularly AAA's top man, Sam Nunis.

Nunis was born on an onion farm in Texas and ran away from home at age fifteen to pursue a racing career. After almost losing his leg in a wreck at a North Carolina race, he switched to promoting races. With his double-breasted suits and slicked-back hair, and with AAA's substantial bank account behind him, Nunis's promotional savvy outclassed France's bootstrap efforts. Nunis hired a stable of PR men (all former newsmen) to help spread word of his races to sportswriters and hired off-duty detectives from the Pinkerton Agency to assist local police with crowd control. Although most of Nunis's races were Indy-style "big car" events, he felt that the postwar appetite for auto racing was on the rise and that there was plenty of room for a few AAA-sanctioned stock car races.

In 1947, Nunis told AAA that its retreat from stock cars a year earlier had been premature. Despite AAA's long-standing uneasy relationship with stock cars, Nunis convinced the organization's Contest Board to give them another chance and to schedule a handful of AAA-backed races that summer. In early 1947, Nunis began advertising those races in auto magazines, declaring in bold black and white his intention to bring AAA into the Bill France realm of southern stock car racing. His ads touted "world's finest talent" and "nation's largest racing schedule."

From Nunis, France learned the importance of strong advertising and good press. That lesson prompted France to befriend sports editors at most of the towns he visited, and early on he became close friends with Bernard Kahn, the well-regarded writer at the *Daytona Beach News-Journal,* who wrote so eloquently about Red Byron.

France and Kahn had met before the war, when France bailed Kahn out of a potential night in jail by paying a parking ticket Kahn couldn't afford. During the war, Kahn served in the navy and would receive long letters from France, rambling about how he believed he could "make some sense out of [the] wildcat" sport of stock cars. They renewed their friendship after the war, and for the next few years, Kahn's exciting stories about stock car races, his heartfelt descriptions of Red Byron, and his promotional references to Bill France played a big role in the coming success of Bill France's sport. Kahn was a good journalist, but hardly an objective one.

France hoarded such allies and alienated those he didn't trust. He would need such partners even more with AAA threatening his control of stock cars. Other racing groups also posed a risk to France's plans. In addition to France's NCSCC, there was the Atlanta-based NSCRA, sanctioning many stock car races in 1946; the Stock Car Auto Racing Society (nicknamed, appropriately, SCARS); the South Carolina Auto Racing Association (SCARA); the United Stock Car Racing Association (USCRA); the American Stock Car Racing Association (ASCRA); and the National Auto Racing League (NARL). In addition to self-proclaimed "national" groups, scores of highly competitive regional organizations mushroomed up and down the East Coast.

Each organization had its own system for assigning points to victories and top-ten finishes and for keeping a tally of how racers performed in their events. Organizations gave a driver anywhere from 100 to 500 points for a victory, 90 to 400 for second place, 80 to 300 for third, and so on. At the end of the year, the driver with the most points would be that specific group's "champion," which would earn him a trophy, maybe a small bonus, and bragging rights. Due to the disparate accounting systems, most groups only counted points earned in *their* races and did not allow victories in other leagues to count toward points in their own league. The term *champion*, therefore, was a measure of how well a racer had performed in one particular group's races and hardly a declaration of overall dominance in the sport. At one point during 1947, Red Byron, Bob Flock, and Buddy Shuman would each rank as points leaders of three different groups.

It had been the same debacle for years, and racers found it maddening to discern which groups were legit. Mainly, drivers followed the money, racing in events offering the largest winner's purses. Sometimes drivers would reach the end of a race only to find the purse had simply disappeared, along with the promoter. Still, most racers cared more about a few five hundred–dollar victories than an end-of-the-year championship trophy.

That would soon begin to change, thanks to Bill France.

Red Byron traveled wherever the dollar signs lured him. He raced to win, but also to earn, and cared little which acronym was printed on his paycheck. France was smart enough to realize that racers such as Byron needed stronger reasons to race in *his* stock car races. They needed financial incentives, winnings large enough to cover the cost of fuel, tires, *and* put a little extra cash in their pockets. If France could buy the loyalty of the best southern racers—and Byron was now soundly one of the best—the crowds that such stars lured to his circus/races would put cash in France's own pockets.

France's task was a mountainous one. Stock car racing, by its very nature, had so far defied efforts to control it because so many racers were law-defying, whiskey-tripping Scots-Irish, whose psyches made them aggressively averse to governance. They just wanted to race, drive fast, win a few bucks, and couldn't give a goddamn which suit-wearing businessman sponsored or sanctioned the event. Racers had little loyalty except to themselves, their cars, and their mechanics. That summer, Bill France made his first major stab at buying drivers' loyalty by announcing that his NCSCC organization would go beyond paying drivers for each individual victory. It would also pay one thousand dollars to the driver who, by year's end, had amassed the most points in NCSCC-sanctioned stock car races. Second place would be worth five hundred dollars. France's offer of cash was a first for stock car racing.

"By establishing the national point ranking system we will be able to guarantee fans, as well as track officials, and a crack field of drivers," France said after announcing his new championship scheme. France's incentive plan would encourage drivers to join as many NCSCC events as they could and seemed aimed directly at Byron, whom he called "the hottest rider in the stock car circuit."

However, France didn't exactly emphasize that his new game plan carried some fine print. Namely: Only races in his organization, the

NCSCC, would count toward his "national" points-ranking system. Victories in other organizations' events, such as AAA's, would be worth *zero*.

At the time of France's announcement, Ed Samples and Bob Flock led NCSCC's point standings. Byron had a better winning percentage but had competed in fewer NCSCC races and was therefore further back in the standings. Whether to prove France's boast that he was the "hottest" driver or to make amends for his embarrassing nonstart at Indy, Byron came back to stock cars with a vengeance.

After returning briefly home to Atlanta, Byron immediately got behind the wheel of the Ford convertible that he had purchased after his release from the hospital in late 1945. Nell—as she often did—rode beside him, and they towed Raymond Parks's number 22 Ford V-8 behind them, the start of an epic, summer-long race-to-race-to-race journey.

Nell rarely witnessed her husband's victories, though, preferring to wait in the car. She loved him, but watching him race made her too nervous. So she was sitting in the parking lot when he set a new track record in Jacksonville, finishing a lap ahead of the field. She was in the parking lot outside Lakewood Speedway when Byron uncharacteristically smashed a competitor off the track. The other driver, Jack Etheridge, had passed Byron and was in a power slide in turn two. Byron accelerated and punched Etheridge's left front, which sent him through a wood-slat fence. Byron later claimed he was only trying to help. "I saw you sideways and thought I could straighten you out," he said, but Etheridge didn't entirely believe him and wished Byron had just let him be.

Nell was also in the parking lot when Byron took his second victory in a row at Lakewood, before twenty-one thousand fans. That second Lakewood win happened to be a AAA event, part of Sam Nunis's recent effort to test France's growing domination of stock cars. France's incentive plan clearly wasn't enough to prevent men such as Byron from racing in non-NCSCC races. The lure of a AAA race was, of course, the money.

Before the war, Nunis and France had actually been friends, and Nunis served as France's announcer at a few Daytona Beach races. The racing world was small and tight-knit. Racers were a constantly moving bunch, like gypsies whose travels often intersected with one another. They helped each other, loaning tools, tires, gas, or cash. But the postwar racing community had become more competitive, and the Nunis-France friendship was a casualty. When Nunis convinced AAA's Contest Board to allow him to try promoting a few stock car races in southern states, he chose Atlanta's Lakewood for his first events, igniting a rivalry with France that would last the rest of the decade.

Nunis called his June event at Lakewood the "National Stock Car Championship Race." When word of the event reached France, he was furious. In retaliation, France announced that Byron would not receive any NCSCC points for that victory, since the Lakewood race hadn't been sanctioned by his "official" stock car racing organization. Men such as Byron would learn, time and again, that France's rule book was a never-ending work in progress and that he could bend, break, or replace his own rules on a whim.

France, meanwhile, was slowly realizing that to wrestle stock car racing into conformity, he might have to do more than buy racers' loyalty. At some point, he'd have to strong-arm them.

France wasn't the only one playing loose with the rules of stock car racing in 1947. At every level, the entire sport had become, metaphorically, a rules-be-damned stock car race, with the front-runners looking nervously over their shoulders at the stalkers. Up-and-coming stock car mechanics were threatening Red Vogt's preeminence. A new gang of investors was throwing money into stock cars, challenging Raymond Parks's role as the sport's first and most successful team owner. A ragged young army of speed-hungry drivers was beginning to haunt Red Byron at every race. And new dirt racetracks began vying for the attentions of racers and fans in places such as Macon, Georgia; Huntsville, Alabama; Danville, Virginia; Martinsville, Virginia; Elkins,

North Carolina; High Point, North Carolina; and North Wilkesboro, North Carolina.

In late June, at the first-ever race at North Wilkesboro's track, nine thousand fans came from as far off as Philadelphia and Miami, quadrupling the town's population. They were not disappointed as they watched Bernard Mitchell's car tumble violently in the first turn of the first lap. The door was shorn off, and the crowd gasped as Mitchell's seat belt snapped and he was thrown into the air. Mitchell seemed to float above his rampageous car before landing face-first on the red-dirt track. Byron and a few other drivers had to think fast and swerve sharply to avoid killing the man. Miraculously, Mitchell was helped off the track with only a broken arm and a body full of bruises. Had his seat belt not snapped, he would have been crushed inside his demolished car. Fonty and Bob Flock took first and second, well ahead of Byron—in a sign of things to come.

Byron was a perfectionist. Bad engines and mechanical problems drove him nuts. Byron was leading a race in Allentown until two flat tires in a row dropped him to sixth place. He was leading a race at Jacksonville until his V-8 began to smoke and sputter, and he pulled off the track to watch Bob Flock race to victory. At Macon, Georgia's new track, Byron's car stayed intact, but Bob Flock pulled ahead of him on the second of fifty laps and stayed there; Byron settled for third, two feet ahead of Fonty Flock. At Trenton, New Jersey, the Flock boys swapped places— Fonty won the race, Byron finished second, with Bob half a car length behind. At Greenville, South Carolina, Byron settled for third—a full lap behind the first two finishers, Bob and Fonty. And at yet another race, Byron was a lap from victory until a broken oil line allowed Fonty to win by a nose.

Flock, Flock, Flock, Flock, *Flock*. Every race swarmed with them.

Even though Bob was a teammate, Byron hated to lose and began to feel the desperate need for an edge, a bit of extra speed. He could deal with the crippled leg, but he couldn't deal with crippled cars. Some drivers were experimenting with alcohol instead of gasoline, but the fumes could be lethal. Byron, desperate to give anything a try, one day nearly passed out in a car powered by alcohol. Other drivers added an occasional drop of nitromethane, a mixture of nitric acid and methane. But "nitro" was also tricky—too much could burn up an engine. Byron finally urged Raymond Parks to purchase a third race car as a backup for the two Fords he and Bob Flock drove. The idea was to have an extra V-8 on hand in case one of the others died, as Byron's had more than once.

The first journey for Parks's three-car team occurred in early August 1947, when the entire Georgia Gang—Parks, Byron, Flock, and Vogt—drove north to a race at the famous track in Langhorne, Pennsylvania. After driving all night, the straggly, Fords-pulling-Fords caravan arrived at dawn at the Howard Johnson's parking lot in nearby Bordentown, New Jersey, which for years had served as Langhorne's unofficial (and reluctant) race headquarters. On race weekends, the lot became cluttered with cars and trailers, its pavement littered with parts and tools.

Drivers loved or hated "the Horn," as they affectionately or disdainfully called the track. The dirt surface of the one-mile circle, created in 1926 on a former swamp, had been blackened over the years by the millions of gallons of used motor oil sprinkled to tamp down summer's dust. A dangerous downhill section on turn three called "puke hollow" got slick and wet sooner than the other turns and claimed many cars and a few lives over the years. One sportswriter called Langhorne "the ultimate test of bravery."

On Saturday afternoon, August 9, after watching his two racers drive their required qualifying laps, Raymond Parks decided with uncharacteristic spontaneity to test his own bravery. Instead of letting his new backup number 22-A Ford sit idle in the pits, he asked the promoters to let him drive a few qualifying laps as well. Parks was surprised to find that his Ford-driving skills from his old bootlegging days were still strong, and he drove fast enough to qualify for the next day's race. That night, Parks barely slept. He had worked himself into a sleepless tizzy over his first-ever stock car race and kept pacing the floor of the room he and Byron shared at the Howard Johnson's. "When that green flag goes down tomorrow they're going to run all over me," he said.

"Ah, don't worry about it," Byron said. "Get some sleep."

But Byron would soon be grateful for Parks's spontaneous decision.

An enormous crowd arrived early, many of the fans wearing paper bags on their heads, the traditional method of combating Langhorne's dust clouds. The cars grumbled to the start line for the two hundred–lap contest. Bob Flock, starting in the enviable "pole" position, stomped on the gas pedal of his number 14 Ford, as forty-five engines and thirty-seven thousand voices merged into a riotous cacophony. In elegiac Roy Hall style, Flock kangarooed ahead of them all. Within three short laps, in less than three minutes, he was already catching up to and then passing the slowest starters. That group briefly included Red Byron, who had clocked a slower-than-usual qualifying time the previous afternoon and had therefore started in the seemingly insurmountable position of number thirty-six.

For Byron to find himself assigned to the extreme latter half of a starting lineup of forty-five cars was very unfamiliar. But he was not unfamiliar with the tactics needed to catch the leader. It took Byron just twenty minutes, nineteen laps, to pass more than thirty other cars—including his boss, Parks—and to grumble up behind the leader, teammate Bob Flock. Byron stayed in the number two slot until the halfway point but then decided to take a chance and vie for the lead earlier than usual. He cut to Flock's inside, and the two drove side by side for a full lap until Byron edged ahead and into the lead. For the next twenty-five laps, the two waged a door-scraping battle. Flock fought back into first place at lap 107, but Byron retook the lead at lap 119, only to give it up a lap after that.

As the two exchanged the lead, Parks found that his dormant whiskey-tripping skills had hardly withered. And he'd quickly gotten used to the awkward bulge of Byron's fatigue pins on the clutch pedal. He picked his way through the field and suddenly found himself in third place, just a few car lengths behind his two drivers.

If the lineup had stayed that way, it would have been the first and probably only time in stock car–racing history that a team owner's cars finished first, second, and third, with the owner driving his own car.

But at lap 123, Flock was forced into the pits with motor trouble. With only Parks stalking him a few dozen yards behind, Byron seemed headed for victory, taking some satisfaction that his teammate was suffering from engine woes, not him. But then it began happening again. The sputters and the misfires and the smoke. Byron cursed and pulled into the pits beside Flock, whose car Vogt had already repaired. Flock sped away and rejoined the race while Byron stewed and cursed. Vogt popped his hood and began to assess the engine, but the prospects of rejoining the race looked grim. Suddenly, Parks and his number 22-A came to a gravel-ripping stop beside Byron.

"Get in," Parks shouted, and Byron didn't hesitate.

Byron flew out of the pits, spewing black dirt behind him, and within ten laps caught up to Flock. But the car didn't have the same zoom as his primary car, and no matter which angle he tried, Byron couldn't find a slot through which to pass. Still, he'd overcome great odds to make it to the front of the pack. The teammates finished 1–2.

As Henry Ford had exclaimed after his one and only race—"*I'll never do that again. . . . I was scared to death*"—Parks was wired, both thrilled and relieved to have competed at such a level and survived. It was satisfying, too, to find his moonshine-driving skills still intact, further proof of their transferability to a racetrack.

Seven days later, the Georgia Gang drove south for Bill France's end-of-summer race at Daytona Beach. Engine problems again created grief for the team. Both of Parks's cars spewed smoke during prerace qualifying laps on Saturday. Flock and Byron were therefore given, as a courtesy, the last two slots in the next day's lineup, starting side by side at the rear of the entire pack. But Byron wouldn't race a lap. On Sunday, his engine wouldn't start, and he was scratched from the race altogether—the second time in a row, dating back to March, that he failed to start at Daytona, the site of his early glory.

Byron had won two of the biggest races of his career here, in 1946 and again in 1947, and was hoping for an unprecedented third victory. But even with a working engine, he might not have succeeded. This, it turned out, was to be Bob Flock's race, one more step toward Flock's seemingly inevitable championship season.

As if the soul of Roy Hall had been transplanted into him, Flock put on an amazing show that Sunday afternoon. Starting last in the field of thirty-one cars, it took Flock just one mile to pass every single competitor. Down the narrow paved backstretch, he rocketed from last place to first, and by the end of the first 3.2-mile loop was firmly in the lead. He stayed there for the next thirty-two laps. No one in the crowd of eighty-five hundred had ever seen a driver bury the entire field in such a short time, *especially* on the paved backstretch, which was barely wide enough for two cars.

"I just drove where they wasn't," Flock said after the race, then gushed that Red Vogt had built "the best car I've ever driven."

Although Parks was thrilled with Flock's victory, as Red Vogt liked to say, speed cost money. Parks's dual patronage of Flock and Byron had put a serious strain on his considerable financial resources. Compared to the seven thousand dollars he'd spent in all of 1941, Parks had already invested twenty thousand dollars halfway through 1947. And, despite having two of the best drivers in the sport, he was still barely breaking even. Parks once told a friend how to make a small fortune: "You take a huge fortune," he said, "and then you go racing."

But Parks's fever for stock cars was as high as ever, the costs be damned. Bob Flock's victory was the fourth straight at Daytona Beach for a Parks-owned car, dating back to Lloyd Seay's victory in 1941. Parks couldn't quit now, and he tried not to think about how long he'd be able to keep pouring money into his team.

Flock's Daytona win moved him into a tie with brother Fonty for the points lead in France's NCSCC. Byron seemed to have lost his edge and became dejected. Maybe it was the bad leg, Parks wondered. Byron's friends knew it hurt more than he ever let on.

Sportswriters were now calling Bob Flock "the Wizard of Whiz" and seemed to have forgotten about the wounded war vet with the makeshift clutch and gimp leg. Byron didn't blame Vogt, though, despite the mechanical difficulties he'd suffered. He knew prewar Fords were getting older and more difficult to keep running at peak speeds, and he still considered Vogt "the best mechanic in the business." He told Bernard Kahn, France's sportswriter friend, "If there was a better mech anywhere, I'd get him. But there isn't."

Through the summer of 1947, Parks and his two drivers dominated the stock car circuit, with Byron or Flock taking the top two spots race after race.

The two weren't as personable or fan-friendly as the duo of Roy Hall and Lloyd Seay had been. Byron and Flock were both quieter, more serious and intense. Still, they were becoming heroes throughout Dixie. After winning a fifty-lap event at a new track in Martinsville, Virginia, Byron sat in the driver's seat, his throbbing left leg dangling toward the ground, as teenage boys crowded around the car, peering inside, running their hands over the hot metal. A photograph in the next day's paper showed the deep lines of Byron's serene face packed with dust, which had also darkened his white coveralls and his muscular, veiny arms. He wore dark sunglasses, a cigarette smoldering in one hand, the other clutching a water canteen. A white helmet covered his bald head, but he appeared grimly content, with an expression that seemed to say, *I needed that one.*

Byron followed that win with a second-place finish at North Wilkesboro, North Carolina, and a win at Elkins, North Carolina, which put him into third place for the overall championship behind the two Flocks. Because he'd driven in nearly all of France's NCSCC races, Fonty was still in the lead, with Bob in second.

Bill France's game plan seemed to be coming together. By awarding 100, 90, and 80 points, respectively, for first, second, and third place (instead of the 500, 400, and 300 some organizations gave), France was keeping his championship contest a close race. Racers hungry for the potential year-end "champion" payoff were following France-sponsored races throughout the South and as far north as Rhode Island. And France couldn't have asked for a better front-runner than Fonty Flock.

Even Parks acknowledged that Fonty was "a Bill France dream."

Fonty and Bob's father had been a carnival daredevil and amateur tightrope walker until he died of cancer, leaving their mother to raise eight children. When the older boys reached their teens, they were sent one by one to Atlanta to help with the successful moonshining business of their uncle, Peachtree Williams, who had been one of Red Vogt's first and best customers, and one of Atlanta's top moonshine suppliers.

After Peachtree was killed in a mysterious car wreck,* his eldest nephew, Carl Flock, took over the family business. Carl became very successful and hired his younger brothers, Bob and Truman Fontello, known as Fonty, to help him with deliveries.

Fonty started racing at age seventeen, sometimes under the name "Wild Bill Dawson," in homage to Dawsonville. In mid-1947, Fonty teamed up with Bob Osiecki, an Atlanta mechanic and car owner whose reputation with whiskey cars rivaled Vogt's. Osiecki also worked on cars for Ed Samples, who ranked in the top five on the NCSCC circuit. The fact that Osiecki now had two of NCSCC's fastest cars, as did Red Vogt, inevitably ignited a bit of competition between the two mechanics. In no time, each man decided to hate the other. Osiecki once called one of Vogt's cars an "also ran," which prompted an extremely foulmouthed retort from Vogt.

---

*Peachtree was killed while he and his chauffeur were driving to Florida for the wealthy bootlegger's annual vacation. The story goes that their car either slammed into a parked flatbed truck or was run off the road by one. Peachtree was killed, but the chauffeur emerged unscratched, which raised the Flock boys' suspicions. Police didn't find any of the gold jewelry or wadded bills Peachtree usually had on him, and the dazed chauffeur gave a confusing account of what had happened. The nephews finally decided that their uncle must have been killed by a rival bootlegger, who had paid off the chauffeur. The police never investigated.

That Flock-versus-Flock competition—with Fonty and Bob each driving the car of a rival mechanic—was exactly the kind of show Bill France had hoped for.

The brothers hardly seemed related. Bob was rail-thin, nervous, and just plain goofy-looking, with wide, wild eyes and a crazy smile of bad, broken teeth. Bob hated to be touched and would wheel around and punch a racer who put a hand on his shoulder. (If he'd been born years later, he could have been cast as an extra in the movie *Deliverance*.) But Fonty was smart, funny, and mischievously handsome, with a pencil-thin mustache, a pudgy, Clark Gable–like face, and a shark's smile. Both Flocks were exciting drivers, both presciently aware that stock car racing was about entertaining the crowds as much as beating the other guy. Bob would feel guilty for cheating the fans if he won a race by a large margin. "I know they like action and they're the ones who make stock car racing possible," he once said. Fonty waved to fans and sometimes drove wearing madras-plaid shorts that he called his "ber-MOO-da" shorts. Younger brother Tim would soon get into the act with a live rhesus monkey named Jocko Flocko as his copilot.

Byron, in contrast to the Flocks, was the intense and mysterious introvert. He had the kind of lurid backstory that appealed to southern racing fans who loved underdogs. But he was also sullen, occasionally moody, and seemed uninterested in self-promotion. He didn't get liquored up on moonshine. He read *books,* for crissake. Stock car fans, as they would half a century later, wanted rowdy, defiant personalities to root for.

Bob Flock, both rowdy and defiant, had recently entered a race at Lakewood, despite the ban against drivers with criminal records. A cop recognized him and literally chased him off the track, tailing him down the straightaway in his patrol car until Flock slipped through an opening in the fence and disappeared into downtown Atlanta.

By late 1947, the Flocks were locked in a race for the NCSCC championship, until Fonty's bid got an accidental boost from Bob, who nearly killed himself.

At a mid-October race in Spartanburg, South Carolina, Bob blew a tire and crashed through a fence, taking a few other cars with him. As the entangled swarm of cars crunched and rolled, the roof of Bob's Ford caved in, crushing him inside—just as Fonty had been crushed in his Ford at Daytona six years earlier. X-rays found shattered vertebrae, and doctors encased Bob's torso in a plaster cast that became his personal prison for months. The career of the Wizard of Whiz seemed over for good.

In Bob's absence, Fonty and Red Byron swapped victories across the final weeks of the season. By December, it seemed to the public that the winner of NCSCC's 1947 championship would be determined by Bill France's final race, a twenty-five-lap contest at Jacksonville Speedway's half-mile dirt track. But a week before that race, France issued an announcement that made the race an afterthought.

As he'd promised earlier in the year, France had pulled together a nice little bonus fund to cap off the 1947 season. France took a portion of the profits from each NCSCC race and stashed it in a bank account, which, by December, held twenty-eight hundred dollars. Of that, one thousand dollars would go to the 1947 champion, the rest to be divvied up by the other top NCSCC finishers. The year-end bonuses would be paid out at a banquet in January, marking the first time in stock car history that drivers got money *after* the season.

Before the December 6 race in Jacksonville began, however, France announced the current point standings. The math made it clear that even with a victory, Byron would not be able to earn enough points to catch the presumptive NCSCC champ, Fonty Flock.

Fonty had only begun racing halfway through the 1947 season, competing in twenty-four races sanctioned by NCSCC and winning seven of them. Byron had raced in a total of thirty-five stock car races that year and won *sixteen times*. But only eighteen of those races were in France's NCSCC league. So, even though Byron won *half* the NCSCC races he'd entered—two more than Fonty—the mathematics of France's incentive plan worked against him. Flock was named the champ simply because

Byron had raced in a number of events not sanctioned by Bill France. And if a race wasn't sanctioned by Big Bill, it didn't count. It turns out Byron's nine NCSCC victories weren't even good enough for second in France's new league. According to France's announcement prior to the Jacksonville race, Fonty Flock had accumulated 1,755 points. Next came Ed Samples and Buddy Shuman, the hard-driving moonshiner from Charlotte, with 1,460 and 1,415, respectively. Byron was way down in fourth place in the NCSCC, with 1,410 points.

Byron hoped to at least climb into second place and to collect the five hundred dollars that came with it. To do that, he'd have to soundly beat Samples and Shuman in France's last race.

Byron climbed into his Ford, angry about losing the championship, and got off to an unusually aggressive start. After just a few laps, Byron was racing side by side with "Wild Bill" Snowden, who'd beaten him back in March by just two feet at this very track. This time, Snowden lost control in the second turn. His car tumbled off the track and came to a stop on its roof. A group of teenage boys ran to the smoking wreckage just as Snowden crawled through the window with only a cut on his eye and a bruised shoulder.

Byron took the lead until Buddy Shuman started to nudge him from behind, a dangerous move that threatened to take them both out of the race. Byron wisely slid right, out of the main groove of the track, and let Shuman pass. As soon as Shuman passed, Byron dropped down into the groove and began shoving Shuman's rear end. The two kept at it for two full laps. Finally, in the north turn, Byron gave Shuman a hard, pissed-off nudge from behind, and Shuman's car fishtailed, then swerved to the right and toward the grandstands. If not for a high retaining wall recently built in front of the grandstands, Shuman would have mowed down hundreds of spectators. Byron roared ahead and lapped the rest of the field, charging on to victory.

Afterward, Byron was restrained, but gracious and gentlemanly. "I am lucky to have Raymond Parks to back me, and I am lucky to have Red Vogt to build my car," he said, before also thanking his pit crew chief, D. C. "Fat" Russell.

Byron had knocked Shuman out of the race, and Ed Samples had finished behind him, in fourth. But Byron's spirits sank when France did a quick calculation and announced the final NCSCC standings. France determined that Ed Samples's fourth-place finish was worth seventy points, enough to put him just ahead of Byron in the standings. Samples would be runner-up in the NCSCC behind Fonty Flock. Byron finished third, followed by Shuman, and then Bob Flock.

Byron won more races than any other stock car driver that year—in the NCSCC alone, he won as many races as Ed Samples and Fonty Flock *combined*. In thirty-five races, Byron's sixteen victories amounted to an incredible winning rate of 46 percent—a feat that would never be repeated in stock car racing. Samples, meanwhile, had won just two of his thirty-four NCSCC races. But he had raced in nearly twice as many France-approved events as Byron and therefore earned points even when he didn't win the race.

The message in all the math was: loyalty to Bill France meant championships—and cash. A writer for a new magazine called *Speed Age* was disgusted. "It is the opinion of this writer, as well as that of many others, that Red Byron was the most successful driver of stock cars this season," he wrote in an editorial.

Byron couldn't have agreed more but had no choice but to swallow France's decree. Despite turning in one of the most successful racing seasons in motorsports history, Byron's achievement would elude the history books, because (a) stock car racing was still considered the equivalent of a circus sideshow, and (b) in stock car racing, Bill France's word was now law.

Nearly all men can stand adversity, but if you want to test
a man's character, give him power.
— ABRAHAM LINCOLN

12

"Next thing we know, NASCAR belongs to Bill France"

peed Age magazine had launched earlier in 1947, a publication geared mostly toward devotees of open-wheel racing, AAA-sponsored events, Indy-style cars, and their miniature versions, the sprints and midgets. In a sign of stock car racing's creeping legitimacy, the editors sent a crew of reporters that summer to both Atlanta and Daytona Beach, ordering them to learn more about this raggedy new kind of racing. In their article "Their Business Is Stocks," the writers told a wide-eyed account of rambunctious southern stock car races, the funny-talking fans, and the scarred, moonshining drivers, as if they'd discovered some long-lost tribe. Using terms such as *gol-durndest* and *hell for leather*, the writers introduced readers to Red Byron, Ed Samples, the Flock boys, Bill France, and Red Vogt, whom they called "the doctor of soupology." They wrote, "It is said that Vogt can get more out of a Ford engine than any man living."

They breathlessly described the race at Lakewood Speedway in which Byron had bumped Jack Etheridge, causing him to swerve crazily through a wooden fence.

"Boards splinter as metal meets wood and the car disappears

through the hole in the fence. The driver steps jauntily from the wreck and lights a cigarette," the story went. "This scene is reenacted time and time again throughout the South . . . and the fans are ready to fight if you should deny that it is the greatest show in auto racing.

"If there's ever a stock car race in your area, don't miss it."

In subsequent months, the Maryland-based *Speed Age* began to receive letters from appreciative southern fans, urging the editors to dedicate even more ink to their sport. "These stock jobs draw larger crowds than any other kind of racing in the South," a writer from Greensboro, North Carolina, said. "If you want your magazine to be a success in this area, you had better include some stories about them, too."

Looking back, the magazine's editors would later acknowledge that they were witnessing the first signs of a revolution in automobile racing. Stock cars and their jockeys were about to grow out of their uncertain, adolescent novelty stage into a viable threat to Indy and AAA dominance. In less than ten years, the world of auto racing would see Bill France and stock car racing dethrone AAA entirely.

By the end of 1947, France had begun to sense some of AAA's vulnerabilities and conceits. He had become a student of AAA, borrowing from the organization some of its rules and regulations, the tools he'd need to enforce consistency and uniformity upon the stock car drivers, tracks, and promoters along the East Coast.

France acknowledged in late 1947 that consistency and uniformity in stock car racing had proved to be a "pretty tough" task, one that had led to many "after-the-race arguments" and even a few fistfights. One problem was that all but a few of 1947's "stock cars" were still prewar Ford V-8s, mostly 1939s that had been so modified over the years they were now anything but "stock."

By definition, a stock car was a pure, unalloyed passenger vehicle without any modifications or alterations. From the beginning, of course, racing *purely* stock cars had proved impossible, with wheels falling off, radiators exploding, and engines seizing. Race promoters and sanctioning bodies made allowances for such nonstock alterations as larger radiators and stronger lug nuts to keep the right-side wheels from tearing off. Without such allowances, they'd never have had enough cars for a good race. But as the list of allowable modifications grew to include extra carburetors and higher-compression manifold heads, the list also began to vary wildly from group to group.

During his racing days, for example, Bill France would travel to Pennsylvania and find that the Northeast's definition of "stock" differed from the Southeast's definition, and he'd have to remove a few modifications in order to race at, say, Langhorne. Some race promoters held fast to a strict definition of stock and called their races "strictly stock." Others acknowledged reality and called their events "semistock." Some preferred the term *modified stocks*. Still others said, *To hell with stocks,* allowing drivers to go so far as to tear off their car's fenders and cut off the roof, creating a motley racer called a "roadster." France and his governing body, the NCSCC, had a nearly impossible time enforcing such a "haphazard" mix of rules and regulations.

Hardly any of the eight-year-old cars competing in the stock car races of 1947 were "stock" cars, by its true definition. Some, such as the contraptions Vogt and Byron created in the black of night, had so many aftermarket, experimental, and homemade parts, they could barely be called "Fords" any longer. Or they contained multiple shades of Ford: a 1934 front end, a 1936 transmission, a 1939 engine.

France knew he'd have to firm up the rules or, before long, jet-powered "stock" cars with wings would be soaring down the backstretch at Daytona. And he knew he had to act fast, to get ahead of the mishmash of groups that continued to flock to stock car racing in 1947. The sport had grown beyond its southern roots and had given rise to the American Stock Car Racing Association in New Jersey, the New England Stock Car Circuit in Rhode Island, and other groups in the West and Midwest.

The most logical group to pull all of the various stock car groups under its ample umbrella would have been AAA, whose Contest Board was approaching fifty years of racing expertise. But France felt that AAA and his rival, Sam Nunis, were elitist, usurious, and dictatorial. Stock car racing needed to remain an affordable, everyman sport. France felt strongly that AAA was an "outsider" and shouldn't be allowed to take over.

AAA had experimented with stock cars over the years but still hadn't resolved what its role should be. Some of AAA's New York–based chiefs still didn't even consider stock car events real races, calling them "junk car events" and part of a fad that was "dying out." They held stock car racing in the same esteem as demolition derbies or stunt driving and advised that the organization keep its distance. Only Sam Nunis seemed to realize that the fast-growing popularity of stock cars had opened the door for someone to step up and take control of the sport's tracks, promoters, schedules, and rules. Nunis continued to tout the potential profits to be made in stock cars, even as AAA's Contest Board kept warily inching away from the dirty, junky sport.

For all those reasons—the lack of consistent rules, the disparate racing organizations, the alphabet soup of competing racing acronyms—Bill France decided in late 1947 to invite all of the big names in stock car racing down to his hometown for a roundtable meeting. With the success of his NCSCC that year, France felt he was in a position to suggest the creation of a more substantial governing body for stock car racing. He also felt sure the drivers, mechanics, promoters, and car owners would follow his lead.

After all, he said, "I was one of them."

France announced his call to arms in *Speed Age* magazine and other racing publications, in which he proposed a meeting of the best minds in stock car racing. Two dozen of the major players in stock cars began arriving at the Streamline Hotel in Daytona Beach on December 14, 1947.* Most were from Atlanta or Daytona Beach, but France had in-

---

*The anniversary of the day Alexander Hamilton proposed taxing whiskey to create the Bank of the United States in 1790. Also the day George Washington died in 1799; at the time, he was the nation's largest whiskey distiller.

vited a number of racers, mechanics, promoters, and car owners from New Jersey, Rhode Island, New York, Ohio, Connecticut, and Massachusetts, including representatives of other regional stock car associations and organizations.

Just past noon on that cool mid-December Sunday, they climbed the stairs to the Ebony Room, a dark, outer-space-themed cocktail lounge with star-speckled walls one flight above the Streamline Hotel. The stated purpose of the gathering was the year-end convention for France's National Championship Stock Car Circuit, at which participants would review the year's racing season and suggest improvements for next year. But over the next forty-eight hours, the meeting evolved into something broader and not entirely expected, birthing a much more profound result than even France foresaw.

After temporary appointments were made—a chairman, secretary, treasurer, and such—France took control of the meeting. Sitting at the head of a handful of pushed-together tables, in his deep, insistent, enthusiastic voice, France gave an hour's worth of cheerleading remarks as the others scribbled notes on cocktail napkins, smoked, and sipped drinks. "Nothing stands still in the world," France began. "Things get better or worse, bigger or smaller. . . .

"Stock car racing has been my whole life," he said. He believed the sport was now at a crossroads—stuck between better and worse. What began as the accidental sport of southern moonshiners had now grown into a legitimate and increasingly popular pastime, solid proof that racing was no longer solely the domain of wealthy northerners. But if stock car racing was to continue its ascent, it had to be standardized and formalized.

France argued that stock car racing offered a simpler, more accessible form of automotive competition than the elitist AAA races with their expensive, tubular racing machines. Southern racing allowed amateurs and hobbyists to take their regular, Detroit-made, off-the-showroom-floor "stock" models to the track. "An average man in a fast automobile can still win races if he's just a reasonably good driver," France said.

With a reasonably strong organization behind it, said France, "I believe stock car racing can become a nationally recognized sport"—*if,* he added, the sport was handled "properly." France looked around the table, into the faces of Red Vogt, Red Byron, Fonty Flock, Ed Samples, and others. "Right here within our own group rests the outcome of stock car racing in the country today," he said.

The meeting broke up at 5:15, with plans to reconvene the next morning. Raymond Parks had chosen not to sit in on the meeting itself but mingled with the others afterward in the bar. France had invited a group of models from a local charm school to mingle with the men. Parks, looking handsome in a tailored suit, crisp white shirt, and dark tie—easily the best-dressed man in the room—sat at the bar between two women in bathing suits, buying them drinks, one of them patting his back.

Fonty Flock flirted with two of the bathing suit–clad models, and one sat in Bill France's lap. Red Byron sat in a corner with Red Vogt and a few others, flipping through the latest issue of *Speed Age* magazine, talking about the new "Tech Topics" column Byron had been invited to write. A few of the men didn't recognize Vogt at first; in place of his white T-shirt and white chinos, he wore a black shirt and gray slacks. But, as usual, he was chain-smoking and cursing. During the meeting, the warning from his ex-wife—"I don't trust that man"—had echoed in the back of Vogt's mind.

Vogt wasn't alone. Some of the participants were wary of France's intentions. He seemed to be mapping out a much more significant role for himself than for anyone else. But by the end of the first night, sufficiently lubricated by free booze and beautiful women, the soon-to-be founders of a new sport seemed ready to follow France's lead.

The next morning, slightly hungover and hoarse, the group met after breakfast back in the Ebony Room. France kicked things off by reminding the men why they were there: to create rules, and possibly a new umbrella group, to govern auto races for "plain, ordinary working people," for mechanically inclined men with a sedan and a dream.

"Stock car racing has got distinct possibilities for Sunday shows," France said. "It would allow race-minded boys that work all week who don't have enough money to afford a regular racing car [to] be competition to the rich guy. It allows them the opportunity to go to a race track on Sunday and show their stuff and maybe win a prize and not make it their full-time job."

France knew some of the attendees were skeptical representatives from other organizations, who had likely agreed to come simply so they could spy. He assigned a couple of them to committees and told them to go off and meet on their own. France later acknowledged his tactic was a "ruse" to get his "rivals" out of his hair.

More than a few of the attendees had been moonshiners and numbers runners, or still were. And to those in the group who'd left school before their teens, France's words sounded eloquent and well reasoned. After years of promoting races, France had become confident and comfortable in front of a crowd of peers. He had always had a strong, loud voice, but now he'd developed a slick salesman's tongue to go with it. Plus, at nearly six and a half feet tall, he loomed inches above nearly every other man in the room.

The three dozen whiskey-sipping cigar-puffers took France's sales pitch and ran with it. They sat around long, narrow tables, surrounded by the star-themed wallpaper and a haze of cigar smoke. The room stayed poorly lit and hazy most of the day as they first argued over how to unambiguously define a "stock" car and then began negotiating which guidelines the sport's promoters and drivers should follow for the 1948 season.

France suggested a point-tallying system for 1948 that would have 5-point increments: 100 points for a victory, 95 points for second place, 90 for third, and so on. The smaller increments of such a system would make the yearlong championship race even closer than it had been in 1947. But Red Byron suggested sticking with the 10-point increments that the NCSCC had used in 1947: 100 points for a win; 90 for second; 80 for third; and so on down to 10 points for tenth place, then 9 points for eleventh place, and on down to zero. The group chose Byron's suggestion.

Next, the men agreed to deposit some of the profits of each race into an escrow account, funds that would be used to pay the year-end bonuses to drivers who'd earned the most points. France stressed that this fund was a crucial financial incentive that would keep drivers loyal to the new organization. France also suggested the creation of a benevolent fund to help injured drivers pay for medical bills, which was approved.

Races for 1948 would be grouped into three different divisions: "modifieds," "roadsters," and a "strictly stock" division. The modified division would essentially be a continuation of the predominant stock car racing of the day. Modified races would host passenger vehicles whose engines and suspension could be altered, but the list of do's and don'ts would be refined so that mechanics such as Vogt didn't get too carried away with their crafty modifications.

The roadster division was also for "stock" passenger cars but would have fewer rules, allowing those cars to be modified even more than the modifieds. Roofs and fenders could be cut off, until the cars looked like California-style hot rods.

Finally, the "strictly stock" division would host new cars and enact much stricter limits on any performance-enhancing alterations, so that the cars were more purely "stock" cars and looked more like a passenger car than a race car. However, because carmakers were still getting up to their full postwar production and hadn't yet introduced too many new models, the strictly stock division would be postponed until 1949.

Since roadster racing was a relatively unproven concept in the South, and the strictly stock events were on hold, the biggest events of 1948 would be the modifieds—off-the-rack, American-made cars, with lights and mufflers removed and doors strapped shut and engines and suspensions altered, albeit within reason, to help them perform on washboard dirt tracks. All three divisions would race on dirt tracks, which France believed "is more than necessary to make stock car racing a good show."

"Stock car races not held on dirt are nowheres near as impressive," he said.

On the final day of the three-day meeting, the participants decided to come up with a new name for the organization. Byron offered up the first suggestion: the National Stock Car Racing Association, or NSCRA, which was seconded and approved. But after a break for lunch, Red Vogt offered an alternative suggestion: the National Association for Stock Car Auto Racing, or NASCAR. France suggested that everyone write down some more ideas on pieces of paper, but the group ignored him and decided to put Byron's and Vogt's suggestions to a vote.

Some of the men liked the idea that Vogt's acronym could be easily pronounced. Others were concerned that it sounded too much like "NASH-car." Nash was, at the time, an automaker, but it didn't make a very good race car. When they voted, seven men chose Byron's NSCRA; four chose Vogt's NASCAR.

Vogt and a few others quickly pointed out that a group called NSCRA already existed in Georgia. So the participants overruled Byron's idea and unanimously approved Vogt's name, NASCAR. As the new word made its entry into the American lexicon, *Speed Age* magazine declared in its next issue the creation of NASCAR to be "the dawn of a new era."

"The eyes of the rest of the auto racing world will watch this experiment very closely," the editors wrote.

Almost as an afterthought, the group chose a few members to serve in various administrative roles. Byron suggested that the group create a governing body consisting of a president, secretary, two promoters, two drivers, two car owners, and two mechanics. He then humbly nominated Bob and Fonty Flock as the two driver representatives. The group instead elected Byron and Buddy Shuman (the moonshiner from Charlotte). Red Vogt and Marshall Teague (a racer and mechanic from Daytona Beach) were chosen to represent the mechanics, and Teague was also chosen to serve as treasurer. Vogt suggested that Raymond Parks serve as one of the owner representatives, but the group ended up voting for two other car owners. Last, they chose two promoter representatives.

E. G. "Cannonball" Baker, a highly respected open-wheel racer from Indianapolis, was chosen as NASCAR's "high commissioner." The men felt Baker's pedigree, and his lofty title, would give NASCAR an added air of legitimacy, which might help in the expected confrontations with snooty AAA. France then suggested that Bill Tuthill, a motorcycle-racing promoter he had invited down from New York, serve as secretary.

Finally came the question of who'd oversee the paperwork, file the incorporation papers, and be given authority to collect and spend money. Byron suggested the obvious: that France serve in that position, as president of the NASCAR governing body.

France never said so publicly, but he believed stock car racing could not survive as a democracy. There'd be too much infighting and what he called "dissidence." Bill Tuthill agreed with him and before the meeting told France, "The democratic method . . . never worked." France and Tuthill had therefore schemed beforehand to prevent representatives of rival organizations from taking a lead role in any new organization. To avoid getting into detailed debates over bylaws and definitions, France and Tuthill hoped to set themselves up as the new organization's top dogs. That way, they could afterward make the rules themselves. Only such an autocracy, they truly believed, could survive.

Other participants in the Ebony Room meetings wouldn't realize until later that they'd given France the power he'd always wanted. Raymond Parks was among those who later grumbled, "The next thing we know, NASCAR belongs to Bill France."

Which, of course, had been France's plan all along.

There are only three sports. Bullfighting, mountain climbing
and motor racing. All the rest are merely games.
— ERNEST HEMINGWAY

13

"Racing Car Plunges into Throng"

History would eventually declare 1948 the year of NASCAR's birth and, to the gall of many who were there in the birthing room, would dub Bill France the sport's lone, heroic founder. At the start of the 1948 season, racers and mechanics who'd only been racing for a few years indeed saw France as their sport's savior. Those who'd known France for a decade, since before the war, knew the more complicated truth.

No one could deny that France worked hard to promote his sport and his vision. Over the years, he did whatever it took to pull off a race. On race day, he was a tornado of energy, seemingly everywhere at once. He sold tickets, sodas, programs. He ran out to rescue injured drivers and constantly shooed spectators back from the track. He started taking flying lessons so he could fly to and from races and visit new tracks, meeting with local promoters interested in hosting their own NASCAR race. He would soon hire NASCAR's first public relations man, a smart smooth-talker named Houston Lawing, who would almost always refer to Red Byron as "the disabled war veteran."

But France wasn't the only one who'd dedicated his life to the sport.

Most of NASCAR's other founders had also been at it since the 1930s. For some, their obsession with stock car racing was progressively taking a significant toll.

For Red Vogt, the start of the 1948 season saw his personal life sink to new lows, depth-charged by his near-maniacal devotion to cars and engines and speed. He was among the first of his day to actually make a half-decent living as a race car mechanic. But that's all he was. Other titles—father, husband, friend—didn't apply.

Twentieth-century history books are filled with tales of iconic men, such as Henry Ford himself, who loved machines more than their wives, children, peers, or selves. Such men became singularly obsessed with the *real* loves of life at the expense of a so-called normal livelihood. An almost sexually charged ardor for machinery could consume the lives of men wooed by mysterious car engines, the smell of burning fuel, the whump of their exhaust. "With the gentleness of a lover, he had stuck his hands into their dark greasy mysteries," one writer said of men such as Red Vogt. But for the mechanical genius who had recently coined the name *NASCAR,* who had suggested many of the new sport's rules and regulations, Vogt's devotion to Ford V-8s had grown far too deep.

Vogt and his wife, Ruth, had split years earlier, before the war. It had never been an ideal partnership. She was educated, headstrong, and impatient. He was *un*educated, headstrong, and impatient. The Vogts' two sons had been raised largely by their maid, Ollie Mae, a heavyset woman who ran the household. Ollie Mae was hired to replace the previous housekeeper, who often ignored the young boys. Ruth came home one night to find one son in his crib, covered in his own feces. Ruth Vogt was rarely at home; Red, even less. On the rare nights when the couple was together for a family meal, the evening often splintered and cracked into a dissonant chirr of curses and angry voices. They screamed at the kids, at each other, at the help. Neighbors wondered how these two embittered screamers, who seemed to despise each other so intensely, had ever been able to procreate, and Ruth once confessed that both pregnancies had been accidents.

Eventually, the sons—Tom and Jerry—were sent away to a military boarding school, the Georgia Military Academy. In their absence, Ruth quit managing the books at her husband's garage to pursue an interest in cosmetics. As her success in that field grew, and Red spent more and more time in his garage, the two agreed to divorce.

One side effect of the divorce was a sharp decline in Red's finances. Ruth had been a shrewd and aggressive business manager, able to collect debts from elusive moonshining clients. Red, on the other hand, was a brilliant mechanic but an inattentive businessman. He wouldn't realize how valuable she'd been to his shop until she was gone. During the breakup, Red accused her of stealing all his money, and she accused him of wasting and mismanaging it. In the end, he had to move out of the large house they'd shared in the upscale East Lake section of Atlanta and into a downtown hotel.

As a divorcé, Vogt worked harder than ever, spending most of his days and nights at his shop. Word of Vogt's mechanical prestige spread, and customers, particularly racing fans, came from all over the Southeast just to have Vogt tune their car to perfection. One customer who drove up from Miami for some engine work had to stay in Atlanta for three days waiting for Vogt to get around to fixing his car. To pay his bills, Vogt took on so much work that he hired a staff of a half dozen mechanics, demanding that they arrive by 7:00 a.m. Vogt would be there when they arrived, and he'd still be working when some of them left twelve to sixteen hours later. After midnight, Vogt would lock himself in the back room and continue working alone. Occasionally, Vogt's young friend from the neighborhood, Billy Watson, would tag along.

Vogt ate erratically scheduled meals at the Davis Brothers Restaurant, the nearest eatery to his shop. After a marathon session with an engine, he and Watson would scuttle across the street for coffee and eggs or a steak. At Davis Brothers, he met an attractive waitress named Betty, who had escaped an alcoholic husband in Kentucky and had brought her sickly daughter, June, to the ostensibly cleaner air of Georgia.

Vogt could be foulmouthed and bitter with other men, with his wife and kids. But he could act surprisingly cordial and polite with strangers, especially women, some of whom he could charm with his hungry eyes and simple tastes. "When Red looks at me, it's like he's taking my clothes off," a family friend once said. Apparently, the false teeth he wore—to replace those knocked out in his motorcycle-racing accident as a teen back in D.C.—shone quite a smile. Red shone that smile at Betty during his visits to her restaurant. He finally invited her on a few dates, often taking her on test-drives into the countryside in a Ford that he'd been working on. In time, she agreed to marry him.

It was an agreement she'd make and break four more times over the years. After first marrying in late 1944, they had already divorced and remarried once by the time they headed to Daytona for NASCAR's first official race in February of 1948.

Betty realized that to be with Red meant coming down to his level. Despite her dreams of a more typical postwar family life with friends and parties and vacations, she had to accept that Red had no real need for a wife. What he cared for most were engines and racing. If she wanted to be part of his life, she'd have to adopt the racing world, too. The more familiar Betty became with that world, the more she realized—as Red's first wife had—what a complicated relationship existed between Red and his childhood friend Bill France. They'd now known each other for decades and during that time had mostly remained friends, even if the friendship bore a slight sully of competitiveness and mistrust. Vogt's first wife had warned him—"*I don't trust that man*"—and though Vogt had initially dismissed them in anger, her words had stayed with him.

One night, a few weeks before driving to Florida for NASCAR's first race in early 1948, Betty found Red sitting at the dinner table, seething. Since he rarely came home to eat, she began putting together a family dinner. Red grumbled through the entire meal. He was pissed-off, he finally admitted, that France had created an association using his ideas, his acronym, but didn't recommend Red for one of the top positions. Instead, France had seemed almost to have conspired with Bill Tuthill, the promoter from New York—a goddamn *Yankee,* no less—who was now NASCAR's secretary. Maybe France felt he needed men around him with business smarts, not just car smarts. But Vogt felt that France, especially in his zeal to lure northern promoters into his southern sport, had stabbed him in the back. "He stayed mad the rest of his days," Vogt's daughter, June Wendt, said many years later. "And yet, he loved Bill France, too."

Despite his simmering anger at France, Vogt mostly kept his complaints to himself. Betty and June sometimes heard him loudly cussing out France over the phone, and a colleague of Vogt's remembers seeing him once punch France in the nose. But strangely, if Vogt ever overheard someone else disparaging France, he'd come to his defense, claiming that France was only doing what needed to be done for the survival of stock car racing.

"Well, you know who the hell would do any better?" he'd snarl at France's critics.

No matter how angry he might have been with France, it wasn't enough to make him quit racing. During the long drive south to Daytona in mid-February of 1948, Betty sat up front beside Red; daughter June sat in the back, looking at picture books and sleeping. Red demanded silence on such long, prerace drives and banned any chitchat or radio listening. Drive time was his thinking time, he explained, snapping at them if they tried to talk. June learned to read and spell in the backseat of the family Ford, picking out letters and words from road signs. Betty brought along self-help books on accounting, intent on teaching herself how to manage the books for Red's garage and to become, at least in some small way, a part of his NASCAR-centric world.

In the silence of that drive to Florida, Vogt had to wonder where he'd now fit in the sport he had named. He'd never been good with numbers or in business. He knew one thing: how to make a Ford V-8 surpass its own capabilities. As he reached the outskirts of Daytona, heading yet again to Big Bill's turf, his thoughts surely turned toward the race. If he was to be denied a role with NASCAR's hierarchy, there was only one place for him to exact any revenge. In this race and every other, he'd have to win—at any cost.

Raymond Parks *(above, on far right)* with three of his sixteen siblings and *(below, right)* with his father, Alfred, who became an alcoholic after Raymond's mother died. Raymond left home at age fourteen, shortly after the picture below was taken. *Courtesy of Raymond Parks*

Parks's moonshining colleagues, fellow "still hands," walking atop wooden "mash" boxes filled with stinky, fermenting corn kernels at a backwoods still. And hauling tin cans full of white lightning out to the delivery car. *Courtesy of Raymond Parks*

Revenue agents inspect a still during a bust.
Courtesy of Library of Congress

Parks graduated from backwoods stills to working for his bootlegger uncle at Hemphill Service Station, which Parks eventually bought. *Courtesy of Raymond Parks*

Below: Parks and his brother count coins collected from Parks's hundreds of slot machines, cigarette machines, jukeboxes, and pinball machines, part of his lucrative Novelty Machine Co. *Courtesy of Eddie Samples*

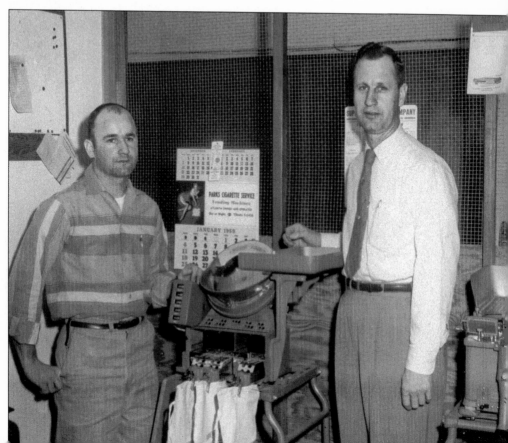

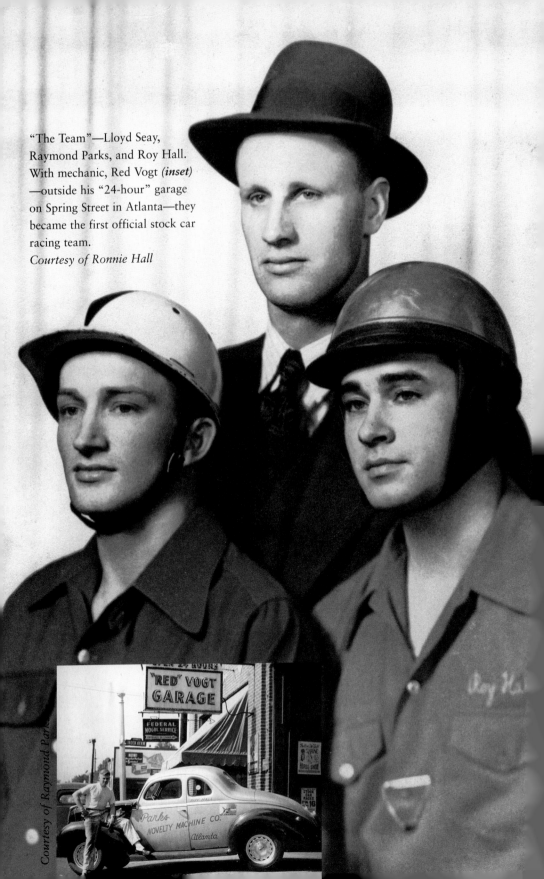

"The Team"—Lloyd Seay,
Raymond Parks, and Roy Hall.
With mechanic, Red Vogt *(inset)*
—outside his "24-hour" garage
on Spring Street in Atlanta—they
became the first official stock car
racing team.
Courtesy of Ronnie Hall

Raymond Parks and Lloyd Seay. *Courtesy of Raymond Parks*

Sportswriters said Lloyd Seay had an "angel face" while his cousin Roy Hall had a "reckless devil spurring him on." Hall's legend as a daredevil bootlegger would become the stuff of folk songs.

Below: Roy Hall with Parks. *Courtesy of Ronnie Hall*

Lloyd Seay carving through the rutted north turn at Daytona, 1941. *Courtesy of Eddie Samples*

Right: Roy Hall at his cousin's grave, beside the headstone Parks bought. Seay was buried just a few yards from the "Whiskey Trail," Highway 9, in downtown Dawsonville. *Courtesy of Ronnie Hall*

Below right: Sheriff Jim Davis carries the pistol that Seay's cousin, Woodrow Anderson, used to shoot Seay and his brother, Jim. *Below:* Lloyd Seay's corpse is being loaded. *Courtesy of Raymond Parks*

WAR

The reluctant soldier.
Courtesy of Raymond Parks

T-Sergeant Parks, in Paris, Texas.
Courtesy of Raymond Parks

Leaving the Cadillac behind, and headed
for the front. *Courtesy of Raymond Parks*

A ravaged German city.
Courtesy of Raymond Parks

Parks survived the wintry, deadly Battle of
the Bulge, and his overmatched 99th
Infantry Division pushed Hitler's Panzer
divisions out of Belgium and back into
Germany. He'd return to Atlanta to learn he
was lucky compared to Red Byron.

Courtesy of Eddie Samples

Courtesy of the Collier Collection

Bill France had been a fairly successful racer before World War II. But after the war, he devoted his energies to organizing the sport of stock car racing. He (and his family) did it all—selling tickets and concessions, timing qualification laps, assisting injured drivers on the track, and cleaning up trash after a race.

Opposite: Early post-war races were filled with inexperienced drivers and frequent wrecks. *Courtesy of Raymond Parks and Eddie Samples*

Roy Hall taking the north turn of the Beach-and-Road course (note sign, lower left: "Danger: Watch for Race Cars"), and *(center)* after the race. *Courtesy of Eddie Samples*

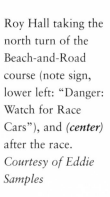

Below: Red Byron in the same turn, years later. *Courtesy of Raymond Parks*

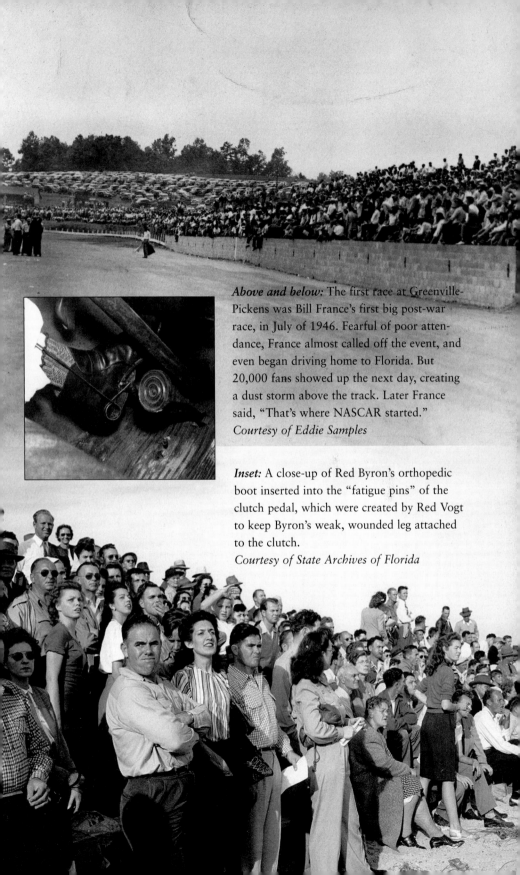

Above and below: The first race at Greenville-Pickens was Bill France's first big post-war race, in July of 1946. Fearful of poor attendance, France almost called off the event, and even began driving home to Florida. But 20,000 fans showed up the next day, creating a dust storm above the track. Later France said, "That's where NASCAR started."
Courtesy of Eddie Samples

Inset: A close-up of Red Byron's orthopedic boot inserted into the "fatigue pins" of the clutch pedal, which were created by Red Vogt to keep Byron's weak, wounded leg attached to the clutch.
Courtesy of State Archives of Florida

MONEY EQUALS SPEED
Red Vogt's skill with Ford V-8 whiskey cars translated perfectly to stock cars.

. . . with Red Byron. *Courtesy of Eddie Samples*

. . . with Byron and Bill France, after a Daytona Beach victory. *Courtesy of State Archives of Florida*

. . . with Fonty Flock. *Courtesy of Eddie Samples*

NASCAR IS BORN

Bill France called on the top forces of stock car racing to meet at Daytona in late 1947 to create a legitimate new organization to oversee stock cars. Two dozen men met for three days in mid-December in the Ebony Room bar above the Streamline Hotel. Among the attendees: Raymond Parks *(center right)*; Fonty Flock and Ed Samples, with women from a local modeling school, hired by Bill France to flirt with the attendees *(top)*; Red Byron, with Fonty *(center left)*; and chain-smoking Red Vogt *(bottom)*. *Courtesy of Raymond Parks*

SPEED EQUALS MONEY

Byron receives a trophy after a victory at Lakewood, in a race sponsored by Sam Nunis *(left)*; with runner-up Fonty Flock *(right)*. *Courtesy of Gordon Jones*

Byron taking his trophy at Jacksonville, Florida, beside runner-up, Fonty Flock, and his patron, Raymond Parks (in hat). *Courtesy of Raymond Parks*

Above: At Spartanburg—the winner's purse awarded to drivers often came in stacks of one-dollar bills, which were collected from ticket sales. *Courtesy of Raymond Parks*

Right: Taking the checkered flag in Atlanta. *Courtesy of Raymond Parks*

After a dusty win at Martinsville, Virginia. *Courtesy of International Motorsports Hall of Fame*

Inset: Byron and Flock with their trophies in front of Raymond Parks's shop. *Courtesy of Raymond Parks*

17 INJURED WHEN RACING CAR PLUNGES INTO THRONG

COLUMBUS, Ga., July 26.—This remarkable photo was made Sunday at the Columbus Speedway at the very instant when a racing stock car veered from the track and hurtled into the crowd. The car, driven by Red Byron, of front tire blew out. This shows spectators in frantic efforts to get out of the way as the speeding car tore through a guard fence. One man lost a leg in the crash and a 7-year-old boy suffered a fractured skull. The

A blowout on the next-to-last lap caused Byron to lose control and plow into the crowd. One man lost his leg and a young boy was killed. *Courtesy of Eddie Samples* *Inset:* The next day's headline.

Byron and Parks beside their 1949 Lincoln at the start of the 2,178-mile Mexican Road race, 1950. It would be one of their last races together. *Courtesy of Raymond Parks*

Other NASCAR participants in the Mexican Road race. *Courtesy of Georgia Auto Racing Hall of Fame*

Vogt wasn't alone in his love-hate feelings for France. While many drivers, mechanics, and car owners were glad to see a new organization that promised to bring consistency and bigger paychecks to their sport, others were wary of France's ambitions. And none of them wanted to be at the mercy of one man. Still, what choice did they have? No one else wanted to handle the business side of things. Many had left school by their teens and didn't have the skills for the job—math, for example, or even the ability to read and write. Many moonshiner/racers wanted simply to race, not shuffle paper. So they allowed France a free hand to create NASCAR however he saw fit.

In the weeks after NASCAR's late-1947 organizational meeting at the Ebony Room, France had ironed out all the financial and corporate details. To help file the incorporation papers, he hired a lawyer, Louis Ossinsky, who was a regular customer at his Daytona Beach gas station. Few drivers knew or even cared about this paperwork stage of NASCAR's creation. But men such as Vogt and Parks knew this much: everyone at the Ebony Room meeting who didn't insist on making the short list of NASCAR's top officers and stockholders was guilty of putting the entire sport in Bill France's hands.*

NASCAR began in a forty-dollar-a-month, second-floor office atop a creaky set of stairs above a defunct bank building, where France and his lawyer decided to create one hundred shares of stock and divide it among three stockholders. Because the corporation was private, the exact details of the stock split would never be fully revealed. But it was

---

*Some details of NASCAR's preincorporation would get lost to history, but a few relatives and friends of both Red Vogt and Raymond Parks would say years later that Vogt and Parks, along with South Carolina race promoter Joe Littlejohn, were initially supposed to have been listed on NASCAR's incorporation papers as either officers or, at least, shareholders. When NASCAR was incorporated in February of 1948, those names were not on any of the corporate documents.

generally understood from the start that Ossinsky received ten shares of NASCAR stock in exchange for his legal services, Tuthill received forty shares, and France took the rest, giving himself fifty shares and half ownership of the entire sport. (By this point, the NASCAR "board" that was elected back in December had become largely inert, and apparently no one questioned France's distribution of stock shares—at least not openly.)

In time, France would own *all* of NASCAR's shares, the start of his family's ironfisted, incredibly lucrative possession of American stock car racing. Tuthill would eventually transfer his shares to another promoter, who, after many disputes with France, would finally sell his shares to France. When Ossinsky died in 1971, France took over his shares, too. Today, NASCAR remains a France-owned business.

No one could have imagined in 1948 that NASCAR would grow to become the world's largest privately held sporting enterprise, nor that France would become a billionaire, ranking—as Henry Ford had— among America's wealthiest men. At the time, stock car racing was hardly a guaranteed moneymaker. But there were a few early suspicions that France was setting NASCAR up as his own personal cash machine.

Yet none of it would have happened without the quiet help of Raymond Parks.

One of the many untold nuggets of NASCAR's unchronicled origins is this: Bill France sometimes needed money to finance races and pay drivers, and he sometimes borrowed that money from Parks. France knew that failing to pay drivers could doom NASCAR, just as it had doomed other race organizations of the 1940s. He needed a backup source of cash in case the ticket sales of a particular race didn't bring in enough to cover the winner's purse. Neither Parks nor France acknowledged their arrangement, but there were signs. Parks once asked Gober Sosebee to deliver a locked briefcase to France at a Daytona race. Parks refused to say what was in the case, as did France, and Parks never publicly admitted to being France's private sugar daddy. But a few of Parks's relatives and friends were aware of the arrangement and have since confirmed its existence.

Parks, therefore, more than anyone else at the time, should have expected an official role within NASCAR or at least a token share of the stock. It was true that France always paid back the money borrowed from Parks and at the time of NASCAR's creation apparently didn't owe Parks a thing. It's also true that Parks did not sit in on the organizational meetings of 1947—he was too busy talking with the pretty charm school girls. Still, he felt cheated that he, along with Vogt, had been left off the list of stockholders. He mostly kept his feelings to himself, swore those who knew of his loans to France to secrecy, and remained France's friend, intent on taking the secret matter to the grave. But he once let slip his true feelings.

"We weren't businessmen, just car owners, drivers and mechanics that wanted to race," Parks said years later. "We had the know-how, but France had the lawyers."

Parks was a self-taught gentleman and fiercely loyal to friends. He had also been a businessman long enough to handle the sharp elbows of a roughly played game. Still, he wasn't entirely prepared for France to play rough with a friend, especially one who had bailed him out financially on more than a few occasions. "He used his lawyers to draw up legal papers giving him all rights to our organization," Parks said.

"That's how Bill France stole NASCAR from the [rest] of us that were there."

For Red Byron, NASCAR's corporate details were of little concern. Though he served as NASCAR's drivers' representative, his official position meant little. There weren't regular board meetings or votes. From the very start, it was a dictatorship, and that wasn't such a bad thing. The sport needed a strong leader, and Byron mostly trusted that France was the right man for the job. Like many drivers of the day, he viewed France as a thin-skinned bully but also a determined leader of a sport that he truly loved.

All Byron really cared about in 1948 was racing. Over the years, he'd convinced himself it was perfectly reasonable to spend all his time and money on races and cars. In the wake of his mother's death and its disruption of his Colorado childhood, he had spent his teens and twenties in peripatetic pursuit of races. Then came the gaping crevasse of world war, and then hospitals and recovery. Then more racing, and now finally some success on the track, although not much money. But now, he thought, maybe this year, with a solid new organization, I might make some cash. He was thirty-three, at least a decade older than most of his competitors, and probably too old and smart to still be pursuing the dream of becoming a champion race car driver. But he couldn't let it go.

Despite their modest income, Byron was settling into his year-old marriage to the stunning, Cherokee-blooded Nell, who was finding her husband to be more contemplative, even sophisticated, than the coarsely handsome, limping war vet she'd first spotted in Daytona Beach. Together, they were enjoying something like a family life, even though much of their time was spent on the road, traveling to races. In fact, at some point during their trip to or from Daytona Beach for the first official NASCAR race, in February of 1948, in the town where they met, Nell became pregnant.

Before that first race, they stopped at Byron's favorite Italian restaurant, on the beach at Daytona, where Red had gotten to know the owner and liked to sample red wines. Nell still wanted to live in Florida someday and surely reminded him of that during their stay at Daytona. But Red wasn't ready for that yet. He wasn't ready to slow down and ease into a safe and healthy retirement. He wanted to achieve something first. And maybe this new NASCAR organization could help legitimize his obsession.

NASCAR's first official race was scheduled for February 15, 1948, a 150-mile contest at Daytona Beach that France promised would be a "real corker."

As the day neared, even jaded veteran drivers got caught up in the excitement of the inaugural race, the new racing organization, and the start of a new season. With all the buildup and the promise of a better stock car–racing system, Tim Flock, competing for the first time at Daytona against his two older brothers, called it "one of the greatest days in stock car history." The only glitch was that Daytona's rich folk and town fathers, who had been accommodating for a decade, had recently decided to put down their collective foot.

France's racecourse had brought stock cars to Daytona in 1936, had hosted scores of races across a dozen years, and earned the city a reputation for speed that would last ever after. But postwar construction had turned the famous Beach-and-Road course's oceanside straightaway into a strip of cottages and motels. Those who'd built homes along the beach preferred seagulls to race cars in their backyards. Led by the Oceanfront Cottage Association, residents' gripes about the noise, wrecks, shards of car parts, spilled oil, and shredded tires on their beach grew louder, finally forcing France to shut down his racecourse in late 1947, a frustrating setback during NASCAR's infancy.

Because France leased the property for the track—from the city, county, and a few private landowners—he was at the mercy of those who owned the land. Luckily, Daytona city officials helped France find property south of town, away from the beachfront cottages, where he scrambled to build a new 2.2-mile oval in time for NASCAR's first big race. France worried that abandoning the old course would damage Daytona's "reputation as the hub of stock car racing." When he finally unveiled the new course in early 1948, just in time, he boasted that the new track was even better than the old one.

"The turns of the new course are something to see," France gushed to the press. "There won't be any dull moments when the boys come roaring through that south turn."

Racers who'd been driving the old Beach-and-Road course for a decade wondered how the new course would compare. Many of them arrived early to scope out the logistics of the historic event. During pre-race practice and qualifying laps, Byron and a few other veterans criticized the south turn. The entrance into the sandy curve off paved

Highway A1A was very tight, with little margin for error. If the timing wasn't perfect, a driver might sail off the crest of the steep bank. Racers were also concerned that the sand of both the north and south turns was too soft. On the old course, that sand had been tamped down by thousands of race cars over the years. The mushy, unpacked sand of this new racetrack was worrisome.

Fans began pouring into Daytona Beach during the days before the race. On the morning of February 15, France opened the gates and began collecting tickets from a streaming crowd of fourteen thousand—one of the largest crowds ever at Daytona. They paid $2.50 apiece and, in the words of one sportswriter, "were thicker than the seeds on rye bread." Fans ran to pick out their spots, most of them choosing the borders of the north and south turns, where the best action would likely occur. There hadn't been enough time to build elaborate new grandstands or safety barriers at the new track. So, on the south turn, spectators stood behind a fence consisting of rope strung between wooden posts. On the north turn, they clustered tightly against the course, creating a narrow chute of bodies, just feet from where the cars would soon barrel past.

As he had done a decade earlier, France had planted signs along the dunes reading "Careful—Rattlesnakes" to prevent gate crashers. Some sneaky spectators just wandered down the beach with fishing poles as props and managed to blend into the crowd. A few of the bolder ones landed on the beach in airplanes and strutted right up to the racetrack.

A record number of drivers entered the historic race, and at 3:30 in the afternoon, fifty-six growling machines—mostly Fords but also a few Buicks and Chevrolets—lined up at the start of a sixty-eight-lap race that would total just shy of 150 miles.

Back in 1941, the first stock car race of the season had been a Bill France–sponsored contest at Daytona that he called the Rayson Memorial, named for a British Royal Air Force pilot killed at the start of World War II. France wanted the Rayson race to become the annual opener of every stock car season. He had a trophy maker create a tall "Rayson

Memorial" loving cup and announced before the 1941 race that the driver who won the event three times during his career would take home the silver trophy.

In 1941, twenty-year-old Roy Hall had won the inaugural Rayson in style. After the war, Red Byron won the next two, in 1946 and 1947. France felt the Rayson Memorial was the perfect event to kick off NASCAR's first season, and the 1948 season, and to inaugurate his new track.

As he sat eight rows back from the front, Byron knew he had a chance to win his third Rayson and end the day with the silver trophy in his hands. But his first two Rayson victories had been on the *old* course, and Byron was concerned about getting a good feel for the tricks and timing of the new track. He also thought about the monkey on his back. He had failed in his last two attempts at Daytona, due to frustrating engine problems. Both times, Bob Flock had led from start to finish.

This time, Flock was a bit handicapped. Bob had still not entirely recovered from his back-breaking accident in late 1947. He had lost weight and appeared frail and disturbingly thin, his fragile body locked inside a constricting back brace that was supposed to prevent him from rebreaking his barely healed vertebrae. Surely his doctors had told him to quit racing, probably for good, if he wanted to live. And yet, looking as if he should be in a hospital bed and nowhere near a racetrack, Flock gingerly slid behind the wheel of Raymond Parks's number 14 Ford, the same V-8 that Roy Hall had raced to victory back in the 1941 Rayson Memorial.

Fonty and Tim Flock were also in the lineup, as were Ed Samples, Gober Sosebee, and a dozen other moonshiner/racers, including a wild and handsome whiskey tripper from Virginia named Curtis Turner, in his first Daytona Beach race.

Byron at least felt good about his number 22 car. After the two engine blowups the previous year, Vogt had decided to build Byron a new V-8 motor for 1948. He'd spent all of January in the back room of his neat-as-a-library shop, working day and night assembling handmade parts into an engine that finally purred like a thousand angry cats.

This time, Vogt wasn't seeking just speed, but stamina. He wanted everything about the engine to be spotless, smooth, and perfect, so that Byron would never again lose a race due to engine problems. Vogt wouldn't let anyone else touch that engine, which is why he kept himself locked in his secret room. As in a hospital OR, the tools were all laid out in perfect rows, the workbench and floors spotless, the overhead lighting just so.

It had gnawed at Vogt that Fonty Flock won the 1947 NCSCC championship driving other mechanics' cars. Vogt was now desperate to recapture something—prestige, glory, or at least respect. Winning NASCAR's first official race, being the mechanic for that historic first victory, might also ease the sting of insult he felt France had inflicted by not including him as an official NASCAR partner or shareholder. It wouldn't bring national fame or fortune, but those within his fraternity would know it had been *his* engine, *his* car. And that meant a lot to Vogt. Because without a fast car, he was just a strange, bulky man with a crew cut, white uniform, and dirty nails; a twice-divorced, chain-smoking, obsessive-compulsive insomniac.

To be safe, Vogt and Parks decided to bring three cars to Daytona. In keeping with the practice he'd begun a year earlier at Langhorne, Parks figured the third car might come in handy if one of the other two wrecked or experienced engine problems. So, in addition to Byron's Ford and Bob Flock's Ford, they towed to Daytona an extra Vogt-tuned '39 Ford, which had briefly been Byron's car the previous year.

At the last minute, a racer who said his name was "J. F. Fricks" decided to race the backup car, numbered "22-A." Byron would be racing against his old car, which had the uneasy feel of racing against an old friend.

With so many cars—and a track that was a mile shorter than the old Daytona track—France was concerned about a massive pileup on the first lap. Rather than start all fifty-six cars at once, he decided to "stagger" the start. Each row of four cars took off at one-second intervals. Local driver (and NASCAR treasurer) Marshall Teague—a happy-go-lucky war veteran who, like Byron, had been a flight engineer on bombers—had qualified with the fastest time and took off with the first group. Byron started eight rows back, with Fonty and Bob Flock nearby.

Teague took the early lead, with Fonty slowly working his way into second. By the midpoint of the race, Fonty finally managed to pass Teague and by lap fifty—with eighteen laps to go—pulled half a mile ahead of Teague and the rest. But as Flock was tearing down the backstretch at one hundred miles an hour, his front wheel spindle snapped, and the wheel twisted off the car. The front wheel hub dug into the pavement and acted as a fulcrum, like a pole vaulter's pole that whipped Flock's car into the air and off the course at full speed. Just as in his horrendous Daytona crash seven years earlier, he roared off the track and into the brush, bounced off an embankment, and commenced tumbling, end over end. The car flipped three times, missed slamming into a telephone pole by mere inches, and finally came to a stop in a clump of palmettos. This time, the car fortunately landed on its wheels, instead of the roof. When the tumbling came to a halt, Flock examined his extremities, shook his head, checked gingerly for broken bones or bloody gashes, and found that he was, remarkably, intact. His race, however, was over.

Brother Bob's race seemed to have ended, too. Despite the painful back brace, which was chafing against his skin, Bob was positioned solidly in fourth place after fifty miles. But when the engine began smoking, he had no choice but to pull into the pits. He and Vogt stood helplessly beside the wounded number 14 car, about to call it quits for the day, when another race car suddenly pulled off the track and roared up beside them. It was the yellow number 22-A Ford coupe, Parks's backup car. The driver jumped out and ran toward Flock—it was Parks himself, who had entered the race under the fictitious name of J. F. Fricks, in his second-ever stock car race.

"Get in," Parks yelled, just as he had to Byron a year earlier at Langhorne.

Because of his back brace, Flock needed help getting into the yellow coupe, but he quickly rejoined the chase behind Byron and the leader, Marshall Teague.

And J. F. Fricks melted into the crowd.

Meanwhile, a number of drivers found themselves unable to handle the tricky south turn. A driver from Indianapolis missed the sharp left off A1A's pavement and sailed over the banked turn to land with a crunch twelve feet below the crest. A few laps later, another driver made the same mistake and landed smack on top of the first car. By the end of the race, five cars would be mashed together in a lifeless heap of smoking metal carcasses at the bottom of the gulley beside the south turn.

With Fonty Flock out of the race, Teague regained the lead, but Byron soon pulled up behind Teague and was driving right on his tail. Byron was about to pass him and take the lead for the first time of the day when another driver nudged up beside him. The fenders of the two cars became locked together, and when Byron tried to pull free, part of his fender ripped off and began clanging against the car, threatening to shred his tire. Furious, Byron pulled into the pits to have Vogt reattach the fender—with a coat hanger. It took fifteen more miles for Byron to again catch the leader. For the next few laps, he kept looking for a slot to Teague's left or right through which to pass.

Byron began to notice that Teague was consistently cutting his turns hard to the inside. He would learn afterward that Teague's brakes had begun to fail, forcing him to use his emergency brake to enter the turns more tightly and slowly. Teague would hug the inside arc of each turn so his momentum didn't carry him too wide and possibly off the track into hundreds of spectators, or off the south turn into the wreckage of cars beside it. After realizing how consistently Teague was cutting to the inside of the turns, Byron decided to make his move—to the *outside*—with sixteen laps remaining.

With his new engine accelerating to nearly 120 miles an hour down the beach, Byron seemed as if he was about to slam right into Teague's rear end. His plan was to slice quickly to Teague's right just as Teague began to hug to the left. As they reached the north turn, Byron made his move and was about to pull beside Teague, but they both were suddenly confronted by the slower car of a driver named Mickey Rhodes. Teague eased off the gas and cut sharply to the left, to the inside of Rhodes. Byron kept his pedal to the floor and swung hard to Rhodes's right, roaring widely and wildly around the outer edge of the turn, his spinning tires spewing rooster tails of sand into the crowd. As fans shielded their faces from the sting of flying grit, Byron churned and bounced through the thick ruts, sliding both sideways and forward at the same time and hoping that the intense strain of the high-speed turn wouldn't snap off his right front wheel.

Losing a right front wheel in a turn was a common and very dangerous affliction in the early days of stock car racing, as Fonty Flock had experienced a few laps earlier. But Byron's wheel and its reinforced lug nuts held fast, and he passed both Teague and Rhodes on the outside, hitting the blacktop of A1A thirty yards ahead of them both.

For the final fifteen laps, Byron blocked Teague's attempts to recapture the lead. On the final straightaway, he pulled far ahead of Teague, again pushing Vogt's new engine to well over a hundred miles an hour, and took the checkered flag of NASCAR's first race. Byron built up such an impressive lead on the final lap that Teague crossed the finish line a full fifteen seconds behind. His Ford immediately ran out of gas and died.

Bob Flock, after pulling out with engine troubles on the twenty-fifth lap and then taking the wheel of the Parks/Fricks backup Ford, had amazingly caught up to the leaders. Across the final laps, he drove like mad to catch Byron, passing car after car, his barely healed back screaming in protest. It was an impressive performance, but he just couldn't match Byron's pace and settled for third place, a half mile behind Teague. When he exited his car at the finish, Flock's shirt was soaked with blood—the metal clasps of his back brace had rubbed his flesh raw.

Byron was exhausted, too, and his leg throbbed as Red Vogt helped him out of his Ford. Looking much older than his years, Byron limped toward a chair and collapsed into it, where he grudgingly spoke with reporters who'd come to chronicle NASCAR's first race. "This was the hardest race I ever won at Daytona Beach," Byron said. "I had to work all the way. Teague was stiff competition. I was lucky to catch him."

With typical humility, Byron thanked Vogt for the new engine he'd recently built for him. "I've always said the car is 90 percent of winning," he said. "The driver and luck take care of the other 10 percent." Byron then reminded the reporter that every major race at Daytona, seven in a row dating back to the prewar victories of Lloyd Seay and Roy Hall, had been won by a Vogt engine in a Parks car.

"You can't win a horse race without a good horse, and you can't win a stock car race without a good car. What the trainer is to the horse, a mechanic is to the car, and I've got the best mech in the racing business," Byron told the press. "Red Vogt is the reason I win. He puts those motors together like a watch. When other mechanics learn his secret gear ratio, there won't be any stragglers in a race. They'll all travel."

When reporters asked Vogt about his new motor, he shooed them away. He'd made his point on the racetrack and didn't need to brag. "What good is a motor if you don't have a jockey like Byron to bring it home for you?" was all Vogt would say.

Bill France chummed with the press, boasting of the thrilling finish and the strong attendance by one of the largest crowds in Daytona Beach history. "What really made me happy was that the race was a good show for the fans," France said.

Raymond Parks, standing quietly off to the side of victory lane, was elated. No reporters came to speak to him. None recognized him as the driver "J. F. Fricks." (In future years, friends would jokingly call him "Mr. Fricks.") Parks preferred shadow to spotlight.

It was his seventh Daytona victory in a row, and his fifth since World War II, a feat that would never be matched by another team owner. His racing fever was soaring. He was still shaky from the nerve-racking pace of driving in NASCAR's first official race. But he was proud of his team and beamed at Byron as if Byron were his own son. (Parks's *real* son, Ray Jr., was now a teen, but the two were largely estranged.) In the same way he had fathered Lloyd Seay and Roy Hall, Parks had nurtured Byron, both financially and emotionally.

Parks knew that winning both the coveted Rayson trophy and the first NASCAR race meant a lot to Byron. If NASCAR survived, Byron's name would be featured in racing's history books. "I know this one was special to him," Parks said.

Red Byron's name was later etched for the third time into the Rayson Memorial loving cup, beneath the name Roy Hall. But instead of taking it back to Atlanta with him, Byron decided to give the trophy to his patron, Parks.

Sportswriters once again adopted Byron as their darling: "Lord Byron . . . the wounded war veteran with a racing heart as big as a steering wheel."

NASCAR's inaugural race had not been a perfect launch. Despite France's promise of a "real corker," drivers had been vexed by the soft, unpacked sand of the two turns. Byron was among many racers who complained that the north turn "got cut up pretty bad." In fact, only twelve of the original fifty-six starters completed the race—a god-awful rate of 21 percent. Every single finisher was driving a 1939 Ford V-8.

Still, with its numerous lead changes, acrobatic wrecks, and dramatic and emotional finish, the race had offered everything a stock car fan could have hoped for. No one had died or been seriously injured. Bill France was a happy man. Red Byron was happy. Raymond Parks was happy. And NASCAR's first season had only just begun.

Soon, the Flock boys would be the happy ones. In fact, the first half of NASCAR's first season should have been renamed the "Flock Family Circus."

The family patriarch, Lee Preston Flock, had been a bicycle racer, an amateur tightrope walker, and the first man in Fort Payne, Alabama, to own a car, which he drove as a taxicab. He named one of his eight children after that car—Reo—and each of the eight kids seemed to absorb more than a one-eighth share of their father's adventurous spirit. The old man died after a mole on his forehead turned cancerous, leaving the family to struggle in his absence. Daughter Reo became a professional daredevil, performing motorcycle stunts, jumping out of airplanes, and walking on their wings. Eldest son Carl earned a world speedboat-racing record and then became a wealthy bootlegger in Atlanta, bringing three of his brothers into the moonshining business with him. Driving Ford V-8s at high speeds on North Georgia dirt roads was the perfect apprenticeship for Bob, Fonty, and Tim, who in 1948 threatened to become NASCAR's first dynasty. Even sister Ethel, named for the gasoline "ethyl" and who drove her dad's taxi after his death, had recently married a bootlegging race car owner and was thinking of joining her three brothers on the stock car–racing circuit. Despite Red Byron's impressive victory in NASCAR's premier, the first few months of NASCAR's existence were dominated by Flocks.

Fonty, Bob, or Tim placed first or second in twenty of NASCAR's first twenty-five races. Byron was always right there with them, finishing among the top three in ten races, including four first-place finishes in a row through April and May.

In no time, the battle for the 1948 season narrowed into a Fonty Flock versus Red Byron contest, an apparent repeat of 1947. In two out of every three races, Fonty or Red—or *both*—finished in the top three. Bill France couldn't have prayed for a better rivalry.

Fonty once ran out of gas on the final lap, allowing Byron to win by a hundred yards. At another race, Byron also won by a football field, but a NASCAR scoring official overturned his victory and declared that Fonty had actually lapped Byron. A few weeks later, Fonty was two hundred yards from victory when another racer's wheel snapped off and smashed into his car, causing a mash-up with three others. Byron swerved sharply around the wreckage and sped past Fonty to take the checkered flag. At another race, Fonty was leading with two laps to go until his foot slipped off the gas and Byron jumped ahead. But Fonty caught him on the final straightaway and won by a few feet. So it went through the first half of 1948. At one point, the "two Atlanta crackers," as one newspaper called them, were tied for the NASCAR points lead. Before race day, other drivers would bet on which of the two would win. Fonty was usually the 2–1 favorite.

Fonty seemed the fans' favorite, too. He was the more natural driver of the two, and clearly the more southern. He waved at fans and drawled a legitimate drawl. Fonty had what one writer called "a bouncing rubber ball of a personality." He dressed loudly and spoke fluently and even occasionally earned extra money selling vacuum cleaners door-to-door. Byron the nonsoutherner, on the other hand, was grave and aloof, stoic and cerebral—"a little older and smarter than the rest of us," Ed Samples once said.

Fans came in droves to catch a glimpse of the Flock-Byron "dog-fight," as the papers began calling it. NASCAR events regularly attracted more than ten thousand fans, lured to remote tracks in the rural Carolinas and Georgia. Sportswriters couldn't have asked for a better story and seemed to love both opponents—Byron was "the red-headed Huck Finn of racing," and Fonty was "the clown prince of racing." Writers would have loved to see them scuffle off the track, too, but had to settle for only subtle signs of the competitive rivalry. "Although there has been no outright hostility between these heavy footed chauffeurs, the air cools noticeably when they meet each other," one writer said.

Byron strung together a few victories to take the points lead away from Fonty. And yet, despite leading NASCAR, Byron still had one eye on Indianapolis.

In 1947, his attentions had been divided between stock cars and AAA/Indy cars, and it had cost him the stock car championship. By missing just a few of the year's stock car races to compete in occasional open-wheel races, he ended up a few points shy of the stock car championship. For 1948, he planned to focus almost entirely on the new NASCAR circuit. Still, Indy had been "his greatest ambition," his wife, Nell, once said.

He had to give it one more shot. So he and Vogt rolled his number 22 Ford stock car into Vogt's garage bay, removed the V-8 engine, and installed it back in the Indy car Byron had raced the previous year. Byron and Nell then towed the car out to Indianapolis. It would be the only vehicle out of nearly seventy hopefuls with a Ford V-8 inside.

Byron called Bill France and told him that he'd miss a few stock car races during his attempt to qualify at Indy. Keeping France in the loop, and NASCAR on his mind, wasn't just a courtesy. To earn points and stay competitive against Flock, Byron had to compete in as many NASCAR races as possible this year. Every day he was away from NASCAR gave Fonty a chance to advance. Plus, he didn't want to offend Big Bill and felt it was better that France hear directly from him about the attempt at Indianapolis instead of reading about it in the papers.

Byron's first qualifying attempt at Indy was scheduled for the Friday before the race, which was typically held on the Sunday before Memorial Day but for 1948 was bumped to Monday. Byron hoped for a perfect alignment of events: to qualify at Indy on Friday, fly to North Carolina for two stock car races Saturday and Sunday, then fly back to race at Indy on Monday.* But the engine was running rough on Friday, and he was unable to drive. On Saturday morning, the engine was still rough, and Byron was faced with a choice. His last chance to qualify at Indy would now be Sunday, which meant he'd miss the two stock car events and maybe lose ground in the NASCAR points standings.

Having already decided to focus on NASCAR and not AAA, Byron reluctantly said good-bye to his Indy car, got on a plane, and flew to Greensboro, North Carolina, where he borrowed another racer's Dodge and raced in a forty-lap event that Saturday night, finishing sixth. Byron then drove over to the North Wilkesboro track for a Sunday-afternoon NASCAR race and finished second. Flock experienced engine problems in both races, so Byron managed to remain in a virtual tie with Flock.

Still, Byron was heart-sunk at failing to qualify at Indy. Again.

After flying back to Indianapolis to pick up Nell and his car, and then driving home to Atlanta, Byron returned to NASCAR and its south-

---

*This was the first attempt at a Memorial Day weekend Indy-NASCAR crossover. From the late 1990s through 2005, a handful of NASCAR drivers would race in the Indianapolis 500, then immediately fly to North Carolina for that afternoon's NASCAR event, the Coca-Cola 500.

ern tracks and the starting lineups that still, as they had for a decade, consisted mostly of Ford V-8s.

Reluctantly, he was coming to terms with the stark truth of his career: he was a dirt-track driver, a Ford-driving stock car racer. If he was something of an outsider among southern stock car drivers, he was even more of an outsider in the elite world of open-wheel racing, whose stars were from New York, Rhode Island, Massachusetts, and Connecticut. AAA drivers liked and respected him, admired the courage it took for a cripple to race on their tracks. But many considered him a good-hearted sideshow and not a dangerous threat. In short, Red Byron was a nice guy, with a good soul.

Which were not exactly common traits among stock car racers.

The 1948 NASCAR season remained as purely southern as its moonshining origins. Its top drivers and mechanics hailed mostly from Atlanta. Over the years, the most notable rivalries—Lloyd Seay versus Roy Hall, Roy Hall versus the Flock brothers, and now Red Byron versus Fonty Flock—had all been Atlanta-versus-Atlanta battles. Still, Byron remained the only one in that group who wasn't *really* southern. He didn't grow up on a farm, didn't learn to drive by delivering the family whiskey, and hadn't seen the inside of a jail cell. He was the rare NASCAR driver without a criminal record.

And yet, he had found his place on the NASCAR circuit. Prior to his Indy attempt in May of 1948, he had won four in a row with NASCAR. Going into a July 25 event at Georgia's new Columbus Speedway, he was in a dead heat with Fonty. Byron even got a little sassy, telling a reporter it was "time to let Fonty eat a little dust."

Fonty, who had recently switched to a new car owner, responded with a promise to arrive at Columbus in a 1939 Ford coupe with a newly built 297-cubic-inch engine tuned just for that event and for Byron (and Byron's smaller 274-cubic-inch engine).

But France's sport was about to be dealt a harsh blow.

Twice. On the same day.

Columbus Speedway was a dusty, half-mile track in central Georgia, across the river from the Alabama town where Roy Hall once hid out from the law. The track—cut into a clump of trees on the outskirts of the town of Midland—was encircled by a ring of five-foot chicken wire fencing, strung between wooden posts, behind which fans began gathering early on a Sunday morning to secure front-row spots for another battle between stock car racing's increasingly contentious top stars, Red Byron and Fonty Flock.

The first-ever race at Columbus had been held a month earlier, on June 20, 1948. Local dignitaries came, along with a few top army officers from nearby Fort Benning. But the race was mostly notable because it was won by Bob Flock at almost the precise moment that brother Fonty was taking the checkered flag at the Birmingham Fairgrounds in Alabama and brother Tim was earning a victory at Greensboro, North Carolina. Three Flocks, three states, and three victories in the same afternoon.

On July 25, NASCAR actually scheduled two races for the same day: the Columbus race and another at Greensboro. France chose to work the North Carolina race, even though his top racers, Flock and Byron, would be racing at Columbus. France's competitor, Sam Nunis, was sponsoring a race at Chattanooga, Tennessee (for the NSCRA, which had decided not to join with NASCAR but instead continued promoting its own events). France hated that Nunis was operating anywhere near one of his own races and wanted to be at Greensboro to make sure drivers who'd promised to attend actually showed up—instead of sneaking off to Nunis's Chattanooga event.

Still, though he chose not to be there on July 25, Columbus Speedway symbolized everything Bill France hoped NASCAR would become. It was a fast, competitive track, which racers loved. It was also the only show in town and drew thousands of fans on an otherwise lazy Sunday afternoon. Prerace photographs of the day captured the devotion to the South's popular new sport. Boyfriends and girlfriends came hand in hand. Parents brought their children. With little space in the small grandstands, many early birds drove their Fords and Chevys right up beside the chicken wire and sat or stood on the hood. Many had attended church that morning and came in their best clothes—cotton dresses, white shirts and ties, straw hats. Others put their daily farm chores aside and came in dirt-smeared overalls. All in all, the scene was like a publicity poster for Bill France's dreams.

As race time approached, Byron seemed calm, confident, and almost serene. He wore a wide-brimmed, safari-style leather hat and dark aviator glasses to counter the insistent Georgia sun. In pit road, he made last-minute checks on his car, testing the "shaker" screen bolted in front of the radiator to keep the red dirt out of his engine—"the most powerful 274-cubic-inch motor in the world today," he boasted. Byron limped among the other cars, nodding at drivers and stopping to chat with a few. It seems he chose not to stop and talk with Fonty Flock, who had arrived that day with his new car.

In recent weeks, tensions between the two front-runners had sizzled. Fonty had nudged Byron from behind in a race the previous week at North Wilkesboro, causing them both to bow out with flat tires. That and Byron's recent "eat a little dust" comment had stoked fans' curiosity about the duel between the two Atlanta crackers.

Byron had always considered himself a smart, fast driver, but ultimately a cautious one. He had an intellectual's regard for the often-overlooked finesse of a race and frowned at recklessness. He preferred to avoid the bumping and bashing that invariably occurred during the early laps. Mostly, he felt it was wiser to use your head, to think and plot and scheme. To him, races were more like high-speed chess matches than all-out sprints. Byron leaned his head into such strategic questions as: When to pit and change tires? All four tires or just two? To pit at all? Did he have enough gas to finish? When to hang back? When to strike? Fifty years later, resolving such queries would earn NASCAR crew chiefs substantial paychecks, often in six figures. In 1948, it was up to the drivers to confront questions of strategy on their own.

Byron was experienced enough to know that some races called for him to simply gun it from the start, or to shove a competitor out of the way, to just go for it. Then again, sometimes a driver's cautiousness or aggressiveness didn't matter. The most freakish things could happen at 150 feet per second.

On July 25 at Columbus, Byron was able to accelerate quickly into the lead, but the half-mile track wasn't ideal for his muscley V-8. The straightaways were too short for him to gain any serious distance on Flock and the others. Byron punched the gas on the front stretch but immediately slowed down to take the next turn and then punched again on the backstretch. And at each turn, Fonty was on his tail, sliding left and right, looking for a gap to pass through. Byron's narrow lead continued for thirty-eight of the forty laps, setting up what seemed surely to be one of the most exciting finishes of the year.

With two laps to go, spectators began inching closer to the flimsy wire fence that separated them from the action. Charles Jenkins had come with his wife and her friend, and they stood between the third and fourth turns. As the crowd pushed itself against the fence, he told his wife he "felt uneasy" and talked her into backing away from the fence to watch the last lap from the bed of a friend's pickup truck.

Which gave him a perfect view of the terrible next moments.

On the next-to-last lap, with less than a mile until victory, Byron approached the third turn and saw in his rearview mirror the car of a young, aggressive Atlanta racer named Billy Carden, who was edging left in an effort to cut to Byron's inside. Fonty followed closely behind Carden. To block Carden's maneuver, Byron quickly nudged left, his car dropping down sharply into the arc between turns three and four. But the sudden turn put too much pressure on his right front tire, which had become weakened by the high-speed miles beneath an intense midsummer sun.

The tire exploded loudly, and the mess of shredded rubber and the exposed wheel hub caught the red dirt and instantly, violently pulled Byron's car to the right. Byron pulled the wheel hard to the left and stood on the brake pedal, a desperate attempt to wrestle the Ford back onto the track and away from the unprotected crowd. When the brakes seemed futile, he decided to punch the gas, while still turning left, trying to spin his Ford's back end away from the now panic-stricken crowd.

But it was all too late, and Byron now saw the bug-eyed faces of a few hundred fans who had nowhere to run. With the chicken wire fence in front, a row of cars behind, and so many bodies packed so tightly together, the fans were trapped. People leaped, shoved, covered their faces, or just froze. They either helped the person beside them or trampled over them. Byron's car climbed the bank and then raked along the fence, his car cutting through chicken wire as if it were a spider web. The Ford's nose plowed through the front edge of the crowd. Bodies bounced off Byron's hood and off one another. The car's shaker screen cut deep into the flesh of legs. Thick fence posts snapped like twigs.

James Brannon had worked as a sales manager at the local dairy company. The family had been looking forward to the race for weeks and arrived early to secure a spot up close. Brannon's seven-year-old son, Roy, sat on the hood of the family Ford, a few feet from the fence, loving every minute of the noisy race. But as Byron's Ford cut an awful swath through the crowd, Roy was looking in the opposite direction, away from the track. His father and mother were standing beside the car and must have seen Byron's car plowing in their direction but were unable to reach their son. Byron's speeding Ford slammed into a wooden post, the last potential obstruction between him and the child.

The long, thick post just bent like a willow and, in the words of one fan, "head-popped" young Roy, who was knocked violently to the ground.

When Byron's car finally came to a stop, scores of bodies lay scattered among the wreckage, beneath a cloud of thick, red dust. Byron, at first unable to get out of the car without assistance, sat there, uninjured but scared to death. *What have I done?* The race came to a halt as drivers and mechanics from pit road all sprinted to the scene of the carnage, frantically tending to the injured, some of them shrieking and terrified.

James Brannon and his wife cradled the body of their unconscious son. Instead of waiting for an ambulance, they put Roy into the backseat of the family car and sped off. As ambulances arrived at the track, Byron seemed discomposed and in shock. He finally managed to get himself out of the car and began limping back toward the pits, dragging his bad leg through the dirt. Charlie Jenkins—who'd moved his wife back from the fence at the last moment—said Byron seemed heartbroken: "helpless . . . a sad sight." Jenkins hadn't realized until that moment the extent of Byron's war injury and became fixated on Byron's lame left foot, which went "flopping" away from the devastation.

Among the first of the victims to reach City Hospital was A. R. Bartram, a forty-six-year-old from nearby Phenix City, Alabama, who was admitted with a badly mangled right leg. The doctors determined they could not save the leg, which they amputated below the knee. A twenty-four-year-old woman was admitted with a broken pelvis; three people had broken legs; and a dozen others were treated for battlefield-like injuries—broken ribs; deep cuts on the arms, legs, and faces; head injuries; bruised and scraped body parts; and shock. Injured worst of all was Roy Brannon. His skull had been pushed in, and he had slipped into a coma. His parents kept a vigil at his bedside, praying for their child to awaken. The next day, a newspaper headline announced Bill France's worst nightmare: "17 Injured When Racing Car Plunges into Throng."

A ghastly photo accompanied the headline. An AP photographer had remarkably captured the precise moment of Byron's car making contact with the frantic, scattering crowd. Roy Brannon, in black-and-white-checked overalls, seems almost to be looking up at the camera, naïvely unaware of the angry machine plowing toward him.

Remarkably, NASCAR's first tragedy was just the start of Bill France's bad day.

At that same moment, four hundred miles to the east, France was officiating his race at Greensboro, North Carolina. Near the end of that race, rookie driver Bill "Slick" Davis rolled his car and was ejected onto the track. Tim Flock and three other drivers slammed into Davis's car, which plowed into its driver's body. Davis died that night of serious head injuries. The next afternoon, seven-year-old Roy Brannon also died. And just like that, NASCAR's first season was marred by two terrible deaths.

France rightly worried that two deaths on the same day—one of them a spectator, and just a child—might tarnish NASCAR right from the start, ruining the league before it had even truly begun. He quickly dispatched emissaries to Columbus to perform damage control, explaining to news writers and locals that the accident had been "strictly unavoidable," that Byron had *not* been driving recklessly or out of control but that the flat tire simply made Byron's Ford "unmanageable."

Byron, meanwhile, felt enormous guilt for his role in the Brannons' loss and the injuries to the others. He would carry that burden the rest of his days.

And Raymond Parks worried deeply for his sensitive driver. Could he sustain the championship race against Fonty? Could he return to a racetrack at all?

I could feel the road some twenty inches beneath me,
unfurling and flying and hissing at incredible speeds. . . .
When I closed my eyes all I could see was the road unwinding
into me. . . . There was no escaping it.
—JACK KEROUAC, *On the Road*

14

An "ambience" of death

NASCAR and its fans tried to shrug off the dark tragedies.

Just a fluke, they told themselves. No one's fault, really. One of the dangers that inevitably accompany a risky spectator sport. But for Byron and some of the other more thoughtful racers, this wasn't so easy, even though the death of racing fans was hardly a new phenomenon, nor an ephemeral one.

Fans had been getting slaughtered by high-speed racing machines ever since those machines had been invented. As early as 1911, a race car had plunged into a race crowd at Syracuse, New York, killing eleven. Over the years, Indianapolis had claimed numerous lives of drivers and fans, including the boy killed in his backyard by a flying tire. But World War II seemed to create a before-and-after demarcation in motorsports. Before the war, death was somehow understandable. Racing was still new and untested, and the death of drivers and fans was to be, somehow, tolerated.

But after the war, death on the racetrack—thanks to safety measures for both drivers and fans—was a bit less frequent and, when it did occur, felt much more unseemly. Racing was becoming a family sport, and death and children didn't mix. The whiff of Roy Brannon's death would hang over NASCAR's entire first season.

For racers—even sensitive ones such as Byron—death was not a sufficient disincentive. They certainly hated to see fans or friends get killed, especially by *their* cars. But they always came back to the track, either by rationalizing or by ignoring the question *Why?* Why would a grown man get back behind the wheel of a murder weapon? Knowing that his health was already at risk—*Why?* Knowing that the last place a crippled war veteran should be is inside a race car with the door strapped shut—*Why?*

Similar questions had been asked of auto racers since Oldfield's day. Over time, drivers and nondrivers grappled for a reasonable explanation, none of them entirely satisfactory. The shortest and maybe best answer was: drivers just can't help it. They're compelled to do the one thing they know they shouldn't. Addiction is an oversimplification, and playing with fire is an insufficient cliché. It's more like dousing yourself and a few others around you with gasoline and then playing with matches.

Buddy Shuman, the Carolina moonshiner/racer, once mangled his hand in a wreck. When it became infected, doctors suggested amputating it. Just as Byron had responded to doctors' plans to amputate his leg, Shuman said, *No way.* Shuman was a racer and would rather be maimed for life than handicapped behind the wheel.

"I'll die with two hands rather than live with one," Shuman told the doctor. Such logic made perfect sense to other racers.

It had been no surprise to Byron, then, when Fonty Flock, after his near-death Daytona Beach crash in 1941, had returned to racing. It had been no surprise when Bob Flock, six months after breaking his back in 1947, returned—in a back brace, no less—to the rutted raceways that could now snap his barely healed spine. Byron knew that Indy racers often drove the cars of their recently departed friends. The mechanics would just wash out the bloodstains, repaint the black burn marks, and pop in a new engine—no reason to scrap a good race car for sentimental reasons.

After Roy Brannon's death, Byron simply kept on racing, far and wide, to prove to himself he still could. As far south as Florida, as far north as Pennsylvania, New Jersey, New York, even Rhode Island, in NASCAR and non-NASCAR races alike, Byron would disappear for days at a time, towing Raymond Parks's car behind. After three or four days with no word, Parks and Vogt would begin to worry they'd never see Byron again. Then he'd show up one morning, looking haggard and exhausted, filthy and grouchy. One morning, he pulled up to Vogt's garage, reached into the backseat, and pulled out a paper grocery bag. He handed it over to Vogt—full of cash.

"Hold on to this for me," he told Vogt, and then went home and collapsed.

Byron was racing harder than ever. And he was eager to get back into the NASCAR fight. In August of 1948, he drove to Daytona for the 150-mile Buck Mathis Memorial, named for a popular driver killed a year earlier, in a race Byron had won.

Bill France was still nervous about the death of a fan—and not just any fan, but a small boy—six months into his new organization's life. His response was to tout NASCAR's safety measures. Prior to the August 150-miler at Daytona, he announced that "extra barricades will be erected between the turns at the track and the spectators for the protection of all concerned." It didn't help that, thanks to Red Vogt and others, the cars were getting faster by the day. Byron's Ford V-8 had recently been clocked at 121 miles an hour.

Parks had been worried about Byron's ability to return competitively to NASCAR after Roy Brannon's death. The late-August Daytona race was the first Parks had attended since the incident, but Byron quickly eased Parks's fears. It seemed that Byron had resolved the accident in his mind. Now, it was either race hard or don't race at all.

So when the 150-miler began, Byron did his Roy Hall imitation, jetting into the lead and staying there. Fonty moved into second place, but Byron loomed a full lap ahead, a seemingly insurmountable two miles, which he soon stretched to four. "Fans marveled at the power and speed Byron had stored under the hood," a newswriter said.

With just four laps to go, Byron bounced through the choppy north turn but wasn't willing to ease up, not even in the turns where fans stood in harm's way. The thick, grabby sand plucked and clawed at Byron's Ford, cloying and insistent, just as the red dirt had been at Columbus. This time, he managed to power through the angry red ruts, but not without injury to his car—a stone punctured a hole in his oil pan, and the black liquid quickly gurgled out. Before he'd even reached the south end of the paved backstretch, his V-8 was gasping and then finally died, ten miles short of victory.

A full two and a half minutes later, Fonty roared past and won the race.

Flock's win put him just ahead of Byron in NASCAR's points race. In victory lane, he complained about the beat-up and difficult turns but sympathized with Byron. "I'm glad I won," he said. "But it was a tough break for Byron."

Byron's performance at Daytona was a message to the others that he was not going to let the tragedy at Columbus slow him down. Fonty's response was to switch teams (for the third time since 1947) and hire a new mechanic, named Joe Wolfe, from Reading, Pennsylvania. The tactic paid off, and Flock raced strongly through September and October. Byron struck back, winning two close races that put him ahead of Flock in the points race. He had amassed nearly three thousand points across the 1948 season but now led Flock by just twenty-five points. By late October, with the season winding down, NASCAR's standings stood: Red Byron, Fonty Flock, Tim Flock, Curtis Turner, Buddy Shuman.

In a remarkable stroke of luck for Bill France, it appeared NASCAR's first championship would be determined on the final race of its first season. This time, France certainly wouldn't declare anyone the champ before the year's last race, as he had in 1947. The final NASCAR race of 1948 was now scheduled for November 7—at Columbus, Georgia, the same track where Byron's car had plowed into the crowd and killed.

A boosterish sportswriter wrote before the race that fatalities such as Roy Brannon's were "very rare" and driver fatalities "almost unheard of." He urged race fans to "get all the thrills and relax and know that the performers have only a minimum of danger," which, of course, was hardly the truth.

The writer failed to mention that a few weeks earlier, Indy racing star Ted Horn had been tossed from his car at a dirt track in Illinois, run over by a peer, and killed. A few days later, Atlanta racer Charles Marks was killed at a fairgrounds track in South Carolina. His car flipped, and Marks was trying to crawl from the wreckage when the other racers, who couldn't see him in the thick cloud of red dust, ran him over. A few months before that, during Red Byron's qualifying attempt at Indy, a veteran named Ralph Hepburn, who had been competing at Indy since 1925, died in a crash during practice. That same day, at a stock car track in Jefferson, Georgia, a rookie named Swayne Pritchett, who'd been inching up in NASCAR's standings and was ranked sixth at the time, took the checkered flag but then inexplicably drove past victory lane and straight into the railing of the first turn at full speed. He was thrown from his car, and his body was run over by the second- and third-place finishers. Pritchett was killed instantly.

So to say that death was "very rare" and that racing carried a "minimum of danger" was hardly an accurate portrayal of the 1940s world of auto racing. Which is why Bill France had reason to be nervous about his final race of the year, where his first NASCAR champion would be determined. If only it weren't the track of Roy Brannon's death.

Two thousand fans arrived early for that November 7 race at Columbus, but AAA and Sam Nunis almost trashed France's season-finale dream race. Besides Byron and Flock, only four other drivers showed up at France's race. France had flown up from Daytona that morning expecting to have a full lineup of seventeen cars, those whose drivers had submitted entry forms the previous week. France was furious to learn that many of those drivers, knowing they weren't in the running for a NASCAR championship, chose instead to race that day at Atlanta's Lakewood Speedway, where Nunis was hosting a AAA race with a larger winner's purse. Scheduling a race on the same day as a competitor was a common and often effective tactic among rival promoters.

Then France's bad day got worse. During a ten-lap warm-up race, Fonty blew his engine, which meant Byron would be racing in the thirty-lap feature race—and for the NASCAR championship—against a field of just four lesser racers.

France decided to call off the race. He grabbed a microphone and lied to the crowd, telling them there must have been a "misunderstanding" about the schedule by the other drivers. He asked fans if they wanted to see the race or postpone it, hoping they'd agree to wait a week. But a majority of fans raised their hands and voted to go ahead with the day's race. France ignored the vote and said he had decided to reschedule the race for the following Sunday and to allow fans to return for free, earning a loud round of "boos."

On the new race day, November 14, twenty drivers arrived, to France's great relief. Byron qualified for the pole position, but Fonty—who had repaired his car during the previous week—lost a wheel during his qualifying race and started seven cars back.

Byron started on the pole and for the first half of the race easily held the lead. Flock started far back in the field but skillfully picked and passed his way through them all. By the eighteenth lap, Flock was right on Byron's tail, and when Byron hesitated in a turn, Flock took advantage and squeezed through a narrow gap and took the lead.

Nell had told Red to be careful, but to win. How could he explain to her that it was often impossible to do both? The memory of Roy Brannon would never leave him, but Byron knew he had to get young Roy out of his head, to race his race, do his job, and win. Isn't that what the fans came for? They were once again pushed against the chicken wire fence, right at the edge of the track, as if the little boy's death had never happened.

Six laps later, Byron found the opening he needed. On the very same turn where his tire had exploded, where everything had changed, he accelerated, and his car leaned up against its two right wheels, sliding and churning, surfing and slicing a crooked line through the red ruts. He weaseled safely past Flock and back into the lead.

Byron stayed there for the last six laps, pushing as hard as possible on every turn of every lap. He couldn't shake Fonty, who drove so close to Byron's rear end, it looked as if the two cars were attached. But Byron found the perfect high-speed groove and thwarted Fonty's every attempt to pass. He finished a scant fifteen feet ahead of Flock.

Afterward, when France tallied up his numbers, he announced that Byron had finished the season thirty-two points ahead of Fonty Flock and would be named NASCAR's first champion. Despite the great cost, the loss of life, he had won a historic championship. And yet, the heavy price he paid would linger. Friends remarked years later that Byron "sort of lost heart after that." Said another, "I truly think the death of that little boy never left him." Charles Jenkins, who was a spectator at the track the day Roy Brannon was killed, said the track forever after carried the "ambience" of death.

Six weeks later, on December 29, Byron's own son was born. They named him Robert Jr. In the days before the birth, Nell had been telling Red it was maybe time to slow down. He'd soon be a father. She knew racing was still his passion, but she reminded him of his less-than-perfect health and their less-than-healthy finances.

"Maybe think about a less spectacular profession," she said, reminding him of the promise he'd made when they first met: to build her a home in Florida.

With an infant son, Red knew Nell would no longer be able to sit by his side as they drove throughout the Southeast in search of races. He'd now have to travel alone. And she was right about his health. Although he rarely talked about it, Byron had come to accept pain as sort of an evil sidekick, the relentless shadow of his professional life. He never went anywhere without his bottle of aspirin, which he popped like candy. Some days were better, and he'd manage to be chatty and upbeat. On his darker days, deep lines would furrow into his face, and he'd appear drawn, gloomy, and prematurely ancient. He'd be in no mood for small talk on those days, which usually occurred after a lengthy race, whose bumps and ruts would terrorize the small shard of shrapnel still lodged deep in his thigh. Even with the help of Red Vogt's specialized clutch pedal, the aftermath of a race involved days of pronounced limping and a sour disposition.

And Byron had to wonder, as did his wife: Would the leg hold out for one more season? Could his body? He would soon turn thirty-four. He had high blood pressure and a weak heart. Army doctors had warned him to go easy on his body, to find a desk job. Instead, he'd pursued one of the most punishing careers a crippled war vet could choose. And now he was facing postwar upstarts ten years younger, such as Tim Flock and Curtis Turner, both twenty-four.

Byron still received a monthly disability check from the army. It was small recompense for his permanent injury, but it helped offset his otherwise shabby income level. He had surely read the recent story in the *Saturday Evening Post* in which Fonty bragged of making between ten thousand and fifteen thousand dollars a year from stock car racing. Even if Fonty was exaggerating, Byron made nowhere near that much. Despite his many victories and his championship season, he still was sharing income from his death-defying stunts with Parks. He was beginning to feel the downside of that arrangement.

When Robert Jr. was born, a few days after Christmas, Byron decided to heed his wife's advice. He met with Parks and told him it was time for them to part ways. He was going to open his own mechanic shop in downtown Atlanta. And instead of racing Parks's number 22 Ford, he would cut back on his racing schedule and begin driving his own race car, also a Ford. Instead of using Vogt, he would be his own mechanic. He wouldn't have to share his winnings with anyone. The number he planned to paint on the door was number 1.

Byron's Speed Shop opened on Hemphill Avenue, not far from Red Vogt's place. Byron had grown beyond his status as a racing oddity into an unlikely southern folk hero. In the sports headlines, he'd become "the Old Master," and Byron counted on his name recognition to lure customers to his shop.

Byron's other stab at domestic peacemaking (and moneymaking) was to visit Atlanta's new, quarter-mile, red-clay racetrack for a chat with the manager. The Peach Bowl was scheduled to open in north Atlanta in 1949, and manager Ray Shoemaker planned to host weekly midget racers, smaller versions of the open-wheel Indy cars. Midgets were easier for a one-legged racer to drive, requiring fewer pumps of the clutch pedal. Byron offered to race once a week at the Peach Bowl, which would draw fans and make some money for Shoemaker. In exchange, Byron would get to do something he loved, but closer to home.

That was the plan, anyway. To stay close to home. Build up a customer base. Join the family for dinner. Race at the Peach Bowl and a handful of other nearby tracks.

But, thanks to Bill France, Byron's new, lower-key lifestyle would not last.

For a decade, stock car racing had been sustained by a pure, very southern us-versus-them attitude. "Us" was the drivers, mechanics, owners, promoters, and fans. "Us" was poor-as-red-dirt farmers, grammar school dropouts, men who knew a mule from an ass. If "us" hadn't made moonshine, "us" had sure as hell tasted it. "Them" was anyone trying to get in the way: revenue agents, Yankees, the AAA, the police. In 1949, "them" was also bankers, lawyers, and more Yankees. That's because 1949 would introduce the previously inconceivable notion that there was real money to be made in stock cars.

Bill France had earned a decent profit during 1948, NASCAR's first season. But 1949 became the year Bill France defected to truly become one of *them*.

France still worked hard on the nuts and bolts of promoting his sport. He still scurried around on race day, selling everything from tickets to hot dogs. But France was also becoming more sophisticated and savvy by the day. After learning to fly, he had recently bought himself a new single-engine airplane to fly to and from races. He wisely remained good friends with Bernie Kahn, the sportswriter for the *Daytona Beach News-Journal*. And as 1949 began, France seemed almost to be gloating about it all.

"Stock car racing has boomed beyond anyone's wildest dreams," he said. "And I feel that we are in for another big year."

Indeed, more people would attend stock car races in 1949 than ever. That meant NASCAR would start collecting fatter sacks of cash, and France would take steps toward his first million. But the drivers would take no such steps, and the fight over stock car racing's growing profits would turn 1949 into a season of chaos, with rifts between France and his racers leading to threats, lawsuits, ultimatums, and other nastiness.

In mid-January of 1949, Byron said good-bye to his wife and infant son and drove to Daytona Beach for an awards ceremony, at which Bill France distributed bonus checks for the 1948 season. NASCAR had taken in sixty-four thousand dollars from the previous year's ticket sales, and, as promised, France had put aside five thousand dollars of that for his end-of-year "point fund."

The top-twenty drivers of 1948, along with their mechanics and sponsors, attended the banquet, held at Daytona's Country Club, their oil-stained fingers clutching cigarettes and cocktail glasses, their ill-fitting suits obvious declarations that they were not club members. After dinner, France quieted the crowd with a tap on his water glass.

Bill Tuthill, NASCAR's secretary and France's right-hand man, took over as emcee and explained, somewhat defensively, that the point fund was no fairy tale. "OK, you guys, this is the point fund you've heard about," he said, holding aloft a thick stack of bank checks, each with a stock car racer's name on it. "I don't care if it takes four hours, you're going to get your money right here in front of everybody."

In recent weeks, Tuthill had become increasingly wary of the whispers among drivers about all that NASCAR money sitting in France's bank account. Tuthill told France the drivers knew how easy it'd be for them to "take some money off the top." After all, promoters had been stealing from the drivers for years. Tuthill warned France that if they didn't "keep everything totally above board," a suspicious driver might sue them and tie up their funds. So they had decided to write the checks weeks before the banquet, to legally and symbolically assure drivers that the money was coming their way.

Tuthill then called the sport's first champ to the podium, and Byron rose from his seat and hobbled forward, dragging his bad leg amid the cheers of his colleagues. Cannonball Baker, NASCAR's commissioner, handed Byron a shiny, three-foot-tall bronze trophy with a miniature '39 Ford on top and "champion" etched into it.

It was a significant moment in motorsports history. After years of being tossed about with abandon, the term *national champion* actually, finally meant something. Without a truly national organization—such as Major League Baseball, formed in 1920 to oversee the American and National leagues—and without a defining year-end contest such as the World Series or football's Super Bowl, the naming of stock car champs had for ten years been a bit of a joke. The trophy declaring Byron the champion of 1948 marked the first time that stock car racing crowned a legitimate single national champ.

France took the microphone, praised Byron's victorious season, and handed him a check for $1,250. Byron was gracious and uttered a few words of thanks, then limped back to his table. At a time when the average annual income in America was less than $10,000, the bonus would have been a welcome dose of cash for the Byron clan—if two-thirds of it didn't belong to Raymond Parks, leaving Byron with just $416.

France and Tuthill then began handing out the rest of the checks, starting with $600 to Fonty for second place and $400 to his brother Tim, who'd finished third.

Afterward, the numbers confounded some of the drivers, at least those who could do math. The top-five finishers of 1948 together won thirty-six out of NASCAR's fifty-two races. Those five men shared $2,700, which meant each of their victories was worth a bonus of just $75. The other fifteen top finishers each received checks of $100 or less. France had intended for the year-end bonuses to inspire drivers' loyalty, to keep them committed to NASCAR and prevent them from wandering off into non-NASCAR events. France would soon learn that it took more than $75 per victory to buy drivers' loyalty.

The question of NASCAR's profitability was one that Raymond Parks was pondering more and more. About the time that Red Byron was receiving his bonus check and trophy, a short news article appeared in the *Atlanta Journal*, praising Parks, the "Atlanta sportsman," as one of the city's finest businessmen and community leaders.

"We congratulate Mr. Parks on his record and sincerely hope that his career will be as colorful and completely successful in the years ahead as it has been in the past," the writer puffed. It was unclear whether "colorful" was a veiled reference to the origins of Parks's success.

In the late 1940s, moonshine still gushed in riverlike quantities from Dawsonville into the homes and nip joints of Atlanta, and beyond. Though liquor in America had been legalized for sixteen years, homemade liquor was still a no-no. Uncle Sam wanted his cut, and the makers of untaxed whiskey were still aggressively pursued by revenue agents throughout the South. In fact, Georgia led the nation with the most moonshining violations in 1948, followed closely by North Carolina, Alabama, and South Carolina.

For Parks, that world was now solidly part of his past, a memory up on a shelf. It had been years since Parks had brokered in untaxed whiskey. He'd quit running numbers, too. The illegal lottery business, the so-called bug, was also now a relic among the many unspoken stories in his rise to prominence.

But the world of crime had served him very well. Except for his three months in jail at age fourteen, and his nine months in prison, he had been lucky. He had snubbed and taunted the law for more than a decade, had earned hundreds of thousands of dollars, and could have paid a much higher price than twelve months behind bars. In fact, learning to read, write, and do math during his 1936–1937 prison term had actually helped him become a legitimate businessman. Parks called it "going to college."

His "Novelty Company" now earned its substantial profits by supplying equipment to Atlanta's *legal* bars and taverns. Parks rented out scores of coin-operated Wurlitzer and Seeburg phonographs—which in the 1930s had earned the name *jukebox*—along with hundreds of cigarette machines, pinball machines, and pool tables to taverns, VFW halls, and private clubs. He and his brother would drive around collecting bags filled with millions of coins, which they'd sort in machines at his office. He also owned at least a half dozen liquor stores. Even if he'd had to pay off some politicians and put the stores in the names of friends or family members, he was now a mostly legal and respected beneficiary of the South's taste for liquor.

At age thirty-five, he attended civic meetings and knew Mayor Hartsfield, the police chief, and various judges by name. He had purchased many acres of land in northwest Atlanta, around Georgia Tech University. He'd even begun giving away some of his fortune, donating large sums to north Atlanta churches and other charities.

Parks had grown, financially and socially, far beyond the crass world of stock cars. Yet there he was, each weekend drawn to some dusty track, in the stands among rowdy, drunken fans. At these raunchy affairs, Raymond Parks—the civic leader, noble citizen, and philanthropist—mingled among the likes of Buddy Shuman, the moonshiner with the mangled hand who once served on a chain gang after getting shot by police.

It would have been easier to rationalize the strange, magnetic pull that stock cars had on him if he had been making money off his hobby. But the truth was, he was still only breaking even on his investment—if that. He had learned enough about business to know when to dump money-losing enterprises. He'd rid himself without emotion of his Polar Bar ice cream shops and a few other business experiments that began losing money.

Racing was different. On paper, his stock car investment was a financial failure. But he knew that Red Vogt, Red Byron, and Bob Flock were all counting on him. They had become members of his dysfunctional family.* And soon, Parks would be rejoined at those tracks by the most infamous and dysfunctional southern bootlegger of all.

Cousin Roy Hall was scheduled to be released from prison in late 1949.

Parks was used to dealing with men incapable of living normal lives. He'd returned from war to learn that Roy Hall, in his absence, had wandered across to the dark side, crossing the line between bootlegger and full-fledged criminal. Before that, he'd watched his intelligent, widowed father drink himself silly.

Parks also knew how an addiction to stock cars could damage a man's life. He watched Vogt grapple with relationships, money, and life in general and witnessed Red Byron's struggles with his demon leg and the ghost of Roy Brannon. Parks knew that Vogt was partly estranged from his own kids, and that Byron was trying not to fall into the same trap. Parks himself was now on his fourth wife. His only son, now a teenager, lived with his first wife. He'd see Ray Jr. now and then, but his son didn't care much for racing. It was understandable, then, for Parks to wholeheartedly believe that Vogt and Byron might not make it without his patronage. They were all three alike, incapable of releasing the grip that racing had somehow gotten on their very souls.

The simple truth was that the three men needed one another. Byron

---

*Parks had recently lost a member of that family. On a cold winter night, Byron's mechanic, Fat Russell, had pulled his car into a garage beneath Parks's office, presumably to keep warm. He closed the door and left the engine running. Russell, a hard-core drinker, must have passed out. They found him the next morning.

needed a wealthy patron for his car and a great mechanic for speed. Vogt needed someone willing to pay extra for his expertise and a driver who could handle the finished product. And Parks needed the best driver and mechanic in the business, men who'd help him win races, maybe earn back some of his investment, or at least witness glory.

Because racing had become more than a fever.

Those weekend trips to Langhorne, Daytona, and Wilkesboro, the trophies now filling his office shelves, the newspaper clippings, and the postrace parties with groupies and beauty queens . . . it was strange and new, sassy and risky. Maybe Parks missed his old bootlegging days, the car chases with revenue agents, and couldn't quite bring himself to shun his daredevil side. Maybe stock cars satisfied some deep, southern instinct. Or maybe, as one southern writer put it, Parks "found God in cars, or if not the true God, one so satisfying, so powerful and awe-inspiring that the distinction is too fine to matter."

Whatever it was, Parks felt powerless to deny his passion. "What else was I gonna do?" he once pondered aloud. "Stay home and listen to radio?"

Byron must have asked himself the same question. The answer, of course, was no. Despite his best intentions—stay home, race less, start a business—Byron realized that racing was undeniably his life's devotion as well.

Racetracks were his church. And victory was his salvation.

Byron met with Parks again just before the 1949 racing season began. Together, they negotiated his return to the Parks-Vogt team, and Parks agreed to share a larger cut of Byron's winnings. The three seemed relieved to be reunited and optimistic about a new season of worship at the altar of speed.

None of them foresaw Bill France's plan to make their church entirely his own.

We are the first nation in the history of the world to
go to the poorhouse in an automobile.
— WILL ROGERS

15

The first race, a bootlegger, and a disqualification

NASCAR had compiled an incredibly busy schedule for 1949, with nearly four hundred races. Entrepreneurs were opening new racetracks all over the Southeast and in turn begging France to schedule a NASCAR race there. Local promoters who wanted to schedule their own race were also seeking out France, requesting that he "sanction" their event. NASCAR expanded into new markets every day.

At established racetracks such as North Wilkesboro in North Carolina, Martinsville in Virginia, and Spartanburg in South Carolina, ten thousand to twenty thousand fans came from far and wide to pay two dollars or more apiece to get through the gates. Fans began arriving a day or two before a race, sleeping in their cars or tents, staking out prime viewing spots beside the track. One writer observed that as race day approached, the parking lot outside the tracks resembled a Civil War encampment, and word began to spread that a NASCAR race was more than just a race. It was a party, a circus, a jamboree, all in one.

With five to ten such races scheduled each week, NASCAR was beginning to take in more money than Bill France could ever have imagined.

NASCAR's expenses were growing, too. France found an insurance agency that agreed to cover drivers' hospital bills. The cost to NASCAR was one hundred dollars per race, and France had to promise the insurance company that he'd host at least three hundred races, guaranteeing the insurance company a total payment of thirty thousand dollars. Also, since NASCAR didn't own any racetracks, essentially borrowing other tracks, France had to share profits with local promoters and track owners. He had to stash some of his profits in the escrow account for the year-end points fund, and he had to make sure he always had enough to cover the winners' purses, somewhere around two thousand dollars per race.

Still, even after all the expenses, NASCAR was collecting many thousands of dollars per race and tens of thousands each week overall. Early in the 1949 season, NASCAR's own treasurer, the Daytona Beach racer Marshall Teague—who had won the 1949 season opener at Daytona—raised what seemed like a logical question:

Where's all the money going?

When NASCAR had been officially incorporated in February of 1948, Teague's "treasurer" title became inconsequential. All fiduciary duties were essentially taken over by the private corporation's three officers: France, Tuthill, and lawyer Louis Ossinsky. Still, Teague was no dummy, and as the 1949 season began to unwind, he noticed that NASCAR's share of the money collected at the ticket gates, even after expenses, seemed significantly more than the amount being offered to drivers.

Teague was soon joined by two moonshiners—Dawsonville's Ed Samples and Charlotte's Buddy Shuman—who began to openly suggest that NASCAR should end its practice of paying a "guarantee." The guarantee was a predetermined winners' purse announced prior to a race, which the top finishers shared. Instead of that flat rate, Teague and the others wanted to compete for a 40 percent share of total ticket sales. That's how AAA and other race-sanctioning organizations usually paid their racers. Some slick race promoters went so far as to promise that every racer would receive twenty dollars just for racing, which at least helped pay for their gas.

In March of 1949, Shuman went public with his complaints, explaining to a North Carolina newsman that NASCAR's "guarantee" at Midland Speedway, northeast of Charlotte, was just two thousand dollars. But at a recent non-NASCAR event at Midland, drivers were paid 40 percent of ticket sales, which amounted to a winners' purse of twenty-seven hundred dollars. Shuman said drivers were "very much satisfied" with that 40 percent approach, adding that he was spreading the word to other racers that non-NASCAR races paid better.

When France refused to eliminate the guarantee, other racers started questioning his use of money collected at the gate. They demanded that France start paying them more. Some followed Shuman's lead and defected to non-NASCAR races. An editorial in a racing magazine defended Shuman and the others, saying that winners' purses comprised of a 40 percent share of ticket sales "looks like a pretty good solution."

France tried to explain that stock car racing was supposed to be a hobby, not a career. Back at the Ebony Room meeting, he'd told the other cofounders that NASCAR should be for "race-minded boys" who work during the week but on the weekends want to "show their stuff and maybe win something, and still not make it a full-time job."

But finally, France quit rationalizing and simply put his foot down. "It's too much," France said of the drivers' 40 percent demands. "We'll be in too-tight a position."

France felt the drivers were being ungrateful and disloyal. He decided, if I can't persuade them to be loyal, I'll force them. Shuman soon received a telegram from France that said, "Drivers who fail to race exclusively for NASCAR will be barred . . . for a period of one year." Other rabble-rousing drivers received similar telegrams.

In protest, Shuman immediately pulled out of a scheduled NASCAR race at North Wilkesboro and signed up for a race at nearby High Point, sponsored by a rival race-sanctioning body, the NSCRA, which was offering a 40 percent payout. (NSCRA—the National Stock Car Racing Association—had been created in Atlanta in 1947 and sponsored a number of races in 1948, when Shuman was named its champion.) Teague also withdrew from NASCAR in protest. The anti-NASCAR protests escalated as Curtis Turner and Bob Flock pulled out to begin following the NSCRA circuit.

That's when things got really dirty. France claimed that three racers—Samples, Shuman, and Speedy Thompson—had scattered thumbtacks on a track before a NASCAR race. France accused the trio, along with Teague and another racer, of "conduct detrimental to the best interests of [NASCAR]." And, as he'd threatened, he banned all five men from NASCAR for a year.

It seemed an excessive step, and one that might backfire on France. But he knew that racers were mostly loyal to one thing: money. He could always win them back with money. France realized that, to earn drivers' patronage at NASCAR races, each individual race had to have an enticing winner's purse, one bigger than AAA's or the NSCRA's. If he could offer bigger payouts, the drivers would come home to NASCAR. And stay there.

France would soon announce an unprecedented five thousand dollar purse. And the five banned racers and other protesters would soon be crawling back to France, begging for another chance with NASCAR. In the meantime, only Red Byron had managed to carefully steer a safe line through the dissention and flak, racing in all circuits, including occasional non-NASCAR races, while somehow avoiding any direct confrontation with Bill France.

But Byron's ability to avoid France's iron fist would not last.

While Byron applauded other drivers' attempts to wrest more money from France—especially Teague, a fellow World War II bomber veteran who had become a friend—Byron was in no position to openly defy France. It was too risky financially.

So he kept his head down as he worked on customers' cars at his Speed Shop during the week, traveling to races each weekend. He had decided to give up on a third attempt at Indianapolis, to devote more time to high-paying events on the NASCAR and NSCRA circuits, and to only dabble in occasional open-wheel events.

Most of the stock car events he joined were, as they had been for years, so-called "modified" races. That meant Byron raced his 1939 Ford against other factory-built "stock" cars that had been modified with all the necessary power-enhancing alterations to help them perform on the corduroy of a dirt track. In such events, nine out of ten entries were prewar Fords. For the 1949 season, Bill France had also introduced NASCAR's experimental new "roadster" division. Some racing fans loved the combination of open-wheel racer and modified racing coupe, although others thought the jalopies looked as if they'd been cobbled together with spare junkyard parts.

Red Vogt chopped up an old Ford coupe and turned it into a roadster, allowing Byron to also compete in NASCAR's roadster division. But it soon became clear that roadsters weren't nearly as popular among fans as the modifieds. Drivers also preferred modified events, and for the first few months of 1949, Byron and Fonty Flock took turns in victory lane in that division. They were once again in a back-and-forth contest for the lead in the points race, followed closely by Curtis Turner and Tim Flock.

Then, midway through the '49 season, Bill France abruptly changed all the rules.

In early 1949, France's rival racing organization, the NSCRA, received a revitalizing jolt from a stocky, aggressive, twenty-two-year-old used-car salesman and part-time race promoter named Bruton Smith, who agreed to take over the floundering organization. Smith was a savvy businessman who began to partner with AAA promoters—most notably France's other rival, Sam Nunis—to sponsor southern stock car races in Tennessee, Georgia, and North Carolina.

At the start of 1949, Smith announced plans for a "strictly stock" race that would only be open to new cars, those built *after* World War II. When France heard about it, he immediately realized he needed to organize a strictly stock event of his own.

Strictly stock races had initially been discussed at the 1947 Ebony Room meeting, when NASCAR's creators voted to establish three tiers of racing: the modifieds, the roadsters, and strictly stock. The strictly stock division never got off the ground in 1948 because there weren't enough new cars coming out of the nation's auto factories. Production was now back to prewar levels, so there were plenty of new car models to choose from. It had already become obvious to France that fans didn't care much for NASCAR's roadsters. And he began to wonder how long fans would continue to pay to see beat-up, decade-old Fords in the modified races. His search for a slick new idea was already leading him toward the creation of a racing series for newer cars.

With Bruton Smith heading in the same direction, France stepped up his efforts. To outdo Smith and lure drivers away from NSCRA, France announced that the winner of *his* strictly stock race would take home two thousand dollars, part of a total purse worth an unprecedented five thousand dollars.

France's attempt to upstage Smith triggered a rivalry that would last half a century. And NASCAR's first strictly stock race would go down as a major turning point in motorsports history, despite a plane crash, state police threats, and a lawsuit.

It had been fifty years since America's first auto races, and nearly fifty years since Henry Ford's prototype had chuck-chucked down Detroit's cobblestones, announcing what that long-ago Detroit newsman had called "civilization's newest voice."

But in the prosperous aftermath of war, with auto factories up and running, there were plenty of loud new voices, shiny new sedans on the road, such as Buick, Cadillac, Chevy, Oldsmobile, Pontiac, Hudson, Chrysler, Lincoln, and Dodge. Race car drivers and whiskey drivers were finding that Ford's postwar V-8s weren't as strong as its prewar engines and that the V-8s of Chevy, Oldsmobile, and Hudson were worthy upstarts.

For Bill France, this was exactly the fan-friendly trend he'd been waiting for.

France wanted the strictly stock division's cars to be identical to those same Chevys and Oldsmobiles that Mr. and Mrs. America drove to the Piggly Wiggly grocery store. A month before the first strictly stock race, France told a sportswriter, "The nice thing about this game is that you don't need a $30,000 special to get started. You just tighten up some old heap, pay your $10 entry fee and start risking your neck."

Simplifying or eliminating some of the technical intricacies of the sport—the superchargers, quadruple carburetors, and handmade camshafts—was key to France's marketing strategy and part of his attempt to appeal to the weekend warrior. The implication was that NASCAR was for everyone, and the drivers are just like you.

However, strictly stock races would also dramatically change the role of the mechanic, whose status would be reduced to that of a mere tune-up man.

For Red Vogt, this was a troubling shift. He'd be a wizard without his wand.

France's new game plan would launch, somewhat poetically, on a former pasture tamed into a racetrack by a couple of moonshiners.

Charlotte Speedway had been built the previous summer and had hosted a half dozen modified stock car races through 1948 and the first half of 1949. In fact, Red Byron had won four times on the track, most recently in May. The three-quarter-mile track sat off Wilkinson Boulevard, west of Charlotte. A farmer named C. C. Allison had leased that portion of his farm to two enterprising young neighbors, Pat and Harvey Charles.

The Charles brothers were among Charlotte's better-known bootleggers, but also pretty handy with tools and heavy machinery. They bulldozed an oval into Allison's field, with banked turns on either end. They built a fence around the oval, wooden grandstands, and a ticket booth. But the Charles boys wouldn't be around to see NASCAR's first strictly stock race. A conviction on bootlegging charges prevented that. Before reporting to the authorities, the Charleses turned the track back over to farmer Allison, who had no idea what to expect from his first big race, scheduled for Sunday, June 19, 1949.

France limited the race to thirty-three cars, as they did at Indianapolis. Drivers were invited to qualify in time-trial heats, which began on Wednesday, June 14. That afternoon, Red Byron posted the fastest qualifying time—a hair under forty seconds for one lap around the three-quarter-mile track. Fan attendance at non-NASCAR races had been declining in recent weeks, which meant that those 40 percent purses some drivers had touted were now worth far less than the purses at most NASCAR races. France's scheme to steal some of the thunder from rival Bruton Smith's NSCRA group seemed finally to be working, and the buzz about the upcoming race on C. C. Allison's farm had grown. As the race date approached, the five drivers who were banned from NASCAR back in March—for "conduct detrimental to the best interests of [NASCAR]"—had been lured into penitence by his five thousand–dollar purse and had asked Bill France if they could rejoin the circuit.

France instructed the men to go to the Selwyn Hotel, where they were called one by one before NASCAR's "high commissioner," Cannonball Baker. France also sat in on the hearings, along with NASCAR's secretary, Bill Tuthill, and lawyer, Louis Ossinsky. Over the course of four hours, the NASCAR officials listened to each man plead his case.

Baker handed down his decision the next day. Baker said he couldn't find enough evidence that Speedy Thompson was involved in dumping the tacks on a NASCAR track earlier in the season and exonerated him. The other four—Shuman, Samples, Teague, and Thompson's brother, Alfred—were found guilty of acting "not in accordance with the best interests of NASCAR." They would all be allowed to return to NASCAR as long as they first paid fines ranging from $50 to $150. But they would also be "under probation" for a year. The Thompson brothers immediately sued NASCAR, but a judge refused to hear their case. The message—from NASCAR and the court—was strong and clear: don't mess with Bill France.

Though NASCAR's ruling was made by Baker, drivers all knew the message had come straight from Bill France, who had become NASCAR's commander in chief. In fact, just eighteen months into NASCAR's existence, France functioned as the executive, legislative, and judiciary branches, without all the messy checks and balances. France believed strongly that for stock car racing to thrive, it couldn't be a democracy.

Tuthill tried to assure drivers and the press of NASCAR's "complete honesty" and once argued that he and France "made an honest effort not to line our own pockets." Then again, France felt that he had sacrificed his own racing career to take on the leadership role that none of the others wanted. As he saw it, he "had done all the spadework." So if he got rich in the process, well, he deserved it. Tuthill also felt that if he and France created a profitable and successful organization, "the money should come along with it."

Despite such rationalizations, complaints about France's slowly growing wealth would follow him the rest of his days. Tim Flock once vented that "Bill was gittin' to be a millionaire and we was still eatin' cornbread and buttermilk."

The rise of Bill France's fortunes, meanwhile, put an even greater strain on those of Raymond Parks. Despite Parks's concerns about pouring more money into the deep pit of his racing team—not to mention his occasional loans to France—he now had no choice but to invest in a new, late-model race car for the strictly stock race.

"We just have to follow his rules," Parks told Vogt.

For a Ford-obsessed mechanic such as Vogt, this new strictly stock business was a problem. He'd now have to transfer his skills to engines and cars *not* made by Henry Ford. And the term *strictly* was like a pair of handcuffs to a mechanic whose legend revolved around the term *modified*. But, like Parks, he had little choice in the matter.

Vogt and Parks discussed their options and decided to buy Oldsmobile's new Rocket "88" for Byron to race. Ford was still making essentially the same flathead V-8 it had been producing for years, but the

more powerful engines of the day were those with overhead valves, especially those made by General Motors for Oldsmobiles and Cadillacs. The
streamlined Rocket 88 and its V-8 would soon replace the old prewar
Fords as the best stock car of the new NASCAR era.

Byron was among the few lucky drivers to be part of a racing team
with a deep-pocketed sponsor such as Parks. Because France's two
hundred–lap, 150-mile strictly stock race was open to "American-made
cars only"—and only those built since 1946—racers had to leave the
'39 Fords at home and scramble to find new rides. Even Fonty Flock
showed up a few days before the big race, looking for a wealthy patron
to loan him a car. Tim Flock also arrived without a car but the day before the race saw a fan he recognized, standing with his wife beside their
new Olds 88.

"Buddy, if you let me drive that car, I'll try to take care of it and not
hurt it," Flock told the man, knowing that the car had just a few hundred miles on it.

"Are you crazy?" the man's wife barked.

The next day, the man arrived without his wife and handed Flock
the keys.

Unlike the anything-goes modified races, the rules for the strictly
stock events would be maddeningly strict and the list of permissible alterations painfully brief. Drivers could tape over the headlights, remove
the muffler, and strap shut the doors—a belt or a dog collar usually did
the trick. They could add safety belts, but few drivers bothered; some
wrapped themselves to the driver's seat with a rubber tire tube. But not
much else was allowed. That meant that mixed in with semiprofessional
drivers who'd been racing for a decade were hopeful newcomers and
amateurs in their seriously *un*modified family sedans—exactly the mix
Bill France was hoping for.

What France did not want was a race dominated by moonshiners,
but that hope would be dashed. Of thirty-three cars at the start line,
roughly half the drivers—including Curtis Turner and the three Flock
brothers—were bootleggers or at least connected to the whiskey business in some way. Many of the car *owners* were bootleggers, too.

The rest of the drivers were a motley cross section of southern culture, including Lee Petty, a bakery truck driver who showed up with his neighbor's Buick Roadmaster; Buck Baker, a bus driver; Otis Martin, a scraggly mountaineer wearing overalls; Herb Thomas, a skinny tobacco farmer; Jim Paschal, a navy vet whose body was half covered with tattoos; and Jim Roper, a part-time midget racer from Kansas who had read about France's race in a comic strip. Also qualifying to start was a lone female racer, Sara Christian, wife of Atlanta businessman Frank Christian (who, like Raymond Parks, had invested moonshining profits in stock cars). Christian would become the first woman to compete in a NASCAR race, and one of the few female racers of the 1940s.

France told reporters it would be the first strictly stock race since before the war. He publicized the event in newspapers and magazines and felt confident he was about to host "one of the biggest crowds we've ever seen. . . . You just wait until Sunday and see."

France nearly didn't make it to his own big race.

On Saturday, he and Tuthill took a ride in a friend's airplane, which France was considering buying, to replace the older plane he flew to and from races. But as the plane came in for a landing at the nearby airport, the pilot overran the runway and rolled onto the highway. Oncoming cars swerved out of the plane's path, narrowly avoiding a collision. The plane landed in a ditch with France and Tuthill shaken up but uninjured.

After speeding back to the racetrack, France watched Saturday afternoon's final qualifying heats. Things didn't look good. The pounding summer sun had dried the track to a parched oval. Crews had watered it that morning, but by afternoon, it was once again a dust bowl. Red dust kicked up by cars taking their qualifying laps had swirled off the track and onto Wilkinson Boulevard, coating the windshields of passing family cars and blinding the drivers. Several fender benders had lured the state police, who ordered France to control the dust. If he didn't, they threatened to shut down the next day's race.

France fortunately found fifty bags of calcium chloride that had been stored in a shed beside the track. Calcium chloride helped reduce dust at racetracks by drawing moisture from the air. He borrowed a fan's pickup truck and drove around the track, dumping the bags over the side, dragging a mesh screen behind the truck to mix the gritty chemical in with the dirt. Normally, it took tens of thousands of pounds of calcium chloride to be effective. But the state police seemed satisfied with France's token effort and allowed the race to proceed.

Race day dawned, a bright sunny day that quickly turned stifling hot.

Previous races at Charlotte Speedway had drawn only a few thousand fans. On June 19, more than twenty thousand arrived for France's show—twice what he had hoped for. They lined up outside the gates, their cars clogging Wilkinson Boulevard and its dirt tributaries for miles around. Roughly thirteen thousand actually paid the entry fee, ranging from $2.50 for general admission to $4.00 for a seat in the grandstands, while more than five thousand gate-crashers swarmed over and around fences, pouring into and spilling over the shaky wooden grandstands. The state police were called to help turn away thousands more.

Fans crowded up against the flimsy wood-post fence that separated them from the racetrack as Charlotte radio personality Grady Cole barked through the loudspeaker his order for the gentlemen—and one lady, Sara Christian—to "start your engines." When the starter's exuberant wave of a green flag signaled the start, the air exploded with the roars and red dust and rebel-yell cheers that were becoming NASCAR's rowdy trademarks.

Bob Flock immediately carved an aggressive path into the lead, but the strictly stock engine of his Hudson was hardly built for fast laps around a cow field and began to overheat. He gave up the lead when his motor blew on lap twenty-five. Bill Blair, an easygoing stock car veteran from nearby High Point, took the lead in a Lincoln he'd borrowed from a stranger the previous afternoon. Blair seemed uncatchable, and at the halfway point, half the other cars sat lifeless in the pits, unable to sustain one hundred miles at the outer limits of their performance. Wheels snapped off, and radiators became clogged with red clay and exploded.

"Strictly stock" cars clearly didn't have the staying power and performance of a whiskey car, nor of a "modified" Ford V-8 racer.

One of the sidelined vehicles belonged to Lee Petty, the bakery truck driver who had come with his wife and two sons, ten-year-old Maurice and eleven-year-old Richard.

The Petty family watched in horror as Lee's suspension cracked in turn three and he lost control of his borrowed Buick. Petty rolled four times, pieces of Buick flying in the air and his body flopping around inside. When the mangled car finally came to a crunching stop, after a tense moment of silence Petty crawled through the window and waved to the relieved crowd to let them know he was okay. Petty then sat beside the track, nursing a cut on his hand, wondering how to tell his neighbor he'd wrecked the guy's family sedan. Another driver said he actually saw Petty cry.

The Petty family would hitchhike home, but the experience apparently had no effect on Petty's son Richard, who would go on to become a NASCAR legend.

One driver rolled his car into a clump of bushes and, though uninjured in the wreck, landed on a bees' nest and was attacked by an angry swarm. He went running toward the pits, wildly waving his arms. Fans thought he was on fire.

Leader Bill Blair came into the pits to get his radiator refilled and take on an extra quart of oil. But a drunk on the pit crew cracked the top of the radiator and couldn't screw the cap back on. Blair had no choice but to rejoin the race and hope for the best.

"It'll burn up!" he warned the car's owner before pulling away.

"Just run it until the motor won't turn no more," the owner said.

Five laps later, at lap 150, Blair's water-depleted engine seized.

A relative unknown named Glenn Dunnaway then pulled to the front of the field. Like more than a few drivers, Dunnaway had shown up that morning without a car of his own. He convinced an acquaintance to loan him a 1947 Ford coupe, one of the few Fords entered in the event. He took control at lap 151 and settled into a winning groove. His

Ford hugged tightly to the track, and nothing that Byron or Flock tried could narrow the growing gap. Dunnaway finished three full laps ahead of the next driver, a Kansan named Jim Roper. Fonty Flock finished third, followed by Byron in fourth.

Contented fans streamed off late that afternoon, their ears still buzzing, and newspaper writers began typing their glowing stories. Everyone, especially Big Bill France, seemed convinced that the first strictly stock race had been a major success. But as dusk turned to night, a mechanic named Al Crisler found something suspicious beneath Dunnaway's Ford.

Crisler's job as NASCAR's first "technical inspector" was to make sure the strictly stock cars hadn't been modified in any way. All of the top finishers' cars were taken to a hangar at the nearby airport and disassembled. Crisler had been suspicious of the way Dunnaway's car carved the tight track's corners, rode smoothly over the bumps, and how he managed to finish two miles ahead of the rest.

Then Crisler found his culprit: steel wedges had been welded to the springs of Dunnaway's suspension—an old bootlegger's trick that helped cars tote heavy loads of moonshine by preventing the suspension from sagging too low. On the racetrack, the wedges had helped keep the car steady, which, in turn, helped Dunnaway drive faster.

Bill Tuthill milled around Crisler during the entire inspection. At one point, Crisler looked up and commented that Dunnaway's probably wasn't the only whiskey car on the track that day. In fact, in Crisler's professional opinion, it was possible that Jim Roper's Lincoln was the only car among the top finishers that *hadn't* been illegally modified. But since they weren't inspecting all of the cars, Dunnaway was merely the only one to get caught. Tuthill called France back at his hotel and broke the news. "Okay," France said. "We'll just have to disqualify Glenn and move Jim Roper up to first."

Dunnaway, of course, claimed he didn't know that his 1947 Ford was a whiskey car, nor that the man who'd loaned it to him, Hubert

Westmoreland, was a bootlegger. It turns out Westmoreland's car had actually been used earlier that week to haul moonshine. But Dunnaway's protests were to no avail.

France's decision bumped everyone up a notch, so that Jim Roper and his borrowed Lincoln won the race—and its two thousand dollars. Fonty Flock came in second, and Byron got credit for third. Other drivers, led by Byron and the Flock brothers, felt sorry for Dunnaway and passed around a hat to raise five hundred dollars for the frustrated racer.

France's decision to disqualify Dunnaway stoked the increasingly uneasy us-against-them relationship between himself and NASCAR's moonshining faction.

Westmoreland, owner of the disqualified car, immediately sued NASCAR, claiming that his car crossed the line first and he had won the race fair and square. In seeking ten thousand dollars in damages, he also argued that inspectors had checked his car before the race and never mentioned the altered suspension. Judge John Hayes, after lengthy testimony from a Ford factory worker and many other witnesses, ruled in France's favor and dismissed the case. Hayes said flatly that Westmoreland's whiskey car was properly disqualified "because of illegal equipment." Hayes's ruling reinforced France's message: there's no room in NASCAR for moonshiners or cheaters. And France's word was final.

France was euphoric over the turnout for his first strictly stock race and was especially happy to pull it off in the hometown of his rival, NSCRA president Bruton Smith. Despite the lawsuits and the plane crash and the flap over Dunnaway's disqualification, France had collected at least $2.50 from more than thirteen thousand happy fans. The "guarantee" paid to the winners was five thousand dollars, which meant NASCAR's take was in the thirty thousand–dollar neighborhood. Even after paying the track owner, the salaries of those who worked the race, the insurance costs, and putting some money into the escrow account for the end-of-year points fund, France made some good money that day.

But the courtroom victory was a particularly important landmark.

France had worried aloud that losing the Dunnaway case would "put a crimp" in his plans by setting a precedent in which race results could be disputed in court. But having a judge declare NASCAR's way of doing things to be legitimate only proved to the racing world that NASCAR was becoming, as France put it, a "stabilizing influence in racing." Hayes's ruling also verified, in a court of law, that France was legally empowered to lead NASCAR as he saw fit, which only engorged his existing sense of authority.

After the success of that first race, France quickly scheduled seven more strictly stock races for 1949, all of them with equally large purses of five thousand dollars or more. He would soon rename the strictly stock series NASCAR's "Grand National" division, a term he borrowed from horse racing. He thought it added a touch of class to NASCAR. (It was later renamed the Winston Cup series and is today known as the Nextel Cup.)

Grand National races quickly surpassed modified races as the fans' favorite, and 1949 would later be known as the year NASCAR truly began; 1948, it turned out, was just a warm-up—a qualifying heat.

The second Grand National race, a 166-miler, was scheduled for July 10 at Daytona Beach. The winner would again earn two thousand dollars— more than Red Byron's entire bonus for the 1948 championship. Byron had hoped to stick to races closer to his wife and child. But if winning a single race in France's lucrative Grand National series could earn him more than a dozen smaller races, he had no choice but to compete.

In fact, he'd follow France's new Grand National circuit wherever it led.

16

"It's not cheating if you don't get caught"

The postwar explosion of newer, faster car models contributed to a growing interest in all kinds of auto racing. Open-wheel races in the Northeast and Midwest were luring record crowds. Even Hollywood latched onto the rising popularity of racing.

The Big Wheel hit theaters in 1949, with Mickey Rooney as the son of a racer who died in a fiery Indy 500 crash. And ten years after starring in *Gone with the Wind*, Clark Gable, a racing enthusiast, had begun filming *To Please a Lady*, in which he played a ruthless Indy driver. In the expanding racing culture of the South, NASCAR's founders and participants were all looking for new ways to make money off engines and cars, to diversify beyond the time-tested formula of stock car racing and moonshining.

Bob Flock had gone into partnership on a new racetrack, with plans to promote his own races. He and his stout, foulmouthed wife, Ruby, had also opened Flock's Restaurant on Spring Street, whose motto was "Hot Biscuits at All Times." In keeping with the hot biscuits theme, Bob and Ruby were rumored to be running a profitable whorehouse on the side. Red Byron had added his Speed Shop to his own racing career and wrote occasional magazine articles about building race car engines. Gober Sosebee, Ed Samples, and Buddy Shuman were also running their own speed shops, while still dabbling in moonshine. Except for Fonty Flock, an admittedly lousy mechanic who supplemented his racing income with door-to-door vacuum cleaner sales, racers and mechanics throughout the southern stock car–racing world were trying to scratch out a living in part by cashing in on the nation's growing taste for speed.

For Red Vogt, selling hot biscuits or vacuum cleaners was hardly an option. He remained—would always remain—exclusively a mechanic. But Vogt worried a little about where his mechanical skills would fit in NASCAR's new strictly stock series.

Vogt's expertise had long been as a master of modification. Through dozens of technical procedures—boring, stroking, and porting; grinding and drilling invasive new holes and shapes into the engine block; casting spells on gear ratios—he could nearly double an engine's horsepower. Those procedures had mostly been permissible during the first decade of organized stock car racing. The new "Grand National" division, however, now banned many of Vogt's proven techniques, and he had to wonder about his future job security in a NASCAR rife with mechanical restrictions.

But Vogt was not one to quit and never exactly viewed the new system as a career breaker. For one thing, he knew engines better than anyone else in NASCAR. And, for that matter, he knew Bill France better and longer than the rest. So he figured, if he could stay one step ahead of France by devising horsepower boosters undetectable by the average NASCAR inspector, he could retain his title as wizard of stock cars.

First, the wizard had to transfer twenty years of experience with Fords to Oldsmobile and its impressive new overhead valve V-8 "Rocket." The first thing Vogt noticed about the Rocket was the oil pressure, which, at fifty-five pounds per square inch, seemed too high. So he drilled tiny holes into the oil pump, which lowered the pressure to thirty-five p.s.i. The holes were intentionally difficult for a NASCAR inspector to detect.

Vogt squeezed extra horsepower from the engine in pony-sized increments, exploiting every crack and imperfection in NASCAR's rule book. If the rules didn't specifically outlaw something, Vogt did it. If the rules banned it, he devised hard-to-detect methods of adding horsepower while eluding a NASCAR inspector's eyes.

He still worked late into the night, often until dawn. Alone in his shop, he experimented with minute reductions in the length of the push rods, or minuscule shavings off the lobes of the camshaft. Vogt was obsessed with perfecting an engine's timing, and much of his creative ingenuity was focused on a dozen or more small procedures that, when combined, improved timing to what he called "the absolute peak of performance."

In tiptoeing around NASCAR's rules, Vogt was establishing unwritten rules of his own. Those rules would be adopted by subsequent generations of NASCAR mechanics, whose greatest thrill was to slip small, creative, undetectable illegalities into an allegedly "stock" race car. Any mechanic who didn't bend the rules as much as possible would not last long. And Red Vogt was their godfather.

One student of Vogt's brand of rule bending, in response to NASCAR limits on gas tank size, developed a huge fuel line that held a few extra gallons. Following a postrace inspection, with the gas tank disconnected and sitting on the garage floor, he fired up the car and drove off. Baffled inspectors reluctantly let him go.

That protégé was Smokey Yunick, a handsome, lascivious, chain-smoking World War II pilot. He had opened a garage in Daytona Beach in 1947 and would spend the next four decades in constant battle with Bill France, often scoffing openly at the idea of a sport in which a driver's fortunes rose and fell not on strict, black-and-white rules but on someone's *interpretations* of the rules. Namely, France's interpretations.

Yunick would say aloud many of the things Vogt only muttered to himself. "How in the hell do you legislate a fraudulent concept?" he'd complain. Stock cars had never been truly stock. Men such as France knew that perfectly stock cars would make for lousy races, which is why modifications had been allowed right from the start. Because the list of allowable modifications was always in flux—and continues that way today—Yunick called stock car racing "at best, a good-natured lie."

Vogt's response to that lie was to beat the rule makers at their own game. Whatever Vogt did during his late-night, chocolate-and-Coke sessions, one thing's for sure: Red Byron's car was more modified than it was supposed to be. But if no inspector figured that out, once the car passed through the NASCAR inspection line, it would be declared legal. That sly game became as much a part of stock car–racing strategy as tires and pit stops. And as Vogt liked to say, "It's not cheating if you don't get caught."

On the afternoon of July 9, 1949, Vogt had the Olds 88 ready and waiting for Byron to tow to Daytona Beach for the next day's race, the 166-miler that would be the second of NASCAR's eight strictly stock races that year.

Byron first squeezed in a Saturday night midget race at Atlanta's Peach Bowl, which he won. He then drove all night and reached Daytona a few hours before race time.

Despite some vocal complaints from other drivers, France allowed three women to race: Sara Christian (the Atlanta bootlegger's wife, who'd raced in the previous Grand National race); Ethel Flock Mobley, sister of the Flock boys; and Louise Smith, a bawdy driver from South Carolina. France hoped the prospect of three women battling crusty moonshiner/racers on the beach, not to mention *four* Flock siblings on the same track, would draw a record crowd. But rainy weather caused a sparse showing of five thousand.

Dawsonville's Gober Sosebee led the early laps, with Tim Flock and Red Byron stalking from behind. Louise Smith flipped her Ford in the chopped-up and rutted north turn, landing upside down and dangling from her seat belt. A dozen fans ran to her aid, but Smith insisted she wasn't hurt and asked if they'd help roll her back over so she could get back in the race. Smith stayed put in the driver's seat while the men flipped her car back onto its wheels, and she took off. Sosebee held the lead until losing a tire with six laps to go. It gave Byron the perfect opening to jump into the lead.

Byron was now a master of the complicated beach course. He knew how to drive at the surf's edge, so seawater could mist up and cool his brakes, but not too close. He knew, when his windshield became gauzy and opaque with salt spray, to eyeball the telephone poles of highway A1A to help him stay on the road. He knew how to shoulder his car into the turns, to broadslide through the knotty, slurried arcs, trusting Vogt's reinforced wheels to withstand the pressure. With no bucket seats in his strictly stock car, he had to hold tight to the steering wheel to keep from sliding into the passenger seat.

He and his Olds 88 kept a steady pace for the final twenty-five miles, and Byron comfortably crossed the finish line nearly two miles ahead of Tim Flock for his fourth Daytona victory, more than any other driver in stock car racing's brief history. This win, however, was worth nearly as much as the previous three victories combined—two thousand dollars.

Ethel Flock Mobley, driving with her AM radio blasting throughout the race, finished an impressive eleventh—ahead of brothers Bob and Fonty. Sara Christian finished eighteenth, and Louise Smith, after her flip, came in second to last. Although all three would continue to race into the early 1950s, resistance from the male racers was strong, and females in NASCAR would not last much beyond that.*

After Byron's victory, NASCAR officials impounded the top-five finishers and began tearing apart the engines, looking for any signs of illegal modifications.

---

*Across the next fifty years, only a handful of women would race with any regularity in NASCAR, most notably Janet Guthrie in 1978 and Shawna Robinson in 2001. In 2005, Danica Patrick finished fourth in the Indianapolis 500, but in NASCAR, while women occasionally compete in minor-league races, no female driver has finished atop any of NASCAR's major races in recent years.

Byron's win was a first for a General Motors car in a NASCAR race. In fact, the top-four finishers were all Oldsmobiles. A Ford didn't even finish among the top ten, lost in a crowd of Chryslers, Mercurys, Hudsons, Cadillacs, and Buicks. Inspectors declared all five of the top finishers to be legit, leaving Byron's victory intact—and giving Red Vogt his own victory over Bill France and his inspectors.

Byron accepted his trophy and envelope of cash, then mingled with other drivers and a few journalists, unstrapping his helmet and firing up the cigar he had chewed during the race. NASCAR's timing official announced that Byron's average speed had been just shy of eighty-one miles an hour—not quite as fast as a modified race car but fairly impressive for an allegedly *un*modified car. When asked by Daytona Beach sportswriter Bernard Kahn about his speed, Byron was unusually defensive. "No way," he snapped, the cigar stuck in the corner of his mouth. "Couldn't have gone that fast. Somebody must have made a mistake. . . . These strictly stock cars are a lot slower." Byron diverted the conversation, telling Kahn that he actually liked the slower pace of the strictly stock cars. "That makes them easier to ride," he said, patting his bad left leg.

Vogt was also asked about Byron's Olds 88 and was equally defensive. He explained that the modifieds could exceed one hundred miles an hour but the strictly stock cars maxed out at ninety-two or ninety-three. For Byron to average eighty for two hours was, Vogt declared, not possible. "I doubt if Red averaged seventy-nine or eighty miles per hour," he growled, then began loading up his tools for the long ride home.

For all his protests, a photograph taken that day shows Vogt uncharacteristically grinning, like a cat with a belly full of canary, like a man with a secret.

Despite the low turnout for that race, Bill France decided to put all his promotional muscle behind his six remaining strictly stock races. Ads in *Illustrated Speedway News* magazine blared, "See the new Oldsmobiles, Lincolns, Fords, Mercurys and other cars at their best," which helped lure 17,500 fans to the third Grand National race, on August 7, at

Occoneechee Speedway in Hillsboro, North Carolina. Byron led until Sara Christian lost her right front wheel and collided with him. He finished twenty-second.

The fourth strictly stock race was held at Pennsylvania's Langhorne Speedway, where twenty thousand spectators watched Byron finish third behind Curtis Turner and Bob Flock.

When France had separated the modified and strictly stock divisions, he decided to tally points separately and award year-end championships for each division. Halfway through the season, Byron's victory at Daytona and third-place finish at Langhorne put him atop the new Grand National division. He decided he could afford to skip the next Grand National race near Buffalo, New York. Instead, he prepared for the sixth of France's eight-race Grand National series, scheduled for late September at Martinsville Speedway in southwest Virginia. But France's popular new Grand National races were in for some competition of their own, and the forces of distrust and dissent were stirring.

Stock car racing was still, to say the least, in its chaotic adolescent stage, and Bill France's foes weren't yet ready to let him take over the whole stock car empire.

AAA and Sam Nunis, who had run a handful of stock car events over the past few years, were making plans for their own series of strictly stock races at Lakewood Speedway in Atlanta later that fall. And NSCRA president Bruton Smith had teamed with the disaffected racer Buddy Shuman to open a new dirt racetrack in Charlotte. Shuman also partnered with the New Jersey–based United Stock Car Racing Club to host strictly stock races that they also decided to call the "Grand National" division. The group audaciously scheduled its first Grand National race (at a paved Connecticut speedway) on the same day as Bill France's sixth Grand National race, September 25, 1949.

The United Stock Car Racing Club's race in Connecticut offered winners a 40 percent share of the ticket sales, but only the size of the crowd would determine whether the purse rivaled that of NASCAR's next big race. For his strictly stock races, France had decided to stick with offering a preset, guaranteed winners' purse, which on September 25 at Martinsville would be four thousand dollars, with fifteen hundred dollars going to the winner. Racers had to gamble: if they drove to Connecticut and the crowd was paltry, the 40 percent share of ticket sales would be far less than the four thousand–dollar "guarantee" France was offering.

France decided to help drivers make their choice by tightening a rule he'd enforced only sporadically. In the past, France had threatened drivers who competed in non-NASCAR races but never officially banned the practice. Instead, he refused to allow victories in another group's races to count in NASCAR. But now France decided to clarify this issue of racing with other organizations. He instructed his right-hand man, Bill Tuthill, to issue a written warning to all drivers that any drivers caught racing in non-NASCAR events would lose all points they'd accumulated in NASCAR. Tuthill assured France it was the right move. "If we back down, we're through," he said.

A number of drivers decided to take a chance and, despite France's threat, raced in a late-summer event at Bruton Smith's new track outside Charlotte. They figured if they stuck together, France wouldn't dare penalize them all. But soon each of the thirteen men received a letter from NASCAR. "If you want to keep racing, you must live up to the rules," it began, then advised them that they had lost *all* of their NASCAR points. Borrowing the term AAA previously used for stock car racers—had in fact used for France himself—France called those who refused to race exclusively for NASCAR "outlaws."

The stripping of points intimidated a few drivers into obedience, but mostly it infuriated them. Many of those who were punished were from Atlanta—so many that Tuthill told France, it's "not safe for any of us to set foot in Atlanta for a long time."

In fact, NASCAR wouldn't hold a race in Atlanta until 1951.

Some shrugged off their frustration, realizing they'd been trumped by France and there was little they could do in return. A few decided to go face-to-face with France, but that route rarely turned out in their favor. At one modified division race that summer, Gober Sosebee was disqualified for what he considered a bogus infraction. He stomped into France's office and called France "a self-made son of a bitch."

"Now, Gober, you didn't mean that," France said patiently.

"I said it and I meant it," the moonshiner drawled back, and stormed out.

At his next race, Sosebee's gas tank got clogged by an errant rag and he was unable to refuel during a pit stop. His mechanic grabbed a gas can and jumped into the backseat of the car. While racing around the track, the mechanic leaned out of the rear passenger window, pulled loose the rag, and filled Sosebee's near-empty tank. Sosebee won the race but was immediately disqualified for having an extra rider in his car. When Sosebee pointed out there was no such rule about extra riders in the NASCAR rule book, France grabbed a pen and wrote "No riders shall be allowed in the back. . . ."

So began the arbitrariness and fluidity of the NASCAR rule book, which—like the Bible—could be interpreted in many ways, depending on the interpreter's intent. If France couldn't find a specific infraction, he'd simply, if ironically, punish a driver or mechanic for "being outside the spirit of competition." Complaints about ever-changing rules and punitive use of the rule book would become hallmarks of the sport.

Red Vogt studied such confrontations closely, and he learned from them.

By late 1949, there wasn't a single track in Dixie at which Red Byron hadn't won. Nor did a track exist where a Red Vogt–tuned car hadn't won multiple times.

But every driver and mechanic had his favorite track. Byron, for example, loved the mile-long Lakewood oval but hated the mile-long Langhorne circle. A driver's love or hate for a track depended on his ability to find the elusive, hard-to-define *groove*. For Byron, finding that groove was a process of elimination. He would try a diamond pattern (picture a round-edged diamond shape superimposed on an oval), with sharp turns and quick shifting from brake pedal to gas pedal. Or he might try a more rounded groove, broad-sliding through each turn and gently accelerating until the car found a grip, then gunning it down the straightaway until the next turn. Byron could always find his groove at Daytona. And in 1949, he found it at Martinsville Speedway, the half-mile red-clay oval in southwest Virginia whose inaugural race Byron had won two years earlier.

The Martinsville track's owner, Clay Earles, would pave the track in 1955, but in 1949, it was still known as one of the South's dustiest red-dirt tracks. Fans left every Martinsville race covered in dust. The photograph of Byron after his 1947 race—dirt-caked, grim-faced, cigarette in hand—became a symbol of NASCAR's glory days. Earles, a self-made promoter who occasionally paid better-known racers to come to his track, had become a loyal friend of Bill France. Clay's devotion to France would help Martinsville keep NASCAR coming back for decades. Martinsville continued to host NASCAR races for the next half century, the only racetrack to span the sport's entire history. Drivers still haggle over how to find the best groove at Martinsville.

NASCAR's sixth Grand National race, on September 25, 1949, drew ten thousand fans to Martinsville. The United Stock Car Racing Club race held the same day in Connecticut didn't seem to hurt France's attendance, and most drivers decided not to take the gamble on that distant event and to stick with NASCAR's four thousand–dollar guarantee.

On such a short track, it was nearly impossible to pass on either of the two eight hundred–foot straightaways, so drivers would make their moves in the turns, often by driving a high groove at the outside of the straightaway and then cutting sharply into the turn, sometimes all the way onto the apron, in an effort to pass. On September 25, Byron couldn't find a route around Fonty Flock. In driver parlance, Flock was "driving wide" and seemed to have the two hundred–lap race wrapped up. But races are often determined by small bits of luck, good or bad, and at the halfway point, Flock's front right wheel snapped off and he crashed, allowing Byron to take the lead and follow his groove for the next hundred laps. He took the checkered flag three laps ahead of Lee Petty.

Byron had now won two of the eight scheduled Grand National races and had twice finished third. He skipped the next race in Pittsburgh, which was won by Lee Petty. Entering the final race of the year, Byron and Petty were ranked first and second in the point standings. Byron was far enough ahead of Petty that he could hold on to first place as long as he just finished in the top twenty at the next race at North Wilkesboro on October 16.

Only some sort of disaster in the season finale would prevent Byron from becoming NASCAR's first two-time champ. Potential disaster lurked. Its name was Roy Hall.

Roy Hall was still a handsome young man of twenty-eight when he was finally released from prison in late summer of 1949, after serving three years. Of course, the first thing he did with his reclaimed freedom was go looking for a race. He borrowed one of Raymond Parks's modified Fords and drove to Spartanburg, South Carolina, for a NASCAR modified division contest. There, despite spinning out wildly in one turn and causing two other drivers to wreck, Hall finished a respectable ninth, half a lap behind Ed Samples's victory.

Parks briefly wondered if Hall might still have a racing career left in him. Bob Flock had left Parks's team to drive his own car. Maybe Hall could rejoin the Parks-Vogt team and, with Byron, become NASCAR's dominant one-two punch. The idea intrigued Parks, but he was also wary of the change he saw in Hall. He'd always been a reckless force on the racetrack, but in his first weeks of freedom, Hall seemed downright scary. He was now a hardened criminal who'd done hard time. Hall seemed almost desperate in his need for a victory, as if it would restore all he'd lost behind bars.

Hall and Byron were about to face off for the first time in many years. For those old enough to have seen Hall race years earlier, this was a thrilling prospect.

Red Vogt once said Hall "could do things with a car which no car was supposed to do." Then again, Vogt also said, "Red Byron was the only one who could sit on Hall's tail and worry him." Vogt had been convinced of Byron's prowess early on, in one of the first postwar races, while watching him hang tight behind Roy Hall's back bumper for the entire race. Vogt said later that it looked "like a car getting towed." Hall was also impressed and after the race asked Byron, "Why didn't you pass?"

"You were going pretty good," Byron responded. "I was satisfied."

Byron respected Hall but had often been wary of going head-to-head with a man who drove with a frenzy and fury that the more cerebral Byron didn't quite understand. Now, with a NASCAR championship and dozens of first-place finishes under his belt, Byron no longer feared moonshining Roy Hall.

On October 16 at North Wilkesboro, it became clear that Hall might still be an instinctively shrewd dirt-track driver but he was now far from the sport's best. Byron led most of the race, making sure he kept clear of Hall, who wasn't necessarily a threat to win the race but could doom Byron's championship chances by running Byron off the track.

Unfortunately, while he managed to keep his distance from Hall, who was scraping fenders amid the pack, Byron had pushed his engine too hard, and it blew up seventy-seven miles into the hundred-mile race. He and his car limped into the pits and watched the rest of the race. Despite a desperate last-lap attempt by Lee Petty, Bob Flock took the checkered flag, followed by Petty and brother Fonty Flock. Hall finished sixth.

Byron was fortunately given credit for sixteenth place, but he would still have to wait for France to tally the season's points and announce whether his sixteenth-place finish was good enough for a championship.

Two weeks later, Hall proved that his audacity now definitely outranked his skills.

He took cousin Parks's Ford to Tri-City Speedway near High Point, North Carolina, for the year's final NASCAR modified division race. Hall had long been a master of sprinting ahead of the rest of the field and into the first turn, then staying there and driving wide to the finish. This time, as Hall punched the gas and tried to take an outside groove around the others, he cut too sharply into the first turn, and the Ford lurched onto its right wheels and kept going. It rolled and rolled. Hall wasn't wearing a seat belt, and his head and body slammed against the roof, the dash, the windshield. When the car finally came to a stop, he was bloody and unconscious.

Hall would spend the next month in the hospital, in critical condition, drifting in and out of consciousness as he recovered from serious head wounds. Friends said he was never quite himself after that. It seemed as if his racing career was really over for good.

Byron, meanwhile, had firmly established himself as the best stock car driver in the land. He didn't attain the folk hero status of murdered Lloyd Seay nor the bootlegger cachet of Hall. No songs would be written about disabled, bald-headed Robert Nold Byron. But over the past eleven years, Byron had learned to combine Seay's intelligent cautiousness and Hall's controlled aggressiveness and had far outlasted them both.

When Bill France tallied the numbers for 1949, he announced that Byron had finished with 842 points to Lee Petty's 725 to become NASCAR's Grand National champ.

This time, there had been no heroics in the season's last race, no poignant, dramatic finale against an aggressive foe at the same track where a boy had been killed. It was a quiet victory for Byron, but hardly insignificant. Byron had won two of the division's eight events and twice placed third. Those four top-five finishes were worth forty-eight hundred dollars, and he'd receive an extra one thousand dollars for being the champ. Combined with the few hundred bucks from his victories in midget races at Atlanta's Peach Bowl that year, and a few wins in NASCAR modified events, Byron's racing income was finally keeping him financially afloat. In November, he competed in a non-NASCAR event at Lakewood Speedway—the same track where his stock car career had begun back in 1938. This time, before thirty thousand fans, Byron was victorious and took another two thousand dollars home to his family.

If stock car racing survived and Byron kept up his winning ways, and the monthly disability checks kept coming from the U.S. Army, it might not be a bad way to string together a living. He had always dreamed of being a full-time professional racer, without the worries of, say, running a garage or a restaurant on the side. Then again, he'd soon learn that Bill France had the final word on who did or didn't make a living in NASCAR.

Despite the approach of war in Korea, the years since World War II had been prosperous ones, and America marched onward as the gas-powered powerhouse of the world. That prosperity was reflected on the highways.

Car ownership was at an all-time high, as were auto accident fatalities, averaging thirty thousand a year. By a two-to-one margin, most of those deaths were on rural roads. But in urban areas, pedestrians comprised the majority of traffic deaths. In downtown Atlanta that fall, Margaret Mitchell was killed by a drunk-driving taxi driver while crossing Peachtree Street on her way to see a performance of *The Canterbury Tales*.

Though Atlanta would fifty years later rank among the nation's more industrial and traffic-choked cities, on the eve of 1950, its soul was still purely southern, which meant corn liquor still reigned among the more profitable industries.

And whiskey trippers still dominated the stock car world.

Not counting Lloyd Seay's championship in 1938, eleven "championship" titles were handed out by southern stock car–racing organizations between 1939 and 1949. Eight of those trophies had a moonshiner's name etched on them, including Roy Hall, Fonty Flock, Eddie Samples, and Buddy Shuman. Two other champions—Bill France in 1941, Red Byron in 1948 and 1949—drove cars owned by ex–moonshine baron Raymond Parks. Furthermore, every stock car champion of merit between 1939 and 1949—except Shuman from Charlotte and Bill France himself—had come from Dawsonville or Atlanta, or divided his time between the two. And nearly all of those championship cars had been created by the best whiskey mechanic of his day, Red Vogt.

As the 1940s came to a close, moonshining Ed Samples was named champion of Bruton Smith's NSCRA group for 1949, having won quite a few lesser-known, non-NASCAR races across the South. (Moonshining Buddy Shuman, who was the NSCRA champ in 1948, would again become NSCRA's champ in 1950.)

But a decade of southern moonshiners dominating all aspects of stock car racing was ending. Indeed, moonshine's dominance of NASCAR had peaked.

As NASCAR transitioned into a new decade, many of the sport's early heroes, founders, and champions would find that NASCAR no longer had room for them. One by one, France would alienate the men—especially the moonshiners, and even his friends—who had helped create his sport but whom he now deemed expendable.

Even Red Byron's NASCAR days were numbered.

SKIMP HERSEY

PART III

A man is divided into two parts, body and spirit . . .
the body is like a house: it don't go anywhere.
But the spirit is like an automobile: always on the move, always.
— FLANNERY O'CONNOR

17

"No way a Plymouth can beat a Cadillac. No <u>way</u>"

If not for the hundred-mile-an-hour pace, they might have been mistaken for a couple of American tourists. Raymond Parks sat in the passenger seat in his straw hat and open-collar shirt, while Red Byron, in his jaunty cap and aviator glasses, manned the wheel of the long, sleek 1949 Lincoln coupe with "26" stenciled on each door.

The Mexican countryside blurred past, fields of farmers and empty stretches of burnt orange desert. As the road entered small villages, it twisted, crossed bridges, and cut close to the roadside homes of the townspeople who'd come out to watch, forcing Byron to ease off the gas a little. In one village, they sped past a small house with a race car punched through the front wall. In another town, they saw the remains of a car that had rolled off a bridge into a dry riverbed. More wreckage littered the mountainsides.

Billed as "the biggest, toughest and most adventurous race ever held," the inaugural Carrera-Panamericana Mexico—the Mexican Road Race, for short—had begun days earlier just across the border from El Paso. Created as a sort of publicity stunt for the completion of Mexico's section of the north-south Pan American Highway system, this was an endurance test to the extreme, a sadistic twist on the famous annual Le Mans twenty-four-hour race west of Paris. The border-to-border race was broken into nine legs over six days, ending at the Guatemalan border. The winner would get six thousand dollars, a purse with enough zeros to lure Parks and Byron farther from home than they'd been since the war.

Byron had kicked off the 1950 season with two top-five finishes and was quickly NASCAR's Grand National points leader once more. Then, just as quickly, he stopped racing. Satisfied with two championships in a row, Byron chose to cherry-pick only a few of the high-paying NASCAR races of 1950. If they added up to enough points for a third championship, fine. But after following Bill France's rules for two years, Byron had decided not to let NASCAR define him and to follow a few of his own rules. He limited his excursions to stock races within a few hours of home, regardless of who promoted the event, and sometimes took Nell along with him, leaving Robert Jr. home with an aunt. The lighter schedule was easier on his leg and gave him more time at home with the family, which would soon include a baby daughter.

But when he heard from other NASCAR drivers about the Mexico race, Byron convinced himself that he could win and bring home his share of the substantial winner's purse. Since most of the 2,178 miles were dirt, the course should have favored a dirt-track racer such as Byron and an ex-bootlegger such as Parks. If they survived.

Some drivers arrived weeks early to scope out the course and practice. But most arrived just in time for the May 5 start and winged it. Parks and Byron drove from Atlanta straight to the starting line, the trunk and backseat crammed with extra tires, tools, and clothes, along with canned food, jugs of water, and tanks of gas.

In no time, they learned that Mexico's new, mostly unpaved highway was far more treacherous than any dirt track they had raced on. Byron had counted on transferring his experience with red-dirt tracks directly to Mexico's orange-dirt highway. But in none of his previous races had he contended with sheer cliffs, loose gravel, hairpin turns, and elevations up to eleven thousand feet. One ill-prepared Guatemalan racer slid off the highway just seventeen miles from the start and was killed. After the body was removed, the codriver, who hadn't been seriously injured, took the wheel and continued racing.

Of the 132 two-man teams from a dozen countries, most were American or Mexican. Among the Americans, most were Indy racers from California and Texas. The southern stock car crowd was barely represented. In addition to Byron and Parks, Bob and Fonty Flock shared a car, as did Bill France and his newfound friend Curtis Turner, who in Byron's recent absence from the NASCAR circuit had become its points leader. France and Turner had become friends during the 1949 season and would drive a Nash sedan loaned to them by a dealer in Texas. They flew together in France's airplane to El Paso, where they picked up the Nash and took a few practice runs outside town. Turner could be a bit too wild in his lifestyle and driving habits for France, but France saw the race as a good promotional opportunity for NASCAR—if they won, that is.

Across the first two days, Byron and Parks lagged far back in the latter half of the pack. But as the heat and the dangerous roads took their toll, handfuls of cars dropped out each day with overheated engines or burned-out brakes or worse, and the Atlanta duo began inching up in the standings. In the fourth leg, they finished sixth out of ninety-three cars and moved into twenty-second place overall. In the next leg, they moved up to nineteenth overall and, on the leg after that, bumped up to eighteenth, with three legs to go.

Bob and Fonty were never even contenders. They had talked a Lincoln-Mercury dealer in Atlanta into loaning them a Lincoln, but the engine block cracked halfway through the race. The Bill France–Curtis Turner team, meanwhile, got off to the fastest start among the stock car teams and after three legs was in third place overall, with Turner behind the wheel averaging ninety-five miles an hour across the first seven hundred miles.

But France was becoming uneasy with Turner's apparent disregard for the sheer drop-offs and the unstable gravel surface. At one point, a small boy ran into the road, waving his arms, and they skidded to a stop. The boy warned them about the upcoming mountain and its dangerous series of esses, where another team had flown off a cliff and crashed five hundred feet below. Still, Turner barely eased up. Churning through back-and-forth turns, to the top of the mountain and down the other side, the twosome sped past yellow highway signs warning *Despacio* (Slow) and *Bajada* (Descent). Finally, Turner encountered a sharp right-angle turn that exceeded his considerable skills. He slammed on his brakes, but the Nash was unable to grab the loose road. The car spun backward and slid toward the edge of a cliff. After an interminable slide, the Nash finally came to a precarious stop with one wheel over the edge. France furiously clambered over Turner and out the driver's door, landing in an angry heap on the dusty road. "I have a wife and kids at home," France yelled. Turner sheepishly promised to drive slower.

The roadside crowds grew thicker as the race entered the outskirts of Mexico City, where half a million spectators lined the route. Mexican soldiers on horseback tried to control the crowds, often yanking on the hair of fans standing too close to the road and flinging them backward away from the course. One racer said that driving so close to the curious crowds was like "rubbing your door handles against their tits." For Byron, it seemed as if he were driving into a wall of people at one hundred miles an hour and surely gave him flashbacks to that terrible day when he *did* drive into a crowd. But every time, just before he slammed into that mass of cheering Mexican fans, the wall would suddenly open a crack and then close in tight again behind him.

Byron and Parks almost saw their race come to an end in Mexico City. After a ceremony at which drivers met Mexico's president, the after-race celebration continued in the streets of downtown, where someone lifted Parks's wallet. It contained more than two thousand dollars, cash they'd need to finish the race. Parks had to call his sister in Atlanta and have her wire him more money, which arrived just in time for the start of the next day's leg.

Parks wasn't the only naïve southerner to lose cash in the big city; Curtis Turner was also pickpocketed. At one point that afternoon, a photographer for *Speed Age* feared for his own welfare when a large, unsmiling Mexican man wielding a three-foot knife approached him and, without a word, hurled his knife into the air. It lopped a coconut off the tree above them. The man hacked the top off the coconut and offered the terrified photographer a drink of its milk.

Back on the highway for the final stretch south to the Guatemalan border, it had become clear to Byron and Parks that they were not going to win. Byron slowed the pace a little, and the two men tried to enjoy the remainder of the race in relative safety. A handful of drivers had already been killed or seriously injured, so Byron figured there was no sense in pushing their luck.

The France-Turner team had also slowed a notch, in keeping with Turner's promise to deliver France home alive. The team began an inevitable slip in the standings, back to eighth, then fourteenth, then fifteenth. They suffered numerous flat tires, the intense heat causing the rubber to slough off in fist-sized chunks. They were so despondent over losing their shot at the six thousand–dollar winner's purse that, during one of their tire-change stops, they even turned down a villager's offer of *cerveza fría*. Only after they were back on the road did they ask each other where a poor farmer would have gotten an ice-cold beer.

On the second-to-last leg, Bill France took over the driving. In an ill-advised attempt at a shortcut, he veered off a highway curve and through a section of grass. The front wheel found a hidden rut, and the sudden jolt cracked the radiator. *Speed Age* photographer Jack Cansler snapped a photo of France and Turner wearing sombreros against the sun, sitting beside a huge cactus trying to hitchhike a ride to the next town.

That night, finding themselves in twentieth place on the eve of the final leg, Turner and France decided to split up. The current eighth-place car was another Nash, whose driver had been stricken with a terrible case of what they euphemistically called "tropical sickness." The driver, a Texas car dealer named Roy Conner, asked Turner to take his place, beside codriver Robert Owens. France agreed to drive the last leg alone, loaning Turner to the team with the better chance at victory. It wasn't generosity. France was relieved to be rid of Turner and his disregard for life and limb. France also figured Turner's chance to actually win the race would be good publicity for NASCAR.

The next day, to prevent a clog on the final, narrow stretch of highway, the cars were started at four-minute intervals, which meant Turner and his new copilot, in eighth place, started twenty-eight minutes behind the leader. Turner drove furiously and, despite his codriver's panicky screams, passed all seven cars that had started ahead of him. He seemed to be headed for victory not only in that particular leg but for the entire race. Then, ten miles from the finish, he had a blowout. While he was changing the tire, two racers passed him. Turner managed to get back on the road and finish. His time was fast enough to win the 160-mile leg (due to the four-minute intervals between starts), but only enough for third place overall. Turned out it didn't matter. When race officials learned he had swapped cars the night before, Turner was disqualified.

As Byron and Parks limped toward the finish line, they were exhausted and eager to be done with it. The two-day drive from Atlanta to El Paso and then two thousand miles of racing, with limited amounts of sleep at night, marked the longest period of time Byron and Parks had ever spent in each other's company. Neither man was a big drinker, so they didn't party late into the night with Turner and the others at the boozy postrace events. They had spent nearly every moment of their six days in Mexico side by side.

These two veterans should have had a lot to talk about, but neither had ever been much for small talk. Above the drone of their Lincoln's engine, one thing they did discuss was their simmering concern about the uncertain future of a career in France's NASCAR.

Byron told Parks he'd been thinking of spending more time on the midget circuit. Those six-foot versions of open-wheel Indy cars had been gaining in popularity. Byron knew it was a compromise. But with his imperfect health and his promise to stay closer to home, racing midgets at Atlanta-area dirt tracks seemed like the perfect plan, like combining his love of open-wheel cars with his dirt-track racing skills.

Parks said he'd give some thought to investing in a new midget car for Byron, and Byron relaxed a little after that. But by the final day of the race, Byron seemed irritable and spent, and Parks began to worry that his partner might just pass out at the wheel. Byron's face was drawn. He had fresh blisters on his calloused hands. Parks could only imagine from the wincing and grimacing what Mexico's highway was doing to Byron's war-wounded leg. But he declined Parks's offer to take the wheel. Then it happened. . . .

With just an hour's drive to the finish, Parks's fear came true and Byron's exhaustion caught up with him. Byron's eyes flickered, drooped, then shut; his head pitched forward; and he slumped against the door. Before Parks knew what was happening, the Lincoln left the road and was barreling toward an embankment. Parks reached over and tried to grab the wheel, barely managing to steer away from a head-on collision with the embankment that might have killed them both. Still, Parks couldn't reach the brake, and the car crunched at an angle against the wall of dirt and rock, the evil sound of sheet metal against rock waking Byron from his brief sleep. The car bounced and bucked, knocking the two into their doors and each other. Supplies in the backseat—including a half-filled gas can, tools, and cans of food—went flying.

Fortunately, they had been traveling at less than full speed, and both were wearing lap belts, or their injuries would have been far worse. Still, the front left of the Lincoln was smashed, and it was no longer roadworthy. As other cars sped past, Byron and Parks sat helplessly by the roadside waiting for a tow truck, bruised and scratched, stinking of spilled fuel and food, but otherwise uninjured.

They weren't alone. Fewer than half of the 132 starters reached the finish line. Byron and Parks joined a casualty list that included Bill France, who crashed into a culvert fifty miles from the finish and again damaged his radiator.

Byron and Parks decided to leave their wrecked Lincoln behind, selling it for a couple of hundred dollars. With that and the cash Parks's sister had wired him, they traveled back to Mexico City, bought plane tickets, and flew home to Atlanta.

Bill France wasn't content to let NASCAR remain a sport in and of the South and had spent much of the previous year flying, in another new plane, to racetracks across the country, negotiating with track owners and promoters in other states. For the 1950 season, only nine of nineteen Grand National races would take place at the racetracks of Dixie. The other ten races would be spread across the eastern half of America.

Byron's talks with Parks during their time in Mexico seemed to have encouraged him to finally, fully break from France's unseemly grip on his career and income. After Mexico, Byron planned to rejoin NASCAR, but only on his terms and in a very limited way, which meant only races with a worthwhile winner's purse.

Rather than chase a third championship by obediently following the NASCAR circuit to Ohio and New York, Indiana and Pennsylvania, Byron stayed close to home, allowing newcomers such as Curtis Turner to dominate in his absence. Byron followed through on Parks's offer to invest in his midget-racing career. Parks bought him an expensive new midget racer called a Kurtis Kraft, and Red Vogt, ever the Ford devotee, removed the car's engine and installed a Ford V-8. They called the rebuilt car the M-1.

Byron began making local headlines for his weekly success at the Peach Bowl. He skipped all of NASCAR's Grand National races that summer.

Then, because it was close to home and at one of his favorite race-tracks, he decided to compete in a non-NASCAR race at Lakewood Speedway, which for years had been dominated by France's rival pro-moter, Sam Nunis. The ban imposed back in 1945 on drivers with criminal records had kept France from bringing NASCAR to Lakewood, since many of his drivers were bootleggers. That had allowed Nunis to make Lakewood his home base, where he hosted some of the largest stock car crowds in history.

A few weeks later, Byron competed in another Lakewood race cosponsored by Nunis and the NSCRA. The field included other veterans who had decided not to abide by France's NASCAR-or-nothing edict and to race wherever and whenever they chose. Ed Samples and Gober Sosebee were there, along with Buddy Shuman, each of whom had at one time been reprimanded by France.

As with Nunis's popular races the previous fall, the grandstands were filled beyond capacity, another message to France that Nunis was a dangerously effective promoter. Byron drove a brand-new 1950 Cadillac that Parks had bought to replace the Oldsmobile 88 and, before twenty-four thousand fans, took the checkered flag. France was furious when he learned that Byron, *his* champion, was an unfaithful NASCAR defector.

Byron drove in yet another NSCRA race in Charlotte a few weeks after that, lured by a five hundred–dollar offer from Bruton Smith just to show up. Prior to that race, Tim Flock—in a naïve effort to be forthright and conciliatory with NASCAR—had called France to ask permission to join the race. In pleading his case, Flock explained that there were no NASCAR races that weekend and that he "needed to feed my family."

"No way," France said.

Clearly, there was no upside to playing by France's rules.

When France learned about Byron's competing in "outlaw" races not sanctioned by NASCAR, he stripped away the points Byron had earned from his top-five finishes in NASCAR races earlier in the year. France also stripped points away from Lee Petty, who had ranked third in the Grand National race at the time, and from Tim Flock, who had been the leader of the modified division.

France felt that he couldn't back down at a time when drivers were testing the limits of his rule book. As an ex-racer, he understood why drivers wanted to compete in every available race. But he was no longer a driver, he was a businessman, and his primary goal was NASCAR's survival. He was also the boss, and not inclined to get his hands dirty by dealing directly with racers' insubordinations. So, as he often did at such times, he dispatched his number two guy, Bill Tuthill, to officially break the news to Byron, Petty, and Flock that they'd have to start accumulating points from zero.

The penalty would cost two of the men a championship.

It seemed that five thousand–dollar purses and end-of-year bonuses *still* weren't enough to guarantee drivers' loyalty to NASCAR. So France decided to prove that he knew just as well as Bruton Smith and Sam Nunis how to get the best drivers to his events.

France announced a new kind of race in South Carolina, a landmark event that would introduce stock cars to a new era of black asphalt instead of red dirt. But it wasn't just the first-ever stock car race on pavement that got every driver's attention. It was the twenty-five thousand–dollar purse.

Sam Nunis was a smart, slick, aggressive promoter who looked more like a Hollywood director or Wall Street broker than a race promoter. He heavily advertised his events in local papers and national magazines and hired savvy PR men to lure fans. At the start of the 1950 season, Sam Nunis had announced plans for a landmark Labor Day race at Lakewood that would be the *longest* stock car race in history: five hundred miles.

France initially scoffed at Nunis's five hundred–mile race. Strictly stock cars were having a hard enough time with one hundred miles and would likely fall to pieces if pushed to five hundred miles. But as Nunis's big race approached and created a buzz among stock car drivers, France—who could never resist a peer's challenge—changed his mind about a five hundred–miler and agreed to meet with a wealthy South Carolina peanut farmer-turned-lawyer, Harold Brasington.

Brasington had raced at Daytona in 1938 and had been smitten by the Indy 500 he attended in 1948. A year later, Brasington bought a farm in eastern South Carolina and began carving a misshapen oval racetrack into the dirt. He planned to call it Darlington Raceway. But unlike every other southern racetrack, it would be paved, just like Indy.

By mid-1950, with his speedway under construction, Brasington teamed with a lesser-known race-sanctioning organization—the Central States Racing Association (CSRA)—to help him promote his own five hundred–mile stock car race. But as race day neared, only one driver had agreed to compete, and the 1.25-mile track was still incomplete, even though twenty-five thousand dollars worth of tickets had already been sold.

Brasington was, in short, screwed. So he called Bill France. France had been seeking a venue for a five hundred–mile NASCAR race—to compete with Nunis's race—but didn't think Brasington's people could pull together such a big event quickly enough. Nonetheless, he agreed to fly to South Carolina and visit the incomplete track.

Despite the ongoing construction, France was impressed by the sprawling complex. It had the makings of stock car racing's largest track, and France envisioned a whole new future for NASCAR. A future of paved speedways, faster cars, huge grandstands, concession stands, campgrounds, and much, much more. France agreed to take over Brasington's race from the CSRA, as both sanctioner and promoter of the event, now scheduled for Labor Day—the same day as Nunis's big five hundred–mile race.

France advertised nationwide. The twenty-five thousand–dollar purse—the largest purse ever in stock car racing—lured so many racers away from Nunis's five hundred–mile race that Nunis eventually was forced to cancel it. He would curse Bill France the rest of his days.

With Nunis's race out of the picture, NASCAR's premier "Southern 500" at Darlington would be the longest stock car race in history and the first on asphalt. The promise of participating in motorsports history, not to mention an unprecedented $10,500 for the winner, lured seventy-five of the nation's best drivers.

Byron was still sore over losing all his NASCAR points and was not in contention for the year's championship. But he found he couldn't stand aside.

Vogt and Parks accompanied Byron and his powerful new Cadillac. Despite his debt to Henry Ford, whose cars had played such a vital role in his lucrative corn liquor career, Parks had always been partial to the more luxurious Caddy. When the carmaker finally introduced a race-worthy car in 1950, with a lightweight overhead valve V-8, Parks abandoned the Olds 88 that had carried Byron to victory earlier in the year and decided to attempt to give Cadillac its first NASCAR victory.

France, meanwhile, bought a secondhand Plymouth sedan for seventeen hundred dollars, a third the price tag of Parks's Caddy. He was on his way to Darlington and found the car at a lot in Winston-Salem, North Carolina. Along for the ride were Curtis Turner, a NASCAR official named Alvin Hawkins, and a California-based AAA/Indy racer driver Johnny Mantz. They towed the Plymouth to South Carolina and parked it out front of the town's lone twelve-room Darlington Motel, where France and other race officials would be staying. The story that France peddled in subsequent years was that he'd purchased the Plymouth to use solely for errands and trips to and from the racetrack. In truth, France, Turner, and Hawkins all pitched in to secretly purchase it for Mantz to race.

Mantz had met France and Turner during the recent Mexican Road Race. In that race, even though he passed out and nearly died from a bad batch of Mexican food, Mantz recovered to finish an impressive ninth. During an after-race party, the NASCAR boys—particularly Turner—convinced Mantz to give NASCAR a shot, so Mantz decided to take a break from AAA and get his chance at Darlington. All he needed now was a car. He'd wrecked his Oldsmobile in a warm-up NASCAR race in Ohio a week earlier. France's purchase of the used Plymouth would prove to be a wise move.

On September 4, 1950, more than thirty thousand spectators fell upon rural Darlington, South Carolina (population six thousand), to watch a whole new kind of race. The journey began days before race time as fans by the thousands arrived early to stake out turf on the brink of Darlington Speedway or inside the oval. It was the first time that stock car fans came a day or two before the race, claimed prime real estate in the "infield," and camped out there. That first pilgrimage to Darlington would evolve into an annual, near-religious ritual, a high holy day on the NASCAR calendar.

With only twelve motel rooms in town, there was no place for fans to sleep, so France opened the gates and allowed the early arrivals to sleep in the infield of the track. Each morning, he detonated a small explosive device to wake everyone up and chased them back outside.

On race day, the alarm clock bomb created havoc as people who'd slept in the infield tried to get out while others tried to get in. With room in the grandstands for just eleven thousand, it bespoke the ingenuity of the thirty thousand fans that they were all able to find a spot from which to view NASCAR's first megarace. France collected so much cash on race day that he and his workers ran out of envelopes and began stuffing it into peach baskets.

Every other driver had arrived with a gusty eight-cylinder engine, including Byron in his spectacular new Cadillac. Johnny Mantz, however, had told France weeks earlier that a lightweight car had the best chance of winning at Darlington. "You know what can win this race?" Mantz told France. "A goddamn Plymouth can win it." As an Indy racer, Mantz was more familiar with asphalt than any of NASCAR's dirt racers and had figured that the lightweight Plymouth—plus some heavy-duty racing tires he'd brought along with him to Darlington—would combine to make a reliable racing package.

Few NASCAR racers had a clue what it'd be like to race five hundred miles, more than twice the length of any race they'd driven. Byron had qualified with one of the fastest speeds, but on race day, he was skeptical about the ability of seventy-five allegedly stock cars to complete such a long race. "There won't be one of these cars at the finish," he said. "Not a damn one." Vogt and a few other mechanics installed jugs behind their drivers' seats, to be filled with each driver's favorite drink—say, whiskey—

which they could sip through a straw during the circuitous marathon. But everyone soon learned what Mantz already knew: what drivers needed most wasn't liquid but rubber.

South Carolina governor Strom Thurmond's wife cut the ceremonial ribbon, and seventy-five cars began winding their way around Brasington's track. Byron knew, from his limited experience on the asphalt-and-brick surface at Indianapolis, that such driving required a very different skill set than dirt-track racing. The turns of a dirt track could be forgiving if a driver knew how to power-slide through them. But on asphalt, the tactic wasn't to slide but to find a groove, hold it tight through the turn, then slingshot into the straightaway, followed by a precise cut back into the chosen groove of the next turn. What Byron didn't fully expect was how quickly his chosen groove would chew up tires.

To soak up excess oil from the freshly paved surface, race officials had dusted sand onto the track. When the scorching South Carolina sun softened the blacktop, it clung to the sand, turning the surface into a sandpaper frying pan. Byron drove steadily, stalking behind early leaders Gober Sosebee and Curtis Turner, only to feel his right-side tires go mushy, then flat. He pulled into the pits to take on a fresh pair. Fortunately, Red Vogt had brought pneumatic wrenches to help quickly unscrew and rescrew the lug nuts. Parks also lent a hand during the furious pit stops, removing his linen jacket and straw hat to help Vogt and his crew change Byron's shredded tires.

Byron was always able to quickly return to the track, but after twenty or thirty miles, he'd have to pull back into the pits for new tires. It was maddening, and by the time the race passed its halfway mark, Byron had replaced dozen of tires, and Vogt was suddenly fresh out. Crew members were sent to the parking lot to buy tires off passenger cars. Parks even donated the tires off his personal Cadillac.

One sportswriter said that racers' tires were "popping like popcorn."

Meanwhile, Johnny Mantz had driven to nearby Myrtle Beach the previous night, partied until dawn, jumped into the Atlantic Ocean to sober up, popped a few aspirin, and drove back to Darlington to pick up Bill France's Plymouth.

According to the story that France and other NASCAR officials adhered to in future years, Mantz didn't even take apart the Plymouth's engine. He and his mechanic just tuned it up, and Mantz began driving. France felt that the story would prove that NASCAR's race cars were truly "stock" cars and, as France put it, "strictly assembly line products." The real story was more complicated.

Mantz's mechanic was Hubert Westmoreland—the North Carolina bootlegger and whiskey mechanic who had owned the car that France disqualified from the first strictly stock race a year earlier. Mantz had qualified in the Plymouth earlier in the week, averaging seventy-three miles an hour, which put him in the thirty-fifth starting spot among seventy-five starters. But after qualifying, Mantz and Westmoreland took the Plymouth to Westmoreland's garage in North Carolina and began souping it up. The key addition was the hard-rubber racing tires that Mantz had brought with him.

On race day, Mantz's six-cylinder Plymouth was still among the slowest cars on the track. Curtis Turner or Red Byron regularly flew past him at one hundred miles an hour or more. But Mantz drove smart and steady, averaging seventy to seventy-five miles an hour in a calm and comfortable groove, away from all the wrecks and blowouts. By lap fifty, he found himself in the lead, the heavy-duty tires helping him avoid costly pit stops. He slowly built an insurmountable gap between himself and the others. The race lasted an incredible six and a half hours, during which Mantz stopped only three times to change tires, compared to Byron's two dozen pit stops. Only a third of the seventy-five starters lasted the entire race.

Despite all the blown tires and time-consuming pit stops, Byron still finished second—nine laps and more than eleven miles behind Mantz. But then, after studying their scoring sheets, NASCAR officials announced that a twenty-one-year-old former baseball pitcher named Fireball Roberts had actually completed one lap more than Byron.

They gave Roberts second place, worth $3,500, and Byron third, worth $2,000.

Mantz earned an incredible $10,510 for his victory, offset slightly by a $2,500 fine imposed against him by AAA for defecting to a NASCAR race. Few could believe that a hungover driver who'd crashed in his only prior NASCAR race, who had driven a car with three-fourths the piston power and at slower speeds than all the others, had somehow won. Tops among the disbelievers were Red Vogt and Red Byron, who angrily demanded that NASCAR inspectors tear apart every nut, bolt, belt, and gear of Mantz's Plymouth, in search of what they assumed would be blatent signs of cheating. Vogt, Byron, and the other top-five finishers knew that Mantz's mechanic, Westmoreland, was a whiskey tripper and mechanic, and they formally protested the legality of Mantz's car, variously claiming it had a nonstock camshaft, shocks, springs. As a virtuoso cheater himself, Vogt knew when to be suspicious. "I *know* there's something phony," Vogt told Bill France's sidekick, Bill Tuthill. "No way a Plymouth can beat a Cadillac. No *way*."

France refused to tear apart his own car. But then he realized it wouldn't look good, especially since Mantz's mechanic was a bootlegger. France finally sent Tuthill to instruct NASCAR's chief inspector, Al Crisler—the same man who'd taken victory away from Glenn Dunnaway and Westmoreland the previous year—to inspect "anything Red wanted checked."

Tuthill called Crisler at the garage first thing the next morning, to ask how the postrace inspection had gone.

"Go?" Crisler shrieked. "It's still *going*. I think you better come over."

When Tuthill and France arrived at the inspection site, Red Vogt was pacing back and forth, muttering to himself. Spread across every inch of the floor were parts of France's Plymouth—the carburetor in tatters; the valves strewn asunder; the pistons lying like six disused limbs; and even the exhaust, wheels, brakes, and gas tank sitting turdlike around the garage. Vogt, having clearly shunned sleep, strode maniacally back and forth. "No way a Plymouth can beat a Cadillac," he said, again and again. "No way."

After a brief consultation, France gave Tuthill the tricky job of telling Vogt that the inspection was, in fact, over, and that they'd found nothing illegal. "It's all there for you to see," Tuthill said quietly, as if speaking to a petulant child. They'd awakened the local Plymouth dealer—*twice*—and the man had verified that Johnny Mantz's winning vehicle was, after all that, *stock*.

"I know, I can see," Vogt growled, breathless, grasping for some other explanation. "But I'm still not *satisfied*."

Tuthill told the inspectors to dump all of the dismembered Plymouth parts into the backseat, his way of telling Vogt the fight was over.

Vogt was right, though. The car wasn't totally stock. The specialized, hard-compound Indy racing tires had helped earn Mantz his victory. But since the rule book didn't specifically prohibit racing tires, they were legal. France wasn't about to revise his rule book this time. Not if it took victory away from his own car.

Vogt's lost battle with NASCAR inspectors that long night at Darlington signaled the beginning of the end of his reign as NASCAR's top mechanic. There were so many rules now, which Vogt felt suffocated his mechanical ingenuity. By ushering in the era of blacktop tracks, Darlington became a turning point for masters of dirt-track racing such as Vogt. It didn't help that Vogt's best driver was veering further away from NASCAR.

Byron's third-place finish at Darlington earned back enough of the points he'd lost earlier in the year to put him in fourth place for the year's championship race. But then he competed in another NSCRA race, and Bill France stripped his points a second time.

Byron wasn't too upset and in fact had expected it. Just as Barney Oldfield had shunned the restrictive AAA Contest Board to race on his terms, Byron seemed willing to let his short-lived NASCAR fame slip away. Byron competed in just four NASCAR races in 1950, but his performance in those events would have been worth fourth place in the year's championship race—*if* he hadn't lost all his points. *Twice.* He ended the 1950 season with zero points. For the first time since World War II, he was no longer a dominant force on the stock car circuit. And he would never again win a NASCAR race.

The 1950 season closed with the naming of a Yankee, a New Yorker named Bill Rexford, as NASCAR's champion.* Rexford had won only once, a one hundred–miler in Ohio, but had competed in all but two of the nineteen NASCAR races and thus accumulated enough points for the championship. Fireball Roberts finished second, followed by Lee Petty, who would have been the champ if France had not stripped away his points earlier in the year.

None of the winning racers of 1950 drove a Ford. In nineteen Grand National races, a Ford won just once. Fords wouldn't return to NASCAR's winner's circle for another five years.

At the end of 1950, during the off-season holidays, Byron and his wife welcomed a baby girl into the family. Parks opened a new sports car dealership, Overseas Motor Agency, which would sell expensive British Austins and other foreign sports cars. Vogt received a peacemaking offer from Bill France to take over a new Nash dealership in Florida and to be the mechanic for a racing team France wanted to finance. France had befriended folks at Nash after they'd loaned him a car for the Mexico race. But in the end, the Vogt-France deal fell apart, and Vogt went back to fixing cars at his Atlanta garage.

Byron, Parks, and Vogt were each taking their first steps away from stock cars. And one another.

---

*A champion from the North turned out to be a fluke. For the next thirty years, Grand National winners would come from one of four southern states: North Carolina (sixteen), South Carolina (ten), Georgia (two), or Virginia (two).

Nothing stands still in the world.
Things get better or worse, bigger or smaller.
— BILL FRANCE

18

NASCAR is here to stay: "Like sex, the atom bomb and ice cream"

In 1951, Detroit invited NASCAR to help celebrate the city's 250th anniversary with a race at the Michigan State Fairgrounds. NASCAR's first event in Henry Ford's hometown, on August 12, came exactly fifty years after Henry Ford had raced his one and only race at the nearby Grosse Point racetrack. But in a clear sign that Fords were no longer considered worthwhile racing cars, only five of the fifty-nine drivers piloted Fords.

One of them was Red Byron, in a borrowed six-cylinder Ford "6."

Byron's friend Marshall Teague drove his Hudson Hornet to victory that day at Detroit. Byron's Ford just didn't have enough horsepower to catch the leaders, and he settled for fourth place—the last top-five finish of his NASCAR career.

Despite his lackadaisical approach to NASCAR the previous year, Byron still had the racing bug and cherry-picked a handful of NASCAR's best races in 1951. He had raced in the season opener at Daytona and at Columbus, Georgia, the track of Roy Brannon's death. He finished eleventh and sixth in those races, earned two hundred dollars and a few NASCAR points. But then he raced in one of Bruton Smith's NSCRA races at Lakewood, and Bill France stripped away all his points once again. (France would go on to strip points from Curtis Turner, Bob Flock, Ed Samples, and others in 1951.)

For Bill France, the Michigan Fairgrounds race was an important introduction to the power players of Detroit, men who in future years would help NASCAR grow into a behemoth. Although France had once declared that NASCAR should be a part-time hobby for weekend warriors, his new vision for a nationwide NASCAR no longer allowed a racer to participate casually. It was all or nothing, and that excluded family men such as Byron, men who didn't want to travel nonstop all year long, following the NASCAR banner up and down the East Coast and occasionally into the Midwest.

For Byron, the Detroit race was more like a death knell, a warning from the racing gods that he was incapable of victory without Parks and Vogt, that NASCAR was no longer his sport, that stock cars were now completely and firmly in Bill France's hands.

Three weeks later, Byron chose a swan song: Darlington, whose winner would receive eighty-eight hundred dollars. Byron towed his Ford there, hoping for one last bit of magic and cash. But his final NASCAR race ended in a violent collision with his friend and fellow "outlaw" Marshall Teague. Teague had been leading the race when a flat tire forced him into the pits. In his attempt to regain the lead, Teague came upon Byron's slower Ford and T-boned it, the nose of Teague's Hudson crushing the driver's door of Byron's Ford.

It was the end of Byron's career. In less than ten years, he would be dead.

Through the 1950s, meanwhile, France expanded his authority in big and small ways, further developing the power to make or break careers, shaping the sport into his image, shaving off the rough edges, always with an eye toward bigger, faster, more. He'd soon be the undeniable mogul of stock car racing and the king of American motorsports.

One day in 1951, France walked through pit road before a race, his 6-foot, 5-inch frame looming above cars, drivers, and mechanics. His eyes scanned the garage until they fell upon a flask of whiskey sitting atop the toolbox of mechanic Smokey Yunick, Red Vogt's protégé, whom France considered a rabble-rousing smart-ass.

Not only had whiskey played a starring role in NASCAR's creation, but it had fueled many drivers through many laps. Some kept a pint under the driver's seat, within easy reach for a nip during races. Buddy Shuman once told a reporter that Lord Calvert, his favorite whiskey, was "my co-pilot." Curtis Turner, the movie-star-handsome ex-bootlegger, had an ample appetite for Canadian Club and Coke. France himself was, according to Yunick, a known drinker—and womanizer. But when France saw Yunick's whiskey that day, he issued a puritanical decree.

"No liquor in the pits," he said.

And just like that, NASCAR took another step away from its bootlegging origins. It was one more turning point in France's mighty struggle to distance NASCAR from its past, to refine it into a clean, modern, moonshine-free American family sport.

With the horrible exception of the boy killed by Red Byron's Ford in 1948, fans were not dying with any regularity on NASCAR tracks. There had been many close calls over the years, especially at Daytona, where fans continued to crowd within feet of the track. A few unlucky accidents could have significantly altered NASCAR's safety record, and its future. But the sport, and France, had been very lucky. The same was not true elsewhere in auto racing, particularly at the more popular open-wheel events, and those fatalities gave a surprising boost to NASCAR's future.

In 1952, a young boy sitting with his father watching a Grand Prix race at Watkins Glen, New York, was struck by an errant race car and killed. A year later, an Indy car flew into the grandstands at a AAA race in Syracuse, New York, landing upside down atop a boy who became jammed in the cockpit. He remarkably survived. Four drivers were killed in the Mexican Road Race of 1954. A year after that, two AAA drivers were killed at Langhorne Speedway, followed by the death of Indy legend Bill Vukovich at 1955's Indianapolis 500, exactly a year after he won the same race. Of the thirty-three men who had raced in the Indy

500 of 1955, eighteen would soon die violent racing deaths, including all of the top-five finishers.

Then came the most tragic racing day of all. Two hours into the twenty-four-hour race at Le Mans in France, Pierre Levegh's Mercedes-Benz clipped the rear end of a slower car and launched into the air, spiraling toward the grandstands at 150 miles an hour. Levegh's car exploded amid a throng of spectators, killing at least eighty and maiming hundreds.

Afterward, a drumbeat of opposition to auto racing grew louder. *Newsweek* called race car drivers "motorized lemmings." A senator from Oregon called for a ban on all racing: "I believe the time has come for the United States to be a civilized nation and stop the carnage on the racetracks." Even the Vatican publicly denounced racing, and the American public began to wonder about AAA's dual role as proselytizer of safe highway driving and promoter of potentially deadly contests on the racetrack.

Finally, in August of 1955, AAA president Andrew Sordoni announced that his group would end all involvement with motorsports. In the early 1950s, AAA had actually begun threatening France's dominance of stock cars by creating its own stock car circuit and luring away a few NASCAR drivers. But the recent racing deaths prompted AAA to end its stock car circuit, to sever its ties to the Indy 500, to dissolve the Contest Board, and to return AAA to its original purpose of helping motorists with broken-down cars, providing road maps and car insurance, and rating motels and restaurants.

For Bill France, this was all good news. AAA's withdrawal opened wide the door for France to become the dominant racing promoter in America. And it happened at just the right time for NASCAR, whose veterans were stepping aside, to be replaced by a new generation of dynamic stars such as Junior Johnson, Fireball Roberts, Herb Thomas, and the ever-entertaining Curtis Turner, with names such as Petty and Earnhardt to follow.

The NSCRA remained France's only real opposition. It wouldn't last long. In 1950, he had met with Bruton Smith, the NSCRA's twenty-three-year-old president, to discuss a merger of NSCRA and NASCAR. "Doesn't sound like a bad idea," Smith said. But a few months later, with the Korean War pulling southern soldiers back to battle, Smith was drafted into the army and trained as a paratrooper. When he returned home to Charlotte two years later, Smith found that the NSCRA had disintegrated amid mismanagement, financial misdeeds, and internal squabbles. France was no longer interested in a merger and, in fact, considered Smith "a pain." Smith would eventually build a vast racing empire of his own,* but during the mid-1950s, he watched from the sidelines as France took absolute control of stock car racing.

Sam Nunis, the scrappy AAA promoter and sometime NSCRA partner, ran short of cash at a few races and was unable to pay drivers. That was a promoter's worst nightmare and, combined with AAA's departure from racing, ended his career. Nunis lived out his days promoting small-time fairgrounds races in Trenton, New Jersey.

Other potential rivals stepped aside or were shoved aside by France. "Outlaw" drivers who'd relied on NSCRA or other racing groups returned to NASCAR, begging France to let them come back. France required men such as Gober Sosebee, Ed Samples, and Buddy Shuman to pay fines or post bonds as assurance that they'd race exclusively for NASCAR.

After AAA's departure in 1955, France went on the stump to tout and overemphasize NASCAR's role in contributing to safety improvements in the automotive industry. His newspaper friend Bernard Kahn at the *Daytona Beach News Journal* helped, awkwardly cheering AAA's departure from racing as a chance for a "blood transfusion in automotive racing . . . from energetic Bill France." In Kahn's words, "automobile racing is here to stay: like sex, the atom bomb and ice cream."

---

*Smith now owns six huge speedways, which host dozens of NASCAR races a year. Like France, he became a billionaire and one of America's richest men.

Drivers lucky enough to be allowed along for the ride simply had to abide by Bill France's rules.

"Stock car racing has boomed beyond anyone's wildest dreams," France once said. Before World War II, he'd been a decent racer and an occasional winner, known more for bluster than skill. He matured into a remarkable salesman, a fearless authoritarian, and a shrewd businessman. And if anyone questioned his authority, he attacked.

In 1961, efforts by Curtis Turner, Tim Flock, and Fireball Roberts to create a drivers' union infuriated France, who called a mandatory meeting before a race.

"Gentlemen, before I have this union stuffed down my throat, I will plow up my track at Daytona Beach . . . and plant corn," he said. "After the race tonight, no known union members can compete in a NASCAR race." France handed out sheets of paper for each of them to sign, rejecting the union. "If you don't sign this form, don't go back and get in your cars," he vowed. "And if that isn't tough enough, I'll use a pistol to enforce it. I have a pistol, and I know how to use it. I've used it before." France quashed a similar attempt to create a drivers' union in 1969, led by Richard Petty.

France and NASCAR got an unintended boost from a 1970 federal ban on televised tobacco advertising. Ironically, it was moonshining racer Junior Johnson who introduced France to the folks at R. J. Reynolds Company, and it was love at first sight—tobacco needed a place to promote its product, and NASCAR needed a sponsor with cash.

Over the years, France expanded his control of stock car racing by building his own racetracks: the Daytona International Speedway in 1959 and, ten years later, Talladega Superspeedway, near the Alabama town where Red Byron once lived.

One of NASCAR's savviest—and more controversial—moves was to create a separate, publicly traded company, called International Speedway Corporation, to buy and run racetracks. ISC grew to own a dozen tracks and acquire part ownership in a few others, along with a radio station, food and beverage concessions, and merchandise operations.

ISC's officers and major shareholders were all France family members, as were NASCAR's top officers and shareholders. Because NASCAR decided which racetracks were allowed to host NASCAR races, the France family essentially controlled the fortunes of racetrack owners, including ISC. Some outsiders complained that there was a built-in conflict of interest and that France-controlled NASCAR favored France-controlled ISC, whose racetracks today host roughly half of NASCAR's top Nextel Cup events. The most vocal opponent has been the France family's only significant rival in stock car racing—Bruton Smith, whose Speedway Motorsports Inc. owns six racetracks.

More than fifty years after his first battles with Bill France Sr., Smith remains as feisty as ever. He has lobbied NASCAR officials to schedule more Nextel Cup races at his tracks and has complained that NASCAR has rebuffed him in favor of ISC racetracks. But those are relatively minor, internal squabbles. For the most part, everybody makes money in today's NASCAR.

It ain't the money. Nor the glory. I just like to drive.
It's that simple. It's my thing. I like the feel of the metal
around me, the feel of the tires under me.
— RICHARD PETTY

19

"I had to start making a living"

POSTSCRIPT: WHAT BECAME OF THEM ALL?

THE FLOCKS

Bob broke his neck in the 1951 season finale—allegedly the only race in which he didn't superstitiously touch the track with his knuckles. He came back in 1952 to beat little brother Tim at the new Asheville-Weaverville Speedway, a North Carolina track that Raymond Parks briefly owned. In the mid-1950s, Bob and Tim raced Chryslers for a race team owned by Carl Kiekhaefer, who sold Mercury boat motors and early on saw the potential for turning NASCAR cars into moving billboards. But Kiekhaefer once jokingly tweaked Bob's chin after a race, and Bob, who hated to be touched, popped his boss in the face. He was fired on the spot. Bob died in 1964 of a heart attack at age forty-six.

Tim, who sometimes drove with a monkey named Jocko Flock strapped in the passenger seat, won NASCAR's 1952 championship. Two years later, France disqualified his victory at Daytona due to an alleged infraction and gave the race to Lee Petty, driving a new Chrysler. Tim suspected the move was France's way of luring Chrysler into racing, and he quit NASCAR in disgust. But a year later, Tim returned to NASCAR when Carl Kiekhaefer offered him a spot on his team. Tim won the 1955 championship, on his way to becoming one of the winningest drivers of the 1950s. In 1961, concerns about increasing speeds, followed by a few drivers' deaths, inspired Tim and a few other racers to create a drivers' union. Bill France angrily banned him from NASCAR for life. Flock quit racing for good in 1962 and died in 1998 at age seventy-three. He is among the few NASCAR pioneers to be named by NASCAR as one of the sport's top-fifty drivers.

Fonty won the big Southern 500 race in 1952 at Darlington (later renamed the "Rebel 500") and afterward jumped onto the hood of his car. Wearing a pair of baggy Bermuda shorts, he led a crowd of thirty-two thousand in singing "Dixie." He raced in several non-NASCAR events in 1954 and was blacklisted by France. He was allowed to return to NASCAR in 1955 after paying a fine and a one thousand–dollar bond. A year later, he joined Tim and Bob's Chrysler-driving team. At Darlington in 1957, he had a blowout, spun and stalled, then got slammed head-on by another driver, who was killed. Fonty retired on the spot. He would never race again but couldn't stay entirely away from NASCAR. In the 1960s, Fonty began working with France on plans to build a new paved speedway in Talladega, Alabama. Fonty also worked for NASCAR's new insurance and road service department (created to compete with AAA) and helped start a fan club program. France later brought in Alabama governor George Wallace (on whose presidential campaigns he served) to help with the Talladega speedway, allegedly shoving Fonty aside. After a long bout with cancer, Fonty died in 1972, at age fifty-one.

LEE PETTY—AND FAMILY

Petty didn't start racing until he was thirty-five. He hit his stride at age forty, when he won NASCAR's 1954 championship, a feat he'd repeat in 1958 and 1959. In 1959, he won the inaugural five hundred–mile race at France's new Daytona International Speedway, in a remarkable two-way finish. It took NASCAR three days of studying photos to declare Petty the winner, by an inch. That same year, Petty protested his second-place finish at Atlanta's Lakewood Speedway. The officials sided with Petty and gave him the victory, taking it away from Lee's own son, Richard, who had begun racing that year and was named NASCAR's rookie of the year. "I would have protested even if it was my mother," Lee said. Richard took the loss in stride and went on to become NASCAR's winningest racer. Richard's son, Kyle, and grandson, Adam, followed him into racing, making the Pettys NASCAR's first four-generation family—until 2000, when Adam was killed practicing for a race in New Hampshire, just a few weeks after Lee, the patriarch, had died. A few other NASCAR family dynasties would emerge, but the only one to rival the Pettys would be the Earnhardts, whose story would also result in tragedy.

THE MOONSHINERS AND THE REBELS

Hard-drinking, hard-living Curtis Turner won hundreds of races and became a crowd favorite through the 1950s. He flew an airplane from race to race, once landing on Main Street in Easley, South Carolina, in search of whiskey; on takeoff, he ripped out the town's main telephone line and lost his pilot's license. He occasionally drove rental cars into motel swimming pools, befriended celebrities, and bedded beautiful women. Turner partnered with Bruton Smith in 1959 to build Charlotte Motor Speedway (later renamed Lowes Motor Speedway), but his financial management was awful—he once bounced a seventy-five thousand–dollar check—and the board of directors ousted him. In 1961, he teamed with Tim Flock and Fireball Roberts to start a drivers' union, and France banned them all from NASCAR for life. France reinstated Turner four years later, and he returned to NASCAR with a vengeance, winning his second start. In 1968, *Sports Illustrated* commemorated Turner's career by putting his face on the cover, calling him "King of the Wild Road" and "the Babe Ruth of stock car racing." Turner was killed in a plane crash in 1970.

Junior Johnson became NASCAR's most famous moonshining racer, considered by many to be the best driver in NASCAR's history. Born into a notorious bootlegging family from North Wilkesboro, he began winning NASCAR races in the mid-1950s, including five Grand National wins in 1955, until a moonshining conviction in 1956 sent him off to Chillicothe federal prison in Ohio, the same prison that had held Raymond Parks twenty years earlier. Johnson was released a year later and in late 1958 began winning once more, including three in a row that fall and 1960's Daytona 500. Johnson became the subject of Tom Wolfe's 1964 profile in *Esquire,* "The Last American Hero Is Junior Johnson. Yes!" But a year later, Johnson abruptly quit racing, at age thirty-three, after winning his fiftieth Grand National race. He soon began a second act as owner of his own successful racing team. In 1972, he introduced R. J. Reynolds tobacco company to Bill France, the result of which was RJR's longtime sponsorship of NASCAR's Grand National division, which became the Winston Cup. In 1985, Ronald Reagan issued a presidential pardon that cleared Johnson's 1956 moonshining conviction.*

Marshall Teague, NASCAR's first treasurer, after initiating the complaints about NASCAR's payouts in 1949, had defected to AAA and was named AAA's stock car champ in 1954. When AAA's stock car circuit ended, he switched to Indy cars and raced at Indy throughout the mid-1950s. In 1959, he was preparing to race his Indy car in a NASCAR-sponsored Indy race at Daytona. He met with France to discuss a return to NASCAR and stock cars, which France agreed to consider. But first, he wanted Teague to try breaking the closed-course speed record (of 176.8 miles per hour) at Daytona International Speedway. France figured it would be great publicity for the new track. While attempting that record, Teague crashed into the wall and was killed. He was thirty-seven.

Fireball Roberts, one of the most dominant racers of the 1950s, and one of the last to have Red Vogt as his mechanic, briefly stood fast with Curtis Turner and Tim Flock in the 1961 effort to start a union. But

---

*In 2005, just days before Christmas, George W. Bush issued eleven presidential pardons. Three of them were to convicted moonshiners.

Roberts resigned as union president, and France allowed him to return to NASCAR. Three years later, at Curtis Turner's Charlotte Motor Speedway, Roberts tried to steer away from the spinning car of Junior Johnson. He collided with Ned Jarrett, and both cars exploded into flames. Jarrett quickly escaped from his car and rushed to help Roberts, who was trapped inside. "My God, Ned, help me! I'm on fire!" he screamed. He died six weeks later and was buried a few blocks from Daytona Speedway, one hundred yards away from Marshall Teague's grave.

Other NASCAR defectors, including Gober Sosebee and Ed Samples, applied for reinstatement to NASCAR in the early 1950s and raced for a few more years before leaving the stock car world to run their garages. Buddy Shuman lasted the longest, racing into the mid-1950s before taking on an administrative role overseeing Ford Motor Company's NASCAR racing program. But the night before a 1956 race in North Carolina, he fell asleep while smoking in his hotel room and died in the ensuing fire.

Billy Watson, the "kid" who used to hang around Red Vogt's garage and whom Roy Hall taught to drive, ran moonshine in the mid-1940s but joined the Marines in 1948 to avoid an indictment on liquor charges. After his return in 1951, he started running numbers, driving Raymond Parks's Cadillac—the one Red Byron had raced in 1949. He was busted in that car in a sting operation and spent seven months behind bars. He considered a racing career after his release, but Parks warned him, "You wanna be broke the rest of your life? If you do, you stay with racing." Instead, Watson created a chain of "Billy's" restaurants throughout Atlanta and became very wealthy. He remained friends with Parks, whom he always called "boss."

ROY HALL

After his critical head injury in the final race of 1949, Hall incredibly returned to race at Darlington in 1952. He drove the only Desoto (numbered "22," in homage to Red Byron) in a field of sixty-six cars. After problems with tires and fuel, he pulled out less than halfway through the race and finished forty-eighth. Except for an ill-advised return to

Lakewood in 1960, where he broke an axle and wrecked, he never raced again. "It's a shame about Roy," a retired Dawsonville whiskey tripper once said. "Folks say he never really was the same after Lloyd Seay's death." Hall lived in downtown Atlanta and sold cars—mostly Chevrolets, which was an ironic career choice for someone who had spent his youth fleeing revenuers and winning scores of races exclusively in Fords. In 1972, Jim Croce immortalized Hall—"Yeah, Roy so cool that racin' fool he don't know what fear's about"—with his song "Rapid Roy (The Stock Car Boy)." He died in 1992 at seventy-two.

DAWSONVILLE, GEORGIA—AND MOONSHINE

After World War II, moonshining arrests shot upward again in the late 1940s and early 1950s, approaching Prohibition-era levels. For many decades, an unwritten code of ethics existed among southern moonshiners, many of whom aspired to create a quality product. But the postwar years saw a decline in scruples: an outbreak of poisoned moonshine in Atlanta in 1951 was blamed for the deaths of forty-two people.

Curtis Turner and Junior Johnson remained the poster boys for moonshining racers through the 1950s and '60s. Two years after Turner's death, NASCAR saw the arrest of its last known moonshiner, Martinsville, Virginia's Buddy Arrington, busted in 1972.

Dawsonville's influence on NASCAR seemed dead and gone, until 1988, when Bill Elliott—"Awesome Bill from Dawsonville"—became NASCAR's champion, exactly fifty years after Lloyd Seay's "championship." In 1991, Elliott drove his number 9 car to victory at Daytona, exactly fifty years after Dawsonville moonshiner Bernard Long had raced his own number 9 car to victory there—just two of the *six* Dawsonville natives to win at Daytona. Photos and news clippings of Elliott today plaster the walls of the Dawsonville Pool Hall, among clippings and photos of Seay, Hall, Parks, Samples, Sosebee, and others. It has become a museum of sorts honoring the symbiotic heyday of stock cars and moonshine.

Local race fans built a twelve million–dollar museum called "Thunder Road" in 2002, displaying a couple of Raymond Parks's cars.

But the venture failed, and Thunder Road is now home to Dawsonville's City Hall. Dawsonville hosts an annual Moonshine Festival, which draws old-timers and replica whiskey cars.

NASCAR, meanwhile, continues to downplay the original link between southern moonshine and the sport's creation. In a DVD called *The History of NASCAR,* the narrator praises the young and talented drivers of the fifties who no longer had the "unsavory pedigree of a bootlegger." And yet, NASCAR's search for profit led to a 2005 decision to lift a ban against hard liquor companies' sponsoring race cars. Fans now cheer for whiskey cars once more: the number 07 Jack Daniels car and the number 7 Jim Beam car, both of them Chevrolets.

FORD MOTOR COMPANY

After getting soundly beaten by Oldsmobile, Plymouth, and Hudson through the early 1950s, Ford introduced a new overhead valve V-8 in 1955 and jumped back into the world of stock car racing, sponsoring the race cars of Junior Johnson, Curtis Turner, and Fireball Roberts. Chevrolet also came on board in 1955 when it introduced a compact but powerful "small block" overhead valve V-8 that was deemed even better than Ford's. Ford and Chevy soon were getting beaten by even faster Chrysler engines. The carmakers of Detroit, after being introduced to NASCAR when France brought his first race there in 1951, were all financing NASCAR teams by the mid-1950s. But then came AAA's 1955 decision to pull out of racing, followed by news reports that fifty thousand people were now dying each year on U.S. highways. Carmakers began to receive bad press for their role in NASCAR racing, and under pressure from the Automobile Manufacturers' Association, Ford, Chrysler, and GM all pulled out of NASCAR by 1957 and would not return until the following decade.

In the 1960s, Henry Ford's grandson, Henry II, led Ford Motor Company back to the sport that its creator so famously "never really thought much of." Fords are now a mainstay of the NASCAR circuit, although in the first years of the twenty-first century, they've been far outnumbered by Chevys and Dodges. The champions of 2003 and

2004 were both driving Fords, but Chevy has twenty-two championship cars compared to Ford's eight. Ford today cohosts NASCAR's annual UAW-FORD 500 at Talladega Superspeedway (near Red Byron's old hometown), an ironic collaboration between Ford and the United Auto Workers, given Henry Ford's notorious union-busting efforts.

Ford Motor Company's century-long presence in Atlanta seemed to be ending. In early 2006, Henry Ford's great-grandson, William Clay Ford, announced plans to lay off thousands and close fourteen factories, including its assembly plant outside Atlanta.

THE CO-FOUNDERS

RED VOGT

In 1951, Vogt had briefly considered Bill France's offer to run a Nash car dealership in Florida and to help France start a Nash racing team. But the two longtime friends and occasional foes could never agree on the details, and the precarious partnership fell apart with the men screaming into their respective telephones.

Vogt remained in Atlanta, working on customers' cars and the occasional race car, until 1954, when he moved to Daytona Beach to work for the well-known carburetor maker Bob Fish, whose drivers included Fireball Roberts. A year later, Fireball Roberts won the season-opening race at Daytona, giving the Fish Carburetor shop its first Grand National victory. But twenty-four hours later, NASCAR commissioner Cannonball Baker announced that Roberts was disqualified. Inspectors had spent all night tearing apart Roberts's Vogt–tuned engine and found a push rod that was .0016 of an inch too short. They gave the victory to Tim Flock and his Chrysler. This was an ironic twist, since Flock had resigned from NASCAR after the previous year's Daytona race, accusing France of disqualifying him in order to award a victory to another manufacturer's car. Vogt suspected—just as Tim Flock had in 1954—that France wanted a Chrysler to win the race and had instructed his inspectors to keep dismantling Roberts's car until they found something to disqualify. It's just as likely that France knew Vogt well enough to believe that if he looked long and hard enough, he'd find a rule violation.

In the wake of that loss, Vogt left Daytona to work in Charlotte for Indy-racing legend Peter DePaolo, who was starting a Ford-sponsored NASCAR team and wanted Vogt as his mechanic. For the 1956 season, DePaolo hired racers Fireball Roberts, Curtis Turner, and Turner's pugnacious friend Joe Weatherly to drive his Vogt-built cars. He also hired a talented mechanic named Ralph Moody, whom Vogt allowed to join his car-building team. Ford factory officials soon decided to add their own guy, John Holman, to keep an eye on Ford's investment. Knowing that Vogt wouldn't agree to partner with a third mechanic, DePaolo was purposely vague about what Holman's exact role would be. One night, Vogt worked on Curtis Turner's car, finished at 5:00 a.m., and went home for a few hours of sleep. When he returned to the shop, he found Holman tinkering on *his* car. He argued with Holman, marched into DePaolo's office, and quit. Holman and Moody later left DePaolo to form their own racing team, taking Turner and Roberts with them.*

After quitting DePaolo's team, Vogt immediately got a call from Tim Flock's sponsor, Carl Kiekhaefer, asking him to work for his Chrysler-Dodge team. Kiekhaefer was a control freak who made his drivers wear uniforms and abide by curfews. Vogt didn't seem to mind the strict culture, and he helped Kiekhaefer's Chryslers dominate NASCAR during the mid-1950s. That success infuriated France, who had initially wanted Chrysler to join NASCAR but didn't want one carmaker winning all of NASCAR's events. France also knew that the cars had been worked on by Vogt and were therefore suspect. He frequently called for inspections of Vogt's Chryslers, until Kiekhaefer quit NASCAR in frustration after the 1957 season and dismantled his team.

Vogt returned to Daytona to work for Smokey Yunick, who called Vogt "Merlin" and "the granddaddy of NASCAR mechanics." Yunick understood that Vogt, now in his fifties, "couldn't handle the bullshitting and political ass-kissing. He was a simple man [who] refused to or

---

*Holman-Moody's Fords dominated NASCAR for the next two decades.

couldn't accept the 'new world' we got flung into." Unfortunately, in the new NASCAR, you had to play politics. Vogt soon left Yunick's shop— Yunick may have understood Vogt, but the two headstrong masters never quite meshed as partners—and in 1958 opened a new garage, where he would spend the next dozen years building special-order racing engines and working on everyday passenger cars.

Vogt retired in 1970 and in the late 1980s managed to rekindle a lukewarm friendship with France, whom he'd known since France was still in utero. The man he once called "watermelon" was now a powerful billionaire; Vogt, on the other hand, lived modestly in the shadow of Daytona Speedway with the woman he'd married five times.

Their different circumstances and many disagreements over the years couldn't undo a deep-rooted connection. Bill France was diagnosed with Alzheimer's, which progressed through the late 1980s, and as his health got worse, he would call his old friend Vogt frequently. Vogt hated to see his formerly cocky and burly friend slowly deteriorate. Once, after visiting France in person and sitting beside his bed and talking about the simple old days of racing, Vogt came home and "cried like a baby," his daughter, June Wendt, recalled. Despite all their battles, "He loved Bill France," she said. Vogt, a chain-smoker for many decades, died of cancer in 1991. He was eighty-seven.

RED BYRON

Byron seemed to feel no sorrow or regret when he left NASCAR after the 1951 season. In fact, he seemed relieved to be moving on. Friends speculated that the ghost of seven-year-old Roy Brannon haunted every race, and many believed he "lost heart" after that tragedy. The NASCAR community had never entirely been his home. Though born in the South, he wasn't raised a southerner, and moonshine never ran in his blood as it had for his patron, his mechanic, and so many of his peers. When he walked away, it was sudden, and without emotion. He and Raymond Parks, after five years as partners and one near-death experience in Mexico, did not call each other up or meet for beers or write letters. Byron never attended NASCAR races as a spectator. He simply drifted south.

Byron finally followed through on his promise to move his wife to Florida and to buy her a house near the ocean. With their son, and now two daughters, Red and Nell moved to West Palm Beach in the mid-1950s where Red took a job with a millionaire sportsman named Briggs Cunningham, a longtime patron of sports car and open-wheel racing. Cunningham wanted to develop a new top-of-the-line sports car—an American version of Italy's Ferrari—to race at the premier events around the world, such as Le Mans. Cunningham built a factory in an airplane hangar in Palm Beach and, in addition to hiring Byron, brought aboard racing legend Phil Walters, a World War II POW with one lung who had frequently raced stock cars under the nom de guerre Ted Tappett (to avoid the wrath of his wealthy Long Island family, who thought stock cars were dirty).

Cunningham introduced Byron to a world of wealth, and he mingled amid the gentlemanly side of motorsports. His friends included famous Indy and Grand Prix racers and racer-playboys such as Porfirio Rubirosa. He was hardly in their league but was earning enough for a few luxuries, including a spectacular two-seater Mercedes ragtop. Byron developed a taste for nice clothes and fine wine and got to know the best restaurants of South Florida. But after the 1955 tragedy at Le Mans, Cunningham decided to close his factory, and Byron went job hunting.

After leaving Cunningham, Byron—now smitten with fancy race cars—worked for a racing team started by Chevrolet for its new sports car, the Corvette. He then opened Red Byron Automotive in Lake Worth, Florida, and worked on the sports cars of wealthy patrons. His love of racing never entirely left him, and he traveled often and for extended periods to work as a mechanic for Sports Car Club of America teams, which raced expensive sports cars on squiggly tracks. He also drove open-wheel cars in a few late-1950s Grand Prix races, including the prestigious "12 Hours of Sebring" in Florida.

Red Vogt used to joke that the Japanese had collected so much American scrap metal for making bombs in World War II—including old Fords—that the first jagged hunk the doctors had pulled out of Byron's wounded leg had the word *Ford* stamped into it. Recycled bits of Ford or not, the remnants of shrapnel still buried in Byron's hip continued to affect his health—and happiness. The withered leg always determined whether it'd be a good day or bad, whether he'd be his usual upbeat and confident self or, as Vogt once observed, "If he wasn't feeling good, he wouldn't say nothin' to nobody."

Byron's health continued to decline in the late 1950s, and he suffered a heart attack in Texas, then another in California, and came home on a stretcher. Doctors insisted that he rest, travel less, slow down. He ignored them.

In 1960, he received a call from Anheuser-Busch, which was considering a sports car team and wanted to hire Byron. He flew to Chicago for a series of meetings. Afterward the Anheuser-Busch people threw a party for the prospective team at a downtown convention hall. Byron caught a chill and went back to his hotel room to rest. He called the front desk to ask them to turn up the heat, and then he lay down.

He never woke up. He was forty-four.

Failed attempts to create drivers' unions during the 1960s meant that veteran NASCAR racers had no health insurance and received no such thing as a pension. What money Byron had managed to save ran out quickly, and his wife eventually moved their family back to the rural Georgia community she'd escaped during World War II. They now live there in very modest obscurity. "He was a good man," says Nell, who now suffers from Alzheimer's. "He was one of the best men I've ever known."

Byron's role as one of NASCAR's creators and its first champ was slowly recognized in the years after his death. In 1966, he was posthumously inducted into the National Motorsports Hall of Fame. Thirty years later, his face appeared on a Kellogg's cereal box. And in 1998—in one of many commemorations of NASCAR's fiftieth anniversary—*Sports Illustrated* named him one of NASCAR's fifty greatest drivers.

RAYMOND PARKS

Parks never wore his racing fever on his sleeve. It didn't cause him to break out in a sweat or froth at the mouth. But if one looked closely, the signs were always there. In business, he strived for honesty (with customers, anyway), cleanliness, and perfection. Similarly, on the racetrack, a Parks car stood out for being the fastest *and* the cleanest. If Hall or Byron crumpled a fender, Parks would have Vogt fix it, even if it didn't affect the performance. Parks wanted his cars to look their best, smooth and polished. But the best cost money. And by 1951, Parks realized for the umpteenth time that, for all his powerful engines and smooth fenders, "I'm spending more than I'm making." Parks's deep pockets had also begun to elicit some suspicion. Sportswriters such as Bill France's friend Bernie Kahn began to wonder in print about the "mysterious young Atlanta millionaire who foots the expensive bills that building these cars requires." Drivers wondered about the fairness of a millionaire's backing in a workingman's sport. "Every car that Byron has driven at Daytona Beach loses $10,000," one racer complained, anonymously. Other car owners didn't have the luxury of throwing away such money, and their drivers suffered for it. Until Kiekhaefer came along, no one in NASCAR was spending as much as Parks on his race cars.

In 1951, Parks finally decided it was time to move on. He sold his race cars and focused on his moneymaking businesses. In 1952, he briefly owned a racetrack—Asheville-Weaverville Speedway in North Carolina. But for reasons that Parks says were never explained to him, Bill France refused to schedule a NASCAR-sanctioned race there. Parks eventually sold out. "I loved racing and I loved winning, but it was costing too much money," he said. "I had to start making a living."

Parks was thirty-seven when he quit NASCAR. Over the years, he had spent tens of thousands of dollars on racing. Parks's moonshine-soaked money supported not only his team but the sport itself. He never spoke of the cash he sometimes loaned Bill France. But colleagues who witnessed such transactions say that that cash helped France and NASCAR get past a few financial rough spots, hard times that otherwise might have compromised NASCAR's ability to survive.

Through the 1950s, Parks sponsored local baseball teams and helped build churches, but a ballpark never gave him the same thrill as a racetrack, his life's true house of worship. Parks acknowledged that

NASCAR was still deeply a part of him. And NASCAR gradually came around to acknowledging the role Parks had played, though it has mostly steered clear of any reference to Parks's prison record or corn liquor career.

Parks eventually bought a condominium in Daytona. During France's long battle with Alzheimer's, when he seemed to want to reconnect with friends from the past, he'd frequently call Parks—sometimes a few times a day—to talk about cars and racing.

At times in his life, if Parks ever felt wronged by a friend or business partner, he could sever the relationship in an instant, often never speaking to the offender again. But he never shut France out of his life, never dwelled on any money owed or wrongs inflicted. Like Red Vogt, he never blamed France for profiting from the sport they all created together. He truly felt that the future success of stock car racing was more important than any hurt feelings, that NASCAR was more vital than any of them.

Dale Earnhardt, Richard Petty, and other legends of the 1960s and '70s, who'd heard about Parks from their fathers, eventually sought out and befriended him. Earnhardt called Parks "the *other* man of Daytona." Parks was sitting in his box seat that day in 2001 when Earnhardt slammed into the wall at Daytona and died.

By the 1990s, a few hard-core NASCAR fans and amateur historians had also pieced together enough bits of Parks's story to know how important he was to NASCAR. They began to visit him at his office on Northside Avenue, next to the liquor store where his brothers and brothers-in-law still worked. The office had become a shrine to Parks's stock car and moonshine days, the walls and shelves busy with memorabilia. Even in his nineties, Parks arrived early at the office each day. There, he was surrounded by the faces in photographs and the names etched on trophies of the men he'd outlived. And it would break the heart of his lovely wife, Violet (his fifth), to see his memory fade each year.

But Parks was never one to dawdle. So he'd work all day, go home for supper, and most nights return to the office and work a bit longer. He remained what he'd always been: a hard worker who took nothing for granted. He was still doing what he did when he escaped from Dawsonville three-quarters of a century earlier, almost as if he couldn't let go of the enterprise that brought him to the big city that changed and defined his life.

He was still selling liquor to Atlantans.

BILL FRANCE AND NASCAR

France dedicated every day of his life, and his family's, to racing. His wife managed the books and tacked publicity posters to telephone poles. His kids sold crushed ice and collected tickets. France handled such menial tasks as directing fans in the parking lot and cleaning up their trash once they'd left. At night, he'd spread all the cash out on the living room floor and start counting. A silver plaque he used to keep on a bookshelf in his in office read, "Money isn't everything, but it does tend to keep the children in touch."

In the late 1980s, after Big Bill was diagnosed with Alzheimer's, the disease progressed rapidly, terribly. At first, he would telephone Red Vogt and Raymond Parks and some of his old friends, men he'd known since before World War II. He seemed to want desperately to talk about the old days. But the disease advanced and his health declined, and as one colleague said, he "wasn't in this world anymore."

In early 1992, France's wife of sixty years, Anne, died. A few months later, France lost his battle with Alzheimer's and died. He was eighty-two.

NASCAR's fan base doubled in the 1990s and was expected, with attendance growing at 10 percent a year, to remain the fastest-growing sport of the new millennium. More and more fans are now college-educated, middle-class, and female. Women and kids are an increasingly attractive target for NASCAR's advertisers.

"It's all about marketing," admits handsome NASCAR phenom Jeff Gordon.

And the numbers are astronomical. NASCAR's top racing series, the Nextel Cup, is one big ad, or as one Yankee writer put it, "40 extremely mobile billboards circle a track for three hours, driven by men in jumpsuits that make bowling apparel look sharp." Cars, drivers, and crews are splashed with the bright colors of benefactors who pay ten to twenty *million* dollars to host "the No. 8 Budweiser Chevy" or "the No. 20 Home Depot Monte Carlo." NASCAR's revenues average more than three *billion* dollars a year—and rising—and NASCAR fans cough up two billion dollars for merchandise each year, with most of the profits going to the lone family that still owns the whole sport.

Bill built family into the business: way back in 1972, France named his son Bill Jr. as NASCAR's president; his grandson, Brian, took over as chairman and CEO in 2003. Granddaughter Lesa France Kennedy is president of ISC, and son Jim is its CEO. Together, the France family is worth billions; the children and grandchildren ranked on *Forbes* magazine's list of richest Americans.

France's own personal legacy remains strong. His name is mentioned during race broadcasts on ESPN, FOX, or NBC. They call him "visionary" and "founder." Even *60 Minutes,* in a late-2005 segment, credited France as the patriarch of "the family that founded" NASCAR, which Leslie Stahl said was "born in Daytona Beach." France would have been pleased that his version of NASCAR's creation survived in his absence.

The story of France's coming to the South and single-handedly creating NASCAR, thereby becoming the savior of redneck racers who couldn't figure out how to run their own sport, is indeed the enduring and romantic legend. Of course, that's just part of the story. Richard Petty once summed up the impression many racers had of France: "NASCAR got this big by being a dictatorship."

France surely deserves his lionized place in automotive history—even Red Vogt once said, "Who the hell would do any better?" Given all the effort France put into stock cars, he never felt guilty when his family business turned into one of the biggest success stories in the history of American sports. But in his final days, with his mind addled by Alzheimer's, he'd get nostalgic and teary-eyed at the sound of long-ago names such as Seay, Hall, Flock, Byron, Vogt, and Parks.

France couldn't have done it without them. Even a dictator has a sense of history. Abraham Lincoln once said, "No man is good enough to govern another man without that other's consent," and Winston Churchill said, "Dictators ride to and fro upon tigers which they dare not dismount." In the end, France had to know that even if they didn't always go along willingly, NASCAR's moonshining cofounders were indeed his heroic tigers.

I feel totally relaxed in the race car. I can tune everything else out.
In a way, it's my retreat. It's probably the place where I'm most at home.
— DALE EARNHARDT, "THE INTIMIDATOR"

Epilogue: This is what NASCAR has become . . .

ATLANTA MOTOR SPEEDWAY, 2005

Half a century after the departure of Raymond Parks, Red Byron, and Red Vogt, NASCAR has changed so much and yet remains so much the same.

Lakewood is no longer a red and dusty racetrack. It's an overgrown field near Atlanta's Hartsfield Airport, which is named for the mayor who had banned bootleggers from racing in the 1940s. The old brick Ford factory that manufactured so many bootleggers' cars during and after Prohibition still stands on Ponce de Leon Avenue. It's now home to the east-side branch of Atlanta's Police Department.

In place of Lakewood, race fans have Atlanta Motor Speedway, twenty miles south, built in 1960 and still owned by Bill France's long-time combatant Bruton Smith. Jimmy Carter once worked as a ticket vendor there and later celebrated his election to the governor's mansion by inviting NASCAR racers to a barbecue dinner. The huge speedway boasts *Gone with the Wind*–themed condos and office buildings such as Tara Place, the Tara Ballroom, and Tara Clubhouse.

To better understand where NASCAR came from, I have tried to grasp what it ultimately became and, in that exploration, enlisted help from two able assistants. In a reprise of my somewhat reluctant childhood trips to races with my father, I have taken my two sons to Atlanta Motor Speedway for their first race, the Golden Corral 500, to get their perspective on NASCAR—and to gauge my own.

I had moved my family to the South in 2002, largely to be near the research for this book. Yet I sometimes worry that my two Yankee-born offspring, who know plenty about life north of D.C., still haven't been sufficiently exposed to southern culture. As we walk toward the enormous racetrack, through a parking lot–sized prerace carnival, my concerns seem justified. The boys walk gape-mouthed through it all, and their questions and comments pop like popcorn beneath a late-winter Georgia sun.

> Daddy, how come there are so many pickup trucks?
> Yeah, and how come almost every car is American, except ours?
> Seems like everyone is white.
> Yeah, Daddy, don't black people like NASCAR?
> Daddy, what's Skoal?
> Who's Jack Daniels?
> Can I get a T-shirt?

We're two hours early for the race, but it seems as if we're latecomers to a party that's been fermenting for quite a while. Apparently, we've missed the point of NASCAR, which goes something like this: the actual race is an afterthought, just the icing on a big, beer-soaked, red-white-and-blue cake that's been baking for three days.

Stock car races have grown too big to be contained in a Sunday afternoon. Fans start surging toward their mecca, often drunkenly, midweek. They come by the busload—church groups and scout troops, bowling leagues and the Sons and Daughters of the Confederacy, husband-and-wife motorcyclists revving engines alongside packs of black-leathery bike gangs. By Thursday, the traveling circus has established its encampment. Gaggles of RVs, big as eighteen-wheelers, with satellite dishes and wooden viewing stands bolted on top, have crammed into the infield and fired up gas grills and generators to power their TVs. Blue tarps shade makeshift patios from the sun. As my observant assistants pointed out, most of those who came on four wheels did so in burly, American-made pickups, nearly every one bearing bumper stickers declaring their favorite driver as "8" (Dale Earnhardt Jr.) or "24" (Jeff Gordon). Or with that cartoon kid Calvin mischievously pissing on "Ford" or "Chevy" or "work" or "24." NASCAR fans are patriots ("These colors don't run") and soldiers' parents ("Bring the troops home"). And if you believe the bumper stickers, God and Jesus are hard-core NASCAR fans, too.

As we join the giddy crowd—nearly two hundred thousand strong, slowly jamming itself into a town-sized stadium—my sons take note of the dress code: cutoffs or jeans and a mostly white T-shirt colored loud with a racer's name or number or some rowdy declaration such as "Born with the Need for Speed." We're among the few families not pulling a wheeled cooler of beer. Confederate flags rival the American flags catching the breeze. As one magazine writer recently put it, after visiting a NASCAR race at Talladega, "It has not come to the attention of eastern Alabama that the Civil War ended."

Race time is still an hour away, but the outer perimeter of the track rages, a pulsing festival of vices—music, food, sexuality, alcohol, tobacco—and marketing. Beautiful women strut beside display booths promoting Viagra, power tools, and Tide detergent. Fans dance inside the Skoal chewing tobacco tent, with its hard-rocking country band and free tins of tobacco. (Me, to Sean: "No, you can't have one.") At a booth promoting a muscle-building protein supplement, chubby men line up to take a shot at an arm-wrestling pro. (Me, to Leo: "No, you can't try it.") The pressure to spend is intense, and I finally cave, contributing fifty dollars to the France family fortune: Sean gets a Dale Earnhardt Jr. T-shirt, and Leo gets an Atlanta Motor Speedway hoodie.

We parade into the stadium and climb grandstands that rise behind thick cables and fencing that will separate us from the potential carnage of the steeply banked, 1.54-mile rectangular track. (In the 1990s, at least twenty-nine NASCAR spectators were killed by cars or debris.) We shuffle away from the more aggressive fans, such as the guy in the one hundred–dollar front-row seat sucking a Bud tallboy, wearing a Confederate flag T-shirt with the Faulkner-esque declaration, "It's a Southern thang, y'all wouldn't understand." We reach the Petty "Family Section," which doesn't allow alcohol, but in a brilliant stroke of forethought, I have brought along a flask of moonshine, compliments of Sean's ex-teacher (procured from a source named One-Eyed Ronnie). It's my tithe to the past, my offering up to the Roy Hall generation and NASCAR's whiskey-making, whiskey-drinking forefathers. Plus, researching this book has required me to become an expert on moonshine and corn-based liquor in general. It's just my job.

But surely not even the flashiest of Roy Hall–era whiskey trippers could have imagined a scene such as this.

Of the scores of football and baseball games I've attended, not one has come close to the emotional intensity accompanying the start of a NASCAR race. Take the National Anthem, which ranks among Leo's favorite songs (along with the theme from "Rocky"); he's got a scratchy LP record version, and I've seen him get beautifully teary-eyed at the crescendo. As a country music star starts singing "The Star-Spangled Banner," Leo looks up at me and screws up his face, as if he'd just swallowed lemon juice. "Sounds weird," he says. But then, at the anthem's off-key climax, all heads tilt backward as a military jet—now a staple of NASCAR races—screams overhead. The hairs on my neck stand up, and I resist an unexpected reaction: I actually choke up. Then a nearby fan screams back, "USA, yeah! Screw the rest of the world!"

The crowd quiets as a preacher thanks Jesus for the freedom to race in America. An announcer then wails the *real* invocation of the day: "Gentlemen, start your engines!" Forty-three cars, most shaped like Chevy Monte Carlos, Ford Tauruses, or Dodge Intrepids or Chargers, blast to life and start their slow, gruff, phlegmy warm-up laps. When the green flag waves, each $150,000 car, about as "stock" as a thoroughbred on a carousel, accelerates to speeds twice as fast as I've ever driven, the angry symphony of 750-horsepower V-8 engines more deafening than the prerace jet. *Noise* is an insufficient word. It's inhuman and inhumane, painful and thrilling. It grinds into the chest, hammers the bones. The air fills with the warm stench of burning tires, burning oil, like the stink of a car fire. "God, I love that smell," a nearby fan screams.

A high-pitched, mechanical whine precedes the pack as it approaches our section, and then the drone of the lead car's engine suddenly drops in pitch as it passes with a "MEEEEE-OW," followed instantly by the staccato rush of forty-two others, "MEE-YOW, MYOW, MYOW, MYOW-YOW-YOW-YOW, YOW-YOW-OW-OW-OW . . ."

Sean and Leo cover their ears. A huge gust of hot, gritty wind follows the pack. Drivers call it "dirty air," and that backdraft of dust, smoke, and microscopic rubber swarms over us, forcing us to squint as the blast knocks off hats and sunglasses, topples cans. A kid in front of us decked out in Jeff Gordon gear turns around grinning; we learn it's his first race, too. His dad, in Dale Earnhardt Jr. gear, puffs out his chest, as if he were absorbing the tsunami of debris-filled air into his very soul. As if it were pure oxygen, the breath that sustains him. But it's soon clear that my sons don't quite get it.

"I'm getting a little bit bored," Leo says a hundred miles into the race. "All it is is going around and around and around." Adds Sean: "When are they going to go faster?"

My sons, with their Yankee-tinged ennui, are clearly part of an ever-shrinking minority. In living rooms across America, millions of men and, increasingly, women—drawn by studly youngsters such as Earnhardt, Tony Stewart, and Ryan Newman—are at this moment watching the same race, contributors to NASCAR's $2.8 *billion* TV contract (which will jump to $4.8 billion in 2007), boosters to NASCAR TV ratings that are double those of baseball, basketball, or hockey, and growing.

Though Sean and Leo aren't yet converts, they can at least at some future date (say, while wooing some southern belle) claim to have personally partaken in the number two spectator sport in America, on its way to overtaking football as number one.

Back in 2001, NASCAR received an unintended boost from former wild child and high school dropout Dale Earnhardt, who had become a NASCAR legend and a multimillionaire. He was modern NASCAR's icon, its Babe Ruth.

Then, on the final lap of the 2001 Daytona 500, Earnhardt's two teammates—snake-bit veteran Michael Waltrip and Earnhardt's rising-star son, Dale Jr.—sped toward a one-two finish. While trying to block other cars and protect his teammates' apparent victory, Earnhardt's black number 3 car—all thirty-four hundred pounds, traveling at 180 miles an hour—got nicked in the butt, veered left toward the infield, and then shot hard right, up the bank and straight into the concrete wall. A split second later, Waltrip took the checkered flag, the first of his career, followed a few feet later by Dale Jr.

Fans stood to see Dale Sr. emerge from his wrecked car and wave. Heck, he'd survived worse-looking wrecks than this. Instead, they waited. As they watched a blue tarp being draped over the number 3, they reluctantly, nervously shuffled toward the exits. Soon, the world learned he was dead. It was NASCAR's most painful loss, and fans to this day will shed tears at the memory of Earnhardt's death.

I've given a lot of thought to what sustains Earnhardt's posthumous, perpetual legend. I've visited his hometown and his former racing headquarters outside Charlotte. I've studied his squinting, Clint Eastwood–like photographs. The Man in Black and the Intimidator, they called him, and he remains—four years dead—NASCAR's biggest star. But why? Even his son, who had a mediocre year in 2005, is one of the most popular drivers. A ten thousand–dollar fine for saying "shit" on national TV only improved his rock-star image. My view is that the Earnhardt family, but especially *the Intimidator,* represents the outlaw spirit that helped create NASCAR in the first place. Dale Sr. was the modern incarnation of Lloyd Seay, Red Byron, Curtis Turner, and especially Roy Hall. Born and raised in the South, Earnhardt had dropped out of school to work at the local mill. But he managed to escape the drab life of his peers because he learned to tame the V-8 beast.

When he died—partly because he died, and NASCAR became national news—NASCAR continued its explosive growth as America's sport. NASCAR fans are wildly attracted to their visceral, animal, *sexual* romp of power and noise, all oomph and brightly painted cars bumping, nudging, and scraping in a high-speed dance. As one modern NASCAR observer said, "Fans get a few beers in 'em, the Dixie comes out."

One of the attendees at NASCAR's 1947 organizational meeting once said that stock car racing was "kind of like country music. Nobody likes it except the public." Maybe my sons are just too young, or too short on Dixie mojo. Whatever the reason, with a hundred miles left in the Golden Corral 500, they ask to leave.

In a sense, I feel I've failed to properly indoctrinate them into the sport whose roots I've spent three years exploring. I try a few statistics on them: the concussive wails pulsing from forty-three engines together equal more than thirty thousand horsepower, enough to blast a rocket into space. Each car gets four to six miles a gallon. Inside, the temperatures reach 150 degrees, and drivers are on their way to losing five to ten pounds. Each driver will grind through thirty to forty tires, each tire worth a dozen of those on our car (about four hundred dollars). Then I explain how a NASCAR rookie named Kasey Kahne nearly won this race back in 2004, after he was hired to replace legendary Bill Elliott— "Awesome Bill from Dawsonville." With his third-place finish in 2004's Golden Corral 500, Kahne became one of the few drivers in NASCAR history to earn three top-five finishes in his first four races. The first to accomplish that feat was Red Byron in 1949.

My sons nod politely, wait to make sure I'm finished, then ask again if it's time to leave. We extract ourselves from Atlanta Motor Speedway, passing an entire trailer dedicated to selling Dale Earnhardt memorabilia. I stop at the trailer selling Jack Daniels merchandise and pick up a T-shirt for my dad.

While driving north toward Atlanta, we learn that the race has been won by Carl Edwards, one of many up-and-comers trying to fill Earnhardt's big shoes. Like many current racers, Edwards is handsome, toothy, charismatic, and well spoken. He's from Missouri, not the South. He won the previous day's minor league "Busch" series race and does backflips off his car after victories. His team owner loves him:

"He's a hunk," says Edwards's team president, Geoff Smith. "They're all good-looking."

Though I'm a bit disappointed to have missed Edwards's backflip, I take comfort in the fact that he was driving a Ford. Although Chevys and Dodges outnumber them, Fords are solidly back in the NASCAR game. There's the Sharpie Ford, the Viagra Ford, the UPS Ford, the Combos Ford, and my favorite, the Trex USG Sheetrock Ford—USG being the company that once employed Red Byron's father. USG also co-hosts the annual USG Sheetrock 400 race at Chicagoland Speedway, not far from where Byron died.

I'm also partial to the Jack Daniels car—which today finished eighth—since that sponsor's Tennessee Whiskey, which my dad favors, is basically charcoal-filtered corn liquor and a descendant of the southern moonshine of Raymond Parks's generation.

Southerners such as Raymond Parks's Uncle Benny had come to rural Georgia to be *separate*. As president of the Confederate States of America, Jefferson Davis once said, "All we ask is to be let alone." In the hills and hollows of the Confederacy, Parkses and other hardy, independent, yet wary and distrustful Irish and Scots-Irish learned to fend for themselves, to live off the land, to build their own homes, to heal themselves with homemade salves and herb poultices, to make their own music—and their own whiskey, whose role in the history and culture of the South is more prominent than even Davis's.

But it has been more than thirty years since a known whiskey tripper spun around a NASCAR track. Except for the new Jack Daniels and Jim Beam cars, the ghosts of southern moonshine have been fully excised from today's NASCAR.

In fact, NASCAR conveniently overlooks (or flat out denies) that it was created by moonshining men such as Raymond Parks. When NASCAR president Mike Helton told reporters, just before the 2006 Daytona 500, that "the old Southeastern redneck heritage that we had is no longer in existence," he was simply echoing similar revisionist efforts by Bill France—senior and junior. Helton was forced to explain his words, claiming that NASCAR wanted to keep its "roots intact." "We're proud of where we came from, we're proud of how we got here," he said, but in the same breath said NASCAR's "heritage" dated to 1948, as if the time line of stock car racing began ticking that year, as if the previous decade meant nothing.

This remains NASCAR's consistent, official stance: the sport was created by Bill France in 1948. Period. NASCAR's website says it was "formed in 1948," and the narrator of the official *History of NASCAR* DVD says, "NASCAR's entire existence in fact is due in large part to the determination and effort . . . of Big Bill France."

If he had lived a bit longer, maybe Big Bill would have come around to defending the redneck heritage, to acknowledging that he did not single-handedly create NASCAR, that he had help, that he couldn't have done it without Raymond Parks, Red Vogt, and the other Atlanta bootleggers. But France is dead, and it's not in the best interests of today's NASCAR conglomerate to contradict France's heroic image nor to embrace the more accurate version of history—the one full of dirt-poor lawbreakers.

It's not just moonshine that's become a buried piece of NASCAR's story. The sport's southernness is disappearing, too. The famed Southern 500 at Darlington, the traditional Labor Day race for half a century, in 2003 was moved to mid-November to allow a California race to become NASCAR's new Labor Day event. The Southern 500 was eliminated altogether in 2004 to make room in NASCAR's schedule for a race in Texas. The racers are becoming less southern, too. Until 1988, when "Awesome Bill from Dawsonville" won the championship, every NASCAR champion except one came from Dixie. Since then, only seven of seventeen champions were southerners, including Dale Earnhardt—four times since 1989 and seven overall—and two Texans.

Even nonsouthern NASCAR champ Tony Stewart has noticed: "I don't think anyone can call it just a Southern sport anymore . . . we're covering all four corners of the United States now." And some fans and old-timers bristle against that. It's like the Civil War diarist Mary Chestnut complained after Dixie's defeat: "They are everywhere these Yankees, like red ants, like the locusts and frogs which were the plagues of Egypt."

After leaving the Golden Corral 500, on a hunch, I drive into northeast Atlanta.

My assistants and I pass the old Ford factory on Ponce de Leon and Red Vogt's old shop on Spring Street and the site of Raymond Parks's first service station on Hemphill Avenue, as I tell the boys bits of the NASCAR story. We finally pull up at the Northside Avenue liquor store, and next to that, I knock on the thick-glass front door.

The lock unclicks, the door opens, and there stands Raymond Parks, can of Coke in hand, looking regal and nowhere near his ninety-one years. I have known him three years now and have been looking forward to introducing my sons to NASCAR's patron saint. Parks is still tall, thin, and, while a bit frail and forgetful, looks sharp in his narrow tie and pressed white shirt; the gray fedora and tan sports jacket hang on a nearby hook.

Almost as if he's been waiting for us, Parks dutifully shows my boys the black-and-white photographs and the pre–World War II loving cups, and lets them run their small fingers over the engraved words "Roy Hall" and "Lloyd Seay." He lets them each hold a replica of the 1949 Oldsmobile Rocket 88 that Red Byron drove en route to becoming NASCAR's first strictly stock car champ. After a while, as he shakes their hands and we begin to leave, a handsome glitter comes to his eye.

"Come back and see us, now," he says.

"Okay," says Leo.

"Okay," says Sean.

Before getting back in the car, we stop in the adjacent liquor store. While my boys run dangerously among aisles of bottles, I chat with Parks's brother-in-law, "Bad Eye" Shirley's brother, Marion. (Bad Eye died in early 2005, taking with him one more of the dwindling pieces of the story of NASCAR.) After Marion and I talk about his own moonshine memories, I buy a bottle of bourbon and say good-bye. The bourbon isn't moonshine, exactly, but corn liquor at least. On the drive home to North Carolina, I explain to Sean and Leo how they have just met the only person alive today who witnessed the full history of NASCAR. And I explain the lineage that ties our own Irish ancestry to moonshine and NASCAR, to Atlanta and bourbon, to Parks himself.

"Cool," says Leo.

"Cool," says Sean.

I visit Raymond Parks a few more times after that. I see him at the birthday party held each year at a racing museum near Greenville-Pickens Speedway outside Greenville, South Carolina. I see him at Dawsonville's Moonshine Festival, where a few NASCAR fans recognize him and ask for his autograph, where Raymond's sister and Billy Watson and Ed Samples's son and Gober Sosebee's son all tell me wonderful old stories, where I walk over to Lloyd Seay's grave and touch his photograph and the cool granite. Whether it's modesty or southern decorum, Parks never talks freely about his moonshining days. I've met with him at least a dozen times across the years, but he'd still sometimes say, "I ain't gonna talk about that," and I'd have to rely on others to fill in some of the blanks.

Still, my most enjoyable moments have been one-on-one with Parks in his office.

I've found myself mesmerized watching him flip through his photo albums, his long, thin, wrinkled fingers turning pages and pointing at long-dead faces and friends, at black-and-white images of his younger self. I've seen his eyes mist up at some unspoken memory. For me to look at those images and then look up into his face and realize he was *there* . . . I mean, he's old, but he doesn't look nearly old enough to be seventy years removed from the events in the fading photographs. Over time, it became moving for me, visiting his office time and again, to see how infatuated he still is with it all.

As if the naïve early days of stock cars had been his first true love.

And each time I visit Parks, I see something new, something I missed.

On one of my final visits, just before Christmas of 2005, I'm about to walk out the office door when I notice a framed letter on NASCAR letterhead hanging on the wall. It was sent to Parks on his eighty-fifth birthday and praised his 1948 and 1949 championships as "an amazing and historical accomplishment." The letter said, "Your place in NASCAR history is unique and enduring." It is signed by Bill France Jr., who closed the letter with this:

"We thank you for being a leading pioneer of NASCAR competitors."

As I drive back home toward the mountains of western North Carolina, I wonder whether the France family knew to be grateful to Parks after all. Maybe the long-ago relationship between Big Bill and Raymond Parks was just a private matter that didn't need to go into the history books. As I drive past the Dawsonville exit off Highway 400, I also find myself wondering—as I often have during my time in the South—if maybe a New Jersey boy can never fully understand all the deeper truths beneath NASCAR's creation and its enduring popularity. Maybe it's as Faulkner said long ago, before there was a NASCAR: "*You can't understand it. You would have to be born there.*"

Notes

A note on sources: Record keeping was sloppy or nonexistent before NASCAR was created. In attempting to unearth relevant details about the years before NASCAR's existence, I tried to be careful to rely on solid, primary sources, such as photographs, interviews, and newspaper or magazine stories. But even then, I found it sometimes difficult to discern from faded articles (in old racers' private scrapbooks, for example) the writer's name and/or the date or even, occasionally, the name of the publication. In cases where I'm unsure of the source, I'll say something like "exact date unknown." Raymond Parks and Eddie Samples graciously shared their scrapbooks; Samples's multi-volume collection was especially useful. But again, details were sometimes missing, which prevented me from providing a perfect and scholarly annotation. Otherwise, every effort has been made to cite and/or explain the source of the information in this book.

1. "NASCAR is no longer a southern sport"

page 6, **TV contract worth nearly $5 billion:** "NASCAR Signs New TV Deal," Associated Press, Jan. 16, 2006.

page 6, **Nextel . . . $750-million deal:** Lisa Napoli, "A New Era in Stock-Car Racing," *New York Times,* July 14, 2003.

page 6, **"NASCAR is no longer a southern sport":** Liz Clarke, "NASCAR Boom Puts South in Rearview," *Washington Post,* Nov. 20, 2005.

pages 8–9, **"the old Southeastern redneck heritage":** Lorenzo Lopez, "NASCAR Still Proud of Its Heritage," *Raleigh News & Observer,* Feb. 17, 2006.

page 9, **"shedding its past as if it were an embarrassing family secret":** Liz Clarke and Dan Steinberg, "The New Language of NASCAR," *Washington Post,* Oct. 6, 2004.

2. White lightning

Unless otherwise noted, the story of Benjamin Parks is from Larry E. Mitchell, "Benjamin Parks Jr.: A Really Golden Heritage," *North Georgia Journal 2,* no. 1 (Spring 1985); Walworth Publishing, *Dawson County, Georgia Heritage, 1857–1996* (Waynesville, N.C.: Walsworth Publishing, 1997); Eddie Samples,

"Garhofa's Raymond Dawson Parks," Georgia Automobile Racing Hall of Fame Association's *Pioneer Pages* 5, no. 1 (Feb. 2002); and interviews with Raymond Parks, Violet Parks, and Lucille Shirley. The story of Parks's childhood, departure from the farm, work as a still hand with Walter Day, and move to Atlanta is also based on Eddie Samples's *Pioneer Pages* story and interviews with Raymond Parks, Lucille Shirley, and Violet Parks. The Civil War reflections and summaries are from various other sources, including E. L. Doctorow, *The March: A Novel* (New York: Random House, 2005). The recipe for southern moonshine and all descriptions of making moonshine are from: Esther Kellner, *Moonshine: Its History and Folklore* (New York: Ballantine Books, 1973); Joseph Earl Dabney, *Mountain Spirits* (Asheville, N.C.: Bright Mountain Books, 1974); Jess Carr, *The Second Oldest Profession: An Informal History of Moonshining in America* (Englewood Cliffs, N.J.: Prentice Hall, 1972); Horace Kephart, *Our Southern Highlanders: A Narrative of Adventure in the Southern Appalachians and a Study of Life among the Mountaineers* (Knoxville: University of Tennessee Press, 1984).

page 11, **"A striking figure"**: Mitchell, *North Georgia Journal.*

page 12, **"a fierce and uncouth race of men"**: Kephart, *Our Southern Highlanders,* 11.

page 12, **"ignorant, mean . . . scum of the Earth"**: James Webb, *Born Fighting: How the Scots-Irish Shaped America* (New York: Broadway Books, 2004), 157.

page 12, **"dear me, how beautiful she was"**: Mitchell, *North Georgia Journal.*

page 12, **"not yet broke in"** and **"the yellow of an egg"**: Ibid.

page 13, **"savage hunters"** and **"civilized population"**: President Andrew Jackson's Case for the Removal Act, First Annual Message to Congress, Dec. 8, 1830.

page 15, **"By God, what will you take for a piece?"** and **"run over and squish"**: Superior Court of Dawson County court files and transcripts.

page 16, **"The mountains didn't have much to offer"**: Samples, "Garhofa's Raymond Dawson Parks," *Pioneer Pages.*

page 16–17, **Day, . . . sentenced for making "illicit . . . untaxed whiskey"**: Superior Court of Dawson County.

page 17, **"to its knees—It'll never rise again"** and **"It's the only thing that lasts"**: Margaret Mitchell, *Gone with the Wind,* audio ed. (Prince Frederick, Md.: Recorded Books, 2001).

page 17, **fistfights . . . you remember most the ones you lost**: Tony Horwitz, quoting Shelby Foote, *Confederates in the Attic: Dispatches from the Unfinished Civil War* (New York: Vintage, 1999), 146.

page 18, **"invaders of your country . . . agrarian mercenaries"**: Shelby Foote, *Shiloh,* audio ed. (Prince Frederick, Md.: Recorded Books, 1993).

page 18, **a bitter sense of tragedy**: Horwitz, *Confederates,* 146.

page 18, **a quarter of the nation's population**: Peter Applebome, *Dixie Rising: How the South Is Shaping American Values, Politics, and Culture* (San Diego: Harvest Book, 1996), 328.

page 18, **Vicksburg . . . little to celebrate in that**: Horwitz, *Confederates,* 146.

page 18, **"all of which . . . can be operated stone drunk"**: Pete Daniel, quoting Rick Bragg, *Lost Revolutions* (Chapel Hill: University of North Carolina Press, 2000), 93.

page 19, **"lewd, crude, half-starved sharecroppers"**: Applebome, *Dixie Rising,* 325.

page 19, ". . . one click away from true reality": Webb, *Born Fighting*, 263.

page 19, "purposely isolated itself . . .": Applebome, *Dixie Rising*, 326.

page 19, a traitor to the South: Ibid., 325.

page 19, within twelve minutes of his arrival . . . : Webb, *Born Fighting*, 262.

page 19, "bunghole of the United States": Applebome, *Dixie Rising*, 11.

page 22, drive-through service station . . . proved a financial boon: Douglas Brinkley, *Wheels for the World: Henry Ford, His Company, and a Century of Progress* (New York: Viking, 2003), 334.

page 22, the creation of the first drive-in restaurants, motels . . . : Ibid., 335.

page 23, a settlement with more saloons than churches: Dabney, *Mountain Spirits*, 132.

page 23, Atlanta started from scratch: Horwitz, *Confederates*, 283.

page 23, "what a quarter million Confederate soldiers died to prevent" and "What is this place?": Ibid.

page 23, streetcars clanging . . . clacking noises coughing out from the textile mills: Tony Earley, *Jim the Boy* (Boston: Back Bay Books, 2000), 122–124.

page 24, Henry Ford . . . farm-bound life . . . "drudgery": Brinkley, *Wheels*, 127.

3. Henry Ford "created a monster"

Unless otherwise noted, all information about "the bug" comes from author interviews with Raymond Parks, his sister Lucille Shirley, Billy Watson, Gordon Pirkle, a few unnamed sources, and a few stories in *Atlanta Constitution*. Information about Parks's arrest and imprisonment comes from interviews with Raymond Parks, Violet Parks, and Lucille Shirley; also Jerry Bledsoe, *The World's Number One, Flat-Out, All-Time Great, Stock Car Racing Book* (New York: Bantam Books, 1976).

page 25, incomes ranked far below the national average: Louis Rubin, ed., *The American South: Portrait of a Culture* (Washington, D.C.: Government Printing Office, 1980).

page 26, "there goes that crazy loon again": Upton Sinclair, *The Flivver King: A Story of Ford America* (Pasadena, Calif.: published by the author, 1937), 4.

page 27, with the isolated, overworked farmer in mind: David Halberstam, *The Reckoning* (New York: Morrow, 1986), 75.

page 27, "Not like any other sound ever heard in this world": Ibid., 76.

page 27, a "fiery Scotsman": Douglas Brinkley, *Wheels for the World: Henry Ford, His Company, and a Century of Progress* (New York: Viking, 2003), 38.

page 28, "fast speed freaks": Peter Collier and David Horowitz, *The Fords: An American Epic* (New York: Summit Books, 1987), 43.

page 28, "I never really thought much of racing": Ibid., 37.

page 28, "sober and honest and hardworking": Sinclair, *Flivver King*, 23.

page 29, "fingers, hands, arms, legs and crushed bodies": Brinkley, *Wheels*, 418.

page 29, equivalent to a six-figure salary: Economic History Services, www.eh.net (an unskilled wage rate of $417 and GDP per capita of $546).

page 30, *Ford* and *car* had become synonyms: Brinkley, *Wheels*, 12.

page 30, "crotchety and mean, frolicsome and full of jokes": Ibid., 350.

page 30, Ford had "inadvertently created a monster": Fred Siegel, "Rebuilding: The

Idea of the City: The Present Crisis in Perspective," www.cooper.edu/humanities/humanitiescities.htm.

page 30, "a colorless liquid poison": Eric Burns, *Spirits of America: A Social History of Alcohol* (Philadelphia: Temple University Press, 2313), 115.

page 31, "Goodbye forever to my old friend booze": Ibid., 188.

page 31, "the beer-drinking German . . .": Halberstam, *The Reckoning*, 69.

page 32, "Do they carry whiskey jugs in their blouses in Kentucky?": Collier and Horowitz, *The Fords*, 39.

page 33, $2,500 . . . worth $29 million: Halberstam, *The Reckoning*, 77.

page 33, "because they wanted America drunk": Sinclair, *Flivver King*, 56.

page 33, "liquor to befuddle the brains of Christian leaders": Burns, *Spirits of America*, 161.

page 34, "the modern world wanted pep, zip, chic": Sinclair, *Flivver King*, 69.

page 34, "a car should not have any more cylinders than a cow": Collier and Horowitz, *The Fords*, 49.

page 34, Model A was "like a friendly farm dog": Brinkley, *Wheels*, 421.

page 35, "I can make any other car take a Ford's dust": Ibid., 421.

page 35, "75% of all crimes . . . the aid of the automobile": Bryan Burrough, *Public Enemies: America's Greatest Crime Wave and the Birth of the FBI, 1933–34* (New York: Penguin Press, 2004), 17.

page 38, "fast as a rabbit": Eddie Samples, "Garhofa's Raymond Dawson Parks," Georgia Automobile Racing Hall of Fame Association's *Pioneer Pages 5*, no. 1 (Feb. 2002).

page 41, Machine Gun Kelley and Baby Face Nelson: Burrough, *Public Enemies*, 18.

page 42, the mayor and police chief announced plans . . . : "Police to Go After Racket 'Big Shots' in Lottery Drive," *Atlanta Constitution*, Aug. 25, 1938.

page 43, "When I sell liquor, it's bootlegging": Burns, *Spirits of America*, 203.

page 43, two dollars a gallon by 1934: Jess Carr, *The Second Oldest Profession: An Informal History of Moonshining in America* (Englewood Cliffs, N.J.: Prentice Hall, 1972), 119.

page 46, "probity and reliability . . . inestimable character": "Raymond D. Parks, Parks Novelty Company," *Atlanta Constitution*, Jan. 2, 1948.

page 46, A rumor spread: Interview with Violet Parks.

page 48, hardworking . . . "rednecks": Tim McLaurin, *Keeper of the Moon: A Southern Boyhood* (New York: Anchor Books/Doubleday, 1991), 14.

4. The bootlegger turn

Unless otherwise noted, the story of moonshine's origins is from: Esther Kellner, *Moonshine: Its History and Folklore* (New York: Ballantine Books, 1973); Joseph Earl Dabney, *Mountain Spirits* (Asheville, N.C.: Bright Mountain Books, 1974); Jess Carr, *The Second Oldest Profession: An Informal History of Moonshining in America* (Englewood Cliffs, N.J.: Prentice Hall, 1972); Horace Kephart, *Our Southern Highlanders: A Narrative of Adventure in the Southern Appalachians and a Study of Life among the Mountaineers* (Knoxville: University of Tennessee Press, 1984); and Eric Burns, *Spirits of America: A Social History of Alcohol* (Philadelphia: Temple University Press, 2003).

page 50, "When I have to turn . . .": Ed Hinton, "The Legend: Lloyd Seay Was the Young Sport's Brightest Star until He Was Gunned Down," *Sports Illustrated Presents 50 Years of NASCAR,* Jan. 28, 1998, 48.

pages 50–51, "devil-may-care" . . . "angel face": Bernard Kahn, "Crown Is Predicted for Stock Car Race," *Daytona Beach News Journal,* 1941 (exact date unknown); also Leroy Simerly, "Auto Race to Be Held Today at Fairgrounds," *Spartanburg Herald,* 1941 (exact date unknown).

page 51, "climb a pine tree": Hinton, *Sports Illustrated,* 46.

page 51, *coolest feller:* Ibid., 48.

page 53, "the dreamers and daredevils": James Webb, *Born Fighting: How the Scots-Irish Shaped America* (New York: Broadway Books, 2004), 87–88.

page 53, "problem children": Ibid., 99.

page 54, tarred and feathered: Alec Wilkinson, *Moonshine: A Life in Pursuit of White Liquor* (St. Paul, Minn.: Hungry Mind Press, 1998), 54.

page 54, "Nonconformity as well as mistrust . . .": Webb, *Born Fighting,* 129.

page 56, George Washington . . . paid his gardener: Philip Brandt George, "George Washington: Patriot, President, Planter and Purveyor of Distilled Spirits," *American History,* Feb. 2004, 73.

page 57, "Booze was food, medicine" and "indispensable accompaniment to liberty": Burns, *Spirits of America,* 8, 5.

page 57, "Amos believed it was his God-given right": Tony Earley, *Jim the Boy* (Boston: Back Bay Books, 2000), 211–213.

page 58, "missed a durned lotsa fun": Dabney, *Mountain Spirits,* 93–101.

page 60, "It was a thousand-dollar-a-week job": Carr, *Second Oldest Profession,* 128.

page 60, "a gentle home pet that grew . . .": Kellner, *Moonshine,* 127.

page 60, thirty-five million gallons . . . produced nationwide in 1934: Ibid., 124.

page 60, a million gallons a year came from . . . Dawsonville: Dabney, *Mountain Spirits,* 132.

page 60, "Virtually everyone in Dawson County was associated": Leigh Montville, "Dawsonville, U.S.A.," *Sports Illustrated Presents 50 Years of NASCAR,* Jan. 28, 1998, 112.

page 61, at age ten and "I couldn't waste all the good liquor": Kim Chapin, "The King of the Wild Road," *Sports Illustrated,* 48–60; D. L. Morris, *Timber on the Moon: The Curtis Turner Story* (Charlotte, N.C.: Colonial Press, 1966), 16.

page 61, In 1935, police and IRS agents pounced: Tom Higgins and Steve Waid, *Junior Johnson: Brave in Life* (Phoenix: David Bull Publishing, 1999), 21; Tom Wolfe, "The Last American Hero Is Junior Johnson . . . Yes!" *Esquire,* Mar. 1965.

pages 61–62, "Lose on the track and you go home": Bill Center and Bob Moore, *NASCAR 50 Greatest Drivers* (New York: Harper Horizon/Tehabi Books, 1998), 21.

page 62, "If it hadn't been for bootlegging and racing": Kellner, *Moonshine,* 128; also Sylvia Wilkinson, *Dirt Tracks to Glory: The Early Days of Stock Car Racing as Told by the Participants* (Chapel Hill, N.C.: Algonquin Books, 1983), 36.

page 63, "It was a game, you against them": Montville, *Sports Illustrated,* 115.

page 63, "I'd start picking my nose": Dabney, *Mountain Spirits,* 164.

page 63, "like a cat in heat": Paul Hemphill, *Wheels: A Season on NASCAR's Winston Cup Circuit* (New York: Berkley Books, 1998), 79.

page 63, "Where are you from?": Montville, *Sports Illustrated,* 115.

page 65, place bets on whose engine they were hearing: Ibid.

page 66, One agent was maimed by a bootlegger: Ralph S. Smith, "An Informal Inquiry into the Dark Science of Bootlegging, A.D. 1920–1932," a three-part series, *Winston-Salem Journal,* Aug. 13–15, 1967.

page 67, "The losers had to play the law": Hemphill, *Wheels,* 96.

page 67, Sherwood Anderson . . . "mostly kids who liked the excitement": Carr, *Second Oldest Profession,* 119.

page 67, "the best automobile driver of [his] time": Dabney, *Mountain Spirits,* 157; Jerry Bledsoe, *The World's Number One, Flat-Out, All-Time Great, Stock Car Racing Book* (New York: Bantam Books, 1976), 80.

page 67, "Maybe you could let me go on through?": Greg Fielden, *High Speed at Low Tide* (Surfside Beach, S.C.: Galfield Press, 1993), 73; Hemphill, *Wheels,* 79.

page 68, "hot with law every night": Hinton, *Sports Illustrated,* 48.

page 69, "He never knew what a brake was": Montville, *Sports Illustrated,* 153.

page 69, One night, two revenue agents . . . : Dabney, *Mountain Spirits,* 164–165.

5. An "orgy of dust, liquor and noise"

Unless otherwise noted, all information on Red Vogt and his friendship with Bill France is from his family: his son, Tom Vogt; his step-daughter, June Wendt; and her son, Steve. Also: Bob Desiderio, "Mechanic Vogt Started Career at Age of 10," *Daytona Beach Morning Journal,* Feb. 24, 1956. Barney Oldfield information is from: Robert Cutter and Bob Fendell, *Encyclopedia of Auto Racing Greats* (New York: Prentice-Hall, 1973), 445; Douglas Brinkley, *Wheels for the World: Henry Ford, His Company, and a Century of Progress* (New York: Viking: 2003); William F. Nolan, *Barney Oldfield: The Life and Times of America's Legendary Speed King* (Carpinteria, Calif.: Brown Fox Books, 2002). And all racing scenes are from various newspaper articles and Greg Fielden, *High Speed at Low Tide* (Surfside Beach, S.C.: Galfield Press, 1993).

page 73, Red took to calling him "watermelon": "Louis Jerome 'Red' Vogt: The Dean of Stock Car Racing Mechanics, 1904–2004," *Crackers and Coffee,* Feb. 7, 2004.

page 73, France secretly raced his dad's Model T: Brock Yates, "The Force: Bill France's Vision Made NASCAR the World's Premier Racing Organization," *Sports Illustrated Presents 50 Years of NASCAR,* Jan. 28, 1998.

page 74, "We had the money and the know-how . . .": Larry Fielden, *Tim Flock, Race Driver* (Surfside Beach, S.C.: Galfield Press, 1991), 33.

page 74, a so-called wet funeral: Ralph S. Smith, "An Informal Inquiry into the Dark Science of Bootlegging, A.D. 1920–1932," three-part series, *Winston-Salem Journal,* Aug. 13–15, 1967.

page 75, Ford . . . a "leader" of the Fascist movement: Brinkley, *Wheels,* 263.

page 75, "a supermechanic with the mind of a stubborn peasant": Upton Sinclair, *The Flivver King: A Story of Ford in America* (Pasadena, Calif.: published by the author, 1937), 110.

page 79, a sleek canvas-and-wood experimental vehicle sped: *LIFE: American*

Speed, from Dirt Tracks to Indy to NASCAR (Time Inc. Home Entertainment, 2002), 14–16.

page 79, **"the absolute limit of speed"**: George Stephens Clark, "Gasoline and Sand: The Birth of Automobile Racing," *Mankind: The Magazine of Popular History* 3, no. 4 (Dec. 1971).

page 79, **"brushed at least a dozen coats while making the turn"**: *LIFE: American Speed*, 19.

page 80, **"the greatest race in the world"** and **"transcendent event"**: Ibid., 22.

page 82, **"barroom brawler, dirt-track daredevil"**: Brinkley, *Wheels*, 45.

page 82, **"rather dull and colorless affairs"**: Randal L. Hall, "Before NASCAR: The Corporate and Civic Promotion of Automobile Racing in the American South, 1903–1927," *Journal of Southern History* 68, no. 3 (Aug. 2002).

page 83, **Henry Ford came to Daytona and Ormond Beach**: Jerry Bledsoe, *The World's Number One, Flat-Out, All-Time Great, Stock Car Racing Book* (New York: Bantam Books, 1976), 32.

page 83, **"rogue, rule breaker, braggart"**: Ibid.

page 84, **"Will the Car Like You Drive . . ."**: Hall, *Journal of Southern History*.

page 86, **a tidy little one hundred–dollar profit**: UMI Publications, *NASCAR: The Early Years* (Charlotte, N.C.: UMI Publications, 2002), 11.

page 87, **"entitled to my winnings"** and **"given a fair deal"**: Fielden, *High Speed at Low Tide*, 32, 31.

page 87, **"The surest way to get a 'hillbilly' to do something"**: Paul Hemphill, *Wheels: A Season on NASCAR's Winston Cup Circuit* (New York: Berkley Books, 1998), 78.

page 88, **the town of Stockbridge**: Fielden, *Tim Flock*, 35; also Sylvia Wilkinson, *Dirt Tracks to Glory: The Early Days of Stock Car Racing as Told by the Participants* (Chapel Hill, N.C.: Algonquin Books, 1983), 35.

page 90, **"I don't know how they got wore out so fast"**: Wilkinson, *Dirt Tracks to Glory*, 36.

page 90, **he once narrowly escaped death**: Eddie Samples, "Lakewood Speedway Continued . . . ," Georgia Automobile Racing Hall of Fame Association's *Pioneer Pages* 2, no. 1 (Mar. 1999).

page 92, **"it doesn't have fenders on it"**: Eddie Samples, "Lakewood Speedway: The Indianapolis of the South, Stock Car Racing Begins," Georgia Automobile Racing Hall of Fame Association's *Pioneer Pages* 1, no. 3 (Aug. 1998).

page 92, **an overflow crowd of fifty thousand had watched Seabiscuit**: Laura Hillenbrand, *Seabiscuit: An American Legend* (New York: Ballantine Books, 2001), 266.

page 92, **"churning up the most interest"**: "Lakewood Trials Are Slated Today," *Atlanta Constitution*, Nov. 10, 1938.

page 92, **"They'll spill speed and maybe some gore"**: "First Race Program Billed in Atlanta," *Anniston Star*, July 1, 1938.

page 95, **"just like the movies"**: "Seay Is Winner of Auto Event," *Atlanta Constitution*, Nov. 12, 1938.

page 95, **insisted that he . . . had really won**: "The Boss of the Beach: Racing's Red-Headed Huck Finn," *Speed Age*, Mar. 1949.

page 97, "the odor of the races has never been too good": *Atlanta Constitution*, June 13, 1950.

page 97, the cutting edge of the wild side: Pete Daniel, *Lost Revolutions: The South in the 1950s* (Chapel Hill: University of North Carolina Press, 2000), 93.

page 97, "The fiercely competitive racing culture" and "orgy of dust, liquor and noise": Ibid., 117, 96.

page 98, "I'm no fool. . . . I guess they melted 'em": Bledsoe, *World's Number One, Flat-Out, All-Time Great, Stock Car Racing Book*, 82.

page 98, "I've got the fever": Ed Hinton, "The Legend: Lloyd Seay Was the Young Sport's Brightest Star until He Was Gunned Down," *Sports Illustrated Presents 50 Years of NASCAR*, Jan. 28, 1998, 47.

6. "All the women screamin' Roy Hall"

Unless otherwise noted, descriptions of Red Vogt's modifications (and stock car modifications in general) are from author interviews with Tom Vogt, June Wendt, George Moore, Billy Watson, Raymond Parks, David Sosebee, and others; also articles in *Speed Age, Motorsport,* and *Pioneer Pages;* Bob Desiderio, "Mechanic Vogt Started Career at Age of 10," *Daytona Beach Morning Journal*, Feb. 24, 1956; and the History Channel's *Automaniac* documentary series (episode, "Moonshine Cars"). All of the Daytona Beach race scenes (and other races), including quotes by and about Roy Hall, are from various newspaper articles in the *Atlanta Constitution, Daytona Beach News Journal*, and *Daytona Beach Sun Record*, as well as Greg Fielden's wonderfully detailed *High Speed at Low Tide* (Surfside Beach, S.C.: Galfield Press, 1993).

page 102, stock car racing's first team owner: Paul Hemphill, *Wheels: A Season on NASCAR's Winston Cup Circuit* (New York: Berkley Books, 1998), 83.

page 104, "The right side of the road is the Atlantic": Interview with Bill Watson.

page 106, "They knew I had money": Hemphill, *Wheels*, 83.

page 106, "The look-alikes could pass for brothers": "Driver, Owner, Mechanic Collaborate to Win Race," *Daytona Beach News Journal*, Aug. 25, 1941.

page 107, "Until then, I have nothing to lose": "Young Atlantan Has No Respect for Life or Limb," *Daytona Beach News Journal*, Mar. 3, 1941.

page 108, "dirt-smeared, wind-burned Georgian" . . . "piloting hooch": Ibid.

page 108, Police . . . cornered him on the highway: "Police Admit Hall Is Demon at Wheel," *Atlanta Journal*, Sept. 3, 1939.

page 108, cop who called Hall "a genius at the wheel": Ibid.

page 109, Bob Flock—the "wild-eyed Atlantan": Fielden, *High Speed at Low Tide*, 44.

page 109, "nerveless . . . no respect for life or limb": "Young Atlantan Has No Respect."

page 109, "Hall had the best of me": Fielden, *High Speed at Low Tide*, 44.

page 114, "Every car owner in the country wants to see . . .": Ibid., 13.

page 114, "The guy who uses his head . . .": Ibid., 15.

page 115, "stay off the track today. . . . A fatal accident": "Stock Car Race at 3 Today," *Daytona Beach News Journal*, Mar. 2, 1941.

page 116, "This is my last race": "Parks Purchased Two Costly Cars and Both Were

Wrecked before Race Started: Happy Ending," unknown Daytona Beach newspaper, 1941, date unknown (from Raymond Parks's scrapbook).

page 119, France . . . known to carry a pistol: Dan Pierce, "The Most Southern
Sport on Earth: NASCAR and the Unions," *Southern Cultures*, 2001.

page 120, "It feels a lot harder to me when I don't win": "Seay Stages One-Man
Race," *Daytona Beach Sun Record*, Aug. 25, 1941.

page 120, "Seay and Hall have a bitter rivalry on the track": "Driver, Owner,
Mechanic Collaborate."

page 121, "one of the finest exhibitions of driving": "Seay Stages One-Man Race."

page 121, "It's about time I won here": Ibid.; and Fielden, *High Speed at Low Tide*,
74.

page 122, Late in life . . . France often put Lloyd Seay on his list: Larry Fielden, *Tim
Flock, Race Driver* (Surfside Beach, S.C.: Galfield Press, 1991), 44.

7. "Yesterday his luck ran out"

Unless otherwise noted, the story of Lloyd Seay's final days and his murder is from
the court documents and trial transcripts of "The State vs. Woodrow Anderson,"
Lumpkin Superior Court, as well as interviews with Raymond Parks. Also: Ed
Hinton, "The Legend: Lloyd Seay Was the Young Sport's Brightest Star until He
Was Gunned Down," *Sports Illustrated Presents 50 Years of NASCAR*, Jan. 28,
1998; Greg Fielden, *High Speed at Low Tide* (Surfside Beach, S.C.: Galfield Press,
1993); Eddie Samples, "Garhofa's Raymond Dawson Parks," Georgia Automobile
Racing Hall of Fame Association's *Pioneer Pages* 5, no. 1 (Feb. 2002); Paul
Hemphill, *Wheels: A Season on NASCAR's Winston Cup Circuit* (New York:
Berkley Books, 1998); and numerous articles in the *Atlanta Journal* and *Atlanta
Constitution*, including "Seay, Winner of Lakewood Race, Is Killed," *Atlanta
Constitution*, Sept. 4, 1941, and "Racer Lloyd Seay Shot to Death in Disagreement
with Cousin," *Atlanta Journal*, Sept. 4, 1941.

page 123, Earlier that summer, a driver from Macon . . . : Hemphill, *Wheels*, 89.

page 124, "the greatest stock car race ever held here": "Dust Being Eliminated for
Labor Day Races," *Atlanta Constitution*, Aug. 28, 1941.

page 124, "Seay . . . just one of the boys": *Atlanta Constitution*, Aug. 31, 1941.

page 125, "the parked cars were red-topped . . .": Malcolm Davis, "Lloyd Seay
Tops Field in Labor Day Races," *Atlanta Constitution*, Sept. 2, 1941.

page 130, Woodrow . . . later worked at Ford's new postwar factory: Samples,
"Garhofa's Raymond Dawson Parks," *Pioneer Pages*.

page 131, "liquor haulers and race fans and thrill seekers: Hemphill, *Wheels*, 80.

page 131, As one southern writer said . . . : Ibid., 81.

8. "MIRACULOUS DEATH ESCAPE"

Unless otherwise noted, all information on Red Byron's childhood is from a lengthy
written response to questions provided by his sister, Virginia Gassaway, as well as
some input from her son, Steve Gassaway. Other information about Byron comes
from Byron's wife, Nell Byron; her sister, Sarah Atha; and Nell's daughters, Beverly
and Betty. Also: various articles in the *Anniston Star* and *Speed Age* magazine; Greg
Fielden, *High Speed at Low Tide* (Surfside Beach, S.C.: Galfield Press, 1993), 80;

and interviews with Raymond Parks and others. Descriptions of Indy cars versus stock cars are from interviews with Dick Berggren and Chris Economacki; David Burgess-Wise's *Ultimate Race Car* (London: Dorling Kindersley, 1999); and Brock W. Yates's *Against Death and Time: One Fatal Season in Racing's Glory Years* (New York: Thunder's Mouth Press, 2004).

page 137, He drove made-from-scratch . . . three-quarter cars: Interview with Buddy Starr.

pages 137, 138, "a disturbance of their peace" and "might as well write our obituary": "Auto Races Today Officially Barred," *Anniston Star,* Aug. 27, 1938.

page 138, "easily the greatest race meet ever conducted in Atlanta": "25,000 Thrilled By 2 Crack-ups at July 4 Races," *Atlanta Journal,* July 5, 1938.

page 139, "a little rough in appearance": "The Boss of the Beach; Racing's Red-headed Huck Finn," *Speed Age,* Mar. 1949.

page 139, "MIRACULOUS DEATH ESCAPE": "25,000 Thrilled By 2 Crack-ups."

page 141, "mass of spilled vehicles and drivers": "Five Drivers Injured on Lakewood Track," *Atlanta Journal,* July 13, 1941.

page 142, By late 1941, he had spent seven thousand dollars: "Driver, Owner, Mechanic Collaborate to Win Race," *Daytona Beach News Journal,* Aug. 25, 1941.

9. Body bags and B-24 bombers

Unless otherwise noted, descriptions of Raymond Parks's wartime experiences come from interviews with and documents provided by Raymond Parks. Also: William C. Cavanaugh, *Dauntless: A History of the 99th Infantry Division* (Dallas: Taylor Publishing, 1994); David P. Colley, *Blood for Dignity: The Story of the First Integrated Combat Unit in the U.S. Army* (New York: St. Martin's Press, 2003); Hugh M. Cole, *The Ardennes: Battle of the Bulge* (published by the Center for Military History, www.army.mil/cmh-pg/books/wwii/7-8/7-8_cont.htm, 1965); and Eddie Samples, "Garhofa's Raymond Dawson Parks," Georgia Automobile Racing Hall of Fame Association's *Pioneer Pages 5,* no. 1 (Feb. 2002). Information on Ford and the B-24 is mostly from Douglas Brinkley's *Wheels for the World: Henry Ford, His Company, and a Century of Progress* (New York: Viking, 2003). Byron's wartime experiences were more difficult to piece together (partly because his ex-wife has Alzheimer's), but the descriptions were assisted greatly by the following wonderful books: Stephen E. Ambrose, *The Wild Blue: The Men and Boys Who Flew the B-24s over Germany, 1944–45* (New York: Simon & Schuster, 2001); Samuel Eliot Morison, *History of U.S. Naval Operations in World War II,* vol. 7, *Aleutians, Gilberts and Marshalls, June 1942–April 1944* (Boston: Little Brown, 1951); and Brinkley's *Wheels.* Also: Elmendorf Air Force Base, 11th Air Force (www.elmendorf.af.mil/11AF/webdocs/history.htm).

page 147, "shot the Seays while their hands were raised . . .": "Justifiable Homicide Is Anderson's Plea in Killing," *Atlanta Constitution,* 1941 (exact date unknown).

page 147, "stand up as free men and fight": "FDR Warns Hitler," *Atlanta Journal,* Sept. 1, 1941.

page 148, the Lloyd Seay Memorial Race . . . : "Full Field of 23 Cars to Race at Lakewood," *Atlanta Journal,* Nov. 3, 1941.

page 149, **In an awkward display . . . :** Vogt's sons are C. Thomas and L. Jerome but went by the names Tom and Jerry.

page 151, **"I hate the cold. Men are miserable, too":** Cavanaugh, *Dauntless*, 60.

page 154, **"They couldn't bag us fast enough":** Samples, "Garhofa's Raymond Dawson Parks," *Pioneer Pages*.

page 160, **"the biggest challenge of my life":** Brinkley, *Wheels*, 459.

page 160, **"Look out, Hitler. Here comes the flood!":** Ibid., 464.

page 161, **a mix of "Daniel Boone and Henry Ford":** Ambrose, *Wild Blue*, 108.

page 161, **". . . exhausted every resource of mind and body . . .":** Ibid., 262.

page 161, **"gaunt and majestic" landscape:** Morison, *History of U.S. Naval Operations*, vol. 7, *Aleutians, Gilberts and Marshalls*, 38.

page 162, **"not smart enough to be afraid":** Ambrose, *Wild Blue*, 184.

page 162, **"the flak was so thick you could walk on it":** Ibid., 161.

page 163, **"hold the western Aleutians at all cost":** Morison, *History of U.S. Naval Operations*, vol. 7, *Aleutians, Gilberts and Marshalls*, 18.

page 164, **not a single U.S. plane was lost:** Norman Bell, "Paramushiro Hit on Schedule," Associated Press, Jan. 24, 1944.

page 165, **one of the only U.S. planes damaged in that campaign:** "Paramushiro Raids Put Japs on Spot," *Seattle Post-Intelligencer*, Feb. 15, 1944.

10. "It's too late now to bring this crowd under control"

The first postwar race scene and all related quotes come from numerous articles and editorials in both the *Atlanta Journal* and the *Atlanta Constitution*, Sept. 2–5, 1945, unless otherwise noted. Red Byron's victory at Daytona Beach in early 1946 is mostly from Greg Fielden, *High Speed at Low Tide* (Surfside Beach, S.C.: Galfield Press, 1993), and Bernard Kahn, "Spins, Wrecks Chill Fans as Bob Byron Whizzes to Beach Race Victory," *Daytona Beach News Journal*, Apr. 15, 1946.

page 168, **always admired the Daniel Boone lifestyle:** Tim McLaurin, *Keeper of the Moon: A Southern Boyhood* (New York: Anchor Books/Doubleday, 1991), 244.

page 169, **"the most intensely patriotic segment of the country":** James Webb, *Born Fighting: How the Scots-Irish Shaped America.* (New York: Broadway Books, 2004), 328.

page 169, **Henry blamed his son's "high flying lifestyle":** Douglas Brinkley, *Wheels for the World: Henry Ford, His Company, and a Century of Progress* (New York: Viking, 2003), 405.

page 170, **"Beat Chevrolet":** Ibid., 506.

page 170, **cars sold faster in the South:** Louis Rubin, ed., *The American South: Portrait of a Culture* (Washington, D.C.: Government Printing Office, 1980).

page 170, **"worship of a newfound power—and freedom":** Jerry Bledsoe, *The World's Number One, Flat-Out, All-Time Great, Stock Car Racing Book* (New York: Bantam Books, 1976), 43.

page 170, **"rude, violent, uncouth, and proud of it . . .":** Pete Daniel, *Lost Revolutions: The South in the 1950s* (Chapel Hill: University of North Carolina Press, 2000), 117.

page 172, **"bootlegger sweepstakes":** "5 Labor Day Lakewood Racers Possess Lengthy Police Records," *Atlanta Constitution*, Sept. 2, 1945.

page 177, **France even told the editor, Wilton Garrison:** Brock Yates, "The Force:

Bill France's Vision Made NASCAR the World's Premier Racing Organization,"
Sports Illustrated Presents 50 Years of NASCAR, Jan. 28, 1998, 70.

page 177, **"Who's going to be in this race of yours?":** Ibid.

page 177, **"We're only interested in big races":** Leo Levine, *Ford, the Dust and the
Glory: A Racing History, 1901–1967* (Warrendale, Pa.: Society of Automotive
Engineers, 2001), 128.

page 178, **Fonty Flock . . . rushed over and scooped brother Bob:** Del Baggett,
"Cracker Driver Is Race Winner Here," *Charlotte Observer*, Oct. 28, 1945.

page 178, **France planned . . . unveiling his own . . . sanctioning body:** Yates, *Sports
Illustrated*, 71; also Mike Hembree, *NASCAR: The Definitive History* (New
York: Harper Entertainment/Tehabi Books, 2000).

page 186, **"I realize I did some things that went against me":** Jack Troy, "All in the
Game," *Atlanta Constitution*, May 9, 1946.

page 186, **"What, no sheets?" Hall complained:** Fielden, *High Speed at Low Tide*, 86.

page 187, **"Give that boy a set of tools . . .":** Jennings, "We Spectators."

page 187, **The next morning, he told Anne . . . they were going home:** Interview
with J. B. Day.

page 187, **"I ain't going back there," he said:** Ibid.

page 188, **Choking traffic jams forced police to turn away another five thousand:**
Greensboro News, July 5, 1946.

page 188, **"That was the start of NASCAR":** Interview with J. B. Day.

page 191, **"Atlanta produce dealer":** "Famous Racer Waives Extradition to
Georgia," *Greensboro Record*, Aug. 5, 1946.

page 191, **charged Hall with abetting the "desperate criminal":** Ibid.

page 191, **"Take care of your momma":** Interview with Ronnie Hall.

page 192, **"I never raced a day in my life":** Eddie Samples, "Garhofa's Raymond
Dawson Parks," Automobile Racing Hall of Fame Association's *Pioneer Pages 5*,
no. 1 (Feb. 2002).

11. Henry Ford is dead

Definitive, comprehensive information about all the racing organizations of the
1940s is hard to come by—no one kept track of such things. Information about
these groups, their championships, and points systems comes from a variety of
sources, including 1940s race programs, newspaper and magazine articles (espe-
cially *Illustrated Speedway News* and *Speed Age*), and the following: Kevin Conley,
"NASCAR's New Track," *New Yorker*, Nov. 2, 2004; Eddie Samples, "Garhofa's
Raymond Dawson Parks," Georgia Automobile Racing Hall of Fame Association's
Pioneer Pages 5, no. 1 (Feb. 2002); Brock Yates, "The Force: Bill France's Vision
Made NASCAR the World's Premier Racing Organization," Leigh Montville,
"Dawsonville, U.S.A.," and Ed Hinton, "The Legend: Lloyd Seay Was the Young
Sport's Brightest Star until He Was Gunned Down"—all in *Sports Illustrated
Presents 50 Years of NASCAR*, Jan. 28, 1998; and A Brief History of NASCAR
(www.mindspring.com/~mike.wicks/nascarhistory.html). Information on Indy rac-
ing and open-wheel cars, unless otherwise noted, is from interviews with Dick
Berggren and Chris Economaki; David Burgess-Wise's *Ultimate Race Car* (London;
Dorling Kindersley, 1999); Brock W. Yates's *Against Death and Time: One Fatal*

Season in Racing's Glory Years (New York: Thunder's Mouth Press, 2004). Details on Byron's attempt to qualify at Indy in 1947 were elusive. I found an article claiming that Byron was in fact struck by a bird. His wife, Nell, also says she remembers the incident. But the *Indianapolis Star* could find no articles about such an event, and none of Byron's peers could recall the alleged incident, so I reluctantly chose to include the bird story.

page 194, **"Be careful, Red,"** she'd say: "The Boss of the Beach; Racing's Red-Headed Huck Finn," *Speed Age*, Mar. 1949.

page 196, **Daytona's Beach-and-Road course:** Interview with Buz McKim (written replies to questions from the author).

page 197, **"The Contest Board is bitterly opposed . . .":** D. Randy Riggs, *Flat-out Racing: An Insider's Look at the World of Stock Cars* (New York: MetroBooks, Michael Friedman Publishing Group, 1995), 36.

page 198, **"I gotta try something safer than moonshine":** Interview with Gordon Pirkle and David Sosebee.

page 199, **In nearly every picture of the Flock brothers:** Kim Chapin, *Fast as White Lightning: The Story of Stock Car Racing* (New York: Three Rivers Press, 1998), 71.

pages 199–202, **[Entire January 26 race]:** Greg Fielden, *High Speed at Low Tide* (Surfside Beach, S.C.: Galfield Press, 1993), 88–90; and Bernard Kahn, "Red Byron Wins Auto Race at 77.4 MPH; 2 Spectators Hurt," *Daytona Beach News Journal*, Jan. 28, 1947.

page 200, **pit road:** Burgess-Wise, *Ultimate Race Car.*

page 202, **"a war injury that rendered his left leg almost useless":** "Byron Rated Tops in Race," Associated Press, Mar. 6, 1947.

page 202, **"filled with Jap shrapnel!":** Smith Barrier, "Three Stock Car Racers Grin at Sports Injuries," *Greensboro Daily News*, Apr. 17, 1948.

page 204, **[the dangers at Indy]:** Yates, *Against Death and Time*, 30–50.

page 205, **[Byron at Indy]:** Interview with George Moore; "Speedy Stock Cars Fill Rain Date at Jacksonville," June 1, 1947 (unknown Jacksonville newspaper); Smith Barrier, "It's a Racing Weekend—at Indianapolis, Too," *Greensboro Daily News*, May 29, 1948.

page 208, **[Henry Ford's death]:** Douglas Brinkley, *Wheels for the World: Henry Ford, His Company, and a Century of Progress* (New York: Viking, 2003), 510–519.

page 209, **Ford . . . reincarnation:** Ibid., 6.

page 209, **"Better drivers mean better races . . .":** *Illustrated Speedway News*, May 2, 1947.

page 210, **"world's finest talent"** and **"nation's largest racing schedule":** *Speed Age*, various issues.

page 210, **[France friendship with Kahn]:** Leo Levine, *Ford, the Dust and the Glory: A Racing History, 1901–1967* (Warrendale, Pa.: Society of Automotive Engineers, 2001), 128.

page 212, **"By establishing the national point ranking system . . .":** "France to Award Stock Car Drivers Trophies—Cash," *Illustrated Speedway News*, May 2, 1947.

page 212, "the hottest rider in the stock car circuit": "40 Car Field Expected for Feature Today," May 11, 1947 (unknown Greenville newspaper).

page 213, "I saw you sideways and thought I could straighten you out": Eddie Samples's 1996 interview with Jack Etheridge, shared with the author.

page 216, "the ultimate test of bravery": Yates, *Against Death and Time*, 77.

page 217, "When that green flag goes down tomorrow . . .": Eddie Samples's 2002 interview with Raymond Parks, shared with the author.

pages 217–218, [Langhorne race] and "Get in": "Flock Wins Langhorne Race," *Speed Age*, Oct. 1947; also various unknown newspapers.

page 219, "I just drove where they wasn't": Fielden, *High Speed at Low Tide*, 93.

page 219, Parks . . . invested twenty thousand dollars halfway through 1947: Sample's, "Garhofa's Raymond Dawson Parks," *Pioneer Pages;* also "Red Byron Wins Feature Race at Martinsville's New Track," Sept. 7, 1947 (unknown newspaper, Danville, Va.).

page 219, still barely breaking even: "Red Byron Wins Feature Race at Martinsville's New Track."

page 219, "You take a huge fortune . . .": Samples, "Garhofa's Raymond Dawson Parks, *Pioneer Pages.*

page 220, "If there was a better mech . . .": Bernard Kahn, "Race Winner Byron Tosses Orchids to Motor Builder Vogt," *Daytona Beach News Journal,* Feb. 16, 1948.

page 221, [Peachtree Williams's story]: Larry Fielden, *Tim Flock, Race Driver* (Surfside Beach, S.C.: Galfield Press, 1991), 36.

page 221, Osiecki . . . "also ran": Vic Brannon, "Red Byron Wins Season Finale," *National Speed Sport News,* Nov. 16, 1947.

page 222, "I know they like action . . .": Fielden, *High Speed at Low Tide*, 91.

page 223, year-end bonuses . . . first time: Ibid., 95.

page 223, France announced the current point standings: All information about the final races of 1947 comes from various unknown newspaper articles, Dec. 6–9, 1947. Also: *Speed Age*, Dec. 1947 and Jan. 1948.

page 224, "I am lucky to have Raymond Parks . . .": *Speed Age*, Jan. 1948.

page 225, "It is the opinion of this writer . . .": Ibid.

12. "Next thing we know, NASCAR belongs to Bill France"

Unless otherwise noted, the entire scene of NASCAR's organizational meeting is based on the following: National Championship Stock Car Circuit, original minutes, "Annual Convention, The National Championship Stock Car Circuit, Ebony Room, Streamline Hotel, Daytona Beach, Florida, Dec. 14–17, 1947"; *Speed Age*, Jan. 1948; William Neely, *Daytona USA: The Official History of Daytona and Ormond Beach Racing from 1902 to Today's NASCAR Super Speedways* (Tucson, Ariz.: AZTEX Corp., 1979); Ben White, "The Formation of NASCAR," *American Racing Classics,* multiple vols. (Concord, N.C.: Griggs Publishing; Talladega, Ala.: International Motorsports Hall of Fame, Jan. 1992); UMI Publications, *NASCAR: The Early Years* (Charlotte, N.C.: UMI Publications, 2002); W. E. Butterworth, *The High Wind: The Story of NASCAR Racing* (New York: Norton, 1971); Greg Fielden, *Forty Years of Stock Car Racing,* 4 vols.

(Surfside Beach, S.C.: Galfield Press, 1992); Greg Fielden, *High Speed at Low Tide* (Surfside Beach, S.C.: Galfield Press, 1993); Mike Hembree, *NASCAR: The Definitive History* (New York: Harper Entertainment/Tehabi Books, 2000). Also: interviews with Raymond Parks, Tom Vogt, Mike Bell, Eddie Samples, and Buz McKim. Also consulted were the following books by Peter Golenbock: *The Last Lap: The Life and Times of NASCAR's Legendary Heroes* (New York: Macmillan Publishing, 1998); *American Zoom: Stock Car Racing—From the Dirt Tracks to Daytona* (New York: Macmillan Publishing, 1994); *NASCAR Confidential: Stories of Men and Women Who Made Stock Car Racing Great* (Osceola, Wis.: MBI Publishing, 2004); and Peter Golenbock, ed., *NASCAR Encyclopedia: The Complete Record of America's Most Popular Sport* (Osceola, Wis.: Motorbooks International, 2003).

page 227, "If there's ever a stock car race in your area . . .": "Their Business Is Stock," *Speed Age,* June 1947.

pages 228–229, France felt . . . AAA was an "outsider": Brock Yates, "The Force: Bill France's Vision Made NASCAR the World's Premier Racing Organization," *Sports Illustrated Presents 50 Years of NASCAR,* Jan. 28, 1998, 87.

page 229, "junk car events" . . . "dying out": D. Randy Riggs, *Flat-out Racing: An Insider's Look at the World of Stock Cars* (New York: MetroBooks, Michael Friedman Publishing Group, 1995), 36.

page 229, "I was one of them": Yates, *Sports Illustrated,* 87.

page 232, a "ruse" . . . "rivals": Neely, *Daytona USA,* 58.

page 234, "the dawn of a new era": *Speed Age,* Jan. 1948.

page 235, "The democratic method . . . never worked": Neely, *Daytona USA,* 58.

page 235, France and Tuthill had therefore schemed: Ibid.

page 235, "The next thing we know, NASCAR belongs to Bill France": Gerald Hodges, "NASCAR Racing—Before There Was NASCAR, There Was Dawsonville," *Susquehanna County Transcript,* Dec. 24, 2002 (http://www.susquehannatranscript.com/archives/12_17_02v4n25/sports.htm).

page 235, France's plan all along: Neely, *Daytona USA,* 58.

13. "Racing Car Plunges into Throng"

All information about the corporate details of NASCAR's creation, the stock split, and the alleged exclusion of Vogt and Parks is from interviews with Raymond Parks, Billy Watson, George Moore, Tom Vogt, and June Wendt. Also: William Neely, *Daytona USA: The Official History of Daytona and Ormond Beach Racing from 1902 to Today's NASCAR Super Speedways* (Tucson, Ariz.: AZTEX Corp., 1979), 58; W. E. Butterworth, *The High Wind: The Story of NASCAR Racing* (New York: Norton, 1971), 19; Jerry Bledsoe, *The World's Number One, Flat-Out, All-Time Great, Stock Car Racing Book* (New York: Bantam Books, 1976), 35, 43; Greg Fielden, *High Speed at Low Tide* (Surfside Beach, S.C.: Galfield Press, 1993); and Ben White, "The Formation of NASCAR," *American Racing Classics* (Concord, N.C.: Griggs Publishing; Talladega, Ala.: International Motorsports Hall of Fame, Jan. 1992). Regarding Raymond Parks's alleged loans to France: Parks has, at times—with the author and with others—denied that he loaned money to France. But his wife, Violet, and sister, Lucille Shirley, have confirmed that he has confessed this fact to them; Lucille said she was personally aware of and witnessed such loans. Others, including Billy Watson and Gordon Pirkle, have backed this up, and some of Parks's colleagues suspect he had vowed never to divulge this information and likely swore many friends to secrecy. The author contacted NASCAR officials about this, but there wasn't enough information for NASCAR to confirm or deny it. Bill France Sr. apparently took the full truth to his grave. The entire Feb. 15 race is from the following: Bernard Kahn, "14,000 Watch Byron Win Auto Race," *Daytona Beach News Journal,* Feb. 16, 1948; *Illustrated Speedway News,* Feb. 1948; Fielden, *High Speed at Low Tide,* 100–102; Larry Fielden, *Tim Flock, Race Driver* (Surfside Beach, S.C.: Galfield Press, 1991); and Tom Higgins, *NASCAR Greatest Races: The 25 Most Thrilling Races in NASCAR History* (New York: Harper Entertainment / Tehabi Books, 1999), 10, 12.

page 237, "With the gentleness of a lover . . .": Harry Crews, *Classic Crews: A Harry Crews Reader* (New York: Poseidon Press, 1993), 340.

page 238, Red accused her of stealing all his money: Interviews with Tom Vogt.

page 239, France had seemed almost to have conspired: Interviews with June Wendt and Billy Watson.

page 240, "He stayed mad the rest of his days": Interview with June Wendt.

page 240, ". . . who the hell would do any better?" Interview with George Moore.

page 243, "We weren't businessmen, just car owners . . .": Gerald Hodges, "NASCAR Racing—Before There Was NASCAR, There Was Dawsonville," *Susquehanna County Transcript,* Dec. 24, 2002.

page 243, "That's how Bill France stole . . .": Ibid.

pages 244–245, a "real corker" and "one of the greatest days . . .": Higgins, *NASCAR Greatest Races,* 10, 12.

page 245, France leased the property for the track: Interview with Buz McKim (written replies to questions from the author).

page 253, [Lee Preston Flock and the Flock family]: Fielden, *Tim Flock,* 14–17; and Russ Catlin, "The Fabulous Flock Family," *Speed Age,* Oct. 1950.

page 254, "two Atlanta crackers": "New Lakeview Speedway to Open for NASCAR in NC," Apr. 11, 1948 (unknown newspaper, Concord or Lexington, N.C.).

page 255, "a bouncing rubber ball . . .": Catlin, "Fabulous Flock Family."

page 255, "a little older and smarter than the rest of us": Transcript of 1990 interview by Rick Minter (reporter for the *Atlanta Journal-Constitution*) with Ed Samples, shared with the author by Samples's son, Eddie.

page 255, "Although there has been no outright hostility . . .": "New Lakeview Speedway."

page 257, "time to let Fonty eat a little dust": "Byron to have 'Indy' Engine for Opening of Lakeview Race," May 2, 1948 (unknown newspaper, Concord, N.C.).

page 260, Which gave him a perfect view . . .: Eddie Samples, "Columbus Speedway's Historic 1948 Inaugural Season; Red Byron's Bittersweet Championship," *Pioneer Pages* 8, no. 2 (June 2005); interview with Charles Jenkins.

page 262, "17 Injured When Racing Car Plunges into Throng": The entire story of this race is from interview with Charles Jenkins; Samples, "Columbus Speedway's Historic 1948 Inaugural Season," *Pioneer Pages;* and Associated Press stories and photographs of July 26 and 27, 1948.

14. An "ambience" of death

page 264, **As early as 1911, a race car had plunged:** Brock Yates, *Against Death and Time: One Fatal Season in Racing's Glory Years* (New York: Thunder's Mouth Press, 2004), 57.

page 265, **"I'll die with two hands . . .":** Smith Barrier, "Three Stock Car Racers Grin at Sports Injuries," *Greensboro Daily News,* Apr. 17, 1948.

page 266, **"extra barricades will be erected . . .":** Greg Fielden, *High Speed at Low Tide* (Surfside Beach, S.C.: Galfield Press, 1993), 103.

page 267, **"Fans marveled at the power . . .":** Earl Kelley, "Fonty Flock Wins Daytona Beach '150'," *Speed Age,* October, 1948.

page 267, **"I'm glad I won":** Fielden, *High Speed at Low Tide,* 104.

page 268, **A boosterish sportswriter . . . "very rare":** "You Have to Ride in a Stock Car before Thrills Really Come Your Way," Sept. 5, 1948 (unknown Columbus, Ga., newspaper).

page 269, **France decided to call off the race.** The entire scene of the final NASCAR race of the year is from Samples, "Columbus Speedway's Historic 1948 Inaugural Season," *Pioneer Pages*; and interview with Charles Jenkins.

page 270, **"sort of lost heart after that":** Interview with Mitzi Teague.

page 270, **". . . the death of that little boy never left him":** Interview with Charles Jenkins.

page 270, **the "ambience" of death:** Samples, "Columbus Speedway's Historic 1948 Inaugural Season, *Pioneer Pages."*

page 270, **"Maybe think about a less spectacular profession":** Race program: "Souvenir Autograph Program—200-Mile Stock Car Race," Jan. 16, 1949.

page 271, **Fonty . . . ten thousand and fifteen thousand dollars:** "You Have to Ride in a Stock Car."

page 271, **[Byron's split from Parks]:** "Byron to Field Own Car," *International Speed Sport News,* Jan. 1949 (unknown writer).

page 273, **NASCAR had taken in sixty-four thousand dollars:** William Neely, *Daytona USA: The Official History of Daytona and Ormond Beach Racing from 1902 to Today's NASCAR Super Speedways* (Tucson, Ariz.: AZTEX Corp., 1979), 59.

page 274, **". . . this is the point fund you've heard about":** Ben White, "The Formation of NASCAR," *American Racing Classics* (Concord, N.C.: Griggs Publishing; Talladega, Ala.: International Motorsports Hall of Fame, Jan. 1992), 11.

page 274, **"keep everything totally above board":** Ibid.

page 275, **the "Atlanta sportsman":** "Raymond D. Parks, Parks Novelty Company," *Atlanta Constitution,* Jan. 2, 1948.

page 275, **Georgia led the nation:** Jess Carr, *The Second Oldest Profession: An Informal History of Moonshining in America* (Englewood Cliffs, N.J.: Prentice Hall, 1972), 129.

page 278, "found God in cars . . .": Harry Crews, *Classic Crews: A Harry Crews Reader* (New York: Poseidon Press, 1993), 325.

page 278, **Parks agreed to share a larger cut:** Interview with Raymond Parks. (Note: Parks couldn't remember what the split was, but typical owner-driver splits at the time ranged from 50-50 to 60-40 to 70-30.)

15. The first race, a bootlegger, and a disqualification

Unless otherwise noted, sources for NASCAR's first strictly stock race include: Gary McCredie, "The First Race," *American Racing Classics* (Concord, N.C.: Griggs Publishing; Talladega, Ala.: International Motorsports Hall of Fame, Apr. 1992); William Neely, *Daytona USA: The Official History of Daytona and Ormond Beach Racing from 1902 to Today's NASCAR Super Speedways* (Tucson, Ariz.: AZTEK Corp., 1979), 64–65; Greg Fielden, *Forty Years of Stock Car Racing*, 4 vols. (Surfside Beach, S.C.: Galfield Press, 1992), vol. 1. References to drivers' protests, NASCAR's "guarantee," and punishment of misbehaving drivers are from Fielden, *Forty Years of Stock Car Racing*, vol. 1, 7; various newspapers, including "Stock Car Drivers Want More Money" (unknown newspaper, Concord, N.C.), Mar. 25, 1949, and "Stock Car 'Jumpers' Reinstated" (unknown newspaper, Charlotte, N.C.), June 19, 1949, and "Jim Roper Wins 'Official' First NASCAR 'Stock' Race," *National Speed Sport News*, June 19, 1949.

page 279, **resembled a Civil War encampment:** Scott Huler, *A Little Bit Sideways: One Week inside a NASCAR Winston Cup Team* (Osceola, Wis.: MBI Publishing, 1999), 35.

pages 279–280, **insurance . . . one hundred dollars per race:** Neely, *Daytona USA*, 59.

page 280, ***Where's all the money going?:*** Fielden, *Forty Years of Stock Car Racing*, vol. 1, 7; and "Stock Car Drivers Want More Money."

page 280, **Teague was soon joined by two moonshiners:** Ibid.

page 281, **Shuman . . . "very much satisfied":** "Stock Car Drivers Want More Money."

page 281, **"It's too much," France said:** Ibid.

page 281, **Teague also withdrew . . . in protest:** Fielden, *Forty Years of Stock Car Racing*, vol. 1, 7.

page 282, **"conduct detrimental to the best interests . . .":** "Stock Car Drivers Want More Money."

page 284, **"civilization's newest voice":** Peter Collier and David Horowitz, *The Fords: An American Epic* (New York: Summit Books, 1987), 35.

page 285, **"The nice thing about this game . . .":** UMI Publications, *NASCAR: The Early Years* (Charlotte, N.C.: UMI Publications, 2002), 35.

page 285, **A conviction on bootlegging charges:** McCredie, "The First Race," 9.

page 286, **"not in accordance with the best interests of NASCAR":** "Stock Car Drivers Want More Money"; and "Stock Car 'Jumpers' Reinstated."

page 287, **Tuthill tried to assure drivers:** Neely, *Daytona USA*, 59.

page 287, **"made an honest effort not to line our own pockets":** Ibid.

page 287, **"had done all the spadework":** Ibid., 58.

page 287, **"Bill was gittin' to be a millionaire . . .":** Jerry Bledsoe, *The World's*

Number One, Flat-Out, All-Time Great, Stock Car Racing Book (New York: Bantam Books, 1976), 43.

pages 287–288, **the more powerful engines ... overhead valves:** D. Randy Riggs, *Flat-out Racing: An Insider's Look at the World of Stock Cars* (New York: MetroBooks, Michael Friedman Publishing Group, 1995), 44.

page 289, **with France and Tuthill shaken up but uninjured:** "Jim Roper Wins 'Official' First NASCAR 'Stock' Race."

page 291, **The Petty family would hitchhike home:** Other versions of this story have Petty there without the family and/or racing his own car, not a friend's.

16. "It's not cheating if you don't get caught"

page 297, **experimented with minute reductions:** Henry "Smokey" Yunick, *Best Damn Garage in Town: The World According to Smokey,* 4 vols. (Holly Hill, Fla.: Carbon Press, 2001), vol. 4, 275.

page 297, **"the absolute peak of performance":** Bob Desiderio, "Mechanic Vogt Started Career at Age of 10," *Daytona Beach Morning Journal,* Feb. 24, 1956.

page 298, **"at best, a good-natured lie":** Yunick, *Best Damn Garage in Town,* vol. 4, 272; Henry "Smokey" Yunick (www.fireballroberts.com/smokey_yunick1.htm).

page 299, **driving with her AM radio blasting:** Suzanne Wise, "Fast Women: Female Racing Pioneers," *Atlanta History: A Journal of Georgia and the South* 46, no. 2 (2004), 57.

page 299, **Across the next fifty years ... :** Ibid.

page 300, **"... Somebody must have made a mistake ...":** Greg Fielden, *High Speed at Low Tide* (Surfside Beach, S.C.: Galfield Press, 1993), 111.

page 300, **"I doubt if Red averaged seventy-nine or eighty miles per hour":** Ibid.

page 302, **"If we back down, we're through":** William Neely, *Daytona USA: The Official History of Daytona and Ormond Beach Racing from 1902 to Today's NASCAR Super Speedways* (Tucson, Ariz.: AZTEX Corp., 1979), 65.

page 302, **"If you want to keep racing ...":** Ibid.

page 302, **"not safe for any of us to set foot in Atlanta ...":** Ibid.

page 303, **"a self-made son of a bitch":** Interview with David Sosebee.

page 303, **France grabbed a pen and wrote ... :** Ibid.

page 305, **Hall "could do things with a car ...":** Robert Cutter and Bob Fendell, *Encyclopedia of Auto Racing Greats* (New York: Prentice-Hall, 1973), 633.

page 306, **"You were going pretty good":** Ibid.

page 307, **Combined with the few hundred bucks:** "1950 NASCAR Yearbook" (Greensboro, N.C.: Bill France Enterprises), 56.

page 308, **auto accident fatalities, averaging thirty thousand a year:** "Motor Vehicle Accidents," *The Lincoln Library of Essential Information* (Buffalo, N.Y.: Frontier Press, 1959), 2081.

17. "No way a Plymouth can beat a Cadillac. No **way**"

Primary sources for the Mexican Road Race include: Jack Cansler, "The World's Toughest Road Race," *Speed Age,* Aug. 1950; Roland Goodman, *Book of the Mexican Road Race* (Los Angeles: Floyd Clymer, 1950); and Robert Edelstein, *Full Throttle: The Life and Fast Times of Curtis Turner* (New York: Overlook

Hardcover, 2005). Sources for the first race at Darlington and Vogt's protests include: Gene Granger, "The 1950 Southern 500," *American Racing Classics* (Concord, N.C.: Griggs Publishing; Talladega, Ala.: International Motorsports Hall of Fame, Oct. 1992); William Neely, *Daytona USA: The Official History of Daytona and Ormond Beach Racing from 1902 to Today's NASCAR Super Speedways* (Tucson, Ariz.: AZTEX Corp., 1979); Greg Fielden, *Forty Years of Stock Car Racing*, 4 vols. (Surfside Beach, S.C.: Galfield Press, 1992); and Tom Jensen, *Cheating: An Inside Look at the Bad Things Good NASCAR Winston Cup Racers Do in the Pursuit of Speed* (Phoenix, Ariz.: David Bull Publishing, 2002).

page 315, **After the body was removed . . . :** Cansler, "World's Toughest Road Race," 22.

page 315, **a few practice runs outside town:** Edelstein, *Full Throttle,* 62.

page 315, **averaging ninety-five miles an hour across:** Ibid.

page 316, **"I have a wife and kids at home":** Ibid.

page 317, **Curtis Turner was also pickpocketed:** Ibid., 61.

page 321, **"No way," France said:** Larry Fielden, *Tim Flock, Race Driver* (Surfside Beach, S.C.: Galfield Press, 1991), 94.

page 322, **he dispatched his number two guy, Bill Tuthill:** Neely, *Daytona USA,* 65.

page 322, **would likely fall to pieces if pushed:** Fielden, *Forty Years of Stock Car Racing,* vol. 1, 20.

page 323, **France envisioned a whole new future:** Ibid.

page 324, **France . . . bought a secondhand Plymouth sedan for seventeen hundred dollars:** Edelstein, *Full Throttle,* 83.

page 324, **In truth . . . :** Granger, "1950 Southern 500."

page 324, **nearly died from a bad batch of Mexican food:** Russ Catlin, "Meet Madman Johnny Mantz," *Speed Age,* July 1951.

page 325, **the alarm clock bomb created havoc:** Leo Levine, *Ford, the Dust and the Glory: A Racing History, 1901–1967* (Warrendale, Pa.: Society of Automotive Engineers, 2001), 199.

page 325, **so much cash . . . peach baskets:** Edelstein, *Full Throttle,* 83.

page 325, **"You know what can win this race?"** Levine, *Ford, the Dust and the Glory,* 200.

page 325, **"There won't be one of these cars at the finish":** Ibid., 199.

page 327, **According to the story that France . . . :** Granger, *American Racing Classics,* 120.

page 328, **Vogt, Byron, and the other top-five finishers . . . formally protested:** Jensen, *Cheating,* 38.

page 328, **"anything Red wanted checked":** Neely, *Daytona USA,* 67.

page 330, **Vogt received a peacemaking offer from Bill France:** Interview with George Moore.

18. NASCAR is here to stay: "Like sex, the atom bomb and ice cream"
Information on NASCAR's first race in Detroit is from William Jeanes, "France and the Motor City," *American Racing Classics* (Concord, N.C.: Griggs Publishing; Talladega, Ala.: International Motorsports Hall of Fame, Apr. 1992). Information

on NASCAR, ISC, and Speedway Motorsports Inc. is from www.nascar.com, www.iscmotorsports.com, and www.speedwaymotorsports.com.

page 333, **Lord Calvert . . . was "my co-pilot"**: Interview with Billy Watson; and Henry "Smokey" Yunick, *Best Damn Garage in Town: The World According to Smokey,* 4 vols. (Holly Hill, Fla.: Carbon Press, 2001), vol. 2, 26.

page 333, **"No liquor in the pits"**: Yunick, *Best Damn Garage in Town,* vol. 2, 26.

page 333, **In 1952, a young boy sitting with his father**: Brock Yates, *Against Death and Time: One Fatal Season in Racing's Glory Years* (New York: Thunder's Mouth Press, 2004), 42.

page 334, **"motorized lemmings"**: Ibid., 117.

page 335, **"Doesn't sound like a bad idea"**: Bob Zeller, "Bruton and the Two Bills: A 50-Year Rivalry," *Car and Driver,* July 2003.

page 335, **France . . . considered Smith "a pain"**: Interview with Buz McKim (written replies to questions from the author).

page 335, **Sam Nunis . . . ran short of cash**: Interview with Billy Watson.

page 336, **"Gentlemen, before I have this union stuffed down my throat"**: Dan Pierce, "The Most Southern Sport on Earth: NASCAR and the Unions," *Southern Cultures,* 2001.

page 337, **More than fifty years after . . .** : Zeller, "Bruton and the Two Bills."

19. "I had to start making a living"

page 338, **the only race in which he didn't superstitiously touch the track**: Kim Chapin, *Fast as White Lightning: The Story of Stock Car Racing* (New York: Three Rivers Press, 1998), 78.

page 339, **allegedly shoving Fonty aside**: Henry "Smokey" Yunick, *Best Damn Garage in Town: The World According to Smokey,* 4 vols. (Holly Hill, Fla.: Carbon Press, 2001), vol. 2, 274.

page 340, **"I would have protested even if it was my mother"**: Frank Ahrens, "Lee Petty Was a Driving Force," *Washington Post,* Apr. 11, 2000.

page 343, **"It's a shame about Roy"**: Charles Duncan, "Hall Won First Time He Raced at Daytona," *Dawson News & Advertiser,* May 8, 2002.

page 343, **an outbreak of poisoned moonshine in Atlanta in 1951**: Jess Carr, *The Second Oldest Profession: An Informal History of Moonshining in America* (Englewood Cliffs, N.J.: Prentice Hall, 1972), 133.

page 346, **DePaolo was purpousely vague about . . . Holman's exact role**: Leo Levine, *Ford, the Dust and the Glory: A Racing History, 1901–1967* (Warrendale, Pa.: Society of Automotive Engineers, 2001), 216–217.

page 346, **"Merlin" . . . "the granddaddy of NASCAR mechanics"**: Yunick, *Best Damn Garage in Town,* vol. 2, 275.

page 346, **"couldn't handle the bullshitting . . ."**: Ibid., 113.

page 349, **[Red Byron's death]**: Interviews with Bev and Betty Byron.

page 350, **"I'm spending more than I'm making"**: Interview with Raymond Parks.

page 350, **"I loved racing . . ."**: Rick Minter, "Lost Tracks of Time: Some of Georgia's Storied Racetracks Are Fading into Memory and Disrepair," *Atlanta Journal-Constitution,* March 23, 2003.

page 351, **"the *other* man of Daytona"**: Eddie Samples, "Garhofa's Raymond

Dawson Parks," Georgia Automobile Racing Hall of Fame Association's *Pioneer Pages* 5, no. 1 (Feb. 2002).

page 352, **"Money isn't everything . . .":** Kevin Conley, "NASCAR's New Track," *New Yorker,* Nov. 2, 2004.

page 352, **"wasn't in this world anymore":** Ibid.

page 352, **"It's all about marketing":** Viv Bernstein, "Good Looks and Good Drivers Join to Complete a NASCAR Package," *New York Times,* Apr. 15, 2005.

pages 352–353, **"40 extremely mobile billboards . . .":** Steve Lopez, "Babes, Bordeaux & Billy Bobs: How I Learned to Love NASCAR," *Time,* May 31, 1999.

page 353, **NASCAR's revenues average more than three *billion* dollars:** Leslie Stahl, transcript of "The Real NASCAR Family," *60 Minutes* (CBS News), Oct. 6, 2005.

page 353, *Forbes* **magazine's list of richest Americans:** Susan Oliver, "Off to the Races! How the Frances of NASCAR Built a Major Fortune in Stock-Car Racing," *Forbes,* July 3, 1995.

page 353, **"NASCAR got this big by being a dictatorship":** Liz Clarke, "NASCAR Boom Puts South in Rearview," *Washington Post,* Nov. 20, 2005.

Epilogue: This is what NASCAR has become . . .

page 357, **"It has not come to the attention of eastern Alabama . . .":** Steve Lopez, "Babes, Bordeaux & Billy Bobs: How I Learned to Love NASCAR," *Time,* May 31, 1999.

page 357, **In the 1990s . . . spectators were killed:** Ames Alexander, "Awareness Grows," *Charlotte Observer,* Nov. 11, 2001.

page 359, **$2.8 *billion* TV contract . . . jump to $4.8 billion in 2007:** "NASCAR Signs New TV deal," Associated Press, Jan. 16, 2006.

page 361, **"Fans get a few beers in 'em, the Dixie comes out":** Scott Huler, *A Little Bit Sideways: One Week inside a NASCAR Winston Cup Team* (Osceola, Wis.: MBI Publishing, 1999), 35.

page 361, **stock car racing was "kind of like country music . . .":** Ibid., 45.

page 362, **". . . Hunk. . . . They're all good-looking":** Viv Bernstein, "Good Looks and Good Drivers Join to Complete a NASCAR Package," *New York Times,* Apr. 15, 2005.

page 362, **"the old Southeastern redneck heritage . . .":** Lorenzo Lopez, "NASCAR Still Proud of Its Heritage," *Raleigh News & Observer,* Feb. 17, 2006.

page 363, **"I don't think anyone can call it just a Southern sport . . .":** "Tony Stewart, Goin' Back to Cali," Tony Stewart press release (True Speed Communication), Feb. 22, 2006.

page 364, **"They are everywhere these Yankees . . .":** Mary Boykin Miller Chesnut, *A Diary from Dixie* (electronic edition: docsouth.unc.edu/chesnut/maryches .html), 379.

Sources

PRIMARY INTERVIEWS

Sarah Atha, Mike Bell, Dick Berggren, Betty Byron, Beverly Byron, Nell Byron, Billy Carden, Betty Carlan, J. B. Day, Willavene Day, Chris Economacki, Dewain Edwards, Sam Edwards, Frances Flock, Ray Fox, Steve Gassaway, Virginia Gassaway, Peter Golenbock, Steve Green, Ronnie Hall, Charlie Jenkins, Buz McKim, George Moore, Jimmy Mosteller, Frank Mundy, Cotten Owens, Raymond Parks, Violet Parks, Virgil Parks, Gordon Pirkle, Eddie Samples, Virginia Samples, Lucille Shirley, Marion Shirley, Ralph Shirley, Louise Smith, David Sosebee, Sarah Sosebee, Vaudelle Sosebee, Buddy Starr, Jimmy Summerour, Mitzi Teague, Terry Terrell, Tom Vogt, Bill Ward, Billy Watson, June Wendt, H. A. "Humpy" Wheeler, Rex White, Suzanne Wise.

BOOKS

Adams, Noah. *Far Appalachia*. New York: Delacorte Press / Random House, 2001.

Ambrose, Stephen E. *The Wild Blue: The Men and Boys Who Flew the B-24s over Germany, 1944–45*. New York: Simon & Schuster, 2001.

Applebome, Peter. *Dixie Rising: How the South Is Shaping American Values, Politics, and Culture*. San Diego: Harvest Book, 1996.

Arthur, Helen. *Whisky: The Water of Life—Uisge Beatha*. Buffalo, N.Y.: Firefly Books, 2000.

Assael, Shaun. *Wide Open: Days and Nights on the NASCAR Tour*. New York: Ballantine Books, 1998.

Bill France Enterprises. *1950 NASCAR Yearbook*. Greensboro, N.C.: Bill France Enterprises.

Bledsoe, Jerry. *The World's Number One, Flat-Out, All-Time Great, Stock Car Racing Book*. New York: Bantam Books, 1976.

Bragg, Rick. *Ava's Man*. New York: Knopf, 2001.

Brinkley, Douglas. *Wheels for the World: Henry Ford, His Company, and a Century of Progress*. New York: Viking, 2003.

Britt, Bloys, and Bill France. *The Racing Flag: NASCAR, the Story of Grand Na-tional Racing.* New York: Pocket Books, 1965.

Burgess-Wise, David. *Ultimate Race Car.* London: Dorling Kindersley, 1999.

Burns, Eric. *Spirits of America: A Social History of Alcohol.* Philadelphia: Temple University Press, 2003.

Burrough, Bryan. *Public Enemies: America's Greatest Crime Wave and the Birth of the FBI, 1933–34.* New York: Penguin Press, 2004.

Butterworth, W. E. *The High Wind: The Story of NASCAR Racing.* New York: Norton, 1971.

Caldwell, Erskine. *Tobacco Road.* Athens: University of Georgia Press, 1995.

Carr, Jess. *The Second Oldest Profession: An Informal History of Moonshining in America.* Englewood Cliffs, N.J.: Prentice Hall, 1972.

Cavanaugh, William C. *Dauntless: A History of the 99th Infantry Division.* Dallas: Taylor Publishing, 1994.

Center, Bill. *Ultimate Stock Car.* London: Dorling Kindersley, 2000.

Center, Bill, and Bob Moore. *NASCAR 50 Greatest Drivers.* New York: Harper Horizon / Tehabi Books, 1998.

Chapin, Kim. *Fast as White Lightning: The Story of Stock Car Racing.* New York: Three Rivers Press, 1998.

Chernow, Ron. *Alexander Hamilton.* New York: Penguin Press, 2004.

Cole, Hugh M. *The Ardennes: Battle of the Bulge.* Published by the Center for Military History, www.army.mil/cmh-pg/books/wwii/7-8/7-8_cont.htm).

Colley, David P. *Blood for Dignity: The Story of the First Integrated Combat Unit in the U.S. Army.* New York: St. Martin's Press, 2003.

Collier, Peter, and David Horowitz. *The Fords: An American Epic.* New York: Summit Books, 1987.

Craft, Dr. John. *Legends of Stock Car Racing.* Osceola, Wis.: MBI Publishing, 1995.

Crews, Harry. *Classic Crews: A Harry Crews Reader.* New York: Poseidon Press, 1993.

Cutter, Robert, and Bob Fendell. *Encyclopedia of Auto Racing Greats.* New York: Prentice-Hall, 1973.

Dabney, Joseph Earl. *Mountain Spirits.* Asheville, N.C.: Bright Mountain Books, 1974.

Daniel, Pete. *Lost Revolutions: The South in the 1950s.* Chapel Hill: University of North Carolina Press, 2000.

Dettelbach, Cynthia Golomb. *In the Driver's Seat: The Automobile in American Literature and Popular Culture.* Westport, Conn.: Greenwood Press, 1976.

Doctorow, E. L. *The March: A Novel.* New York: Random House, 2005.

Earley, Tony. *Jim the Boy.* Boston: Back Bay Books, 2000.

Edelstein, Robert. *Full Throttle: The Life and Fast Times of Curtis Turner.* New York: Overlook Hardcover, 2005.

Faulkner, William. *The Reivers.* New York: Vintage, 1992.

———. *The Sound and the Fury*. London: Picador Classics, 1989.

Fielden, Greg. *Forty Years of Stock Car Racing*. 4 vols. Surfside Beach, S.C.: Galfield Press, 1992.

———. *High Speed at Low Tide*. Surfside Beach, S.C.: Galfield Press, 1993.

———. *NASCAR Chronicle*. Lincolnwood, Il.: Publications International, 2005.

———. *Real Racers: Heroes and Record Writers from Stock Car Racing's Forgotten Era*. Surfside Beach, S.C.: Galfield Press, 1998.

Fielden, Larry. *Tim Flock, Race Driver*. Surfside Beach, S.C.: Galfield Press, 1991.

Foote, Shelby. *Shiloh*. Audio ed. Prince Frederick, Md.: Recorded Books, 1993.

Gabbard, Alex. *Return to Thunder Road: The Story Behind the Legend*. Lenoir City, Tenn.: Gabbard Publications, 1992.

Golenbock, Peter. *American Zoom: Stock Car Racing—From the Dirt Tracks to Daytona*. New York: Macmillan Publishing, 1994.

———. *The Last Lap: The Life and Times of NASCAR's Legendary Heroes*. New York: Macmillan Publishing, 1998.

———. *NASCAR Confidential: Stories of Men and Women Who Made Stock Car Racing Great*. Osceola, Wis.: MBI Publishing, 2004.

———, ed. *NASCAR Encyclopedia: The Complete Record of America's Most Popular Sport*. Osceola, Wis.: Motorbooks International, 2003.

Goodman, Roland. *Book of the Mexican Road Race*. Los Angeles: Floyd Clymer, 1950.

Halberstam, David. *The Reckoning*. New York: Morrow, 1986.

Hembree, Mike. *NASCAR: The Definitive History*. New York: Harper Entertainment / Tehabi Books, 2000.

Hemphill, Paul. *Wheels: A Season on NASCAR's Winston Cup Circuit*. New York: Berkley Books, 1998.

Higgins, Tom. *NASCAR Greatest Races: The 25 Most Thrilling Races in NASCAR History*. New York: Harper Entertainment / Tehabi Books, 1999.

Higgins, Tom, and Steve Waid. *Junior Johnson: Brave in Life*. Phoenix, Ariz.: David Bull Publishing, 1999.

Horwitz, Tony. *Confederates in the Attic: Dispatches from the Unfinished Civil War*. Paperback ed. New York: Vintage, 1999.

Howell, Mark D. *From Moonshine to Madison Avenue: A Cultural History of the NASCAR Winston Cup Series*. Bowling Green, Oh.: Bowling Green State University Popular Press, 1997.

Huler, Scott. *A Little Bit Sideways: One Week inside a NASCAR Winston Cup Team*. Osceola, Wis.: MBI Publishing, 1999.

International Motorsports Hall of Fame. *American Racing Classics*. Multiple vols. Concord, N.C.: Griggs Publishing; Talladega, Ala.: International Motorsports Hall of Fame, 1992–1994.

Jensen, Tom. *Cheating: An Inside Look at the Bad Things Good NASCAR Winston Cup Racers Do in the Pursuit of Speed*. Phoenix, Ariz.: David Bull Publishing, 2002.

Kellner, Esther. *Moonshine: Its History and Folklore.* New York: Ballantine Books, 1973.

Kephart, Horace. *Our Southern Highlanders: A Narrative of Adventure in the Southern Appalachians and a Study of Life among the Mountaineers.* Knoxville: University of Tennessee Press, 1984.

Kollock, John. *These Gentle Hills.* Clarkesville, Ga.: Habersham House Publishers, 1992.

Lazarus, William P. *The Sands of Time: A Century of Racing in Daytona Beach.* Champaign, Il.: Sports Publishing, 2004.

Levine, Leo. *Ford, the Dust and the Glory: A Racing History, 1901–1967.* Warrenton, Pa.: Society of Automotive Engineers, 2001.

Libby, Bill. *Heroes of Stock Car Racing.* New York: Random House, 1975.

MacDonald, Charles B. *A Time for Trumpets: The Untold Story of the Battle of the Bulge.* New York: Quill / William Morrow, 1985.

MacGregor, Jeff. *Sunday Money: Speed! Lust! Madness! Death! A Hot Lap around America with NASCAR.* New York: HarperCollins, 2005.

McCarthy, Cormac. *The Orchard Keeper.* New York: Ecco Press, 1965.

McCrumb, Sharyn. *The Ballad of Frankie Silver.* Paperback ed. New York: Signet Books, 1999.

———. *Ghost Riders.* Paperback ed. New York: Signet Books, 2004.

———. *St. Dale: A Novel.* New York: Kensington Books, 2005.

McKay, Don. *Wild Wheels: Thrilling Adventures of Men and Cars.* New York: Dell Publishing, 1969.

McLaurin, Tim. *Keeper of the Moon: A Southern Boyhood.* New York: Anchor Books / Doubleday, 1991.

Martin, Mark. *NASCAR for Dummies.* Hoboken, N.J.: Wiley Publishing, 2005.

Menzer, Joe. *The Wildest Ride: A History of NASCAR (or How a Bunch of Good Ol' Boys Built a Billion-Dollar Industry out of Wrecking Cars).* New York: Simon & Schuster, 2001.

Mitchell, Margaret. *Gone with the Wind.* Audio ed. Prince Frederick, Md.: Recorded Books, 2001.

Morison, Samuel Eliot. *History of U.S. Naval Operations in World War II.* Vol. 7, *Aleutians, Gilberts and Marshalls, June 1942–April 1944.* Boston: Little, Brown, 1951.

Neely, William. *Daytona USA: The Official History of Daytona and Ormond Beach Racing from 1902 to Today's NASCAR Super Speedways.* Tucson, Ariz.: AZTEX Corp., 1979.

Nelson, Derek. *Moonshiners, Bootleggers & Rumrunners.* Osceola, Wis.: Motorbooks International, 1995.

Nolan, William F. *Barney Oldfield: The Life and Times of America's Legendary Speed King.* Carpinteria, Calif.: Brown Fox Books, 2002.

Reed, John Shelton. *My Tears Spoiled My Aim—and Other Reflections on Southern Culture.* San Diego, New York: Harvest / HBJ Book, 1993.

————. *Whistling Dixie: Dispatches from the South.* San Diego, New York: Harvest / HBJ Book, 1990.

Riggs, D. Randy. *Flat-out Racing: An Insider's Look at the World of Stock Cars.* New York: MetroBooks, Michael Friedman Publishing Group, 1995.

Rubin, Louis, ed. *The American South: Portrait of a Culture.* Washington, D.C.: Government Printing Office, 1980.

Sinclair, Upton. *The Flivver King: A Story of Ford America.* Pasadena, Calif.: published by the author, 1937.

Sowers, Richard. *The Complete Statistical History of Stock-Car Racing: Records, Streaks, Oddities, & Trivia.* Phoenix, Ariz.: David Bull Publishing, 2000.

Spiegel, Marshall. *NASCAR: 25 Years of Racing Thrills.* New York: Scholastic Book Services, 1974.

Stanchak, John. *Civil War.* Eastbourne, England: Gardners Books, 2001.

St. John, Warren. *Rammer Jammer Yellow Hammer.* New York: Three Rivers Press, 2004.

Time Inc. Home Entertainment. *LIFE: American Speed, From Dirt Tracks to Indy to NASCAR.* Time Inc. Home Entertainment, 2002.

UMI Publications. *NASCAR: The Early Years.* Charlotte, N.C.: UMI Publications, 2002.

Walsworth Publishing. *Dawson County, Georgia Heritage, 1857–1996.* Waynesville, N.C.: Walsworth Publishing, 1997.

Webb, James. *Born Fighting: How the Scots-Irish Shaped America.* New York: Broadway Books, 2004.

Wilkinson, Alec. *Moonshine: A Life in Pursuit of White Liquor.* St. Paul, Minn.: Hungry Mind Press, 1998.

Wilkinson, Sylvia. *Dirt Tracks to Glory: The Early Days of Stock Car Racing as Told by the Participants.* Chapel Hill, N.C.: Algonquin Books, 1983.

Yates, Brock W. *Against Death and Time: One Fatal Season in Racing's Glory Years.* New York: Thunder's Mouth Press, 2004.

————. *NASCAR off the Record.* Osceola, Wis.: Motorbooks International, 2004.

Yunick, Henry. *Best Damn Garage in Town: The World According to Smokey.* 4 vols. Holly Hill, Fla.: Carbon Press, 2001.

ARTICLES AND OTHER SHORT WORKS

Cansler, Jack. "The World's Toughest Road Race." *Speed Age,* Aug. 1950.

Carlson, Peter. "American Bacchanal." *Washington Post Magazine,* Sept. 2, 1999.

Clark, George Stephens. "Gasoline and Sand: The Birth of Automobile Racing." *Mankind: The Magazine of Popular History* 3, no. 4 (Dec. 1971).

Conley, Kevin. "NASCAR's New Track." *New Yorker,* Nov. 2, 2004.

Granger, Gene. "The 1950 Southern 500." *American Racing Classics.* Concord, N.C.: Griggs Publishing; Talladega, Ala.: International Motorsports Hall of Fame, Oct. 1992.

————. "Tim Flock." *American Racing Classics*. Concord, N.C.: Griggs Publishing; Talladega, Ala.: International Motorsports Hall of Fame, Jan. 1993.

Hall, Randal L. "Before NASCAR: The Corporate and Civic Promotion of Automobile Racing in the American South, 1903–1927." *Journal of Southern History* 68, no. 3 (Aug. 2002).

Hembree, Mike. "Raymond Parks." *American Racing Classics*. Concord, N.C.: Griggs Publishing; Talladega, Ala.: International Motorsports Hall of Fame, 1994.

Hinton, Ed. "The Legend: Lloyd Seay Was the Young Sport's Brightest Star until He Was Gunned Down." *Sports Illustrated Presents 50 Years of NASCAR*, Jan. 28, 1998.

Hodges, Gerald. "NASCAR Racing—Before There Was NASCAR, There Was Dawsonville." *Susquehanna County Transcript*, Dec. 24, 2002, http://www.susquehannatranscript.com/archives/12_17_02v4n25/sports.htm.

Ingram, Jonathan. "Last of a Breed." *Speedway Illustrated*, Oct. 2004.

Jeanes, William. "France and the Motor City." *American Racing Classics*. Concord, N.C.: Griggs Publishing; Talladega, Ala.: International Motorsports Hall of Fame, Apr. 1992.

Lopez, Steve. "Babes, Bordeaux & Billy Bobs: How I Learned to Love NASCAR." *Time*, May 31, 1999.

McCredie, Gary. "The First Race." *American Racing Classics*. Concord, N.C.: Griggs Publishing; Talladega, Ala.: International Motorsports Hall of Fame, Apr. 1992.

Montville, Leigh. "Dawsonville, U.S.A." *Sports Illustrated Presents 50 Years of NASCAR*, Jan. 28, 1998.

National Championship Stock Car Circuit. Original minutes. "Annual Convention, The National Championship Stock Car Circuit, Ebony Room, Streamline Hotel, Daytona Beach, Florida, Dec. 14–17, 1947."

Oliver, Susan. "Off to the Races! How the Frances of NASCAR Built a Major Fortune in Stock-Car Racing." *Forbes*, July 3, 1995.

O'Reilly, Don. "Bill France." *American Racing Classics*. Concord, N.C.: Griggs Publishing; Talladega, Ala.: International Motorsports Hall of Fame, Jan. 1993.

Pierce, Dan. "The Most Southern Sport on Earth: NASCAR and the Unions." *Southern Cultures*, 2001.

Samples, Eddie. "Columbus Speedway's Historic 1948 Inaugural Season; Red Byron's Bittersweet Championship." *Pioneer Pages* 8, no. 2 (June 2005).

————. "Garhofa's Raymond Dawson Parks." Georgia Automobile Racing Hall of Fame Association's *Pioneer Pages* 5, no. 1 (Feb. 2002).

————. "Lakewood Speedway: The Indianapolis of the South, Stock Car Racing Begins." Georgia Automobile Racing Hall of Fame Association's *Pioneer Pages* 1, no. 3 (Aug. 1998).

————. "Lakewood Speedway Continued. . . ." Georgia Automobile Racing Hall of Fame Association's *Pioneer Pages* 2, no. 1 (Mar. 1999).

Stahl, Leslie. Transcript of "The Real NASCAR Family." *60 Minutes* (CBS News), Oct. 6, 2005.

White, Ben. "The Beach." *American Racing Classics.* Concord, N.C.: Griggs Publishing; Talladega, Ala.: International Motorsports Hall of Fame, July 1992.

———. "The Formation of NASCAR." *American Racing Classics.* Concord, N.C.: Griggs Publishing; Talladega, Ala.: International Motorsports Hall of Fame, Jan. 1992.

Wise, Suzanne. "Fast Women: Female Racing Pioneers." *Atlanta History: A Journal of Georgia and the South* 46, no. 2 (2004), 42–59.

Wolfe, Tom. "The Last American Hero Is Junior Johnson . . . Yes!" *Esquire,* Mar. 1965.

Yates, Brock. "The Force: Bill France's Vision Made NASCAR the World's Premier Racing Organization." *Sports Illustrated Presents 50 Years of NASCAR,* Jan. 28, 1998.

FILMS

Automaniac documentary series. "Moonshine Cars" episode. History Channel, 2005.

Gone with the Wind. Warner Home Video, 2004.

Greased Lightning. Good Times Home Video, 1998. (Original: Warner Bros., 1977.)

Great Racing Movies, Burning Rubber Thrillers. (Includes: "The Fast and the Furious"; "The Big Wheel"; "Hot Rod Girl.") American Home Treasures, 2002.

The History of NASCAR. BSC Entertainment, 2003.

The Last American Hero. CBS/Fox, Key Video, 1985. (Original: Twentieth Century Fox, 1973.)

NASCAR's Great Moments: The Early Years. Sony Music Entertainment, 1997.

The NASCAR Story: From Thunder Road to Victory Lane. Vol. 1, *1947–1958.* Charlotte, N.C.: Creative Sports, 1993.

NASCAR—The IMAX Experience. IMAX, 2005.

Tell about the South: Voices in Black and White—The History of Modern Southern Literature, 1915–1940. Charlottesville, Va.: Agee Films, 1999.

Thunder Road. MGM, 1997.

WEB SITES

www.fireballroberts.com

www.fordracing.com

www.garhofa.com

www.henryfordestate.com

www.iscmotorsports.com

www.juniorjohnson.com

www.library.appstate.edu/stockcar

www.livinglegendsofautoracing.com

www.motorsportshalloffame.com

www.nascar.com

www.nationalspeedsportnews.com

www.ncarhof.com

www.speedwaymotorsports.com

www.racing-reference.com

Acknowledgments

I wish I'd started on this project sooner. So many moonshining NASCAR pioneers have passed on—including a few who died during the course of my research—and so much of the early history of the sport has been lost. That is why I'm grateful to Raymond Parks for remembering so much, saving so much, and sharing it all with me. I truly enjoyed the many hours I spent with him and his wife, Violet. Parks wasn't entirely sure he wanted to see his life on display like this. He remains a southern gentleman, and I could tell he felt there was something unseemly in talking to a stranger about his past. But over time, he warmed up to me, sometimes nudged along by Violet or his brother Virgil or sister Lucille. I'm grateful to them all. Without them, this book would not have happened.

Nor would this book have been possible without the generosity of Eddie Samples (son of 1940s stock car racing legend Ed Samples) and Mike Bell, both with the Georgia Auto Racing Hall of Fame. Eddie and Mike welcomed me into their homes and shared their massive collections of stock car research. Thank you both for preserving an important piece of southern history. Another invaluable resource, which grows larger by the day, is the Stock Car Racing Collection at Appalachian State University. My thanks to its creator and curator, Suzanne Wise, for all she's done to help a Jersey boy understand NASCAR. The International Motorsports Hall of Fame and Museum in Talladega was another invaluable resource, and I thank Betty Carlan for her assistance.

Enormous thanks go out to the families of Red Vogt and Red Byron . . . to Tom Vogt, June Wendt, and George Moore; to Nell, Betty, and Beverly Byron; to Virginia and Steve Gassaway; and to Roy Hall's son, Ronnie. I'm also grateful to the following: Billy Watson; David, Sarah, and Vaudelle Sosbee; Gordon Pirkle; J. B. and Willavene Day;

Terry Terrell; the folks at the Dawson County Chamber of Commerce and the Dawson County Courthouse; Dan Pierce of UNC-Asheville and participants in his excellent "Mountain Thunder" program at the Asheville library in 2003; Dick Berggren, Chris Economaki, and Peter Golenbock, for the occasional dumb question; Buz McKim and Nancy Kendrick at ISC. Thanks to Catherine Taylor for introducing me to the writings of Horace Kephart and to Cara May for introducing me to the novels of Sharyn McCrumb, which were part of my southern education. That education continued with McCrumb's 2005 book *St. Dale,* and I feel fortunate to now consider Sharyn a friend.

This book was helped greatly by the weeks spent at the wonderful Hambidge Center's residency program in Georgia (thanks, Fran and Cindy; I hope to be back soon) and the days spent lingering at Malaprops Bookstore in Asheville (thanks, Emoke, Linda, and Andrew). Thanks also to Erik Larson, Buzz Bissinger, Bob Timberg, Homer Hickam, David Hartman, and Robert Hicks for advice at crucial moments along the way.

Family and friends who suffered through early drafts or offered support, advice, or food include Larry Chilnick, Mike Hudson, Pauline and Bill Trimarco, Katherine and David Reed, Brian and Cheryl Klam, Brooke Hopkins, Gerry Fabbri, Ellen Phirrmann, John Plemmons, J. D. Kramer; the Terlingua contingent, Rob and Blaise; and the Yankee contingent, John Mooney, Tom Moran, and Jim Haner. My thanks to them all, and to my father, Phil.

Tommy Hayes, head of the Great Smokies Writing Program, was a reliable source of sound advice and empathy. "Mr." Adams and his supply of corn liquor (compliments of One-Eyed Ronnie) helped me blast through anything resembling writer's block. And the Drive-By Truckers— with their savvy tunes about bootleggers, stock car racers, and the South—became the loud sound track for the writing of this book.

My deepest thanks go out to my editors: Caroline Sincerbeaux, for her steady hand over the course of two years, and Shana Drehs, for driving this project to the finish line. I'm grateful to everyone at Crown for their continued support—from copy editors to proofreaders, designers to lawyers, publicists to marketing folks, I couldn't have asked for a more professional team. Thanks to Andrew Levine, Beth Davey, and everyone at Inkwell Management. And to my outstanding agent, Michael Carlisle, I say: thank you, and onward.

Finally, much love to my wonderful, lush, zany, inspiring family: Mary, Leo, and Sean. I could neither have started nor finished this without you by my side.

Index

AAA (American Automobile Association), 84, 85, 137, 177, 189, 190, 209, 211, 213, 227, 230, 235, 269–270, 280, 283, 301, 341
  Contest Board of, 81–82, 196, 197, 210, 214, 228, 229, 334
Alabama Racing Association, 137
Aleutian Islands, 149, 158–159, 163, 164
Alfa Romeos, 203, 205
Allentown, Pennsylvania, 113, 120, 215
Allison, C. C., 285, 286
All the King's Men (Warren), 168
Altoona, Pennsylvania, 73
American Medical Association, 30
American Stock Car Racing Association (ASCRA), 211, 228
Anderson, Sherwood, 67
Anderson, Woodrow, 126–130, 147
Anheuser-Busch, 349
Anti-Saloon League, 30, 32
Anti-Semitism, 33, 75
Appalachian Mountains, 54
Arrington, Buddy, 343
Asheville-Weaverville Speedway, North Carolina, 338, 350
Assembly-line concept, 29
Atkins, Elbert, 117
Atkins, Massey, 117
Atlanta Motor Speedway, 355–359
Atlantic City, New Jersey, 73
Automobile Manufacturers' Association, 344

B-24 bomber ("Liberator"), 160–165
Babylonians, 20

Baker, Buck, 289
Baker, E. G. "Cannonball," 125*n*, 235, 274, 286, 345
Barrow, Clyde, 35
Bartram, A. R., 262
Baseball, 7, 10, 80, 92, 137, 274, 359
Basketball, 10, 80, 359
Beach-and-Road course, Daytona, 4, 83–88, 109–111, 113–121, 177, 182–183, 196, 199*n*, 200–201, 203*n*, 218–219, 245
Big Wheel, The (movie), 295
Birmingham Fairground, Alabama, 137
Black, Blackie, 95
Black migration, 36
Blair, Bill, 290, 291
Bonneville Salt Flats, Utah, 83
Born Fighting: How the Scots-Irish Shaped America (Webb), 54, 169
Brannon, James, 261–262, 265, 266
Brannon, Roy, 261–262, 268, 270, 277, 331, 333, 347
Brasington, Harold, 322–323
Brinkley, Douglas, 208
Brogdon, Jap, 124, 148
Buck Mathis Memorial, 266
Buicks, 182, 246, 291, 300
Bulge, Battle of the, 143, 149, 152–156, 158, 161
Burns, Eric, 57
Burt, Clifton, 15
Bush, Ernest, 94–95
Bush, George W., 341*n*
Byron, Elizabeth, 133–135

Byron, Eva Nellis Davis, 184, 194–195,
198, 202, 204, 206, 213, 244, 255,
270–271, 314, 330, 348, 349
Byron, Jack, 133–135, 140, 141, 165–167
Byron, Peg, 135, 140, 166
Byron, Robert, Jr., 270–271, 314, 354
Byron, Robert Nold "Red," 5, 7, 8, 10,
59*n*, 96, 148, 309, 360
as auto mechanic, 134–136, 272, 282,
296, 348
birth of, 132
birth of children, 270–271, 330
birth of NASCAR and, 231, 232, 234,
243
childhood of, 133–134, 244
death of, 332, 349
death of mother, 35, 244
dual loyalties of, 140, 184–185, 189,
255–257
family of, 133, 134
France and, 282, 321
Hall and, 305–306
Indy dreams of, 203–206, 255–256
joins army, 141, 142
leaves home, 135
as NASCAR's first champion, 270,
274–275
Oldfield as hero to, 136, 190
Parks and, 142–143, 179, 180, 200,
202, 252–253, 263, 266, 271–272,
277, 278, 318–319, 330
personality of, 179, 198, 222
physical appearance of, 140
press on, 138, 181, 183–184, 200–202,
210, 211, 225, 255, 272
racing by, 91, 93–95, 116, 137–142,
176, 178, 179, 181–185, 190,
198–207, 211–220, 223–225, 226,
244, 247, 248, 249–263, 265–270,
283, 285–288, 292–294, 298–301,
303–308, 314–321, 323–332, 342,
348, 361, 364

recognition of, 349
retirement from racing, 332
rivalry with Fonty Flock, 254–259, 267,
283
trademarks of, 136
tragedy at Columbus Speedway and,
260–263, 266, 267, 270,
277, 347
Vogt and, 179, 180, 202, 204,
206, 252
war injury of, 165–167, 175, 180, 202,
220, 262, 271, 319, 348–349
wife of, 184, 194–195, 198, 213, 244
in World War II, 143, 149, 158,
161–165
Byron, Virginia, 133–135, 140, 161, 167

Cadillacs, 288, 300, 321, 324–326, 329,
342
Caesar, Julius, 12
Caldwell, Erskine, 18–19, 29, 131
Calhoun, John, 13
Campbell, Sir Malcolm, 83
Cansler, Jack, 317
Cantlon, Shorty, 206–207
Cantrell, Jack, 172
Capone, Al, 25, 43, 62, 66
Caren, Billy, 260
Carnegie, Andrew, 32
Carpetbaggers, 18
Carr, Jess, 60
Carrera-Panamericana Mexico (Mexican
Road Race), 313–320, 324, 333
Carter, Jimmy, 355
Central States Racing Association (CSRA),
323
Charles, Harvey, 285
Charles, Pat, 285
Charlotte Speedway, 176–177, 285–286,
289–292, 340, 342
Chattanooga, Tennessee, 258
Cherokee Indians, 12–14, 54–55, 93

Chestnut, Mary, 363–364

Chevrolets, 34, 193, 246, 343–345, 348, 362

Christian, Frank, 289

Christian, Sara, 289, 290, 298, 299, 301

Chryslers, 300, 338, 339, 344–346

Churchill, Winston, 354

Circular tracks, creation of, 79

Civil War, 13, 17–18, 23, 53, 57, 168, 205n, 207, 209, 363–364

Clemson, Thomas, 13

Cobb, Ty, 7, 30

Coca-Cola 500, 256n

Cole, Grady, 290

Columbus Speedway, Georgia, 257–263, 268, 331

Conner, Roy, 318

Constitution of the United States, 57

Contest Board of the AAA (American Automobile Association), 81–82, 196, 197, 210, 214, 228, 229, 334

Corn whiskey, 55–56

Cortez, Ramon, 93

Corvettes, 348

Cotton, 14, 35

Cotton, P. W., 137

Creek Indians, 13

Crisler, Al, 292, 328

Croce, Jim, 192, 343

Crockett, Davy, 123

Cromwell, Oliver, 53

Cronkite, Walter, 161

Cummings, Wild Bill, 84

Cunningham, Briggs, 348

Cunningham, Ucal, 110

Dahlonega, Georgia, 12

Daniel, Pete, 97

Danville, Virginia, 215

Darlington Raceway, South Carolina, 323–329, 332, 339, 342, 363

Davis, Bill "Slick," 262

Davis, Jefferson, 362

Davis, Joe, 130

Dawsonville, Georgia, 12, 14–15, 18, 36, 37, 40, 45, 48, 50–52, 126, 198, 221, 343–344, 365

Dawsonville-to-Atlanta run, 51, 60

Day, Walter, 16–17, 19, 21, 36, 40

Daytona Beach, Florida, 4, 5, 79, 80, 83–88, 109–111, 113–121, 177, 182–183, 196, 199n, 200–201, 203n, 218–219, 245–251, 253, 266–267, 341, 359–360

Daytona International Speedway, 336, 340, 341

Declaration of Independence, 57

Decoration Day, 205

Deland, Florida, 113

DePaolo, Peter, 346

Detroit, Michigan, 26, 27, 29, 331, 332

Dick, Robert, 57–58

Dillinger, John, 34, 35

Distillation, 20

Dodges, 345, 362

Doubleday, Abner, 7, 10

Doublings, 20

Dreyer, Pop, 184

Driver injuries and fatalities, 5, 7, 8, 119, 125n, 142, 183, 199, 206–207, 215, 223, 264, 265, 268, 291, 307, 315, 333–334, 338, 341, 342, 351, 360

Duesenbergs, 203

Dunnaway, Glenn, 291–294, 328

du Pont, Pierre, 32

Duryea brothers, 79

Dyer, Carson, 124, 125, 192n

Earles, Clay, 304

Earnhardt, Dale, Jr., 8, 360

Earnhardt, Dale, Sr., 4, 111, 355, 359, 361, 363
  death of, 5, 7, 351, 360

Earnhardt, Ralph, 7

Edwards, Carl, 361–362

Eisenhower, Dwight D., 156

Eleventh Air Force, 161

Elkins, North Carolina, 215, 220

Elliott, Bill, 343, 361, 363

Emerson, Ralph Waldo, 28

Esquire magazine, 341

Etheridge, Jack, 201, 213, 226

Eyston, G. E. T., 83

Faulkner, William, 3, 11, 170, 366

Female drivers, 289, 290, 298–299, 299*n*,
    301

Fields, W. C., 31

Fish, Bob, 345

Fitzgerald, F. Scott, 33

Flivver King, The (Sinclair), 33

Flock, Bob, 226, 234, 295–296, 332, 339,
    353
  as bootlegger, 109, 172, 176, 221, 254,
    288
  family of, 221, 253
  injuries of, 223, 265, 338
  personality of, 222
  in prison, 172
  racing by, 113, 124, 125, 140, 148, 176,
    178, 181, 190, 191, 198–199,
    201–203, 211, 213, 215–223, 225,
    247, 249, 251, 253, 258, 265, 282,
    290, 301, 306, 315, 338
  in World War II, 199

Flock, Carl, 221, 254

Flock, Fonty, 178, 226, 231, 234, 271,
    275, 296, 339
  as bootlegger, 109, 116, 221, 254, 288
  death of, 339
  family of, 221, 253
  injuries of, 199, 223, 265
  personality of, 222, 255
  physical appearance of, 222
  racing by, 113, 116, 119, 120, 140, 148,

    198–199, 215, 219, 247, 249–251,
    253–260, 265, 267–270, 288, 292,
    293, 304, 306, 308, 315, 339
  rivalry with Byron, 254–259, 267, 283

Flock, Lee Preston, 253

Flock, Reo, 253–254

Flock, Ruby, 295–296

Flock, Tim, 271, 283, 287, 339
  as bootlegger, 62, 254, 288
  Jocko the monkey and, 222, 338
  racing by, 199, 245, 247, 258, 262, 267,
    275, 288, 298, 299, 321, 338, 345
  unionization issue and, 336, 340, 341

Floyd, Pretty Boy, 34–35

Fontello, Truman, 221

Football, 7, 80, 274, 359

Ford, Clara, 27, 32, 208

Ford, Edsel, 32, 169–170, 207

Ford, Henry, 10, 24, 35, 137, 194, 345
  cars built by, 26–30, 32–34, 48
  death of, 208
  death of mother, 26, 59*n*, 133
  as defense contractor, 149, 159
  Edsel and, 169
  education of, 75
  family of, 26
  funeral of, 209
  Hitler and, 75, 159
  leaves home, 26
  liquor, distaste for, 31–33, 43, 208
  old age of, 207–208
  racing by, 27, 218, 331
  racing cars and, 27–28, 78–79, 83
  as role model, 74
  Vogt, meeting with, 99*n*
  World War I and, 159
  World War II and, 149, 159–160

Ford, Henry, II, 170, 207, 344

Ford, William Clay, 345

Ford Motor Company, 169–170, 344–345
  creation of, 28–29
  growth and financial success of, 32–33

Ford V-8 cars, 4, 9, 10, 34–35, 48, 49, 63,
    76, 85, 86, 92, 94, 98–99, 102,
    198, 204–207, 216, 227, 247, 253,
    256, 257
Fort Wayne, Indiana, 107
France, Anne, 187–188, 352
France, Bill, 5, 8–9, 74, 126, 131, 139,
    172*n*, 187, 258, 332, 363 (*see also*
    NASCAR [National Association of
    Stock Car Auto Racing])
  as auto mechanic, 73, 85
  birth of NASCAR and, 229–236,
    241–243
  Byron and, 282, 321
  championship scheme of, 212–213,
    219–221, 223–225, 232
  death of, 352
  disputes with drivers, 86–88, 90, 119*n*,
    273–275, 281–282, 286–287, 293,
    302–303, 321–322, 335, 336
  expansion of authority of, 332–336
  health of, 347, 351, 352–354
  legacy of, 353
  NCSCC (National Championship Stock
    Car Circuit) and, 178–179, 189,
    190, 197, 199, 212–214, 219,
    223–225, 228–230, 232
  Nunis and, 214, 228, 323
  Parks and, 91, 242–243, 350–352, 366
  personality of, 88
  physical appearance of, 232, 332
  as promoter, 86, 114–115, 121–122,
    177–179, 187–189, 190, 196, 197,
    199, 209–212, 236, 273, 352
  racing by, 86, 91, 93, 95, 109,
    111–121, 123–125, 148, 174, 178,
    181–183, 187, 190, 209, 308,
    315–318
  reaction to tragedies by, 262–263, 266
  stock shares of NASCAR and,
    241–242
  unionization issue and, 336, 339, 340

  Vogt and, 73, 90, 100, 239–241, 296,
    345–347, 351, 352
  in World War II, 149
France, Bill, Jr., 353, 363, 366
France, Brian, 353
France, Jim, 353

Gable, Clark, 161, 295
Garrison, Wilton, 177
General Motors, 29, 288, 300, 344
Georgia State Highway 9, 51, 65, 68
Gettysburg, battle of, 209
Golden Corral 500, 356, 361
Gold rush, in Georgia, 12–14
Gone with the Wind (Mitchell), 14, 17, 88,
    108, 295
Gordon, Jeff, 352
Grady, Henry, 23
Grand National division, 294, 296,
    300–301, 304–307, 320, 321, 330,
    341
Grant, Larry, 110
Great Depression, 9, 19, 35, 67
Greensboro, North Carolina, 113, 120,
    191, 256, 258, 262
Greenville, South Carolina, 215
Greenville-Pickens Speedway, South
    Carolina, 187, 188, 190, 365
Guthrie, Janet, 299*n*

Hall, Elizabeth, 192
Hall, Eula May, 59
Hall, "Reckless" Roy, 7, 48, 49, 104, 124,
    125, 132, 134, 139, 198, 217, 219,
    220, 252, 342, 353, 360
  ancestors of, 54
  arrests and run-ins with law, 108,
    172–173, 175, 178, 179, 185, 187,
    191–192
  as bootlegger, 59, 60, 64–66, 68–70, 107
  Byron and, 305–306
  death of mother, 133

Hall, "Reckless" Roy *(cont'd)*
  driving skills of, 68–70
  family of, 59, 105–106
  injury to, 307, 342
  Parks and, 173, 185–186, 193, 252, 277
  personality of, 106, 107
  physical appearance of, 59, 106, 173, 192
  press on, 108, 109, 111, 118, 174–175
  in prison, 111, 116, 192, 197, 277
  racing by, 48, 62, 91, 93, 95, 106–121,
    140, 172–175, 177–178, 181–183,
    185–187, 191, 192, 197, 203n,
    247, 305–308, 342–343
  release from prison, 305
  Seay and, 105, 120, 343
  songs about, 112, 192–193, 343
  Vogt and, 76, 185, 186
Hall, Ronnie, 192
Hamilton, Alexander, 229n
Hankinson, Ralph, 112–113
Hartsfield, William B., 171, 175, 276, 355
Hawkins, Alvin, 324
Hayes, John, 293, 294
Heads, 21
Heller, Joseph, 161
Hellmueller, Bert "The Flying Dutchman,"
  92
Helmets, 205
Helton, Mike, 8–9, 362–363
Hemingway, Ernest, 236
Hemphill, Paul, 87
Henderson, William "Big Six," 62
Hepburn, Ralph, 268
Hersey, Skimp, 125, 177
High Point, North Carolina, 113, 120,
  123–124, 215, 281
Hitler, Adolf, 75, 151, 152, 159
Holland, Bill, 184, 204, 206
Holman, John, 346
Horn, Ted, 184, 204, 205, 268
Hornsby, Marion, 173–175
Horse racing, 92

Hudsons, 290, 300, 331, 332, 344
Huntsville, Alabama, 215

Indianapolis, 75, 79–80, 82, 97, 102, 139,
  185, 186, 196, 203, 255, 256, 264,
  299n, 333–334
Ingle Hollow, North Carolina, 61
Internal Revenue Service (IRS), 57, 61, 62
International Speedway Corporation (ISC),
  336–337, 353
International World Speed Trials, 83
Ireland, 52–53

Jackson, Andrew, 12–13
Jacksonville, Florida, 215, 223, 224
James I, King of England, 53
Jarrett, Ned, 342
Jefferson, Thomas, 56
Jenkins, Charles, 260, 262, 270
Jocko Flocko (monkey), 7, 222, 338
Johnson, Robert, Sr., 61
Johnson, Robert Glenn "Junior," 7, 61–62,
  334, 336, 341–344

Kahn, Bernard, 201, 210–211, 220, 273,
  300, 335, 350
Kahne, Kasey, 361
Kelley, Machine Gun, 41
Kennedy, Lesa France, 353
Kerouac, Jack, 264
Kerry, John, 165n
Kiekhaefer, Carl, 338, 339, 346, 350
Kiska, battle of, 163–164
Korean War, 308, 335
Ku Klux Klan, 30
Kurtis Kraft, 320

Lakewood Speedway, Atlanta, 90–91, 106,
  108, 113, 118, 120, 123–125, 130,
  138–140, 171–175, 178, 196, 213,
  214, 222, 269, 301, 303, 307,
  320–321, 340, 343, 355

Langhorne Speedway, Pennsylvania, 107, 112, 216–218, 228, 248, 301, 303, 333
Lardner, Ring, 31
Laurel, Maryland, 73
Law, Glenn "Legs," 49, 172, 173n, 179
Lawing, Houston, 236
Lee, "Light-Horse" Harry, 54
Lee, Robert E., 13
Le Mans, France, 334, 348
Lemonade Lucy, 30
Leonard, Walter, 191
Levegh, Pierre, 334
Lincoln, Abraham, 30, 101, 226, 354
Lincolns, 290, 292, 313, 319
Lindbergh, Charles, 160
Littlejohn, Joe, 117, 182, 183, 241n
Lloyd Seay Memorial Race, 148
London, Jack, 132, 133–134
Long, Bernard, 120, 343
Long Island, New York, 79
Lowes Motor Speedway, 340

Mackenzie, Doc, 114, 182
Macon, Georgia, 215
Mantz, Johnny, 324–329
Marion, Milt, 85
Marks, Charles, 268
Marshall, George, 158
Martin, Ola, 15
Martin, Otis, 289
Martinsville Speedway, Virginia, 215, 220, 279, 301, 302, 304
Maseratis, 203, 205
Mathis, Buck, 266
Maude, Aunt, 25, 36
Mays, Rex, 204
McGovern, George, 161, 163
McTell, Blind Willie, 112, 192
Melrose Park, Alabama, 137
Mencken, H. L., 19, 43
Mercedes, 203, 334

Mercurys, 300
Mesopotamia, 52
Michigan State Fairgrounds, Detroit, 331, 332
Midgets, 272, 318–320
Midland Speedway, Charlotte, 281
Miller, Uncle, 22, 25, 35–37, 41, 44
Mitchell, Bernard, 215
Mitchell, Margaret, 14, 72, 88, 295, 308
Mitchum, Robert, 31, 66
Mobley, Ethel Flock, 254, 298, 299
Model A Ford, 34, 79, 139
Model T Ford, 21–22, 31, 33, 79, 134, 135
  introduction of, 29
  sales of, 29–30
Modified division, 228, 233, 283, 284, 288
Monroe, Rose ("Rosie the Riveter"), 160
Moody, Lloyd, 87
Moody, Ralph, 346
Moonshine
  alcohol content (proof) of, 21
  creation of automobiles and, 31–32, 34, 35
  Flock brothers and, 62, 109, 116, 172, 176, 221, 254, 288
  Hall and, 59, 60, 64–66, 68–70, 107
  Parks and, 3–9, 7, 19–21, 36–40, 42–45, 48–49, 63, 98, 150, 275, 276, 350, 362, 363, 365
  in postwar years, 343
  process of making, 19–21
  recipes for, 20
  Seay and, 9, 51, 55, 60, 64–67, 107, 126–131
Moultrie, Georgia, 45
Mundy, Frank, 172n
Murphy, Dan, 95

Naismith, James, 10
NARL (National Auto Racing League), 211

NASCAR (National Association of Stock
Car Auto Racing), (*see also* France,
Bill; Moonshine; Stock car racing;
specific drivers)
  benevolent fund of, 233
  birth of, 8, 229–236, 361
  corporate sponsorship, 6, 336, 341, 344,
    353, 362
  Darlington Raceway, 323–329
  decision-making style of, 119
  divisions of cars, 233
  Earnhardt's death and, 5, 7, 351, 360
  fan base, 6–7, 352
  female drivers, 289, 290, 298–299,
    299*n*, 301
  first blacktop race, 322–328
  first championship, 5, 7, 267–270, 274
  first strictly stock race, 284–294
  first tragedy (Columbus Speedway,
    1948), 260–263, 265
  governing body of, 234
  Grand National division, 294, 296,
    300–301, 304–307, 320, 321, 330,
    341
  inaugural race (1948) of, 244–253
  incorporation of, 241*n*
  lawsuits against, 293–294
  naming of, 7, 234
  1947 organizational meeting of, 8,
    229–236, 361
  origins and evolution of, 5, 6, 7–10,
    25, 188, 209, 333, 343–344,
    362–363
  purses, 5, 115, 280–282, 302, 322, 323,
    328
  racetrack ownership and, 336–337
  revenues of, 273–274, 279–282, 287,
    293, 353
  safety measures taken by, 266
  stock shares of, 241–242, 243
  televised races, 6, 359
Nash cars, 315, 317, 345

Nation, Carry, 30
National Motorsports Hall of Fame, 349
NCSCC (National Championship Stock
    Car Circuit), 178–179, 189, 190,
    197, 199, 212–214, 219, 223–225,
    228–230, 232
NCSRA (National Championship Stock
    Racing Association), 197
Nelson, Baby Face, 41
Ness, Elliot, 62
New England Stock Car Circuit, 228
Newsweek magazine, 334
Nextel Cup, 6, 7, 294, 337, 353
Ninety-ninth Infantry Division, 150–158
North Wilkesboro, North Carolina,
    215, 220, 256, 259, 279, 281,
    305, 306
NSCRA/NSRA (National Stock Car
    Racing Association), 190, 197, 211,
    234, 258, 281–283, 286, 293, 309,
    321, 329, 331–332, 335
Nunis, Sam, 209–210, 213, 214, 228, 229,
    258, 268–269, 283, 301, 320–323,
    335

Occoneechee Speedway, North Carolina,
    301
Offenhauser (Offys), 203, 205
Ohio River, 54
Oldfield, Bernd Eli "Barney," 27, 28, 79,
    87, 137, 203, 329
  birth of, 80
  as hero to Byron, 136, 189
  personality of, 82
  physical appearance of, 81
  racing by, 79–83, 90
Olds, Ransom, 79
Oldsmobiles, 287–288, 296–299, 300,
    324, 329, 344, 364
On the Road (Kerouac), 264
Open-wheel cars, 81, 137, 140, 175, 184,
    203, 295

Orr, Will, 15
Osiecki, Bob, 221–222
Ossinsky, Louis, 241, 242, 280, 286
Owens, Amos, 57–58
Owens, Robert, 318
Oxford, Alabama, 137

Paramushiro raids, 164–165
Parker, Bonnie, 35
Parks, Alfred, 15, 16, 45, 277
Parks, Benjamin, Jr. (Uncle Benny), 11–14,
    54, 362
Parks, Etna, 15
Parks, Ila, 15–16
Parks, Leila, 15
Parks, Leman, 15
Parks, Lois, 44, 46
Parks, Ray, Jr., 154, 252, 277
Parks, Raymond, 39, 108, 125, 133, 198,
    234, 343, 353
  ancestors of, 54
  as auto mechanic, 35, 37
  birth of, 14
  birth of NASCAR and, 231, 235, 241,
    243, 366
  as bootlegger, 3–9, 19–21, 36–40,
    42–45, 48–49, 63, 98, 150, 275,
    276, 350, 362, 363, 365
  Byron and, 142–143, 179, 180, 200,
    202, 252–253, 263, 266, 271–272,
    277, 278, 318–319, 330
  car dealership of, 330
  death of mother, 133
  death of Seay, 131, 132
  education of, 19, 47
  family of, 14–16
  France and, 91, 242–243, 350–352, 366
  Hall and, 173, 185–186, 193, 252, 277
  leaves NASCAR, 350
  liquor store ownership by, 44, 46, 98,
    149, 276
  lottery business of, 41–42, 98, 150, 276
  marriages of, 44–46, 150, 277, 351
  moves to Atlanta, 22–24
  personal cars of, 21–22, 38, 46
  personality of, 44
  physical appearance of, 21, 25, 106,
    231, 364
  police and, 38–40, 42, 47
  in prison, 16–17, 47, 62, 276, 341
  racing by, 216–218, 248, 249, 252
  as racing team owner, 98–99, 102, 109,
    116, 121, 214, 216, 219, 248, 252,
    277, 287, 288, 305, 308, 313, 314,
    316–318, 324, 326, 350
  real estate holdings of, 44, 46,
    150, 276
  reputation of, 46–47
  runs away from home, 16–17, 19, 352
  Vogt and, 76, 77, 105, 277, 278, 330
  in World War II, 143, 149–158
Parks, Rufus, 15
Parks, Sally Henderson, 12
Parks, Violet, 5, 6, 351
Paschal, Jim, 289
Paterson, New Jersey, 112, 189
Patrick, Danica, 299n
Peach Bowl, Atlanta, 272, 307, 320
Pearl Harbor, attack on, 148, 160
Penson, Henry, 41
Petty, Adam, 340
Petty, Kyle, 340
Petty, Lee, 7, 289, 291, 304–306, 321,
    330, 339–340
Petty, Maurice, 291
Petty, Richard, 6, 78, 291, 336, 338, 340,
    351, 353
Peugeots, 203
Pike's Peak, Colorado, 136
Pinkerton Agency, 210
Plasterco, Virginia, 133
Ploesti, Romania, 162–163
Plymouths, 324, 325, 327–329, 344
Pritchett, Swayne, 268

Prohibition, 10, 16, 19, 30–33, 65, 74, 208
  repeal of, 43, 44, 60
Purser, Smokey, 86–88, 116, 118, 182
Pyle, Ernie, 50, 66

R.J. Reynolds Company, 6, 336, 341
Rankin, Robert, 208
Rayson Memorial, 246–247, 252–253
Reagan, Ronald, 341
Reconstruction, 18
Reese, Charlie, 86, 87
Revolutionary War, 52, 54, 56, 157
Rexford, Bill, 330
Rhodes, Mickey, 251
Ride in the Storm, Chief, 93, 95
Roadsters, 228, 233, 283, 284
Roberts, Fireball, 7, 327–328, 330, 334,
  336, 340–342, 344, 345, 346
Roberts, Floyd, 90
Robinson, Shawna, 299n
Robson, George, 186
Rockefeller, John, 32
Rogers, Will, 279
Rooney, Mickey, 295
Roosevelt, Franklin D., 18, 43, 147, 157
Roper, Jim, 289, 292, 293
Rose, Mauri, 184, 204, 207
Rubirosa, Porfirio, 348
Rum, 55, 56
Russell, D. C. "Fat," 200, 204, 205, 224,
  277n
Ruth, Babe, 7, 359

Salisbury, North Carolina, 107, 109
Samples, Eddie, 124, 125, 182, 188, 190,
  197–201, 213, 221, 224–226, 231,
  247, 280, 282, 286, 296, 305, 308,
  309, 321, 332, 335, 342, 343, 365
Sanctioning organizations, emergence of,
  196–197
Scopes Monkey Trial, 19
Scotland, 52–56

Scots-Irish, 52–57, 169, 212
Seabiscuit (horse), 92
Seat belts, 205, 215, 288, 319
Seay, Jim, 126–130, 147
Seay, Lloyd, 7, 48, 49, 179, 182, 183n,
    193, 197, 198, 203, 220, 252, 307,
    308, 343, 353, 360, 365
  ancestors of, 54
  birth of, 58
  as bootlegger, 9, 51, 55, 60, 64–67, 107,
    126–131
  death of, 129–130, 132, 147, 343
  driving skills of, 50, 51, 62, 68, 131
  family of, 58–59, 105–106
  funeral and gravesite of, 131
  Hall and, 105, 120, 343
  personality of, 106
  physical appearance of, 51, 106
  press on, 106, 120, 124, 130–131
  racing by, 9, 91–95, 106–109, 111–122,
    123–126, 130, 139, 141
  Vogt and, 76
Seay, Ray, 51, 59
Seay, Robert, 148
Second Oldest Profession, The (Carr), 69
Seminole Speedway, Orlando, 178, 181,
  182
Seton, Ernest Thompson, 134
Sherman, William T., 13, 17, 18, 23, 47,
  53, 147
Shirley, Lucille, 45
Shirley, Marion, 364
Shirley, Ralph "Bad Eye," 44–45, 47, 49,
  148, 192, 364
Shoemaker, Ray, 272
Shorty (friend of Byron), 136, 137, 143,
  179
Shuman, Buddy, 177, 181, 211, 224–225,
  234, 265, 267, 276, 280–282, 286,
  296, 301, 308, 309, 321, 333, 335,
  342
Sinclair, Upton, 29, 33, 75

Singleton, Red, 91, 125

Singlings, 20

Slave trade, 56

Smith, Bruton, 283, 284, 286, 293, 301, 302, 309, 321, 331, 335, 337, 340, 355

Smith, Geoff, 362

Smith, Louise, 298–299

Snowden, "Wild Bill," 224

Sordoni, Andrew, 334

Sosebee, Gober, 123, 124, 182, 198, 199, 242, 247, 296, 298, 299, 303, 321, 326, 335, 342, 343, 365

Sour mash, 20

South Carolina Auto Racing Association (SCARA), 211

Southern 500, 323–329, 339, 363

Southern States Fairgrounds, 176–177

Spartanburg, South Carolina, 223, 279, 305

Spectator injuries and fatalities, 80, 97, 115, 117, 201, 204, 261–265, 268, 270, 277, 331, 333, 347, 357

Speed Age magazine, 225, 226–227, 229, 231, 234

Speedway Motorsports Inc., 337

Sports Car Club of America, 348

Sports Illustrated magazine, 340, 349

Steinbeck, John, 30, 161

Stewart, Jimmy, 161

Stewart, Tony, 363

Stockbridge, Georgia, 88

Stock Car Auto Racing Society (SCARS), 211

Stock car racing (*see also* France, Bill; NASCAR [National Association of Stock Car Auto Racing]; specific drivers)
    Armistice Day race (1938), 90–95
    battle between two factions, 170–171
    at Beach-and-Road course, Daytona, 4, 83–88, 109–111, 113–121, 177,

182–183, 196, 199n, 200–201, 203n, 218–219, 245
    bounties, 123
    Daytona-vs.-Atlanta, 90, 95–96, 112, 118
    definition of stock car, 227–228
    disputes in, 85, 86–88, 90, 119n, 273–275, 281–282, 286–287, 293, 302–303, 321–322, 335, 336
    driver injuries and fatalities, 5, 7, 119, 125n, 142, 183, 199, 215, 223, 264, 265, 268, 291, 307, 338, 351, 360
    drivers banned from, 171–172, 175, 178, 188
    emergence of sanctioning organizations, 196–197, 211
    fans of, 96–97, 115
    inspections, 86, 115, 292–293, 297, 299, 303, 328–329, 345–346
    modifications to cars, 91–92, 94, 101–105, 115, 228, 292–293, 296, 297–300
    movie newsreels of, 199–200
    1939 season, 106–108, 114, 115, 140
    1940 season, 109–111, 113–115
    1941 season, 113–121, 123–125
    1946 season, 181–190
    1947 season, 194, 199–202, 210, 213–225
    origins of, in Florida, 83–88
    origins of, in Georgia, 88–89
    postwar, 170–179, 197–198
    press coverage of, 97, 106, 108, 109, 111, 118, 120, 124, 130–131, 138, 174–175, 181, 183–184, 200–202, 210, 211, 225, 255, 272
    spectator injuries and fatalities, 115, 117, 201, 261–265, 268, 270, 277, 331, 333, 347, 357
    sponsorship, 6, 89, 336, 341, 344, 353, 362

Stock car racing *(cont'd)*
    superstitions and, 124–125, 338
    World War II and, 147
Strictly stock division, 228, 233, 283–294,
        296–302
Sunday, Billy, 30, 31, 82
Sweet mash, 20
Syracuse, New York, 264, 333

Tails, 21
Talladega Superspeedway, Alabama, 336,
        339, 345, 357
Tax, on liquor, 54, 56, 57, 60
Taylor, Harley, 94, 95, 124, 125
Teague, Marshall, 234, 248–251, 280–282,
        286, 331, 332, 341, 342
Teeter, Lucky, 147–148
Thomas, Herb, 289, 334
Thompson, Alfred, 286
Thompson, Speedy, 282, 286
Thunder Road (movie), 31, 66
Thurmond, Mrs. Strom, 326
Time magazine, 209
To Please a Lady (movie), 295
Trail of Tears, 13
Trenton, New Jersey, 215, 335
Tri-City Speedway, North Carolina, 306
Troy, Jack, 185
Turner, Curtis, 7, 61, 247, 267, 271, 282,
        283, 288, 301, 315–318, 320, 324,
        326, 327, 332, 333, 334, 336,
        340–344, 346, 360
Tuthill, Bill, 235, 239–240, 242, 273, 274,
        280, 286, 287, 289, 292, 302, 322,
        328, 329
Tyler, Swift, 38, 47

United Auto Workers (UAW), 345
United States Car Racing Association
        (USCRA), 211
United States Gypsum Company, 133, 362
United States Stock Car Drivers Association,
        190

United Stock Car Racing Club, 301, 304
Updike, John, 170

Vanderbilt, W. K., 79
Vanderbilt Cup, 79, 97
Vogt, Betty, 238–240, 347
Vogt, Caroline, 73
Vogt, Charles "Louie," 73
Vogt, Jerry, 74, 76, 149*n*, 237–238
Vogt, Louis Jerome "Red," 7, 8, 125, 139,
        140, 172*n*, 198, 216, 219, 342, 353,
        363
    as auto mechanic, 25, 49, 65, 72–77, 90,
        91–94, 99, 102–105, 109, 111, 115,
        116, 149, 200, 214, 218, 220, 221,
        226, 237–240, 247–250, 283, 285,
        287, 296–300, 303, 309, 326,
        328–330, 341, 345–347
    birth of, 72
    birth of NASCAR and, 231, 234,
        239–240
    Byron and, 179, 180, 202, 204,
        206, 252
    death of, 347
    education of, 103
    France and, 73, 90, 100, 239–241, 296,
        345–347, 351, 352
    Hall and, 76, 186
    marriages of, 74, 237–239, 347
    meeting with Henry Ford, 99*n*
    motorcycle accident of, 73
    Parks and, 76, 77, 105, 277, 278, 330
    personality of, 74, 75–76, 238–239
    physical appearance of, 74, 77–78, 239,
        248
    Seay and, 76
    in World War II, 149
Vogt, Ruth, 73–75, 77, 99*n*, 100,
        237–239
Vogt, Tom, 74, 75–76, 99*n*, 103, 149*n*,
        237–238
Volstead Act of 1920, 31
Vukovich, Bill, 333

Walden, J. R., 191

Wallace, George, 339

Walters, Phil, 348

War Admiral (horse), 92

Warren, Robert Penn, 168

Washington, George, 54, 56, 229n

Washington Post, The, 9

Watkins Glen, New York, 333

Watson, Billy, 104–105, 173n, 179, 185,
        238, 342, 365

Weatherly, "Little Joe," 125n, 346

Webb, James, 54, 169

Weldon, A. J., 136–137, 175

Wendt, June, 238, 240, 347

Westmoreland, Hubert, 292–293, 327, 328

Wheeler, Wayne, 32

Wheels for the World (Brinkley), 208

Whiskey, history of, 52–57

Whiskey Rebellion of 1794, 54

Wilderness Trail, 54

Willard, Frances, 30

Williams, Peachtree, 74, 221

Winston Cup, 294, 341

Winton, Alexander, 27, 79

Wolfe, Joe, 267

Wolfe, Tom, 341

Women's Christian Temperance Union, 30

World War I, 159

World War II, 67, 141, 147–165, 168–169

Wrigley, Norman, 104

Yunick, Smokey, 297–298, 333, 346–347

ABOUT THE AUTHOR

NEAL THOMPSON (www.nealthompson.com) is a veteran journalist who has worked for the *Baltimore Sun, Philadelphia Inquirer,* and *St. Petersburg Times* and whose magazine stories have appeared in *Outside, Esquire, Backpacker, Men's Health,* and the *Washington Post Magazine.* He teaches at the University of North Carolina–Asheville's Great Smokies Writing Program and is author of the critically acclaimed biography *Light This Candle: The Life & Times of Alan Shepard.* Thompson, his wife, and their two sons live in the mountains outside Asheville, North Carolina.